M000283009

Jim Murray's
WHISKY BIBLE
～ 2004 ～

The world's leading whisky guide from the world's leading whisky authority

CARLTON
BOOKS

Contents

Introduction

Not since Ernest Hemingway's creative (and digestive) juices were in full flow has so much been written and so much whisky consumed at one and the same time. Well, perhaps that's not quite true. The majority of the whisky reviewed here ended up in a spittoon, which was not, most likely, the case with Hemingway.

Even so, this book does enjoy the distinction of a number of firsts. The first to give an analytical breakdown of the strengths and weaknesses of individual whiskies, rather than having a random number seemingly plucked from somewhere out of the ether (or should that be Angel's Share); the first to have detailed notes on over 1,000 single malts; the first to include over 2,000 whiskies overall; the first tasting guide to include all the world's whisky styles between one set of covers; the first (to my knowledge) to be linked to its own exclusive website so readers can gain maximum information; the first (amazingly – and sadly – this is quite true) to cause the author both a callus and repetitive strain syndrome through opening so many sample bottles ...

Over two thousand whiskies. Why should a book go to so much detail, you may wonder. Well, the answer is because of the enormous interest that has been generated among the public in whisky. And not just Scotch. People are, these days, alive to the beauties of Japanese and Irish; bourbon and rye; blends and grains. But also they are wary. Spirits are not cheap. Buy a bottle of wine that is below par and you make a mental note not to get it again. Buy a dud bottle of whisky and it can be a costly learning experience.

Whilst travelling around the world in recent years, either visiting distilleries or giving tastings, it became apparent that people were in constant need of sound, up-to-date and consistent advice. The number of whiskies being made available for selection was increasing week by week and so the choice was getting larger and harder. And through listening to the needs and wishes of whisky lovers the seeds for *Jim Murray's Whisky Bible* were sown.

By rule of thumb, distillers and bottlers prefer not to have their whiskies given numerical ratings for public consumption. Not least because one bad review from a perceived prominent nose can do significant harm to sales after a lot of hard marketing graft or capital outlay. However, this book has been written for the aid and enjoyment of the consumer, plus also the liquor store owner or manager (and, I can assure you, quite a number in the trade itself). And the average whisky drinker much prefers to have a simple, easy-to-understand rating system to help them in their choice, irrespective of what the distiller wants. And so, after writing a number of ratings-free guides, I have gone down the marking route – and make no apology for it. To further help the whisky drinker I have clearly displayed just where I have docked marks – or added them – by breaking the evaluation down into four distinct segments: nose, taste, finish and balance. Doubtless I will surprise, annoy and/or offend some people I have known for a long time in the industry with a number of my ratings and observations; others will be delighted. Whatever, my phone is in for a busy time over the next few months and I may need less room to hang my Christmas cards ...

Every whisky within this book has been rated entirely on merit and for consistency tasted – or in the vast majority of cases re-tasted – by me in the last twelve months, a massive percentage in a liquid golden three-month period between May and August 2003 at my tasting lab in England. Single cask bottlings by their nature need tasting only once. But with each subsequent yearly edition other bottlings will be re-evaluated because, contrary to industry edict, whiskies as often as not shift slightly in character from batch to batch.

As this book is designed for international use there's no mention about value for money. Instead, I have opted for marking up style and quality, a factor that comfortably transcends international exchange rates, tax variations and the health and colour of people's credit cards. The decision to buy, then, must be made by the purchaser after he or she has taken this advice into consideration. Or not, as the case may be.

Originally I had planned to include the whiskies from all the world's distilling nations in this book. But the Sars outbreak put paid to that and I made an editorial decision to include Asian and Indian whiskies – Japan excepted – in the 2005 edition onwards. Also, we had hoped to answer one of the most common questions I am asked: just how many whiskies are there? Even with over 2,000 whiskies specially tasted for this book, still we don't know. There was also a problem of space. The idea was to give full tasting notes on all whiskies rated 85 and over and summary notes on those marked below. However, by the time the tasting notes were completed there was less space for additional features than had been envisaged. And as the purpose of *Jim Murray's Whisky Bible* is to be the ultimate tasting guide, the notes came first.

For that reason we will see *Jim Murray's Whisky Bible* evolve in future years with extra space created for forthcoming editions. To keep in touch with new releases and other news in the whisky world, contact **www.whiskybible.com**. This website will also include information about the distilleries featured in this book but for which there was insufficient room to give detail in print. I have tried to include as many whiskies as are likely to be found around the world's market place. It has not been possible to find them all and some I did not include if the sample I had was too out of date. If I have somehow missed your favourite whisky, then I beg your forgiveness. Please contact me or my team on **jimmurray@whiskybible.com** so we can track down a sample and rectify my oversight for the next edition.

Finally, a word about my tasting notes. In recent years I have sat back and read some whisky descriptions made by others and felt nothing but perplexity, frustration and, to be honest, irritation. For if I didn't understand what they were talking about, or in any way recognise the whiskies so floridly described, it was highly unlikely anyone just getting their feet under the whisky table would either, thus possibly creating an inferiority complex and scaring away potential converts to this most glorious of spirits. Of course, tasting whisky is subjective and a matter of individual opinion: that is half the fun. And it is quite likely you may not agree with each and every one of my evaluations: I would be entirely astonished and mildly disturbed if you did. But my experience of giving tastings quite literally from New York to New Zealand means that I have learnt along the way the language that the average whisky lover understands and is entirely comfortable with. It is unlikely you will find much here in the way of references to "marigolds on a bed of nutmeg" and "two-week old, lightly boiled asparagus with a distant hint of briny anchovies" or some other pretentious twaddle written by someone with a limited knowledge of whisky but a boundless ability to massage their own ego. This, proudly, is a bullshit-free book designed to help people discover and enjoy a spirit that can, in one form or another, entertain and seduce even the most hardened and cynical palates.

Enjoy the book. But better still, enjoy the whiskies ...

Jim Murray
Borat's Glade
Wellingborough
August 2003

How to Read The Bible

The whole point of this book is for the whisky lover – be he or she an experienced connoisseur or, better fun still, simply starting out on the long and joyous path of discovery – to have ready access to easy-to-understand information about as many whiskies as possible. And I mean a lot. Thousands.

This book does not quite include every whisky on the market ... just by far and away the vast majority. And those that have been missed this time round – either through accident, logistics or design – will appear in later editions once we can source a sample.

Whisky Scoring

The marking for this book is tailored to the consumer and scores run out just a little higher than I use for my own personal references. But such is the way it has been devised it has not affected my order of preference.

Each whisky is given a rating out of 100. Twenty-five marks are given to each of four factors: nose (**n**), taste (**t**), finish (**f**), balance and overall complexity (**b**). That means that 50% of the marks are given for flavour alone and 25% for the nose, often an overlooked part of the whisky equation. The area of balance and complexity covers all three previous factors and a usually hidden one besides:

Nose: this is simply the aroma. Often requires more than one inspection as hidden aromas can sometimes reveal themselves after time in the glass and increased contact with air. The nose very often tells much about a whisky, but – as we shall see – equally can be quite misleading.

Taste: this is the immediate arrival on the palate and involves the flavour profile up to, and including, the time it reaches maximum intensity and complexity.

Finish: often the least understood part of a tasting. This is the tail and flourish of the whisky's signature, often revealing the effects of ageing. The better whiskies tend to finish well and longer without too much oak excess.

Balance: This is the part it takes a little experience to appreciate but it can be mastered by anyone. For a whisky to work well on the nose and palate, it should not be too one-sided in its character. If you are looking for an older whisky, it should have evidence of oak, but not so much that all other flavours and aromas are drowned out. Likewise, a whisky matured or finished in a sherry butt must offer a lot more than just wine alone and the greatest Islay malts revel in depth and complexity beyond the smoky effects of peat.

Each whisky has been analysed by me without adding water or ice. I have taken each whisky as it was poured from the bottle and used no more than warming in the glass to extract and discover the character of the whisky. To have added water would have been pointless: it would have been an inconsistent factor as people, when pouring water, add different amounts at varying temperatures. The only constant with the whisky you and I taste will be when it has been poured directly from the glass.

Even if you and I taste the same whiskies at the same temperature and from identical glasses – and even share the same values in whisky – our scores may still be different. Because a factor that is built into my evaluation is drawn from expectation and experience. When I sample a whisky from a certain distillery at such-and-such an age or from this type of barrel or that I would expect it to offer me certain qualities. It has taken me 25 years to acquire this knowledge (which I try to add to day by day!) and an enthusiast cannot be expected to learn it overnight. But, hopefully, *Jim Murray's Whisky Bible* will help...!

Score chart

Within the parenthesis () is the overall score out of 100.

0–50	Nothing short of absolutely diabolical.
51–64	Nasty and well worth avoiding.
65–69	Very unimpressive indeed.
70–74	Usually drinkable but don't expect the earth to move.
75–79	Average and usually pleasant though sometimes flawed.
80–84	Good whisky worth trying.
85–89	Very good to excellent whiskies definitely worth buying.
90–93	Brilliant.
94–97	Superstar whiskies that give us all a reason to live.
98–100	Better than anything I've ever tasted!

Key to Abbreviations

% Percentage strength of whisky measured as alcohol by volume. **b** Overall balance and complexity. **bott** Date of bottling. **db** Distillery bottling. In other words, an expression brought out by the owners of the distillery. **dist** Date of distillation or spirit first put into cask. **f** Finish. **n** Nose. **nc** Non-coloured. **ncf** Non-chill-filtered. **sc** Single cask. **t** Taste.

Finding Your Whisky

Worldwide Malts: Whiskies are listed alphabetically throughout the book. In the case of single malts, the distilleries run A–Z style with distillery bottlings appearing at the top of the list in order of age, starting with youngest first. After age comes vintage. After all the "official" distillery bottlings are listed, next come other bottlings, again in alphabetical order. Single malts without a distillery named (or perhaps named after a dead one) are given their own section, as are vatted malts.

Worldwide Blends: These are simply listed alphabetically, irrespective of which company produce them. So "Black Bottle" appears ahead of "White Horse" and Japanese blends begin with "Amber" and ends with "Za". In the case of brands being named after companies or individuals the first letter of the brand will dictate where it is listed. So William Grant, for instance, will be found under "W" for William rather "G" for Grant.

Bourbon/Rye: This is one of the most confusing types of whiskey to list because often the name of the brand bears no relation to the name of the distillery that made it. Also, brands may be sold from one company to another, or shortfalls in stock may see companies buying bourbons from another. For that reason all the brands have been listed alphabetically with the name of the bottling distiller being added at the end.

Irish Whiskey: There are four types of Irish whiskey: (i) pure pot still; (ii) single malt, (iii) single grain and (iv) blended. Some whiskies may have "pure pot still" on the label, but are actually single malts. So check both sections.

Bottle Information

Because there are no labels included in this book in order to save room I have tried to include all the relevant information you will find on the label to make identification of the brand straightforward. Where known I have included date of distillation and bottling – to day, month and year if known. Also the cask number for further recognition. At the end of the tasting notes I have included the strength and, if known, number of bottles released and in which markets. So NL will mean it is available in the Netherlands.

Bible Thumping The Evils of Colour Prejudice

Admit it: it's happened to you, hasn't it. You know that feeling. You grab a new bottle of one of your favourite whiskies, one you haven't tasted for a while. In your mind are memories of great moments of just you, a glass, the whisky. Kids listening to music upstairs, your partner on the phone or computer. It's just the three of you to resume that sacred trinity.

But before you open it you can't help just looking a second time at the colour of the whisky. Your brow furrows slightly. It seems darker than how you remember it. But you don't worry. It simply means that they are using more sherry than before, right?

You pour. Yes, it's definitely a shade darker. Then you nose ... aaahhh there's those deep orangey notes, but the barley ... where's the barley? And there's no evidence of sherry ... what's going on? You are not salavating like you used to ... you taste, first a sip then a real mouthful. There's a tingling sensation, the malt arrives to sing to your tastebuds and now you swallow and wait for the big finish ... which doesn't come. Where has it gone? Where are those high notes you remember that made your nerve-ends tingle? Why has most of the flavour already vanished? You take another mouthful ... the same thing happens ... no, the finish is even shorter this time. You look at the bottle with suspicion ... yep, it's definitely the same whisky you drank two years ago ... even the label's the same. Yet it is different. It is darker. It is duller ... it's been caramelised!!!

It's happened to you. It's happened to me ... oh, how it's happened to me.

Too often in recent years. And particularly in the last six months. To the point where you have reached that certain moment when you know you have to have a rant. It is one of those things that come over you and nothing short of being hit by a rampaging elephant will stop you from having your say.

For this book it happened when I was about a quarter of the way through all those tasting notes. I was trying to hit a tight schedule but I had to quit for the day about four hours early. The reason? I had tasted so much caramel in the whiskies I had been analysing that the build up was dulling my tastebuds sample by sample. I could no longer trust what my senses were telling me.

Now how can this be? Listen to the average marketing guy and he will tell you that caramel is purely a colouring agent and doesn't have a single say in the smell or taste of whisky. In fact, it's not just the marketing men. I know a blender or two who reckon exactly the same thing.

It's all our fault

Frankly, I don't think anyone could be wider of the mark. Caramel, when overused, can kill a whisky dead. Even in moderate amounts it can clip a whisky's wings to dramatic effect: instead of soaring it will crash towards the finish. When you look through this book you will see which brands have been marked down for excessive caramel use: look for the term "toffee". True, a whisky can pick up natural caramel notes from the oak. But they usually (though not, admittedly, always) tend to blend and balance in. And when they've been heavy-handed on the caramel I the bottling hall, toffee is the finish you often get instead of the more complex tones that should herald the finale of decent whisky.

In fairness to the industry, we can easily understand why caramel is used. It's our fault. It's the trait of the consumer that wants to see every whisky look exactly the same: if two bottles of the same brand have a fractionally different colour, then surely there is something wrong with one of them. We have been brought up on a diet of sameness. When just a fraction of caramel is added simply as a way of guaranteeing colour consistency, often the effect is negligible. Though, of course, that depends on the kind of whisky. If it is light in character then its tolerance to caramel is less. Sadly, the suspicion is there that caramel is added to give some whiskies that older look. Or more powerful. How many times have you been at a tasting or in a bar and seen someone hold a dark whisky to the light and tell his friend sitting next to him: "Wow, that looks strong"? When in fact it is just a coloured dram at 40% while a cask strength Islay sitting next to it is gives the insipid appearance of Riesling yet is ready to blow the guy's socks off.

Perhaps that's one of the factors as to why I enjoy bourbon and rye so much. Talk about "here's looking at you, kid ... ." The beauty of bourbon is that what you see is, roughly, what you get. It's the law: no additives. Sure, they have filtration. But just looking at a bourbon tells you much about its history: the darker it is the more action the whiskey is likely to have seen inside the barrel. A lighter bourbon may not be younger: it could have been lurking in the lower reaches of the warehouse keeping away from the heat and be lighter in colour and character than something a few years younger but merrily broiling away beside the rafters.

But with whisky from elsewhere, you never quite know. Unless the label specifies that you are dealing with something uncoloured. Or you are in an enlightened country that decrees that if a whisky includes caramel that should be stated on the label.

There will be those in the industry who will be shaking their head disagreeing with every word I have written here. I can hear their voices now: "Listen, they have been using caramel in whisky since the year dot. It doesn't make a bit of difference to the taste of the whisky. You are talking out of your arse, Jim." It has been said to me by one or two already.

Interestingly, one who executive said it to me a little more courteously changed his tune when I got him inside a lab and started adding caramel to the base whisky before it was bottled and got him to taste it at five different colour levels.

And if caramel really makes no difference, explain this. When I blend rum, to give it a specific "Naval" style I add caramel. Without it, it would just be golden in colour. But not only does the colour change, so too does the entire flavour make-up. This happens even when dealing with high-ester rums of massive character. In the old Naval dockyards of Deptford caramel was always added to British naval rum. And as caramel is made from sugar in the first place, it tends to sit quite naturally with rum which is distilled from the same substance.

Just the other month, I was reading somewhere some rubbish to the effect that if a rum is dark then it is aged. This, of course, is nonsense: there are any number of dark rums around which is basically new crop (rum from straight off the still and never seen the inside of a barrel) sent over to Europe in stainless steel or plastic drums and then mixed with caramel. Likewise, it was common practice in Guyana to pre-colour some of their Demerara rum. In other words caramel is put into the barrel along with new spirit and then left to age. The difference in both colour and flavour between pre-coloured rum and identical spirit left to mature in an identical cask without caramel is stark and dramatic.

So if it can have this effect on rum, why not whisky – which is made from grain, not sugar? Of course the answer is that it does. For that reason I never use caramel when working with whisky. I don't want to do anything that subtracts from the natural charisma of the whisky, which caramel invariably does. It dulls. It blunts.

That is one of the reasons I was so taken with a new vatted malt called Six Isles. The fact there was no colouring absolutely screamed at you; the flavours are natural, fresh and unhindered. Of course when it enters the Far Eastern markets, especially Taiwan, the pressure will be on for the company to add some caramel and colour it up. Well, I'm praying they don't. I have already done that in my lab to see what happens and the result is something markedly inferior.

Of course the marketing guys will point out, with some justification, that if that is what a specific market wants, then that is what they should get. But wouldn't it be great to see a company stand it's ground and say: "this is the way we present our whisky: totally natural and in peak condition. Now you learn to appreciate it."

It all comes down to education. I like to feel I do my bit when giving tastings, but I can't be everywhere or hope I will convert all I meet. Which is why I mention it here: it is a topic in need of a good crusade.

The distillers must have the confidence to go for it, too. They can take a leaf out of the book of those independent bottlers who are going down the uncoloured, unchill-filtered route. They, in turn, had followed the example set by Springbank and you don't hear many calls to add caramel to that. One of those independents, Whisky Galore, launched their range a year or two ago with a disastrous bunch of frankly uninspiring, caramel-flattened malts. They soon discovered their mistake and now their natural coloured range is as good as any around and even contains a true classic or two.

No spirit, it seems to me, is more natural or as indicative of its environment than whisky, nor so delicate and fragile. Perhaps now it is time for some bravery from the big boys. And not just in Scotland, but worldwide.

We all know the old Scottish joke that a Scotsman likes his whisky the same way he likes his women: naked. Here's praying it won't be too long before that means without caramel, as well as water ...

Review of the Whisky Year

Did you blink at any time in the last year? Then you probably missed something happening in Scotch during 2003, by far the busiest whisky sector in the world.

And, for once, the majority of the news has been good. None better for me has been the buying – rescuing some might say – of Bunnahabhain and Glengoyne. Both distilleries and their respective blends, Black Bottle and Langs, had been shunted into the sidings by their owner in recent years while the Edrington Express stopped only at Macallan, Highland Park, Famous Grouse and Cutty Sark, with the odd excursion to Glenrothes and Glenturret.

Bunna has been bought by Burn Stewart, which is also great news for their Deanston distillery. That has been suffering in recent years in its single malt form through insufficient high quality stocks being available at most ages, the malt being a major constituent in many Burn Stewart blends. But of their many brands, none have quite the cache of the extraordinary, ultra-smoky Black Bottle, easily one of the finest blends around. And Bunnahabhain as a distillery, looking a bit bedraggled in its final days under Edrington, will also profit from some tender loving care. Expect to see a peaty version (from experimental stocks made by Edrington but mysteriously kept by them away from public consumption) of one of the two unpeated Islays – with Bruichladdich – to appear on the market during 2004. But equally important for those who remember Bunna as one of Scotland's greats is the returning of the standard 12-year-old to a much less sherried form, where the astonishing salty freshness can be bracingly savoured as it was two decades ago.

Buying distilleries is an entirely new venture for Broxburn-based blenders Ian MacLeod & Co. But as owners themselves of a fair number of brands, including the excellent and also heavily peated Isle of Skye blend, the move from blenders to distillers was a natural, sensible and – with the number of either silent or surplus distilleries around these days – inevitable one. Glengoyne and Langs may not have fitted into Edrington's plans, but both will be reintroduced to once fertile markets during 2004. I hope the emphasis on the malt is put on the younger, 10-year-old versions rather than the older ones: Glengoyne at 10–12 really can offer something worth discovering.

Good news all round

It's a happy story all round: two companies needing to expand are happy: Edrington, looking to see two proud old distilleries go to good homes (and earn some cash in the process), are happy; two sets of employees are happy; whisky lovers are happy. If only all whisky tales could conclude with so many genuine smiles.

Two other distilleries have changed hands, both being brought back from the dead. Allied have sold the small but perfectly formed Glencadam distillery at Brechin to Angus Dundee. Glencadam now partners up with Speysider Tomintoul, relieving some of the workload. And, most astonishing of all, the near-forgotten Perthshire distillery of Tullabardine has also been snapped up after nearly a decade of silence having been included in a tourism-led land deal that should see it re-opened by early 2004, great news to those of us who used to savour this most creamy of drams.

Will there be any distilleries changing hands during 2004? Almost certainly. Chivas would like to unload a number of theirs, especially Braeval and Allt-a-Bhainne. But if you are inclined to bet it might be worth putting a few bob on their smaller and much more traditional Speysider Benriach being the first to move.

In some ways the most curious development was the re-naming by Diageo of their Cardhu distillery back to its original Cardow. The reason behind this is because the malt, in some ways the most sensuous in all Speyside, is in short supply and demand is outstripping the efficiency of the stills – especially since sales of it went through the roof in Spain. So instead they launched in August a vatted Speyside malt called Cardhu Pure Malt. Very decent stuff, but just not pure Cardhu. There are no plans just now to bottle Cardow as a singleton, though doubtless it will happen in time, in limited editions most likely and, I would guess, at a premium price. While understanding the move, a part of me is uncomfortable with the Cardhu name being used this way: the packaging is very similar and I will be surprised if some unsuspecting or uninitiated souls don't buy Cardhu Pure Malt mistaking it to be the original single version. Cardhu is not a malt that other companies have been able to fill for their own blends for a good many years (especially when so much was required for their own massive Johnnie Walker portfolio) so the chances of it arriving as an independent bottling are slim to nil. Even so, the thought that several thousand casks of single malt bearing the name Cardhu exist while it is marketed as a vatted malt just goes against the grain for purists like me. I certainly hope it won't be the start of a trend. How ironic that the waters should be muddied by the cleanest malt on all Speyside.

Irresistible

On the subject of going through the roof, what an amazing year for what is fast being rightly recognised as the world's most extraordinary distillery: Ardbeg. Apart from being closed in January 2003 for three weeks of maintenance, the distillery has been operating a six-day week, taking its annual output to 950,000 litres of alcohol – some way removed from the 250,000 when Glenmorangie first began running things in 1997. In the same period, sales have moved from 200 nine-litre cases a year (of which I normally bought two) under Allied to a staggering 28,000 last year, marking a 33% increase in sales in the last year alone. Now, normally I make a point of never, ever getting all trade writer-ish when it comes to whisky. But in the case of Ardbeg it is something I can't resist, considering the long, lonely and sometimes heated campaign I waged for Allied to sell the distillery for it to achieve the world recognition it rightly deserved. The only blip in the last year or so, for me, has seen the 17-year-old lose some – occasionally all – of the peaty balance in recent bottlings. Though this is understandable due to the shortfall in old stock perhaps it would be wise to call a premature day on the 17-y-o while it is still very fondly remembered. However we were all more than compensated by the one off bottling of single cask '76 that almost defied description. Meanwhile the almost insatiable world demand for Ardbeg goes on. I remember – at the first meeting on Islay – of the Glenmorangie management, just days after they acquired the distillery, how they were worried that few people had ever heard of it. I assured them that if they played their cards right, they would have a cult brand on their hands. If the results of 2002–03 are anything to go by, it looks as though they are now holding four aces and three kings. It just shows what a little bit of faith can do.

Which reminds me. At a time when the marketing people in the industry try to confound you with the mysteries of whisky that may or may not exist, there is one that is genuine and is still to be explained: why is Ardmore, one of the world's greatest whisky distilleries, never brought out by its owners, Allied, as a single malt? Independent and special anniversary bottlings apart, it's a whisky earmarked for that brilliant and underrated blend, Teacher's. Frankly, it beggars belief, and the scores here in *Jim Murray's Whisky Bible* given to the handful of expressions available goes some way to underline what once was a hunch, now a firmly held belief. I am sure my friends in the Allied blending labs are happy to see just about all the make heading towards Teacher's. And that is a blend not to be tampered with. But, surely, Allied can find 25 casks from somewhere that they can dump as an official 10-year-old each year ...

And on the subject of Teacher's. Well, the worst news of the year by far was the confirmation of the closure of the magnificent Dumbarton grain distillery once and for all. Although originally it was supposed to be a mere mothballing – the temporary closure until stocks are required again – some of us were never quite convinced (especially in view of the commanding position it held by sea and city – perfect for upmarket re-development) and there was no great surprise when the grim news was announced. If the blenders at Allied tell me they are happy with the upgraded spirit coming from Strathclyde, then I believe them, because any team capable of putting together blends like Teacher's and Ballantines 17 must know what they are talking about. But even so ...

The grain at Dumbarton always seemed that little different: firm yet sympathetic. There was certainly nothing quite like it about and I now wait with not a little trepidation to see how the improved Strathclyde fits the bill. Dumbarton will be a hard act to follow: just not too hard I hope. (For the story of Dumbarton and how Strathclyde's grain was changed, read my feature to appear on **www.whiskybible.com**.)

Silence of the drams

And, just down the road from Dumbarton, while this book was being written, pen was being put to paper for the sale of one of the world's oldest distilleries: Littlemill. To add to the pathos, its ageing stock is enjoying a reputation it failed to attain in its working days, the trademark roughness being blunted by time. The stillhouse had already gone and soon the remainder is to follow now owners Loch Lomond have sold the land to developers. With all distilling equipment long removed, it was unlikely there would be much of a chance of a reprieve; the additional cost of installing more up to date effluent treatment was another large nail in its coffin. When neighbouring distilleries Dumbarton and Littlemill are flattened in fact three distilleries will vanish. The lowland distillery Inverleven was located within Dumbarton and I remember the sadness of the manager when I spoke to him the day it distilled for the last time a decade ago. He hoped it would reopen but a sadness and resignation in his voice suggested that his head told him something other than his heart.

But, as I say, most of the news is good. There are four planned new distilleries. One should be up and running soon in Campbeltown; there's a move afoot to build a tiny Lowlander; aborted plans are being re-worked to build Islay's smallest and a larger and financially well-backed concern in the entirely non-distilling island of Shetland, thereby stripping Highland Park of it's age-old title of Scotland's most northerly distillery.

Great and old oaks wither and fall. But green shoots are sprouting just about wherever in Scotland you look.

It goes without saying that things have been happening elsewhere in the whisky world. Not least in Kentucky where at last the pot still bourbon made at the refurbished Labrot & Graham Distillery has made its bottled bow. For those of us who remember the old plant as an elegant ruin in a beautiful hollow beside a lazy creek, it is hard not to pinch yourself to believe it true. A review of that and the most significant developments elsewhere will be found within the introductions of each section of the *Whisky Bible*.

Jim Murray's Whisky Bible Award Winners 2004

To save you reading over 2,000 whisky tasting notes one by one I have made life easy for you. Each year *Jim Murray's Whisky Bible* will announce a World Whisky of the Year selected from the winner of one of at least 18 categories. It is not only to help you. But it is to personally pay tribute to those who have created something exceptionally special in an already high quality industry.

As well as listing those that I believe have topped their particular tree we also have a roll of honour for all those elite brands which have scored 93 marks or above. During the research and writing of this book it has become apparent that the marking system has something of the Richter Scale about it: the higher the marks, the more pronounced it becomes. In other words, there may be little difference between whiskies marked at 69 and 71, but the gap between 89 and 91 becomes very large indeed.

With well over 2,000 whiskies evaluated for *Jim Murray's Whisky Bible*, it is obvious that the 85 whiskies making it to a score of 94 and above does represent the very highest peak of the mountain. Likewise the similar number on 93 itself represents the crème rather than double the crème.

For those of your wondering why the masterful Old Malt Cask Ardbeg 1975 doesn't pick up a gong, it was bottled in 2000 and therefore doesn't represent a recent bottling – even though a few unclaimed bottles can still be found here and there.

It is a strange thing, this tasting whisky for a living. Every day you sample a whisky for the first time, or re-sample it for the umpteenth, and over the years you get a feel for the best distilleries. Perhaps, then, it is no surprise that those I consider the top three in the world, Ardbeg, Buffalo Trace and Wild Turkey are all Award Winners, yet curiously not always with the brands I expected to see running away with the prizes. Also I was disappointed to see neither the 10 years olds of Laphroaig and especially Talisker make it to the 93 mark, let alone win their category.

But as little as a year ago I would have been genuinely surprised to see Jameson top the bill for the Irish and an obscure distillery in Oregon pick up the small batch award. Biggest surprise of all though was when I made it to a tiny Oat Whisky distillery in Austria and found an entirely new species of whisky and one, it must be said, of astounding beauty.

The question is what will *Jim Murray's Whisky Bible 2005* unearth? As this book amply demonstrates, absolutely nothing can be taken for granted as far as whisky is concerned ... except that true genius will always be celebrated within these pages.

Award Winners

2004 World Whisky of the Year
George T. Stagg

Scotch Single Malt of the Year
Ardbeg 1976 Single Cask No. 2390

Scotch Single Cask Single Malt of the Year
Ardbeg 1976 Single Cask No. 2390

Best New Scotch Single Malt Bottling (from more than one cask)
Macallan ESC IV

Best Scotch Single Malt 12 years Old and Under
Scotch Malt Whisky Society Cask 93.10 Aged 11 Years *(Glen Scotia)*

Scotch Blended Whisky of the Year
William Grant's 21 Year Old

Scotch Blended Whisky of the Year (Aged)
William Grant's 21 Year Old

Scotch Blended Whisky of the Year (Standard)
Teacher's Highland Cream

Best New Scotch Brand
The Six Isles Pure Island Malt

Bourbon of the Year
George T. Stagg

Best Bourbon Aged 10 Years or Under
Wild Turkey Russell's Reserve Aged 10 Years

Rye Whiskey of the Year
Sazerac Rye 18 Years Old

Irish Whiskey of the Year
Jameson

Japanese Whisky of the Year
Pure Malt Black

Japanese Single Malt of the Year
Hakushu 1984

Japanese Blended Whisky of the Year
Special Reserve 10 Years Old

Canadian Whisky of the Year
Seagram's VO

Best Small Batch Whisky of the Year
McCarthy's Oregon Single Malt Aged 3 Years

"New World" Whisky of the Year
Waldviestler Hafer Whisky 2000 *(Austrian Oat Whisky)*

The Rankings (97–93)

97

Scotch Single Malt

Old Malt Cask Ardbeg 1975 Aged 25 Years *(bottled Oct 00)*

Bourbon

George T. Stagg

96

Scotch Single Malt

Ardbeg 1976 Single Cask 2390
Ardbeg 1977
Ardbeg Committee Reserve
Ardbeg Provenance 1974
Old Malt Cask Ardbeg 25 Years Old (dist 75, bottled May 01)
Hart Brothers Glen Grant Aged 29 Years
Isle of Jura Aged 36 Years

Blended Scotch

Ballantine's 17 Years Old
William Grant's 21 Year Old

Bourbon

Elijah Craig 12 Years Old
Wild Turkey Russell's Reserve Aged 10 Years

Straight Rye

Sazerac Rye 18 Years Old

95

Scotch Single Malt

Ardbeg 21 Years Old
The Dalmore 62 Years Old
Glenglassaugh 1973 Family Silver
Private Collection Glen Grant 1953
Highland Park Aged 18 Years
Scott's Selection Longmorn-Glenlivet 1971
The Macallan ESC IV
Cask Port Ellen 1980
Springbank Aged 35 Years
Talisker Aged 20 Years

Blended Scotch

Black Bottle
The Royal and Ancient 28 Years
Royal Salute 50 Years Old
Teacher's Highland Cream
William Lawson's Founder's Reserve Aged 18 Years

Blended Irish

Jameson

Bourbon

Daniel Stewart Aged 12 Years *(aka Original Barrel Bourbon Aged 12 Years)*

Japanese Single Malt

Hakushu 1984
Suntory Pure Malt Hakushu Aged 12 Years
Yoichi 20 Years Old

Japanese Vatted Malt

Pure Malt Black

94

Scotch Single Malt

Aberlour a'bunadh 12 Years Old Stirling Silver Label
Old Malt Cask Ardbeg 1975 Aged 24 Years
Ardmore 100th Anniversary 12 Years Old
Old Master's Ardmore 1980
Bladnoch Aged 10 Years (Flora and Fauna)
Bowmore Voyage
Caol Ila Aged 21 Rare Malts Selection
Blackadder Raw Cask Clynelish 1976
Dalwhinnie 15 Years Old
Glenfiddich 1937
Adelphi Glen Grant 31 Years Old cask 1706
Old Masters Glen Grant 1969
Glenmorangie 10 Years Old
The Glenrothes 1967
Scotch Malt Whisky Society Cask 93.10 Aged 11 Years *(Glen Scotia)*
Highland Park Aged 25 Years *(50.7%)*
Mission Range Highland Park 1979
Knockdhu 23 Years Old
Laphroaig Aged 30 Years
Laphroaig Aged 40 Years
Old Malt Cask Millburn Aged 34 Years
Adelphi Port Ellen 24 Years Old
Rosebank Aged 20 Years Rare Malts Selection
Royal Lochngar Aged 23 Years Rare Malts Selection
Old Malt Cask Scapa Aged 25 Years (dist Nov 74)

Unspecified Single Malt Scotch

Finlaggan Old Reserve Islay Single Malt
The Ileach Peaty Islay Single Malt

Vatted Scotch Malt

Century of Malts
Safeway Islay Pure Malt 10 Years Old
The Six Isles Pure Island Malt

Blended Scotch

Chivas Brothers Oldest and Finest
William Grant's Family Reserve

Irish Single Malt

Knappogue Castle 1992

Blended Irish

Jameson 1780 Matured 12 Years
Jameson Gold

American Single Malt

McCarthy's Oregon Single Malt Aged 3 Years

Bourbon

Buffalo Trace
Eagle Rare 17 Years Old
Jefferson's Reserve 15 Year Old
Old Forrester Birthday Bourbon Vintage 1989
Vintage Bourbon 1976
Wild Turkey Rare Breed *(batch W-T-02-91)*

Single Malt Rye

Old Potrero *(Essay 8 RW ARM 8 A)*

Japanese Single Malt

Suntory Pure Malt Hakushu Aged 20 Years

Shirakawa 32 Years Old Single Malt
Yoichi 15 Years Old
Scotch Malt Whisky Society Cask 116.1 Aged 16 Years *(Yoichi)*

Japanese Blended

Special Reserve 10 Years Old

Canadian

Seagram's VO

Austrian Oat Whisky

Waldviestler Hafer Whisky 2000

93

Scotch Single Malt

Aberlour Aged 15 Years Cuvee Marie d'Ecosse
Ardbeg 10 Years Old
Ardbeg 1976 Single Cask 2395
Connoisseurs Choice Ardbeg 1974 *(bottled 95)*
Old Malt Cask Ardbeg Aged 29 Years
Provenance Autumn Distillation Ardbeg Over 9 Years
The Balvenie Aged 15 Years Single Barrel
The Maltmill Speyside (Balvenie) Single Malt 11 Years
Peerless Benriach 1968 (cask 2590)
Bowmore 17 Years Old
Platinum Brora 1972
Old Malt Cask Bunnahabhain Aged 16 Years
Adelphi Dailuaine 22 Years Old
The Dalmore 1973 Gonzalez Byass Sherry Cask Finish
Glenfiddich Aged 15 Years Solera Reserve
Cadenhead's Glenglassaugh 25 Years Old
Glengoyne 1985 Cask 103
Peerless Glen Grant 1974
Scotch Malt Whisky Society 18th Anniversary Cask No. 9.30 *(Glen Grant)*
The Glenlivet Cellar Collection 30 Years Old American Oak Finish
The Glenlivet Vintage 1970
Berry's Own Selection Glenlivet 1975
Glenmorangie Distillery Manager's Choice 2001
Blackadder Glenturret 17 Years Old
Highland Park Bicentenary Vintage 1977 Reserve
Old Malt Cask Highland Park Aged 25 Years
Isle of Jura 1973 Vintage
Laphroaig 10 Years Old Original Cask Strength
Private Cellar Longmorn-Glenlivet 1970
The Macallan 1946 Select Reserve
The Macallan 1972 29 Years Old
Oban Bicentenary Manager's Dram 16 Years Old
The Whisky Shop Port Ellen 1978
Coopers Choice Rosebank 1993
Scotch malt Whisky Society Cask 25.30 Aged 13 Years (Rosebank)
"Green" Brackla 1975 27 Years Old
Springbank Wood Expression 12 Year Old Rum Wood
Juul's Private Bottling Springbank Vintage 1966 Aged 34 Years
Murray McDavid Springbank 1965
Cask Strathisla 1974

Vatted Scotch Malt

Compass Box Eleuthera All Malt

Blended Scotch
  The Bailie Nicol Jarvie
  Buchanan's Special Reserve
  Compass Box Asyla *(2003 bottling)*
  Islay Mist Premium Aged 17 Years
  Isle of Skye 8 Years Old
  Royal Salute 21 Years Old
  Royal Silk Reserve
  Whyte & Mackay 30 Years Old
  William Grant's Classic Reserve 21 Year Old
Irish Pure Pot Still
  Knappogue Castle 1951
Irish Single Malt
  Bushmills 16 Years Old Triple Wood
Blended Irish
  Golden Irish
  Midleton Very Rare 1990
Bourbon
  Ancient Ancient Age 10 Years Old
  Blanton's Gold Edition
  Booker's 7 Yrs 3 Months
  Maker's Mark (Black Wax Seal)
  Old Heaven Hill Very Rare Aged 10 Years 100 Proof
  Rip Van Winkle 15
  Old Heaven Hill Very Rare Aged 10 Years 100 Proof
  Rip Van Winkle 15 Years Old
Single Malt Rye
  Old Potrero *(Essay 5 RW ARM 2 A)*
Straight Rye
  Jim Beam Rye
Japanese Single Malt
  Scotch Malt Whisky Society Cask 120.1 Aged 21 Years *(Hakushu)*
  Nikka Single CaskMalt Whisky 10 Years Old *(Yoichi)*
  Yoichi 10 Years Old
Japanese Vatted Malt
  Southern Alps Pure Malt
Japanese Blended
  Golden Horse Busyuu Deluxe
  Hibiki 21 Years Old
  The Nikka Whisky Aged 34 Years
  Super Nikka
  Tsuru
Canadian
  Crown Royal
  Gibson's Finest Rare
  Lot No 40
  Schenley OFC Aged 8 Years
  Wiser's De Luxe 10 Years Old

Scottish Malts

For those of you deciding to take the plunge and head off into the labyrinthine world of Scotch malt whisky, a piece of advice. And that is, be careful who you take your advice from. Because, too often, I hear that you should leave the Islays until you have tackled the featherlight Speysiders and the bolder, weightier Highlanders. This is just complete, patronising nonsense. The only time that rings true is if you are tasting a number of whiskies in one day. Then leave the smoky ones to last, so the lighter chaps get a fair hearing.

I know many people who didn't like whisky until they got a Talisker from Skye inside them, or a Lagavulin to swamp their tastebuds with oily iodine. The fact is, you can take your map of malt whisky, start at any point and head in any direction you feel. There are no hard and fast rules. Certainly with well over 1,000 tasting notes here you should have some help in picking where this journey of a lifetime begins.

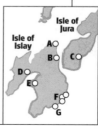

Isle of Skye

8

29

Isle of Mull

DISTILLERY LOCATOR

1	Highland Park	21	Tullibardine	H	Glasgow
	Scapa	22	Glengoyne	I	Edinburgh
2	Pulteney	23	Loch Lomond	J	Perth
3	Clynelish		Littlemill	K	Dundee
4	Balblair		Auchentoshan	L	Aberdeen
5	Glenmorangie		Interleven	M	Inverness
6	Dalmore	24	Rosebank	N	Ben Nevis
	Teaninich	25	St. Magdalene		
7	Glen Ord	26	Glenkinchie		
8	Talisker	27	Isle of Arran		
9	Ben Nevis	28	Sprinbank		
10	Dalwhinnie		Glen Scotia		
11	Royal Lochnagar	29	Tobermory		
12	Glen Garioch	A	Bunnahabhain		
13	Oban	B	Caol Ila		
14	Edradour	C	Jura		
15	Fettercairn	D	Bruichladdich		
16	Blair Athol	E	Bowmore		
17	Glencadam	F	Ardbeg		
18	Aberfeldy		Lagavulin		
19	Glenturret		Laphroaig		
20	Deanston	G	Port Ellen		

Isle of Jura

Isle of Islay

A

B C

D

E

F

G

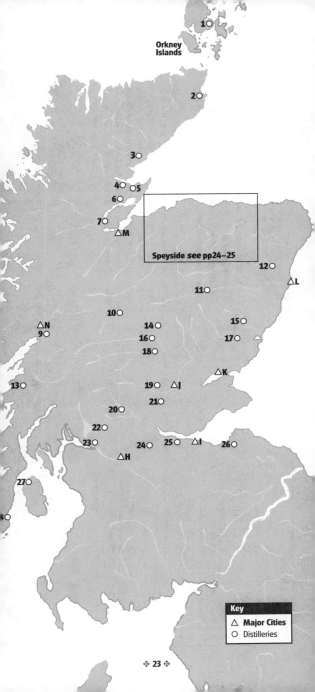

Orkney
Islands

1○

2○

3○

4○ 5○
6○
7○
△M

Speyside *see* pp24–25

12○

△L

11○

△N
9○

10○

14○

15○

16○

17○

18○

13○

19○ △J

21○

20○

22○

23○

24○ 25○ △I 26○

△H

27○

△K

Key	
△	**Major Cities**
○	Distilleries

Speyside

No other area on earth has such a concentration of whisky distilleries as Speyside. And although they are falling out of fashion somewhat – Macallan apart – the last year has seen some impressive new offerings, especially from older bottlings.

The most common style of Speyside malt is a mouthwatering one, not dissimilar to chewing on the stem of freshly picked young grass. However, that was not always the case, and Speyside – or Glenlivet malts, as they were once known – tended to have a weightier, smoky style, evidenced by some bottlings of Macallan from the 1940s. Only Ardmore continues this tradition though Gordon & MacPhail's Benromach distillery after a few years of experimentation have now decided to go down that route. The results, perhaps to be released in a decade's time, should make fascinating dramming.

DISTILLERY LOCATOR

1	Speyside	15	Cardhu	28	Knochdhu
2	Tomatin	16	Benrinnes	29	Ardmore
3	Tomintoul	17	Aberlour	30	Glendronach
4	Braeval	18	Macallan	31	Glenglassaugh
5	Tamnavulin	19	Craigellachie	32	Macduff
6	The Glenlivet	20	Glen Elgin		
7	Tormore	21	Glenlossie	**A**	**Dufftown**
8	Royal Brackla	22	Mannochmore		Glenfiddich
9	Cragganmore	23	Miltonduff		Balvenie
10	Glenfarclas		Benriach		Kininvie
11	Allt - A - Bhainne	24	Longmorn		Glendullan
12	Dailuaine		Linkwood		Mortlach
13	Tamdhu	25	Glenburgie		Dufftown
14	Knockando	26	Glenmoray (Elgin)		Pittyvaich
	Imperial	27	Inchgower		

B	**Rothes**
	Speyburn
	Glen Grant
	Caperdonich
	Glenrothes
	Glen Spey
C	**Mulben**
	Auchroisk
	Glentauchers
D	**Keith**
	Altmore
	Strathmill
	Glen Keith
	Strathisla

Key

△ Major Cities
○ Distilleries

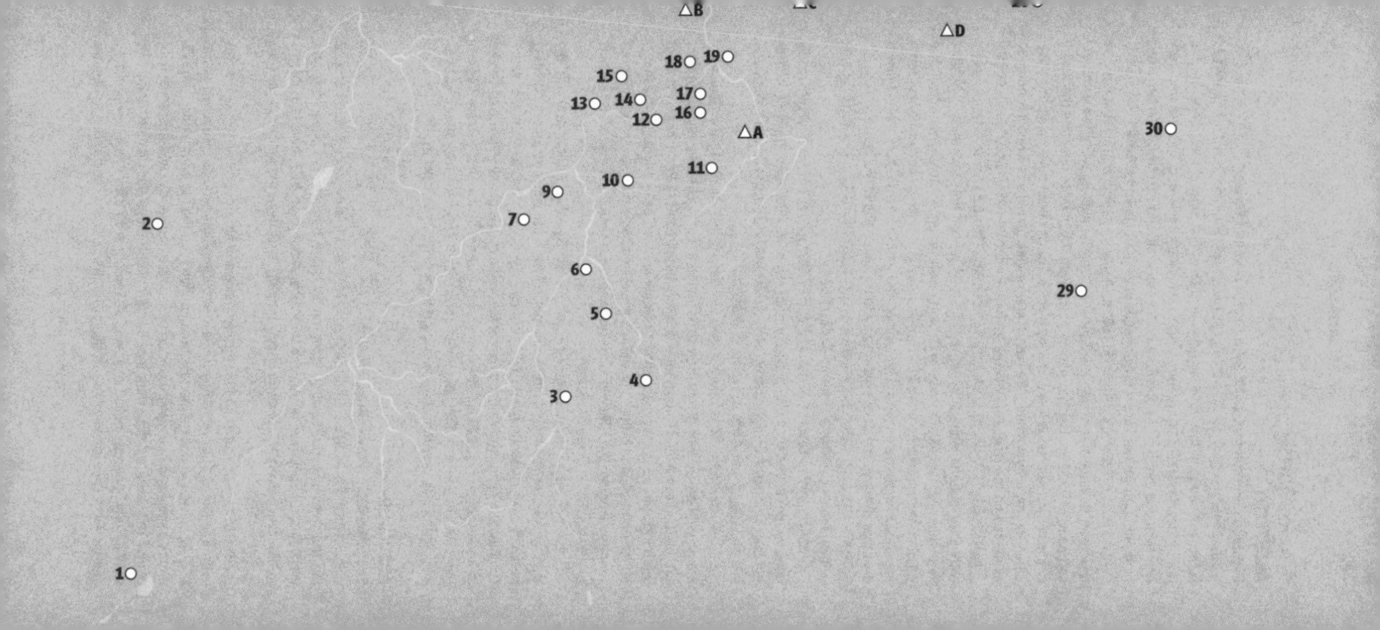

B
D
18
19
15
17
13
14
16
12
A
30
11
10
9
2
7
6
29
5
4
3
1

Single Malts
ABERFELDY
Highlands (Perthshire), 1898. John Dewar & Sons. Working.

Aberfeldy Aged 12 Years db **(89) n**22 softly honied, rich and clean; **t**23 lighter in body than the nose suggests, a prick of first smoke, then spice, but the honey develops; **f**22 pretty long with developing vanilla and soft oils and very late honey again; **b**22 I have long loved this malt and it shows to good effect here although I'm not sure if the strength does it any favours. **40%**

Aberfeldy Aged 25 Years db **(85) n**24 this might fool a few Highland Park devotees: heather and honey in abundance, and beautifully weighted with very soft peat, too; **t**21 the oak has played havoc with the balance here and the honey is patchy and sparse; **f**19 dry, chalky, tired; **b**21 just doesn't live up to the nose. When Tommy Dewar wrote, "We have a great regard for old age when it is bottled," as quoted on the label, I'm not sure he had as many as 25 years in mind. **40%**

Aberfeldy 1980 Cask Strength bott 97 db **(92) n**23 some serious weight with juicy sultana alongside honey, crushed green leaf and malt; **t**24 pure Perthshire: honey all the way with soft, lush, intense malty mouthfeel. The vaguest hint of delicate peat; **f**22 more smoke and now a heather-honey depth appears, though the finale is a bit toffeed and vanilla intense; **b**23 this is brilliant malt that displays the distillery's beauty to its fullest extent. **62%**

Connoisseurs Choice Aberfeldy 1975 **(81) n**20 **t**22 **f**19 **b**20. Slightly smoky and sweet. **40%**. *Gordon & MacPhail.*

Connoisseurs Choice Aberfeldy 1977 **(83) n**20 **t**21 **f**22 **b**20. A soft, mildly honied dram with a surprising appearance of shy peat. **40%**. *Gordon & MacPhail.*

Connoisseurs Choice Aberfeldy 1978 **(84) n**22 **t**22 **f**20 **b**20. Floral and lots of barley sugar. **40%**. *Gordon & MacPhail.*

Old Malt Cask Aberfeldy Aged 23 Years dist Oct 78 **(86) n**22 a salty aroma with an old wooden garden shed feel to it. Perhaps a little too much oak; **t**20 big and not a little coastal for a distillery in the heart of Perthshire! Briny, but the honey thread unravels and intensifies towards the oaky middle; **f**24 lashings of rich honey, a little burnt toast around the edges, remaining spicy and salty, but seriously yummy; **b**20 there is an oaky stand-off at first, but the finish is the stuff of dreams. **50%**. *Douglas Laing.*

Scotch Malt Whisky Society Cask 60.25 Aged 27 Years **(89) n**22 big stuff: curiously coastal for a Perthshire malt with a briny, citrus freshness blending perfectly with seasoned oak; **t**22 no less shy on the palate with the same combination restructuring in a different formation on the palate. A touch of smoke is added for effect; **f**23 such a tease: softens down towards a more coffee-demerara finale with the oak threat receding; **b**22 absolutely stunning stuff playing the oak brinkmanship card to perfection. **55.2%. nc ncf sc.**

ABERLOUR
Speyside, 1826. Chivas Bros. Working.

Aberlour 10 Years Old db **(86) n**20 mint and freshly sliced cucumber; **t**22 big fruit presence but teasing, spicy malts battle through; **f**23 very long and weighty for a Speysider of this age with formulating fruit; **b**21 there is evidence of a decent percentage of clean sherry butts at work here: the spiciness stars for the malt. **43%**

Aberlour a'bunadh db **(88) n**23 liquorice and hickory, coal dust, oloroso and even a gentle waft of peat. Any heavier and the aroma wouldn't leave the glass; **t**22 big spice and oak hit the tastebuds running, the malt is an afterthought; **f**21 remains spicy and heavy with a return of liquorice (red candy style, this time); **b**22 phew! This is heavy-duty malt that blasts holes through your palate, unique in style for any Speyside malt. If anything, it's too big at **59.8%**! This is a single malt that varies in style slightly from bottling to bottling. Sadly the bottling marks are often too small to make head or tail of, or I would include different tasting notes as I have done with Yoichi. However below, to give some idea of the variance in style, are the notes and evaluation from one of the earliest bottlings in 1998.

Aberlour a'bunadh db **(91)** n23 firm malt and sherry but punctuated by over-ripe mango and rich honey tones; t23 immediate spice and then an eruption of honey and barley with some liquorice diving in. A soft dispersal of peat around the palate adds an extra surprise; f22 the intensity remains at first but quietens as vanilla makes its mark and some cocoa trickles in; b23 brilliantly balanced and displaying a fruity-malty and mildly peaty complexity which is jaw-dropping. **59.6%**

Aberlour a'bunadh 12 Years Old Sterling Silver Label db **(94)** n24 stupendous stuff: heavier and oakier than the age suggests but with a big, waxy sherry note offering a cleaner, richer dimension; t22 quite massive with a big sherry and ripe date surge that breaks against a malt middle and delicious spices; f23 long, magnificently oaky and proud. Pure cocoa and clean sherry fight for the finish but intertwine for a dead heat; b23 don't try and convince me all the malts in here are 12 – the average age seems a whole lot greater. Just startling and just about deserving a 24-carat gold label. **58.7%**. *Limited edition.*

Aberlour 12 Years Old Double Cask Matured db **(79)** n19 t21 f19 b20. Fresh mint on the nose and finish but the taste, though rich, lacks structure. **43%**

Aberlour 12 Years Old Sherry Cask Matured db **(85)** n20 bizarrely toothpastey; what is it about mint and Aberlour? t22 stunningly textured, rich fruit, with succulent grape edging out the malt; f22 long, with fingers of oak on the malt; b21 this is a big, clean dram where the malt is just about strong enough to hold onto the sherry. **40%**

Aberlour Aged 15 Years Cuvee Marie d'Ecosse db **(93)** n23 sublime fresh sherry with kumquats and lime for extra zest; t24 beautifully ethereal with the malt drifting in all directions while the fruit, though rich, has virtually no weight at all, magical malt; f22 some light vanilla apologetically drifts in to replace what appeared to be a hint of smoke; b24 this, and the a'bunadh Sterling Silver, lift Aberlour into the super league of malt whiskies. It is sold primarily in France, and one can assume only that this is God's way of making amends for that pretentious, over-rated, caramel-ridden rubbish called Cognac they've had to endure for the last couple of centuries. Hope there'll be enough to go around the rest of the world one day. **43%**

Aberlour Aged 15 Years Sherry Wood Finish db **(84)** n19 t21 f23 b21. The sherry slowly builds to a chewy, spicy crescendo. **40%**

Aberlour Aged 21 Years db **(77)** n21 t21 f17 b18. Hard as nails with the finish really closing in with little compassion. **43%**

Aberlour Aged 30 Years db **(89)** n23 a clean, deep sherry aroma with a lemon and mint residue: compelling stuff; t22 deep, moderately dry throughout with a slow build-up of spices and smoke. Malty, grapey succulence together with some cocoa bitterness adds extra complexity; f22 long and brilliantly weighted, the fruitiness helps sweeten the malt gracefully; b22 a classy Aberlour with great complexity. **43%**. *1,000 bottles.*

Aberlour 1976 db **(85)** n22 suety, sultanas, lots of vanilla; t20 a sweet malt blast is immediately swamped by wave upon wave of encroaching oak; f22 more vanilla but malt stretches complicate the length; b21 pleasant and well-measured; lacking complexity until the finish. **43%**

Aberlour 1980 db **(89)** n21 sawdust and sultanas; t22 exceptionally clean malt and fruit with a subtle prickly backdrop; f24 immensely complex with warming hints of everything from spice to sherry with malt and smoke in between: a legendary phase for any whisky; b22 a quality dram offering enormous subtlety and charisma. **43%**

Aberlour 1988 Distillers Selection db **(69)** n17 t19 f16 b17. Sulphur tainted, I'm afraid. **40%**

Aberlour 100 Proof db **(91)** n*23* beneath this sherried, volcanic start there is something rather sweet and honied. One of the most two-toned noses you'll find in a long while; t*23* sweet to begin and honied, too. The maltiness keeps its shape for some time. Between the middle and end an ebulliient spiciness takes hold; f*22* massively long and fruity; b*23* stunning, sensational whisky, the most extraordinary Speysider of them all ...which it was when I wrote those official notes for the bottling back in '97, I think. Other malts have superseded it now, but on re-tasting I stand by those original notes, though I disassociate myself entirely with the rubbish: "In order to savour Aberlour 100 at its best add 1/3 to 1/2 pure water". **57.1%**

Aberlour Warehouse No. 1 Aged 12 Years cask 11552 filled into cask 12/12/90, first-fill bourbon cask db **(86)** n*22* nutty, biscuity; t*22* sweet with ripe cherries and rich malt; f*21* long and slightly toasty, good sweet malt follow-up; b*21* great to see a bourbon-cask Aberlour for once. Strength not stated – around **60%. sc.**

Aberlour Warehouse No. 1 Aged 13 Years sherry cask matured 6524 filled into cask 26/5/89 db **(90)** n*22* raw oloroso but not even a hint of an off-note: almost overpowering; t*23* just about the cleanest oloroso you could wish for: thankfully the malt has body enough to pick a spicy hole through the fruity onslaught; f*22* the fruit slowly subsides leaving a slightly roasty, burnt oaky note at the death: even a pinch of salt and smoke, maybe; b*23* for those who love their sherried whisky. Come and get it! No strength stated – about **59%.**

Blackadder Raw Cask Aberlour 1990 sherry hogshead 3318, dist 7 May 90, bott Apr 02 **(70)** n*17* t*19* f*17* b*17*. Rich, but a poor cask. **59.9%. nc ncf sc.**

Blackadder Raw Cask Aberlour 1990 bourbon hogshead 3319, dist 7 May 90, bott Mar 03 **(87)** n*21* fresh, immature for its age, but quite mouthwatering and appealing; t*23* classic, sharp, grassy notes, enormous gristy malt; f*22* clean, malty, chewy; b*21* lack of complexity thanks to almost zero oak input but a delicious Speysider. **60%. nc ncf sc.**

Cadenhead's Aberlour-Glenlivet 13 Years Old dist 89, bott 03/03 **(86)** n*21* fresh, grassy; t*22* mouthwatering, fresh, uninterrupted malt; f*22* medium length, remains grassy and clean; b*21* if you ever wanted to know what a blender looks for in 12-ish-year-old Speyside from a cask that is on its second or third filling, this is just about the perfect example. **46%**

Old Malt Cask Aberlour Aged 12 Years (83) n*21* t*21* f*20* b*21*. Demure and subtle, a textbook quality Speysider. **50%.** Douglas Laing.

The Single Barrel Collection Aberlour 1987 dist Mar 87, bott Dec 01, cask no. 1806 **(77)** n*19* t*18* f*21* b*19*. Pleasant but rather one-dimensional. **55.43%. nc nf.**

Whisky Galore Aberlour 1989 14 Years Old (84) n*19* t*23* f*21* b*21*. Really clean and delicious (especially on the mouth arrival), the malt running riot unimpeded by oak. But perhaps too young for its age. Even so, just so massively drinkable! **46%.** Duncan Taylor & Co.

ALLT-A-BHANE
Speyside, 1975. Chivas Bros. Silent.

Old Malt Cask Allt A Bhainne Aged 16 Years dist Apr 85, bott May 01 **(66)** n*15* t*18* f*16* b*17*. Allt-a-sorts. **50%. nc ncf.** Douglas Laing. 114 bottles.

ANCNOC (see Knockdhu)

ARDBEG
Islay, 1815. Glenmorangie Plc. Working.

Ardbeg 10 Years Old db **(93)** n*23* oily, slapped-on-all-over-with-a-trowel-peat that leaves nothing uncoated. A lovely salty tang gives an extra tweak; t*23* sweet, equally oily arrival with a massive malt surge. When that has passed the serious work of picking out the intense seaweedy, oaky complexity begins; **f**24 stupendous spices add an extra dimension to the already complex story unfolding on the palate; **b**23 close your eyes and enjoy. **46%**

Ardbeg 17 Years Old (earlier bottlings) db **(92)** n23 a gentle, seductive, sweet peat leads the way to a complex arrival of malt and vanilla; **t**22 soft and languid at first, brilliant, sweet chewy malt with just a shade of cocoa adding depth and balance; **f**23 a delightful level of residual peat which ensures a long, sophisticated finish and just shows the extent of Ardbeg's complexity even without peat screaming at you; **b**24 OK, I admit I had a big hand in this, creating it with the help of Glenmorangie Plc's John Smith. It was designed to take the weight off the better vintages of Ardbeg whilst ensuring a constant if limited supply around the world. Certainly one of the more subtle expressions you are likely to find, though criticised by some for not being peaty enough. As the whisky's creator, all I can say is they are missing the point. **40%**

Ardbeg 17 Years Old (present bottlings) db **(90)** n22 enormously fruity and flighty. The peat though present is just a mere echo of what it once was, with lashings of sweet marmalade where peat used to be, but still lightly salted and malty; **t**23 moist Madeira cake with cherries; softly malted and sweet with a lovely encrustation of salt that slowly grows; **f**22 the sweet fruit continues on its classy course; the shape in the mouth is sublime, the smoke almost a mirage; **b**23 the peat has all but vanished and cannot really be compared to the original 17-year-old: maybe it's time to give this beauty a new name. It's a bit like tasting a Macallan without the sherry: fascinating to see the naked body underneath, and certainly more of a turn on. Peat or no peat, great whisky by any standards. **40%**

Ardbeg 21 Years Old db **(95)** n24 the kind of aroma that has made a legend of a distillery: marmalade on slightly burnt toast while in the background a peat fire smoulders and salt melts on porridge; **t**24 arrives on the palate like a snowflake, deft, weightless for all its enormity of character, lush citrus fruits for all the rich peat; **f**22 for its age, sweet and tender: the oak is taking a day off and offers no more than a token bitterness to counter the malt, beautifully spiced; **b**25 we all have bad days, weeks, months in our life when we wonder why we were put on this earth then you open a bottle like this and discover the reason. This is a dram of dreams, an inspiration and reminder that something does not have to be perfect to achieve greatness. The distillery manager Stuart Thomson oft told me of his affection for this bottling. It was one of the few Ardbegs that had slipped through my net over the last 25 years. So I tasted it for the first time to mark the 1500th whisky for this book. Stuart's confidence was well-founded: the remaining few hundred bottlings have a tough act to follow. **56.3%.** *Limited edition from 12 casks.*

Ardbeg Guaranteed 30 Years Old db **(91)** n24 slightly burnt toast, raisins on the highest point of a freshly baked bun; sensuous malt and peat-reek on a vanilla bed; **t**23 silky and increasingly sweet, none of the enormity one might expect and the oak plays lip-service; **f**21 perhaps too gentle for an Ardbeg with limited shoreline complexity; **b**23 an unsual beast, one of the last ever bottled by Allied. The charm and complexity early on is enormous, but the fade rate is surprising. That said, still a dram of considerable magnificence. **40%**

Ardbeg 1975 Single Cask No. 4701 db **(87)** n22 dry and oaky, the peat arrives in salty waves; **t**22 rich and estery with a distinct maltiness that is set apart from the smoke; **f**21 more salty esters and vanilla; **b**22 unusual mouthfeel for an Ardbeg: hard and relatively unyielding for this distillery. **46.4%**

Ardbeg 1975 Single Cask No. 4703 db **(91)** n22 hard, flinty malt, peat hovers around, complex salts; **t**23 brilliantly fills the mouth with an ever-increasing smoke presence, begins dry and then sweetens out: a profound malt; **f**23 softens but the complexity levels refuse to fall, quite salty by the end with rich fruit adding depth; **b**23 a lovely Ardbeg that is quite lethargic despite its obvious riches. The bitter-sweet balance nears perfection. **47.7%**

Ardbeg 1975 Single Cask No. 4716 db **(86) n**21 dank stables, smoke and salt; **t**22 sweet malt with some vanilla and peat giving something to chew on; **f**22 light vanilla, cocoa, oranges and smoke; **b**21 doesn't quite take off and develop like the average Ardbeg of this era. Still a little gem, though. **45%**

Ardbeg 1975 Single Cask No, 4718 db **(83) n**20 **t**22 **f**20 **b**21. The least inspiring of the individual casks, revealing that Ardbeg is mortal after all. Still amasses a complexity other whiskies dream about but the finish, like the nose, is bitter and less than perfect. **46.7%**

Ardbeg 1976 Single Cask No. 2390 sherry butt filled 24 Nov 76, hand bott at dist 27 Apr 02 db **(96) n**24 biting brine despite the sherry. The cask seems to have been held under water for 25 years, not in a warehouse: remarkable and quite brilliant; **t**25 a stupendous marriage of ripe grape, perfectly weighted peat-reek and juicy malt. It simply doesn't get better than this. Come to think of it, few things in life actually do; **f**23 relatively medium but again it is the brine that stars, bringing out the intensity of the barley yet keeping the oak at bay, some deep liquorice underlines the age; **b**24 when you die, have a bottle of this put beside you in the coffin to take to the afterworld: this is just one of those drams of a lifetime. Distillery manager Stuart Thomson has proved to be an inspired choice: not only can he make a fine malt, he can pick a bloody incredible dram. Respect. **53.1%**. *494 bottles; sold only at distillery.*

Ardbeg 1976 Single Cask No. 2395 db **(93) n**24 salty and a lot peatier than the sherry usually allows. Let it lay, unwatered, in the glass for 10 minutes for the most extraordinary results. Then it becomes farmyardy, organic and just so alive; **t**23 very sweet malt arrival then an explosion of peat, big with some juicy fruit; **f**22 decent oak arrival and teasing spices and chocolate; **b**24 really supremely weighted malt with a bit more oak than it needs but enough charisma to see it off. **54.4%**

Ardbeg 1976 Single Cask No. 2396 db **(91) n**24 mildly hot and nippy, even so, just wonderful peat complexity. No joking: take 5–10 minutes over this one before drinking. Incredible; **t**23 labyrinthine peat and malt delve deep into the oak, liquorice and aniseed form a fascinating sub committee; **f**21 mildly tame compared to the complexity of earlier, sweetens with vanilla and gristy malt starring. The final burst is pretty hard and brittle; **b**23 at first this was marked in the mid-80s. Then I tasted again ... and again ... and again.... Superb. **53.5%**

Ardbeg 1976 Single Cask No. 3275 db **(85) n**22 thin, quite hard, orangey and bourbony; **t**21 biting. malty, soft peat; **f**21 lots of vanilla and custard; **b**21 a quite different, light dram highlighting the scope of the peating levels in those own-made malt days. Those who thought the lightly peated 17-year-old vatting a recent un-Ardbegian invention and vociferously decried it are in for a reality check and a large slice of humble pie. **44.6%**

Ardbeg 1977 db **(96) n**25 an aroma your nose sinks into and you have to prise it away from the glass: thick, weighty, gently oiled peat offers so much more. The barley is still intact, there is coke smoke and a million things you might find from the sea. Never sweet, never dry; **t**24 probably the sweetest Ardbeg arrival on the palate of all time: an absorbing mixture of one part sugar cane juice to 20 parts concentrated malt, and heavily peated malt at that; **f**23 lighter here than I might have expected when I first tasted the casks in '97, the oak has fizzed through like I anticipated, so there is a lightness towards the end slightly unusual for an Ardbeg. Even so, the mouthfeel remains nothing short of perfect; **b**24 when working through the Ardbeg stocks, I earmarked '77 a special vintage, the sweetest of them all. So it has proved. Only the '74 absorbed that extra oak that gave greater all-round complexity. Either way, sweet, or slightly dryer, the quality of the distillate is beyond measure: simply one of the greatest experiences – whisky or otherwise – of your life. **46%**

Ardbeg 1978 db **(91)** n23 dry, the oak has already made telling inroads, but kept in check by brilliant salty, coastal notes; t24 wave upon wave of peated malt crashes on the tastebuds, the sweetness level rising with each landing, quite salty and chewy; f22 the oak remains confident but allows the mildly sweet malt a very free hand, slightly bitter towards the end; b22 an Ardbeg on the edge of losing it because of encroaching oak, hence the decision made by John Smith and I to bottle this vintage early alongside the 17-year-old. Five years on, still looks a pretty decent dram, though slightly under strength! **43%**

Ardbeg Committee Reserve bott 02, db **(96)** n24 punchy, salty and oily, there is a mildly Taliskeresque, peppery bite to this one ... perfect for starting the tasting day at 7am!!! My God, am I awake now, or what??? t24 brilliant spray of all things sweet and salty and so much more besides. The peat seems to operate on several different levels, each one displaying slightly different coastal tones or pure vegetable: outstanding; f23 surprising toffee-fudge finish but before then the quality of the chocolate would shame the Belgians; b25 absolutely faultless balance: Ardbeg personified. You take the first mouthful and wonder: is this the best Ardbeg of them all? Had I been drinking this at the distillery and not in my tasting lab, I would probably have said yes. But this lab is a great leveller, devoid of all romantic contact with the exception, perhaps, of sultry, dark brown Brazilian eyes flashing at you at the other side of my desk ... but I digress. What a way to start the day ... does this rate alongside the OMC '75 or the Provenance '74, or even the Ardbeg '77? It is a hard choice. More mouthfuls are required at full cask strength: it's a tough life. But then that toffee note detected is further concentrated upon: this is not something normally in the the Ardbeg armoury and is for me, I decide, a chink. A mark is lost. The ACR is not the greatest Ardbeg of all time. It's not yet 8 in the morning. Nearly an hour has passed in near silence trying to unravel this conundrum. Time for breakfast after Ardbeg. Do I have any caviar left ...? **55.3%**. *3,000 bottles.*

Ardbeg Lord of the Isles db **(87)** n23 as if two peat types are working in tandem: one soft, toffeed and lilting, the other firmer, drier; t23 big peat kick at first then a more sombre maltiness; f20 slightly flat and disappointing; b21 a dram that starts well enough but complexity becomes scarcer as a cream-toffee effect mingles with the peat. **46%**

Ardbeg Provenance 1974 bott 99, db **(96)** n24 the peat courses through the aroma in perfect balance and harmony with the soft, gently spiced and salted peat, touches of something citrus here and there, too; t25 the malt is soft and sweet at first but then the peatiness gathers momentum and intensity until it absolutely glows; f23 the oak bourbon-malt-peat-cocoa characters all ebb and flow but are joined by a more bitter note that counters the earlier sweet maltiness, some toffee-character in there as well: all-in-all, pretty enormous; b24 this is an exercise in subtlety and charisma, the beauty and the beast drawn into one. Until I came across the 25-year-old OMC verson during a thunderstorm in Denmark, this was arguably the finest whisky I had ever tasted: I opened this and drank from it to see in the year 2000. When I went through the Ardbeg warehouse stocks in 1997 I earmarked the '74 and '77 vintages as something special. This bottling has done me proud. **55.6%**

Connoisseurs Choice Ardbeg 1974 (bottled 95 – old-fashioned cream label) **(93)** n24 massive depth that cocks a snook at the 40% strength. Complexity goes off the scale here as orangey-fig notes dovetail with brooding, mildly sinister smokiness, ye olde Ardbeg at its most nose-tweaking; t23 beautiful marmalade notes melt into the peaty inferno, lots going on here, but in a very gentlemanly way; f23 fruit and malt sit comfortably with the bitter cocoa and lingering peat, the fade is a slow one; b23 a dram that is etched in the hearts of many Ardbeg lovers discovering the distillery for the first time. Understandably and rightly so. **40%**. *Gordon & MacPhail.*

Connoisseurs Choice Ardbeg 1974 (bottled 97 – newer, purple label) **(89)** n22 pines among the peat; t22 very sweet malt, the peat level has dropped on the previous bottling though the complexity continues along a fruity path; f23 long, light and flighty, the malt is fabulously textured and offers a late, salty burst; b22 a slightly different animal to the previous bottling, lacking a kind of all-round brilliance in a way that is so subtle you struggle to put your finger on exactly why, no matter how many times you taste it and re-taste it ... (hic!) On such is the finest line between genius and mere excellence drawn. **40%.** *Gordon & MacPhail.*

Connoisseurs Choice Ardbeg 1990 (88) n23 like much of 1990-distilled Ardbeg drawn at this time, the peat is pastel-shaded rather than punchy, fragile rather than forceful; t22 sweet and almost a little green, the style that was preferred in the 50s: chewy, though; f22 the smoke drifts effortlessly to the end where it meets a slight bitterness, moderate complexity; b21. **40%.** *Gordon & MacPhail.*

Connoisseurs Choice Ardbeg 1991 (88) n22 young in character and light, the peat drifts effortlessly about but hasn't cranked up the phenols; t23 oily and genuinely mouthfilling. The new Ardbeg texture begins here, with the malt being slightly like grist dissolving on the tongue with an extra sprinkling of sugar for good measure: this is one of the sweeter renditions; f22 soft with just the merest detail of oak, otherwise it's peated malt grist all the way; b21 sweet, oily and so easy to drink. **40%.** *Gordon & MacPhail.*

Glen Denny Ardbeg 1990 Aged 11 Years (91) n21 a dry marzipan nose almost outweighs the sweeter peat-reek. Light and refined by Ardbeg standards, there is marmalade to enrich it slightly; t23 so soft it dissolves on the palate, leaving a sweet, smoky residue. Waves of vanilla and peat vie for control, but neither take it; f24 long, enormously complex, a touch salty with the peat now taking a warming, spiced form. Ardbeg at its most teasing and luxurious; b23 cracking stuff that, despite the lazy nose, dominates, confuses, confounds and tantalises the tastebuds. Wonderful. **43%.** *Hunter Hamilton Co. 419 hand-filled bottles.*

Kieler Whisky Club Ardbeg Germania dist 26/12/75, bott 26/03/02, cask no. 4716 **(88)** n22 dry, oak chippings; sappy peat; t23 dry, then a roast coffee middle builds into a fuller peaty effect; f21 very laid-back with sweet malt; b22 a gentle, softly bodied, complex dram that thankfully doesn't deliver the oak threatened on the nose. **44.8%.** *35 samples issued for the Kiel Whisky Club, Germany.*

Murray McDavid Ardbeg 1991 bourbon cask MM2999, dist Feb 91, bott Feb 00 **(86)** n20 green, young, lots of nibbling, flapping, nowhere near fully fledged peat; t22 massively lively, as might be expected, the youth of the dram finding a mouthwatering barley note through the thickish peat; f22 very light vanilla picks a course around the smoke, some light oils maintain a sweetness while the barley continues to offer fresh complexity; b22 an intriguing and genuinely fun Ardbeg that helps complete a learning curve. **46%. nc ncf sc.**

Old Malt Cask Aged 11 Years dist May 90 **(84)** n20 t22 f21 b21. Curiously over-sweet and, for all the moutainous peat, the usual Ardbeg complexity fails to fully materialise. **50%. nc ncf.** *342 bottles.*

Old Malt Cask Ardbeg 1975 Aged 24 Years dist Oct 75, bott May 00 **(94)** n23 salty and slightly sweaty, the seaweed and peat form enticing layers; t24 fabulous bite, then soft peat arrival allowing a multi-layered, lingering attack on the tastebuds in which cocoa plays no little part; f23 elegantly brawny, muscles everywhere but the complexity is superb: just so amazingly bitter-sweet; b24 this is a dram that will be preferred over the 25-year-old version (75/00) by those looking for raw aggression over finesse. I won't argue either way – it's a personal thing. **50%. nc ncf.** *Douglas Laing. 713 bottles.*

Old Malt Cask Ardbeg 1975 Aged 25 Years dist Oct 75, bott Oct 00 **(97)** n25 the peat is big, but like all great Ardbegs, its intensity is diffracted through several layers of malt. Some salt adds piquancy and as the malt warms in your hand some orangey fruit arrives, but under the heavy guard of the firm peat. Both dry and sweet, heavy and light, salty and peppered, flowery yet a little fruity, this has it all. There is even that lovely, oiled smell of a warm-running model train. As close to perfection to make no difference; **t**24 mouthfilling and chewy, the peat shows the soft and delicate side to its nature at first before becoming pretty firm. Almost Taliskeresque peppers pummel the tastebuds, but these, too, are fleeting. There is a quick outburst of something honied and fruity and then wave upon wave of gristy malt and toffee; **f**23 eventually, much drier with 25 years of oak having a calming influence. Even so, the peat returns with soft ripples of smoke and vanilla acts as a mute recipient; **b**25 is this the best independent bottling of whisky of all time? I would say yes. And it would be a hard job to find a better single cask throughout Ardbeg's warehouses. I have tasted more individual casks of Ardbeg than any other whisky critic living, but never have I found one that so captures the brilliance of the world's greatest distillery – even my mark of 97 is me just nit-picking and being mean! Just one single glass at bottle strength – don't you dare add a single drop of water to this one – a quiet room, and you will be lost in the labyrinth of this great whisky for hours if not days. Will you ever get to the bottom of it? I very much doubt it. **50%.** *Douglas Laing. 702 bottles.*

Old Malt Cask Ardbeg 25 Years Old dist Oct 75, bott May 01 **(96)** **n**23 curiously less prominently peated than other OMC '75 bottlings with a much heavier oak influence, remains coastal and cunning, though, with a tidal, salty impact to add to the abrasiveness; **t**25 a dry initial impact that slowly and gloriously increases in sweet-malty intensity as it spreads around the palate. This is the stuff of genius; **f**24 salty, cocoa-crusted, a devaluing of the sweet peat that has gently gathered on the palate. The perfect climb-down to the perfect build-up; **b**24 just a little imbalance on the nose and slight bitterness to the finish dock a few points – but who cares? If you don't have this in your Ardbeg collection, consider it incomplete. But don't let it sit there gathering dust: experience ...! **50%. nc ncf.** *Douglas Laing. 243 bottles.*

Old Malt Cask Ardbeg Aged 27 Years dist Mar 75 **(92)** **n**22 amazingly delicate peat that meanders around the equally soft sherry, fabulously clean and complex, everything is gentle and understated. Everything is hinted at, but nothing stated, except the obvious magnificence of this aroma; **t**24 nothing short of outstanding: the arrival on the palate is a fanfare of sweet malt followed by soft murmurings of peat then no less delicate lush sherry. The oak arrives last, almost apologetically, alongside some gentle spice; **f**22 a gathering of warming, peppery spices – not unlike a Talisker – but the sherry remains clean and the peat simply flickers around the palate; **b**24 proof positive that to be a great Ardbeg it does not have to be swimming in peat. We are talking sheer unadulterated elegance and complexity from the world's greatest distillery when it was in its prime. What more can one say? **50%. nc ncf.**

Old Malt Cask Ardbeg Aged 28 Years dist Nov 72, bott 01 **(87)** **n**20 hot and biting; toasty and dry, the peat is heavy but quite dull, almost sinister, in character; **t**22 hard malt meets even harder oak. An early oak bitterness is softened by some battling sugars; **f**23 very light, showing signs of a little wear and tear but still enormous and chewy, brilliant late rallying complexity with spices and more waves of malt; **b**22 vaguely battered and bruised, but some genuine class shines through.

Old Malt Cask Ardbeg Aged 29 Years dist Mar 72 **(93)** **n**24 much of the distillate of '72 possessed a deep, earthy resonance to the peat, as if they were using fuel cut from the deepest parts of the bed. This enormous character is in full play here; **t**24 enormous sweet and lush, though not in the oily style of today. Chewy, big malt and some liquorice-toffee oak add extra depth. Lovely marmalade fruitiness clings to the mouth, too; **f**22 surprisingly light, as if spent. The oak hangs around to add a bitterish edge though doesn't intrude too much on the dying embers of peat; **b**23 a malt on the cusp of brilliance, but just a summer or two over its time. Good to see a '72 vintage showing its own peculiar qualities, though. **50%. nc ncf.** *Douglas Laing. 432 bottles.*

Premier Malts Ardbeg 11 Years Old dist 28/3/91, bott Nov 02 **(88) n**22 the peat is thick, punchy and intense; **t**23 this is a rich dram, an Ardbeg of the full, fat variety where oak is still to play a key role; **f**22 remains oily so the peat barely subsides; **b**21 a big, uncomplicated Ardbeg of the new oily school. **60.6%.** *Malcolm Pride.*

Provenance Ardbeg Autumn Distillation Over 9 Years dist Autumn 90, bott Summer 00 **(93) n**23 young, vibrant, lively and drenched in peat. Fresh it may be, but the complexity of that peatiness takes some unravelling. All the usual suspects with iodine, seaweed, salt and so on, but this time with the sweet malt is dried peppers – not a usual Ardbeg feature in bottled form; **t**23 a pounding mixture of concentrated grist and hot peppers. An oily sweetness creeps across the palate to offer a cocoa-peat middle. Very chewy and uncompromising, but the complexity is in saga form; **f**23 so enormously long that, after the third mouthful, you can just sit back and enjoy the long-haul flight. It all ends in vanilla but the peat refuses to go away; **b**24 this one takes me back, about the closest bottling to the first Ardbeg I tasted 20 years ago I have found. The Lagavulin may be a little more intense than this, but you will be hard pushed to find any other whisky offering such complexity. Though unusually spicy and dry, this is a classic for Ardbegophiles. **43%.** *Douglas McGibbon & Co.*

Provenance Ardbeg Autumn Distillation Over 10 Years dist Autumn 90, bott Winter 00 **(83) n**19 **t**23 **f**20 **b**21. Brilliant middle, a tad off the mark elsewhere. Not to be confused with Ardbeg Provenance! **43%.** *Douglas McGibbon & Co.*

Symposium International Ardbeg 1991 (89). n22 thick and oily, lots of vegetation among the liquid barley, dense and uncompromising; **t**23 a very sweet, malty arrival that then takes off as the peat leaves, clean and attractive; **f**22 yields seriously to reveal the barley; **b**22 unambiguous Ardbeg.

ARDMORE
Speyide, 1899. Allied. Working.

Ardmore 100th Anniversary 12 Years Old db dist 86, bott 99 **(94) n**24 beautifully clean, sweet peat with none of the salty freshness that one associates with island malts. A crisp, firm almost hard and angular nose that displays heaps of character; **t**23 intense and complex from the start with a wonderful shape-changing style. One moment it is hard and biting into the roof of the mouth, the next it is soft and sweet and caressing the tastebuds, peaty and smoky throughout and fabulously malty and intense; **f**23 sweet, flour-gristy softness at first, smoky and then it sharpens and becomes steely hard, delicate vanilla oak and for the first time a touch of honeycomb; **b**24 this was to be one of the great whiskies of 1999. As this didn't get Allied switched on to what a truly great malt this is, nothing will. Quite fantastic.

Ardmore 100th Anniversary 21 Years Old db **(91) n**24 lovely weight of smoke to counter the confident fruit and oak; **t**22 silky, gently peated malt and lush fruit make for the most gentle combination; **f**22 very light vanillas and an echo of smoke and spice; **b**23 a malt which simply caresses the tastebuds. The fruit influence is important but the malt and smoke are intriguingly subtle. It just gets better each time you taste it. **43%** *Very rare. One or two only available exclusively at Glendronach distillery shop and the odd one has slipped into specialist outlets. Bottled exclusively for guests of the distillery's centenary bash.*

Gordon & MacPhail Ardmore (91) n23 perfectly peated, soft and lumbering, allowing some wonderful malty tones egality. Just sniff and enjoy! **t**24 the arrival on the palate is a tapestry of all things magical. The peats are subtle, complex and a little spicy, there is early chocolate as the oak grabs hold and then there is an oaty, honeycomb thread. Just staggering; **f**21 flattens a little, but the honeycomb and spice continue; **b**23 arguably the best Gordon and MacPhail standard bottling of the last decade. **40%**

Gordon & MacPhail Ardmore 1985 **(90)** n23 classic Ardmore charm: delightfully smoky yet offering a hint of lavender and bitter-sweetness among the complex malts. Exhilarating; **t**22 there is a controlled surge of smoke that immediately rises and then levels off as a superbly textured almost biting maltiness comes through; **f**22 very similar to a Very Old Barton bourbon with the mouth popping with oaky-malty notes that keep the lips smacking; **b**23 considering the main theme is peat-oak-malt, the complexity is truly astonishing. One of G&M's most assured malts and worth hunting down. **40%**

Gordon & MacPhail Ardmore 1987 **(85)** n21 honied and surprisingly peatless; **t**22 silky sweet, ultra intense malt with a whiff of smoke; **f**21 a procession of vanillas; **b**21 a silky, sweet expression with little more than a hint of smoke. **40%**

Old Malt Cask Ardmore 21 Years Old dist Nov 79, bott Mar 01 **(90)** n23 charming display of untarnished softly peated barley: just so subtle! **t**23 follows on from the nose without missing a beat: glorious malt with a touch of smoke and oil; **f**21 light and vanilla-rich; **b**23 probably from a second or even third-fill bourbon cask, the malt has almost unrestrained dominance. Just sniff the glass after it has gone! **50%**. *Douglas Laing. 648 bottles.*

Old Masters Ardmore 1980 bott 98 **(90)** n21 loads of fruit, oranges in particular, marry with an oily, oaky, smoke background; **t**23 prickly spice and wafting smoke blend brilliantly with the concentrated malt and brilliant oaks. Fabulous bitter-sweet balance; **f**22 long and lush and remains spicy to the end; **b**24 a melt-in-the-mouth gem that underlines the brilliance of this distillery. **51.4%**. *James MacArthur.*

Ultimate Selection Ardmore 1992 dist 25/2/92, bott 28/11/02 **(86)** n21 oily smoke diffuses with clean barley; **t**22 sweet and oily with intense, chewy maltiness; **f**21 simmering peat just gets above the gathering oak; **b**22 a bold and classy version. **43%**. *Van Wees. NL.*

ARRAN (see Isle of Arran)

AUCHENTOSHAN
Lowlands, 1800. Morrison Bowmore. Working.

Auchentoshan 10 Years Old db **(79)** n17 t21 f21 b20. A lively, malty chap that coats the mouth with a soft oil and cocoa. **40%**

Auchentoshan 18 Years Old dist 78 db **(87)** n22 gooseberries and riesling with fresh barley; **t**21 rich, busy malt with complex oak infusion; **f**22 soft brown sugars mixing with the rich malt. Long and lingering; **b**22 a really delightful Lowlander full of complexity. **58.8%**

Auchentoshan 21 Years Old db **(84)** n20 t20 f23 b21. Recovers from a surprisingly hot start to generate some really gorgeous spicy and ultra malty complexity for the outstanding finale. **43%**

Auchentoshan 29 Years Old dist 73, cask 793 db **(89)** n24 exceptional sherry butt: a touch of coffee fringes the fruit, slightly salty and dry. Oloroso is near peak performance; **t**24 my, oh, my: a supreme combination of seasoned, clean oloroso and bourbon. The malt kicks in to add further sweetness. Simply sublime; **f**19 oak begins to make its mark with a touch of bitterness, but the complexity remains; **b**22 maybe one or two summers too long – the oak has crept in to unravel the finish, but until then the experience is one of sheer joy. **55.8%**

Austentoshan 1978 (see Austentoshan 18 Years Old)

Auchentoshan Select db **(72)** n18 t19 f17 b18. Malty but thin and a little hot. **40%**

Auchentoshan Three Wood db **(74)** n*19* t*17* f*20* b*18*. An attractive finish. The mouthfeel still isn't right, but this is so much better than the dreadful first-ever bottling. **43%**

Cadenhead's Auchentoshan 10 Years Old dist 92, bott 03/03 **(85)** n*20* Clean, attractive though a bit thin and lifeless; t*23* superb maltfest arrival on the palate, aided by some weak spices; f*21* slightly oily, sweet malt; b*21* the fun is all upfront: brilliant malt sparkle. **46%**

MacLeod's Lowland Single Malt Aged 8 Years (74) n*17* t*20* f*18* b*19*. Thin, malty and cream-toffee sweet. **40%**. *Ian MacLeod (Auchentoshan, though not stated).*

Old Malt Cask Auchentoshan Aged 33 Years dist Nov 67, bott Feb 01 **(77)** n*21* t*21* f*17* b*18*. Inside of garage showroom: new car smell. Hot and biting. **45.3%. nc ncf.** *Douglas Laing. 162 bottles.*

Old Masters Auchentoshan 1992 bott 02 **(79)** n*18* t*22* f*19* b*20*. Rougher than an oil-less engine. But the malty punch on the palate is memorable. **64.2%.** *James MacArthur.*

Scott's Selection Auchentoshan 1978 bott 96 **(72)** n*20* t*18* f*16* b*18*. Has some sweet, bourbony moments. **51.2%.** *Robert Scott & Co.*

Whisky Galore Auchentoshan 1992 Aged 10 Years (88) n*21* deliciously young and undermatured, so fresh and malty; t*23* mouthwatering grassy, clean malt... amazingly a slight hint of peat! f*22* more of the same, sweetens out and spices arrive; b*22* just so rare to find Auchentoshan of this age that is so brilliantly distilled. A treat. **46%**

AUCHROISK
Speyside, 1974. Diageo. Working.

Auchroisk Aged 10 Years db **(75)** n*19* t*20* f*17* b*19*. The really disappointing, toffee-laden and bitter finish undermines the sweet, grassy, malty intensity on the arrival on the palate. One of Speyside's lighter, most delicate drams, this has to be treated with very tender care and sensitivity which appears not to have happened here. **43%**. *Flora and Fauna.*

Old Malt Cask Auchroisk Aged 27 Years dist Dec 74, bott, Dec 01 **(83)** n*21* t*22* f*19* b*21*. A light, malty, grassy Speysider, even after all these years in the cask. Thoroughly enjoyable. **43.8%. nc ncf.** *Douglas Laing. 246 bottles.*

The Single Barrel Collection Auchroisk 1989 12 Years Old dist June 89, dist Dec 2001 cask no. 30257 **(69)** n*17* t*18* f*17* b*17*. Too oaky and aged, despite little colour. **65.92%. nc nf.**

AULTMORE
Speyside, 1896. John Dewar & Son. Working.

Aultmore 1983 Cask Strength bott 97 db **(79)** n*20* t*19* f*20* b*20*. Some pleasant malt-barley sugar notes, but it's some battle to get there. **58.8%**

Adelphi Aultmore 14 Years old cask 2900 dist 85, bott 99 **(69)** n*17* t*19* f*17* b*16*. A less than impressive cask – sulphur tainted. **60.1%. sc.**

Hart Brothers Aultmore Aged 10 Years dist 1990 **(86)** n*21* crispish barley; t*22* clean, refreshing malt, a blender's delight; f*21* firm oak and malt with waves of spice; b*22* nothing flash or spectacular, just extremely good quality and very well-made Speyside malt. **43%**

Inverarity 10 Years Old Speyside (81) n*19* t*22* f*20* b*20*. A light, flitting malt, but with the toffee on the finish, not quite light enough. Exceptional, faintly smoked, ultra-malty middle. **40%**. *From Aultmore, though not stated.*

Old Malt Cask Aultmore Aged 16 Years dist Apr 84, bott Jul 01 **(77)** n*18* t*22* f*18* b*19*. A light Speysider slightly out of breath at this age on nose and finish but glories in a sensational cream toffee-rich arrival on the palate. **50%**

BALBLAIR

Highlands (Northern), 1872. Inver House. Working.

Balblair 10 Years Old db (75) n24 t18 f16 b17. The mild, peated nose is just amazing: just like being by the sea, with salt and seaweed etc. But to taste: bland, bland, bland!!. Too much caramel. **40%**

Balblair 16 years Old db (78) n21 t21 f18 b18. Sweet and enticing at first but lacking depth and complexity on the finish. Not a patch on previous bottlings. **43%**

Balblair 27 Years Old Limited Edition Sherry Cask db (91) n23 coffee and intense sherry: a dense aroma for wine lovers especially; t23 the sherry influence is profound, though not overwhelming. Sparks fly as the peppery spices arrive; f22 thick oak softened by and sweetened by raisins. Heavy roast Java returns for the finale; b23 an outrageously big sherry cask of the old school that has much to say and is worth listening to. Fabulous. **46%**

Balblair Aged 33 Years db bott 2002 (89) n22 sweet, ripened peaches despite the marauding oak. Excellent charm and balance. The complexity is understated; t23 Quite a sugary offering: the sweetness runs from start to middle. Not unlike German coffee biscuits with the barley flour crisp then chewy. The oak is telling and fabulously controlled with a lovely mocha layer; f21 long, even and sweet with gentle spices drifting around. The oak is deft and balances supremely with some very late orangey notes; b23 sexy stuff designed for late nights, a silent, gently lit room and an elegant, blonde and beautiful woman, the same age as the whisky, called Andrea by your side.... Everything is softly done and the complexity is almost alarming. **45.4%**

Balblair Elements db (87) n22 heather-honey and clean malt; t22 very sweet start, lush with developing malt and spice; f21 slightly bitter fruit, with compensating smoke; b22 This is such an improvement on the first, elementary, Elements that it is barely comparable. Much sweeter and confident. **40%**

Adelphi Balblair 37 Years Old cask 893 dist 65, bott 02 (82) n21 t19 f22 b20. A shade too much sap to make this a great whisky, but the honey and kiwi fruit on the finish is sublime. **54.3%**

Gordon & MacPhail Balblair 10 Years Old (85) n21 honey, spice and chalky oak; t22 brilliant malt flourish that runs through from dry and chewy to sweet; f21 tails off towards oak, but always remains intact; b21 a chewy, clean dram. **40%**

Old Malt Cask Balblair Aged 35 Years dist May 66, bott Aug 01 (85) n22 the most extraordinary, unique fruitiness tinged with smoke; t21 liquid velvet, but a surge of over-eager oak dampens the proceedings; f22 settles down and returns to sultanas and smoke; b20 just a few years beyond brilliance, but still packs a punch. **40.4%. nc ncf.** *Douglas Laing.* 151 bottles.

BALMENACH

Speyside, 1824. Inver House. Working.

Balmenach 27 Year Old db (86) n21 unusual mixture of peat and coal smoke and some sharpish oaky notes; t22 a thread of peat weaves its way around the toasted honeycomb: silky and sexy; f21 long, silky, smoky, spiced; b22 confirmation of this distillery's ability to dazzle at great age. **46%**

Balmenach Aged 25 Years Golden Jubilee db (89) n21 towering vanilla, slightly chalky and dry where the oak is beginning to gain hold. Decent if unsophisticated spices kick but interweave attractively with the stewed apples. Threatens to be slightly too oaky but just enough sweet honeycomb keeps it under control; t23 spicy, robust and bourbony. Now complexity is the key word as the peppers buzz around the palate and the charging oak clashes head on with the roasty, malty notes. Some burnt honeycomb in there, too. Delicious cocoa peaks very early on; f22 perhaps slightly on the tired at first side but enough demerara sweetness carries it through to a fabulously long and beautifully weighted conclusion. Lots and lots of toffee hangs around seemingly forever; **b**23 What a glorious old charmer this is! An essay in balance despite the bludgeoning nature of the beast early on. Takes a little time to get to know and appreciate: persevere with this belter because it is classic stuff for its age. Bottled in special still-shaped decanter to mark the occasion of the Queen's Golden Jubilee. **58%**. *Around 800 decanters.*

Adelphi Balmenach 13 Years Old cask 3560, dist 90, bott 03 **(88) n**21 firm and malty; **t**23 massive malt, absolutely mountainous stuff; **f**22 a saner, more complex phase, lightened by a subtle citrus note; **b**22 I have never come across a malt from this distillery with such a massive malt character. Incredible. And so delicious! **60.1%**

Connoisseurs Choice Balmenach 1973 (72) n17 **t**19 **f**18 **b**18. Not quite the cleanest of drams. **40%**

Connoisseurs Choice Balmenach 1974 (86) n22 hints of honey and smoke; **t**22 fine malt-honey oak-cocoa balance, lovely texture; **f**20 dries gently and reintroduces the smoke; **b**22 a Speyside, laid-back version of a Highland Park! **40%**. *Gordon & MacPhail.*

Deerstalker Balmenach Aged 12 Years (85) n21 really excellent malt-oak balance: complex; **t**22 sheds of honey and rich oak suggest something older than 12; **f**21 delicate malt and butterscotch, more hints of age; **b**21 an elegant, beautifully structured Speysider. **40%**. *Aberfoyle & Knight.*

Deerstalker Balmenach Aged 18 Years (81) n20 **t**21 **f**19 **b**21. A delicate, butterscotch malt with charm, character and a touch of age. **40%**. *Aberfoyle & Knight.*

Hart Brothers Balmenach 18 Years Old dist 1979 **(81) n**21 **t**21 **f**19 **b**20. Silky, sweet and gently oaked. **43%**

Hart Brothers Balmenach Aged 30 Years dist Jan 72, bott 02 **(85) n**20 a few signs of oak bruising, but the fruit patches it up; **t**22 massive sherry, spice and chocolate, powering and majestic; **f**22 long with continued and absolutely delicious sweetened cocoa notes; **b**21 this is big, impressive whisky that should keep sherry lovers amused for a while. **50.1%**

Inverarity Ancestral 14 Years Old (74) n18 **t**19 **f**19 **b**18. Fusty and fruity with toffee on the finish. 40% Although not stated on label, this is Balmenach. **40%**

Scott's Selection Balmenach 1979 bott 96 **(83) n**21 **t**21 **f**20 **b**21. A highly drinkable expression from a distillery that rarely stands up so contendedly at this kind of age. **62.4%**. *Robert Scott & Co.*

The Single Barrel Collection Balmenach 1988 13-y-o cask 2774, dist Oct 88, bott Dec 01 **(85) n**19 dusty/fusty at first, saved by grapey-sultana fruitiness, chalky and dry; **t**23 fantastically rich with lively blast off of mouthwatering, oiled fruit-basket of flavours; thumping malty middle and lots of subtle spices. Fabulous; **f**21 calmed by lashings of vanilla and barley. Slightly brooding; **b**22 An absolute treat: the arrival on the palate is near flawless. **59.79%. nc nf.**

THE BALVENIE
Speyside, 1892. William Grant & Sons. Working.

The Balvenie Aged 10 Years Founders Reserve db **(90) n**23 astonishing complexity: the fruit is relaxed, crushed sultanas and malty suet. A sliver of smoke and no more: everything is hinted and nudged at rather than stated. Superb; **t**24 here we go again: threads of malt binding together barely detectable nuances. Thin liquorice here, grape there, smoke and vanilla somewhere else; **f**20 Light muscovado-toffee flattens out the earlier complexity.The bitter-sweet balance remains brilliant to the end; **b**23 just one of those all-time-great standard 10-year-olds from a great distillery. **40%**

The Balvenie Aged 12 Years Double Wood db **(79) n**22 **t**21 **f**17 **b**19. Sledgehammer sherry offers the fruitiest of welcomes while good spice doubles up on the malt-sherry front. The caramel has a too leading role on the finish, though. Usually better than this. **40%**

The Balvenie Aged 15 Years Single Barrel db **(93)** n23 cracking vanilla-malt split. Complex, intriguing, something to really get your nose into. Quite maltings-floorish; t24 massive malt surge is invigorating and mouthwatering. Glorious; f22 keeps clean and relatively oak-free; b24 just one of those drams that should be within touching distance at strategic points around the house. **50.4%** *Being single barrel the bottlings do change quite regularly: fortunately the magnificence of the quality rarely does.*

The Balvenie Aged 21 Years Port Wood db **(87)** n23 clean, mouthwatering evidence of fresh port pipes; t22 the wine swamps the malt for a while, but being Balvenie the complexity returns, a softly smoked, sweet maltiness leading the way; f21 vanilla and toffee; b21 using port pipes like this can backfire on a malt as complex as Balvenie, but this one comes through with flying Scottish and Portuguese colours. **40%**

The Balvenie 25 Years Old Single Barrel cask 14439 **(88)** n23 sturdy yet fresh malt surrounded by soft mint. The oak is wheezing a bit, but beautifully couched; t22 lively and minty with intense malt of varying sharpness; f21 some late oiliness, then vanilla and a sprinkling of spice and cocoa; b22 tremendous stuff: complex and charming.

The Balvenie Aged 50 Years db cask 191 **(87)** n23 coffee and biscuits alongside the ultra-ripe, thick sherry, not unlike moist cherry fruitcake. Smoke remains after the sherry is burnt out; t23 some suppressed oak does its best to escape, but has a major battle to fight its way through the layers of big grape. Lovely spices point in the direction of some peat; f19 pretty shattered oak offers a bitter finale, but the fruit does all it can to soften things and lengthen out matters; b22 a noble dram battered by oak but comes through with a degree of nobility. Natural strength.

The Balvenie 1967 Vintage Cask db **(89)** n24 beautifully delicate and floral with a layer of peat. Bourbon-style vanilla adds age, approaching perfection in Balvenie terms; t22 oily rush of malt. Now Canadian-style vanilla infuses with spices and dry cocoa; f21 dries to become vanilla-rich, remains cocoa dominant; b22 dry and complex.

The Balvenie 1968 Vintage Cask db **(86)** n23 firm and flinty, deep oak with a hint of the berry fruit about it, and buttered crumpets for good measure; t22 creamy malt then a surge of unspecified fruitiness; f20 hardens into brittle toffee with the Balvenie-esque light muscovado sweetness lingering from the middle until it fades as the oak grabs hold; b21 the delicate sweetness accentuates the dry finale. Pretty delicious. **50.8%**

The Balvenie 1972 Vintage Cask db **(88)** n22 melon and ginger: beautifully oaked, bourbon style; t23 immediate spices, more ginger plus peppers and a touch of apple then bright malty notes; f21 some smoke appears with the cocoa and a late touch of honey; b22 a superb, lightly smoked Balvenie that shows some age but wears it well. Natural strength.

The Balvenie 1989 Port Wood db **(83)** n20 t22 f21 b20. The nose is remarkably undemonstrative, all the fruity action arriving up front early on the tastebuds. Good follow-through. **40%**

The Maltmill Speyside Single Malt 11 Years cask 3008, dist 1990, bott 2001 **(93)** n24 lavender and moist ginger cake combined. Beautifully complex and weighted: the stuff of legend; t24 the ginger is there on the arrival with some delicate honey, too. Gloriously spiced and a little oily; f22 long vanilla trail that dries quickly after all the action; b23 exquisite stuff: Balvenie unplugged in some ways. It would be great to see the distillery carry on where the Germans left off. **55%**. Is it Balvenie? "The distillery founded in 1892 in Dufftown is named after the castle nearby. It is still owned by an independent company and uses its own malting...." Sadly, I understand The Maltmill in Hamburg who bottled this are no longer in business. William Grant keeps a close eye on each and every Balvenie cask so it doesn't find its way as a single malt onto the open market. So a real collector's item ... in every sense. **55%. sc.** Germany.

BANFF
Speyside, 1863–1983. Demolished.

Chieftain's Choice Banff Aged 18 Years dist 80 **(80) n**19 **t**22 **f**19 **b**20. Excellent coppery texture; big and chewy. **43%**. Ian MacLeod.

Connoisseurs Choice Banff 1974 **(74) n**17 **t**20 **f**18 **b**19. Slightly feinty when warmed, so big and oily, too. Sweet and malty. **40%**. Gordon & MacPhail.

Connoisseurs Choice Banff 1976 **(76) n**19 **t**20 **f**19 **b**18. Soft with chalky oak. **40%**. Gordon & MacPhail.

Coopers Choice Banff 1978 Aged 22 Years bott 01 **(82) n**22 **t**21 **f**19 **b**20. Struggles at the end, but the nose and mouth arrival in particular are excellent for a Banff. **56%**. Vintage Malt Company.

Old Malt Cask Banff Aged 24 Years dist Dec 77 **(88) n**19 grinding oak appears to knock the wind out of the lighter, slightly honied orangey tones, just a fraction sappy; **t**24 outstanding mouthfeel and arrival on palate. The sweet malt is also fantastically spiced and for a moment all-consuming. A hint of peat wafts across the mouth but the rich honeycomb is a meal in itself. The intensity and complexity has to be tasted to be believed! **f**22 long, tapering, clean with a build-up of some piney, oaky notes. Lots of natural caramel with chewy cream toffee and again some attractive soft orange. Perhaps a fraction overcooked in the oak department at the absolute finale ... though not by much; **b**23 only the nose prevents this from hitting the 90s. This is heady and unquestionably beautiful stuff: the sweetness is almost liquor-like at times and women will adore this one. **50%**. Douglas Laing.

Old Malt Cask Banff Aged 31 Years dist Nov, 66 bott Aug 98 **(88) n**23 big age oakiness, hints of lavender and a pleasing saltiness, malty, lightly smoked; **t**22 sweet and bourbony early on with lashings of honied finesse, intense and pleasantly oily, slightly plummy; **f**21 remains thick on the palate for a long time; **b**22 hangs together well with the oak having the final say. Good whisky for its age. **50%. nc ncf**. Douglas Laing. 181 bottles.

Old Malt Cask Banff Aged 35 Years (Sherry) dist Feb 66, bott Mar 01 **(76) n**19 **t**19 **f**19 **b**19. A tired old soul, but one with a dry, spicy tale to tell. **46.4% nc ncf**. Douglas Laing. 192 bottles.

Old Masters Banff 1976 bott 01 **(86) n**20 foraging oak; **t**22 brittle barley and excellent mouthfeel; **f**22 loads of oak-barley character with late cocoa and smoke; **b**22 fit for its age. **57.1%** James MacArthur.

BEN NEVIS
Highland (Western), 1825. Nikka. Working.

Ben Nevis Ten Years Old db **(85) n**19 oily, nutty but a little off-key **t**22 such a massive introduction to the palate: soft oils, citrus notes and very big oak on the malt but sweet enough to chew for ever; **f**23 the integration of the oak really makes for some finish: long, hints of bitter roast coffee against the sweet oils; **b**21 the nose makes you say oh-oh, but you need a knife, fork, spoon and napkin for the taste. **46%**

Ben Nevis 21 Years Old db dist 74, bott 95 **(91) n**23 lime and under-ripe Seville oranges and crushed black peppers abound: the oak is of bourbony character with some hickory and old, dusty leather **t**23 absolutely sensational mouthfeel: the most delicate coating of oil is sweetened with brown sugar. The malt remains big and roasty. Just sit back and enjoy the ride; **f**22 remains fat and very, very long. Intense vanilla dissipates, leaving a buttery cream-toffee residue, always sweet; **b**23 although bottled in 1995 and from a single cask spotted for its brilliance by the manager, apparently some bottles are still doing the rounds at great prices as this is regarded as near enough the ultimate Ben Nevis. I, for one, will not disagree too loudly. This bottling underlines the enormity of this great distillery. **60.5%.** 192 bottles.

Ben Nevis 1973 Age 26 Years cask no. 747, bott 99 db **(91) n**22 honied and biting, this is a really big, bruising whisky. There are bourbony notes depicting decent age but the underlying malt is powering and complex: not a nose for the faint-hearted; **t**23 for the nose read the taste, except the bourbon, though apparent, lays low and instead big honey and now even some smoke appears. Watch out also for the green apples and kumquats that somehow make their presence felt amid all the action. Breathtaking; **f**23 long, with toast and toffee and a light roast coffee blend. Some sweet bourbony notes re-emerge: stupendously complex; **b**23 Ben Nevis has its detractors, though I have never been entirely sure why. This bottling was one of my favourites in the world through 1999 and firmly put the distillery among the greats of Scotland. This is lush and magnificent: cask 747 produced a jumbo of a malt that has no problem taking off. When it'll land, your guess is as good as mine! **52.7%. sc.** 252 bottles.

Ben Nevis 26 Years Old cask 952, dist 75, bott 01 db **(91) n**23 salty and dry: an amazing cross between Springbank and single distillation pot-still demerara; **t**23 loads of salt and sugar together push forward the amazingly intense malt, hints of citrus, then some thuggish oak; **f**21 drier still now the malt has worn off with some lovely spices nipping and biting here and there; **b**24 another cask from the Ben Nevis of Improbable Complexity. A connoisseur's dram and a half. **53.9%**

Ben Nevis 30 Years Old cask 2519 db **(86) n**22 ripe dates concentrate, soft bourbon and lemon: this is a big nose with oak and age stamped all over it; **t**22 sweet malt, amazingly, to the fore then a surge of big cocoa-led oak; **f**20 bitter with heavy roast Costa Rican coffee joining the cocoa, but finally the oak takes complete control; **b**22 a malt living on the edge: just about over the top oak but there is enough sweetness around not only too see it through but to make for a fascinating dram. **56.9%**

Blackadder Raw Cask Ben Nevis 1984 sherry cask 258, dist 21 Nov 84, bott May 02 **(83) n**21 **t**21 **f**21 **b**20. Good, clean sherry butt, blackberries on the middle, a little hot. **61.2%. nc ncf sc.**

Blackadder Raw Cask Ben Nevis 1992 bourbon hogshead 687, dist 24 Feb 92, bott Apr 03 **(77) n**18 **t**20 **f**19 **b**20. Light and mouthwatering, but not entirely on song. **59.6%. ncf nc sc.**

Cadenhead's Ben Nevis 17 Years Old dist 86, bott 03/03 **(86) n**22 fit-to-burst gooseberries, newly mown hay and a touch of honey: entrancing; **t**22 rich malt that becomes slightly oilier as it develops with spice arrival; **f**21 more low-key simple malt; **b**21 one of the lightest examples of Ben Nevis bottled in recent years. **46%**

Hart Brothers Ben Nevis Aged 35 Years sherry wood dist 67 **(84) n**21 **t**22 **f**21 **b**20. Enormous ginger through the middle and finish. A hard-punching middleweight. **50.1%**

Old Malt Cask Ben Nevis Aged 34 Years dist Apr 66, bott Jan 01 **(78) n**18 **t**22 **f**19 **b**19. Flavoursome but hot and slightly off key. **50%. nc ncf.** Douglas Laing. 168 bottles.

Old Malt Cask Ben Nevis Aged 36 Years dist Dec 64, bott Mar 01 **(87) n**23 big sweet oak, giving a top-rate bourbon style; **t**22 oak and fruit dominate; **f**21 a waft of smoke gets amongst the overworn oak; **b**21 this bourbon-style is not unusual in a well-aged Ben Nevis. Excellent. **50%. nc ncf.** Douglas Laing. 156 bottles.

BENRIACH
Speyside, 1898. Chivas Bros. Silent.

Benriach 10 Years Old db **(77)** n*18* t*22* f*18* b*19*. Disappointing, non-existent nose but a really excellent malty mouth arrival. Lost in toffee on the finish. **43%**

Cask Benriach 1982 casks 5211–3, dist 4/5/82, bott Sep 93 **(89)** n*22* stupendous cut-grass nose, clean and pure Speyside; t*23* the malt is intense and oily, wrapping itself around the palate; f*22* more malt and soft cocoa; b*22* this was for a long time the finest Benriach ever bottled. Although bottled 10 years ago, if you still see the odd bottle around, treat yourself. **60.6%**. *Gordon & MacPhail.*

Connoisseurs Choice Benriach 1980 **(71)** n*20* t*19* f*16* b*16*. Charisma bypass. **40%**. *Gordon & MacPhail.*

Connoisseurs Choice Benriach 1981 **(78)** n*20* t*21* f*18* b*19*. Beautiful grassy nose and mouth arrival, but otherwise typically thin. **40%**. *Gordon & MacPhail.*

Connoisseurs Choice Benriach 1982 **(83)** n*21* t*21* f*20* b*21*. Excellent example of a fresh, light Speysider offering a clean, unpretentious blending malt. **40%**. *Gordon & MacPhail.*

Peerless Benriach 1968 cask 2590, dist Nov 68 **(93)** n*23* deft oak, hints of chocolate lime; t*24* brilliantly mouthwatering, fruity with sharp malt; f*23* lots of natural caramel softens the oak, sweet malt continues; b*23* this bottling puts Benriach into another dimension. Superb. **50.4%**. *Duncan Taylor & Co.*

Peerless Benriach 1968 cask 2593, dist Nov 68 **(76)** n*22* t*20* f*17* b*17*. Delightfully fruity, bit over-oaked **51.4%**. *Duncan Taylor & Co.*

BENRINNES
Speyside, 1826. Diageo. Working.

Centenary Reserve Benrinnes 1978 bott 95 **(78)** n*20* t*22* f*17* b*19*. A so-so dram with a hint of peat to mark the centenary of G&M, not the distillery. **40%**. *Gordon & MacPhail.*

Connoisseurs Choice Benrinnes 1972 **(79)** n*18* t*22* f*19* b*20*. Not convinced about the nose, but nothing wrong with the big sultana middle. **40%**. *Gordon & MacPhail.*

Connoisseurs Choice Benrinness 1973 **(79)** n*20* t*21* f*18* b*20*. Clean, oily and malty. Very sweet. **40%**. *Gordon & MacPhail.*

Dun Bheagan Benrinnes Aged 20 Years dist 79, bott 00 **(74)** n*19* t*20* f*17* b*18*. Trademark coal-gas nose and pleasant spice, but rather caramel-jaded and ordinary. **43%**. *William Maxwell.*

Milroy's Benrinnes Over 11 Years Old dist 89, bott 00 **(79)** n*21* t*20* f*19* b*19*. A pretty biggish version of this unusual, triple-distilled dram. **43%**

Old Malt Cask Benrinnes Aged 19 Years Sherry dist Jul 81, bott Jan 01 **(79)** n*18* t*22* f*20* b*19*. Big and chewy, but if anything slightly too sweet and cloying. **50%. nc ncf.** *Douglas Laing.*

BENROMACH
Sepyside, 1898. Gordon & MacPhail. Working.

Benromach Aged 18 Years db **(78)** n*18* t*21* f*20* b*19*. Rich textured. **40%**. *Gordon & MacPhail.*

Benromach 19 Years Old Port Wood Finish db **(91)** n*22* incredibly fresh, winey, juicy fruit gums and clean; t*23* mouthwateringly clean and juicy with a sensational mixture of ultra-clean barley and quite amazing sweet grape; f*22* some lazy spices and bristling oak marry superbly with that elegant barley thread; b*24* these must be absolutely brand new, first-fill sherry pipes to get this intensity of flavour. A classic among port finishes, reminding others how it should be done. **45%**. *Gordon & MacPhail.*

Benromach 25 Years Old db **(85)** n*21* a waft of oak interrupts a blanket of barley concentrate; t*22* staggeringly intense malt: sweet, lip-smacking stuff; f*21* remains unbelievably sweet and relatively oak-free until the very dying moments; **b**21 very sweet, highly enjoyable but lacking the all-round complexity or even age one might expect of a 25-year-old. *Gordon & MacPhail.*

Benromach 1973 Vintage db **(80) n**22 **t**20 **f**19 **b**19. Bitter oak finish compliments the light, sweet barley. **40%**. *Gordon and MacPhail.*

Benromach 1974 db **(79) n**21 **t**21 **f**18 **b**19. A delicate flower lacking any sort of "ooomph". **40%**. *Gordon & MacPhail.*

Benromach Centenary 17 Years Old db **(80) n**20 **t**21 **f**19 **b**20. Light and elegant, a delicate malt selected to mark the re-opening of this excellent Speyside distillery. Some undertstated sherry and soft malt make for a typically understated dram **40%**. *Gordon & MacPhail.*

Cask Benromach 1982 db casks 1335, 1341, dist 15/10/82, bott Jun 96 **(92) n**23 textbook rich, intense yet faultlessly clean oloroso; **t**24 fruit and spice in perfect proportion: not a single blemish; **f**23 the malt arrives at last with rich grape still evident; **b**22 it was probably bottlings like this that convinced G&M of the need to buy this distillery. Masterful. **63%**. *Gordon & MacPhail.*

Cask Benromach 1982 db casks 112, 114, dist 2/2/82 bott 24/10/01 db **(84) n**20 **t**22 **f**22 **b**20. Incredibly sweet and almost syrupy. One of the most intensely malted drams on the market, but perhaps lacks balance – even with some late spices. **59.7%.** *Gordon & MacPhail.*

Connoisseurs Choice Benromach 1969 **(82) n**21 **t**22 **f**19 **b**20. One of those annoying G&Ms from that period that starts off brightly and then just dies on you! Probably caramel is to blame. **40%**. *Gordon & MacPhail.*

Connoisseurs Choice Benromach 1971 **(90) n**22 heavy sherry nose, soft spices; **t**23 clean sherry, really juicy grape with a sweet malt counter thrust; **f**23 a hint of smoke digs in as the sherry continues its mouthwatering cruise around the palate; **b**22 one of the most memorable CCs from that period, hoisting the sherry flag with some aplomb. **40%**. *Gordon & MacPhail.*

BEN WYVIS
Highland (Northern) 1965–1977. Demolished.
Ben Wyvis Aged 27 Years cask 1061, dist 72 db **(78) n**21 vanilla, soft oak with a sweet structure and the malt is intact – amazing for a light whisky for this age – with some softening caramel; **t**20 big malt, toffee presence then becoming gradually hotter, not peppery, simply from the way it has been distilled; **f**18 very thin, surprisingly little oak, meagre malt and more bite: the finale is sweet and coated with late oil; **b**19 this is by no means great whisky, but it is certainly among the most rare you will ever locate. There are hints here of why the distillery closed: certainly even after all these years the oak cannot paper over the cracks. That said, you are drinking history and romance and it should be enjoyed with due reverence. **43.1%**. *146 bottles.*

BLADNOCH
Lowland, 1817. Working.
Bladnoch Aged 10 Years db **(94) n**23 lemon and lime, marmalade on fresh-sliced flour-topped crusty bread; **t**24 immensely fruity and chewy, lush and mouthwatering and then the most beguiling build-up of spices: the mouthfeel is full and faultless; **f**23 long, remains mildly peppery and then a dryer advance of oak. The line between bitter and sweet is not once crossed; **b**24 this is probably the ultimate Bladnoch, certainly the best I have tasted in over 25 years. This Flora and Fauna bottling by then owners United Distillers should be regarded as the must-get-at-all-costs Bladnoch. If the new owner can create something even to hang on to this one's coat-tails then he has excelled himself. For those few of us lucky enough to experience this, this dram is nothing short of a piece of Lowland legend and folklore. **43%** *For those of you with a nervous disposition, the*

author would like to point out that not a single drop of this whisky was spat out during the creation of these tasting notes.

Cask Bladnoch 1985 cask nos 318, 352, 870–1, dist Jan/Feb 85, bott Jun 96 **(88) n**22 toast and marmalade; **t**22 amazingly fruity with a hint of marzipan; **f**22 long, malty and no little fruit; **b**22 a charming, slightly unusual Bladnoch: fruity, as is its wont, but in a quite unusual direction. Lovely stuff. **56.8%.** *Gordon & MacPhail.*

Connoisseurs Choice Bladnoch 1980 (77) n19 **t**20 **f**19 **b**19. Easy-going and malty. **40%.** *Gordon & MacPhail.*

Gordon & MacPhail Bladnoch 1988 Cask Strength (81) n20 **t**21 **f**20 **b**20. Well-structured and beautifully chewable. **58.8%**

James MacArthur Bladnoch 10 Year Old (78) n22 **t**19 **f**18 **b**19. Immensely chalky and dry despite some rich early malt. **43%**

Old Masters Bladnoch 1992 bott 02 **(88) n**22 big malt and oak sitting comfortably; **t**22 fabulous, mouthwatering bitter-sweet chap and so, so malty; **f**22 a zesty fruitiness, marmalade and malt with some chunky oak arriving; **b**22 classically clean, fresh Lowland whisky. I would use this in any blend. **58.5%.** *James MacArthur.*

Private Cellar Bladnoch 1987 bott Feb 03 **(77) n**20 **t**20 **f**18 **b**19. A bit lively and nippy with thin malt. Charactertul and hot to handle despite a begrudging sweetness. **43%.** *Forbes Ross Co. Ltd.*

Royal Mile Whiskies Bladnoch 16 Years Old dist Jun 80, bott Jan 97 **(87) n**22 firm, with a solid texture of crisp malt, softened only by oak; **t**22 mouth-filling and sweet, the malt is really quite outstanding; **f**21 long, hints of cocoa with the oak and spices; **b**22 absolutely top drawer Bladnoch. **??.?%** *From RMW shop, Edinburgh.*

The Ultimate Selection Bladnoch 1991 bourbon barrel 4011, dist 17/7/91, bott 11/9/02 **(77) n**17 **t**20 **f**20 **b**20. Not quite firing on all cylinders but there is good cocoa at the finish. *Van Wees NL.*

BLAIR ATHOL
Highlands (Perthshire), 1798. Diageo. Working.

Blair Athol Aged 12 Years db **(77) n**18 **t**19 **f**21 **b**19. Thick, fruity, syrupy and a little sulphury and heavy. The finish has some attractive complexity among the chunkyness. **43%.** *Flora and Fauna range.*

Old Malt Cask Blair Athol Aged 25 Years dist March 75 **(80) n**21 **t**20 **f**19 **b**20. Don't look for complexity, but still one of the better – and these days few – Blair Athols on the market. **50%.** *Douglas Laing.*

BOWMORE
Islay, 1779. Suntory. Working.

Bowmore 12 Years Old db **(85) n**21 delicate, buttery peat; **t**22 sweet intense malt with a peaty shadow; **f**21 light, clean, hint of vanilla; **b**21 a real sweetie in every sense. **40%**

Bowmore 17 Years Old db **(93) n**23 the peat could be made from helium, so light is it. Even so, it remains the dominant feature in a complex aroma; **t**23 sweat peat at first, then juicy malt; **f**23 long, fragile with the peat lingering but refusing to undermine the complexity; **b**24 a masterpiece. Back to its old self: an exercise in understatement and refinement. Always my favourite aged Bowmore of them all – with only Voyage offering something more extraordinary and beautiful – and this bottling shows exactly why. Sublime.

Bowmore 25 Years Old db **(90) n**21 nutty, toasty; **t**23 silky fruit, glazed cherries and tantalising spices; **f**22 a final tilt of clean sherry then creamy malt and vanilla; **b**24 bit of a tastebud Lothario, seducing the palate with a cool, oozing charm. Beware. **43%**

Bowmore 1957 db **(91) n**23 tangerines and marzipan: Lubec's finest. The peat is so laid back it could be chewing straw. So, so delicate and attractive; unobtrusive oak; **t**23 firm malt with a chewy, oily coating. The peat offers itself as a volley of prickly spice, followed by the softest, most gentle malt follow-through; **f**22 long, more malt oil and a reintroduction of something vaguely fruity and juicy; **b**23 nothing from 1957 has the right to be this well preserved and sophisticated. It appears I have a challenger... **40.1%**

The Vintage House Bowmore 20 Years Old (91) n22 a curious lacing of bourbon and distant peat with something heathery thrown in. Delicate and complex; **t**23 big and explosive from mouth entry with dry oak booming through but softened by rich malt and touch of honey; **f**23 long, sweetening despite the growling, deep oak and spicy peat. Enormously big finale with liquorice and toast and cocoa powder; **b**23 another brinkman's malt with the oak going as far as is safe. Enormous depth and complex peat that, beyond the spice, has to be sought. **52.7%. ncf.** *From The Vintage House, London only.*

Bowmore 1964 Vintage Bourbon Cask db **(86) n**23 the oak, perhaps in conjunction with the apparently vanished peat, has given an attractive rye character; **t**21 fruity and mouthwatering start but the malt gives way to budding oak; **f**21 dry finale as the oak makes its stand; **b**21 just about holds together for a very enjoyable dram. The peat has been absorbed to create an unusual rye effect – and for those new to this game, this has nothing to do with the fact that this was matured in a bourbon cask: that spirit has had no influence whatsoever. **43.2%**

Bowmore 1964 Vintage Fino Cask db **(90) n**21 biting and hot, but the malt is impressive as is the sultry, fleeting fruit; **t**23 gentle fruit now but still there is bite and truculence; **f**23 long, lots of sultanas and still that lovely malt/spice mix; **b**23 sheer quality. Curiously, much more Bushmills in style than Bowmore. Exquisite stuff. **49.6%**

Bowmore Cask Strength db **(80) n**19 **t**21 **f**21 **b**20. A buttery, malt-rich very lightly smoked dram which lingers on the oil. **56%**

Bowmore Claret Bordeaux Wine Cask db **(62) n**16 **t**16 **f**17 **b**13. When this first came out the then distillery boss Jim Mcewan and I fell out (temporarily, of course!): he loved it, I loathed it. For the sake of this book (and it needed a good reason) I re-visited this whisky. And I still loathe it. The whisky has been swamped by the wine, is raw and the character of a distillery I love has been obliterated with all balance sacrificed. Oh dear, oh dear. **56%**

Bowmore Darkest db **(69) n**18 **t**18 **f**17. **b**16 Raw and slightly wild. I adore youth on a whisky but this is just not my scene at all. **43%**

Bowmore Dawn db **(89) n**21 busy, complex, firm peat; **t**23 mouthwatering, malty and full bodied; **f**22 lovely fruit follow-through then long, long toasty, vaguely honied malt; **b**23 there appears to be some youngish malt in this, but it has been superbly honed to create a malt of blistering complexity. Superb. **51.5%**

Bowmore Dusk db **(80) n**18 **t**19 **f**23 **b**20. Another youngster, almost a mirror image to the Oddbins exclusive bottling of Bowmore or Islay (can't remember) of about 12 or 13 years ago. Memorable for the astonishing finish after a so-so start. Love it!! **50%**

Bowmore Legend db **(80) n**19 **t**21 **f**20 **b**20. A very even, almost docile Bowmore but possessing great shape around the palate. The peat is raw but well-mannered. **40%**

Bowmore Mariner db **(89) n**20 young and ungainly; **t**23 packs a stupendous punch. Young this malt may be, but it's as clean as a whistle and the peat is unfettered and rich; **f**23 long, smoky with brilliant malt complexity; **b**23 a big, peaty number, lumbering but genuinely charismatic and delicious This is sheer, unpretentious fun – a session dram for when you are wanting to rough it like an old tar... and I speak as a former member of the

Swedish Merchant Navy (well, I had to escape from Lagos somehow), I'll have you know. Talk about ship shape. **43%**

Bowmore Surf db **(75)** n*19* t*20* f*18* b*18*. More of a ripple. **40%**

Bowmore Voyage db **(94)** n*24* salt spray and peat-reek on a cottage lumb: intoxicating, but not from the alcohol; t*24* an intriguing display of young and old malts clashing together then harmonising with a massive sweet malt heave-ho; f*23* longer than a sailing to Sydney. The peat simply moulds into every crevice in the mouth; b*23* a more apposite name I can't think of. Despite some apparent youth, this whisky has done the rounds and has the salty scars to prove it. Brilliant, me 'arties. Ah, ha, an' don't ye all knock it back at once. **56%** *(the Moody Blues obviously had a premonition of this whisky's arrival when in the 70s they wrote: "My ship's sailed stormy seas/battled oceans filled with tears/At last my port's in view/now that I've discovered you…")*

Blackadder Bowmore 25 Years Old cask 3174, dist Apr 73, bott Apr 98 **(89)** n*22* gentle orangey, biscuit-dough sweetness, with no more than a pinch of peat: so elegant; t*23* outrageously charming mouthfeel: delicate pitter-patter of flavours ranging from fruity to oaky-earthy but mainly malt and peaty with a little salt tossed in for a coastal feel; f*20* dries towards the oak but that lovely, fragile mouthfeel remains intact; b*24* a supremely balanced whisky.

Blackadder Raw Cask Bowmore 1989 cask 22533, dist 21 Sep 89, bott Apr 02 **(79)** n*20* t*19* f*20* b*20*. Clean, lightly peated dram with mouth-filling sweet properties but a bit hot, alcohol apart. **63.3%. nc ncf sc.**

Blackadder Raw Cask Bowmore 1989 bourbon barrel no. 22535 dist 21 Sep 89, bott Mar 03 **(79)** n*20* t*19* f*20* b*20*. As cask 22533 above. **62.9%. nc ncf sc.**

Blackadder Raw Cask Bowmore 1991 cask 15093, dist Sep 91, bott Apr 02 **(89)** n*22* gristy, lively and fresh; t*23* exploding peat then malty-peaty shockwaves;f*22* amazingly long with sublime cocoa and hints of Columbian coffee; b*22* Just a really superb malt, full of character and life. Brilliant for its age. **61.2%. nc ncf sc.**

Blackadder Raw Cask Bowmore 1991 refill sherry cask 22535, dist Sep 91, bott Mar 03 **(89)** n*22* t*23* f*22* b*22*. A complete re-run of cask 15093. I suspect the cask number for this bottling is a mistake. **60.7%**

Coopers Choice Bowmore 1990 bott 03 (12 Years Old) **(88)** n*21* still slightly green, but the peat is gentle and sensuous; t*22* early sweet malt start, then a fascinating bitter oak surge before the sweetness returns; f*23* quite long with this toing-and-froing between oak and barley continuing for some time; b*22* as impressive an example of Bowmore of this age as you could hope for. **43%.** *The Vintage Malt Whisky Co.*

Dun Bheagan Bowmore Aged 21 Years dist 80, bott 01 **(79)** n*19* t*21* f*19* b*20*. Very unusual Bowmore, much more peppery and fragmented than the norm for this age. Lively but not quite in tune. **43%.** *William Maxwell.*

Hart Brothers Bowmore 11 Years Old dist 90 **(84)** n*22* t*22* f*21* b*19*. The serious lack of colour suggests, correctly, that this is taken from a pretty well-used cask. The result is a new-make, youngish single malt, one of not inconsiderable charm and clarity of nose and taste. Love it! **46%**

Hart Brothers Bowmore Aged 34 Years dist Feb 68, bott Oct 02 **(85)** n*21* gooseberry jam and a hint of smoke; t*22* silky fruit and incredibly sweet malt; f*21* a puff of smoke and some buzzing spices remind you it's an Islay dram; b*21* amazingly delicate and beautifully preserved. **40.2%**

Old Malt Cask Bowmore Aged 18 Years dist Mar 83, bott Feb 02 **(91)** n*24* peat and raspberries (seriously folks, it really is!!): what a fabulous and nearly unique combo! t*23* mouthwateringly fruity with the peat leaking about palate amid firm malt; f*22* loads of light muscovado amid the dying malt; b*22* question: what kind of whisky do you buy a person (like me) whose favourite fruit is raspberry and who is a bit partial to some peat? Answer: this. Absolutely unique. Take my word for it. **50%. nc ncf.** *Douglas Laing. 270 bottles.*

Old Malt Cask Bowmore Aged 34 Years dist May 66, bot Mar 01 **(79)** **n**22 **t**20 **f**18 **b**19. Bowmore by name, certainly not by nature. The fruit pastel fruitiness is lovely, but something essential is missing. **45.15%. nc ncf sc.** *Douglas Laing. 96 bottles.*

Old Malt Cask Bowmore Aged 35 Years dist May 66, bott May 01 **(86)** **n**22 Golden Grahams with a splash of lime; **t**22 fruity, then clean malt; **f**21 gentle vanilla and more citrus; **b**21 they must have run out of peat on the island. Very unusual, amazingly fruity. **44% nc ncf sc.** *Douglas Laing. 192 bottles.*

Old Masters Bowmore 1990 bott 02 **(77)** **n**17 **t**21 **f**20 **b**19. Liqueur-sweet, but a tad out of kilter. **56.7%.** *James MacArthur.*

Peerless Bowmore 1966 cask 3311, dist May 66 36-y-o **(84)** **n**22 **t**19 **f**22 **b**21. Astonishing array of orange-related fruits, kumquats at the fore; the arrival is oaky-tired but the finish is full of soft, spicy life. Virtully peatless. **42%.** *Duncan Taylor & Co.*

Peerless Bowmore 1968 cask 3819, dist Oct 68 34-y-o **(83)** **n**21 **t**22 **f**20 **b**20. Another curiously peatless offering, though the depth of the sweet malt is very impressive. **40.3%.** *Duncan Taylor & Co.*

Peerless Bowmore 1969 cask 6085, dist Nov 69 33-y-o **(77)** **n**21 **t**20 **f**18 **b**18. Thin and a bit oaky. **42.5%.** *Duncan Taylor & Co.*

Murray McDavid Bowmore 1989 bourbon cask MM5133 bott 00 **(86)** **n**22 clean and gristy with an above-average peaty character for this distillery; **t**22 enormously sweet arrival, slightly oiled; **f**21 oily, vanilla and peat; **b**21 a full-on Bowmore that lingers around. **46%. nc ncf sc.**

Murray McDavid Bowmore 1989 bourbon cask MM20975, dist Jun 89, bott May 02 **(87)** **n**22 softly peated, sweet, almost winey; **t**22 sweet, moderately spiced malt. The oak says no more than hullo; **f**21 vanilla and deft smoke; **b**22 this is about as gentle a peaty dram as you could ask for. **46%**

Scotch Malt Whisky Society Cask 3.77 Aged 13 Years **(83)** **n**20 **t**22 **f**21 **b**20. For all the natural colour, a pretty youthful aroma and mouthfeel; the peat pretty chilled and allowing barley-character to help provide something fruity and eventually chalky. **55.9%. nc ncf.**

Signatory Bowmore Rare Reserve 33 Years Old dist 28/2/68, bott 23/7/01 cask 1431 **(91)** **n**23 old airing cupboards: soft honey outguns the peat; **t**23 incredibly sweet peat coats the mouth with the thinnest layer possible and still the honey persists but in a toasty way; **f**22 the vanilla is a bit tired but the malts come to the rescue; **b**23 seriously remarkable malt that needs a bit of time in the glass to get going. A classic Bowmore of its genre without doubt and proof to some that you don't need cart-loads of peat to be a great Islay. **46.2%.** *218 bottles.*

Signatory Bowmore 11 Years Old Unchill filtered Collection hogshead 2220, dist 6/5/92, bott 26/3/03, **(88)** **n**22 peat kilns or Scottish coastal villages on a cold day; **t**22 soft, intensely sweet at first with the malt; **f**22 some black coffee with the peat, but sugared; **b**22 a cask just about every blender in the country will recognise: Bowmore at 10–11 years of age that is clean with a delicate peaty punch. Spot on..**46%.** *378 bottles.*

Ultimate Selection Bowmore 1992 cask 2216 dist 6/5/92, bott 11/9/02 **(85)** **n**20 young, fresh barley, scarcely peated; **t**22 refreshing grassy malt with an echo of smoke; **f**22 long, incredibly clean and beautifully sweet; **b**21 a near colourless dram untroubled either by oak or, by Bowmore standards, even peat. That said, it is so faultless in construction that it makes the perfect summer quaffing dram. **43%.** *Van Wees NL.*

Whisky Galore Bowmore 1989 **(70)** **n**16 **t**18 **f**18 **b**18. Hugely disappointing from the off-note nose to the lifeless finale. **46%.** *Duncan Taylor & Co.*

BRAES OF GLENLIVET
Speyside, 1974. Chivas. Silent.

Connoisseurs Choice Braes of Glenlivet 1975 (89) n23 sexy and alluring, gristy and fresh despite so many years in wood, even a touch of peat; t23 just astonishingly fresh and grassy despite the massive age, mouthwatering, clean, sweet, deftly smoked and glorious; f22 light, the softest of oak presence; b21 there will be those that argue that such an old whisky should offer more. Obviously the cask has done the rounds, but one must judge on quality. And in this context we are talking really first-class Speyside malt that is sensuously lip-smacking. I could start the day on this anytime. **40%**. *Gordon & MacPhail.*

BREAVAL (see Braes of Glenlivet)

BRECHIN (see North Port)

BRORA
Highland (northern), 1819–1983. Diageo. Closed.

Brora Aged 22 Years Rare Malts Selection dist 72 db (87) n21 smoking bonfires and a few chunks of peat tossed in; pretty dry; t22 firm entrenched oak at first then a sweet malty rush; f22 dries again with the oak returning nipping and biting; bitter chocolate on the late finish; b22 much more there than a cursory tasting will reveal. Big, big stuff. **56.7%**

Celtic Cross Brora 1980 (92) n23 one of the best Brora noses of recent years: lively peat, a dash of salt yet somehow not coastal in style. With some delicate oak around, this is beautifully weighted and complex; t23 intricate patterns of malt and spice, a touch of sugar here, dryer oaks there, totally harmonious and symmetrical; f22 dries but slowly and in sychronisation with everything else around it: almost like a green olive by the finish; b24 a gem of a bottling. There have been some run-of-the-mill Broras of late as age has taken its toll, but this is absolutely top of the tree. **46%**. *Scotch Malt Sales Ltd According to bottle code, bottled in 02.*

Connoisseurs Choice Brora 1972 (74) n18 t19 f19 b18. One of those malts that doesn't quite gel, the peat in particular being off beam. **40%**. *Gordon & MacPhail.*

Connoisseurs Choice Brora 1982 (74) n19 t20 f17 b18. Very lightly peated with sweet vanilla. **40%**. *Gordon & MacPhail.*

Old Malt Cask Brora Aged 19 Years Sherry dist Sep 81, bott Dec 00 (86) n21 lovely honey; t22 more acacia honey and the deftest wisps of smoke on the chewy barley; f22 velvety spices and melt-in-the-mouth fruit; b21 genuine charm. **50%. nc ncf**. *Douglas Laing. 564 bottles.*

Old Malt Cask Brora Aged 19 Years dist Nov 82 (75) n18 t20 f19 b18. Warms the tastebuds and lacks the normal peaty glow. **50%**. *Douglas Laing. 744 bottles.*

Old Malt Cask Brora Aged 20 Years dist Jun 81, bott Jul 01 (86) n21 pungent, uncluttered peat with a floral tone, too; t22 enormous, with chunky peat in tandem with something honied and malty and a shaft of oak; f22 long, saline and smoky; b21 this is a really big, smoky, salty, mother-of-all peated mainlanders. **50%. nc ncf**. *Douglas Laing. 560 bottles.*

Old Malt Cask Brora Aged 26 Years dist Nov 74, bott Apr 01 (82) n19 t23 f20 b20. The nose, though smoky, is delicate, so what follows next is big honey-peat surprise. **50%. nc ncf**. *Douglas Laing. 258 bottles.*

Scotch Malt Whisky Society Cask 61.15 Aged 26 Years (83) n18 t22 f21 b22. Quite a hot, nippy chap this. The smoke has burnt itself out slightly leaving an attractive, naturally sugared malt-oak bitter-sweet finish. A dram with attitude. **54.8%. nc ncf sc.**

Signatory Brora 20 Years Old Cask Strength cask 273, dist 25/2/82, bott 11/11/02 **(82)** n*18* t*22* f*21* b*21*. A seeringly hot dram with little or no peat to soften the blow. The intensity of the sweet, sugared malt is attractive, though. **58.6%.** *292 bottles.*

Platinum Brora 1972 (93) n*22* sharp, brittle grassy/malty notes get the mouth salivating. A hint of something peaty can be found amid something fruity and, to be honest, something a little farmyardy, too! t*24* big and even more salivating! Sweet, mildly sugary start with some soft peats arriving at the middle: massive yet fabulously subtle; f*23* loads of silky, gristy malt that revels in its clean, peaty smokiness. This is big stuff that just gets better the longer it stays on the palate; b*24* you taste a whisky this magnificent, and you can't help but wonder as to the thinking behind closing down such a brilliant distillery. There must be good reasons, but they are entirely lost in the stunning beauty and enormity of this classic bottling. **59.5%.** *Douglas Laing.*

Platinum Brora Aged 30 Years dist Mar 72, bott Jan 03 **(91)** n*24* the closest aroma to a peat-reeked distillery kiln I have ever come to: an old-fashioned maltings in a bottle; t*23* a big fruit influence – tinned peaches and sultana – helps play down the sweet peat and threatening oak; f*22* the oaky tones fade, kept in their place by roasty, gristy, smoky malt that lingers to the nth degree; b*22* a real one-off whisky that tells its very own story. **49.7%.** *Douglas Laing.*

Provenance Autumn Distillation Brora Over 25 Years dist Autumn 75, bott Winter 01 **(87)** n*22* a strange union of kippers and honey. The vanilla is the go-between and ensures an even weight: wonderfully refined; t*22* the peat booms loud and long, but has little of the seaweedy quality of an islander: salty nonetheless with the oak charging towards the middle. The malt holds firm and offers sufficient sweetness; f*21* hints of cocoa butter and dry, overdone toast, chewy and smoky to the last ember; b*22* decidedly non-Islay in style and quite magnificent in every respect. However, you can only wonder at the enormity of this had it been delivered at full cask strength. **43%. nc ncf.** *Douglas McGibbon & Co.*

BRUICHLADDICH
Islay, 1881. Bruichladdich Ltd, Working.

Bruichladdich Aged 10 Years db **(88)** n*21* beautifully clean and zesty, the malt is young and almost juvenile; t*23* a sweet, fruity then malty charge along the tastebuds that gets the mouth salivating; f*22* soft vanilla and custard tart; b*22* this is really great stuff: a whole lot lighter and less oily than a generation ago with the casks appearing to have limited influence. Few island whiskies come more refreshing than this. **46%**

Bruichladdich Aged 15 Years db **(89)** n*22* quite salty with just a faint honey note; sea-breezy and fresh; t*22* lots more saltiness alongside the firm oak and gentle malt; f*22* long and malty with developing spice brushed with cocoa; b*23* a very coastal, laid-back dram where the complexity has to be spotted by the tastebuds in the same way that eyes become accustomed to the dark. One of Scotland's more subtle malts worthy of time and exploration **46%**

Bruichladdich XVII db **(87)** n*22* pears and clean malt; t*21* an oily signature heralds some enormous malt; f*22* quite long with a steady build-up of vanilla and salt, offset by some sweeter malty tones; b*22* another sensuous and well-balanced dram. **46%**

Bruichladdich Aged 20 Years db **(87)** n*19* malty but a little soapy; t*21* warming, massive, sweet malt; f*24* roast chestnuts and brilliant bitter-sweet malt: fabulous complexity unravels; b*23* not a confident start, but well worth a long hard study. Brilliant complexity. **46%**

Bruichladdich Legacy 1966 db **(92)** n*23* a yielding aroma not short on fruit and a vague smokiness: dreamy stuff; t*23* stupendous softness, so the malt moulds itself to the mouth while the fruit offers something mouthwatering ... at this age! There really is a hint of something smoky in there, which fits beautifully with mercurial oaky notes; **f23** the oak is so in tune with the malt: no sappiness or bitterness here, just grace, charm, melting malt, cocoa ... oh, and that hint of smoke again! **b23** that's my laddie! **40.6%**

Bruichladdich Vintage 1970 db **(87) n**23 all the weight on this is oak but it harmonises impeccably with a barley-sugar, honey sweetness; **t**23 again the skeleton is oak, the meat is a chewy, oily maltiness; **f**20 dries to leave a salty, slightly sappy shadow; **b**21 before the oak kicks in it is utter bliss. **44.2%**

Bruichladdich Vintage 1984 db **(86) n**22 new-mown grass and honey. How un-Islay can you get?!? **t**22 wonderful oily character that coats the roof of the mouth with soft malt-vanilla **f**21 very dry with a marked degree of saltiness; **b**21 surprising amount of age present considering the richness of the malt. **46%**

Blackadder Raw Cask Bruichladdich 1970 hogshead 4840, dist 16 Nov 70, bott Apr 02 **(89) n**23 teasingly sweet, honey, heather and very fresh malt; **t**23 brilliantly lush as spices add an extra dimension to what is otherwise repeated from the nose; **f**21 dry oaky tones with a touch of salt; **b**22 first-class aged Islay. **53.8%. nc ncf sc.**

Blackadder Raw Cask Bruichladdich 1991 hogshead 3264, dist 22 Nov 81, bott Apr 02 **(83) n**19 **t**22 **f**21 **b**21. Typically oily and extremely malty and clean. **56.1%. nc ncf sc.**

Cadenhead's Bruichladdich 16 Years Old dist 86, bott 03/03 **(88) n**20 very flakey oak lightens what appears to be delicate peat-reek; **t**23 massive malt arrival, enormously rich, sweet ... and smoked? **f**22 long with some trace elements of peat: just so beautifully weighted malt; **b**23 if I didn't know better, I'd say there was some peat influence in there somewhere. In fact, I will say there is some ... what a collector's item! **59.9%. nc ncf sc.**

James MacArthur Bruichladdich 10 Years Old **(89) n**21 over-ripe bananas and sweet malt; **t**23 flawlessly intact malt and soft oak, brilliantly made whisky with not a single off-note or blemish; **f**23 more bananas and malt; **b**22 pastel-shaded flavours that are fruity and invigorating. A little gem. **43%**

Gordon & MacPhail Bruichladdich 1969 Cask **(77) n**19 **t**20 **f**19 **b**19. Very sweet and intense, but the oak just takes too large a slice of the action. **52.5%**

Gordon & MacPhail Bruichladdich 1969 Cask **(82) n**21 **t**22 **f**19 **b**20. Lightly oiled, not unlike Canadian with the cream toffee oak effect. **54.2%**

Gordon & MacPhail Bruichladdich 1988 Cask **(86) n**22 the vaguest touch of smoke on the deeply malty nose; **t**22 enveloping oils help the sweetish, malty vanilla cling to the palate; **f**21 lazy wafts of smoke re-surface as some drier, oaky, cocoa notes drift in; **b**21 a collector's item: peat on a Bruichladdich. It is barely detectable, but it is there. A very more-ish dram. **54.2%**

Lochindaal 10 Years Old Bruichladdich **(78) n**18 **t**20 **f**20 **b**20. A pleasant malty dram once you get past the mildly off-key nose. **43%.** Associated Distillers Ltd.

Murray McDavid Bruichladdich 1986 cask MM514, bott 03 db **(80) n**21 **t**20 **f**20 **b**19. Good oak and gooseberries on the nose and malty-salt on the body. **46%**

Old Malt Cask Bruichladdich Aged 13 Years dist Oct 88 **(79) n**19 **t**21 **f**20 **b**19. Rather charming – Speyside in style. **50%.** Douglas Laing.

Peerless Bruichladdich 1969 cask 2329, dist May 69 33-y-o **(88) n**22 very softly honied with honeysuckle, too, and the very faintest trace of peat; **t**23 brilliant mouth arrival with a rich, coppery texture then a riot of clean, gently sugared malt; **f**21 dries as the vanilla arrives; **b**22 certainly one of the richest and most distinguished unmalted Islays bottled in the last decade. **48.7%.** Duncan Taylor & Co.

Royal Mile Whiskies Bruichladdich 12 Year Old dist Jul 85, bott Apr 98 **(88) n**21 apples and very soft vanilla; **t**23 gloriously oily texture holds fast to the palate, sumptuous malt with a hint of salt and honey; **f22** the oiliness continues, as does the vanilla influence and spotless malt; **b22** this is one of the few Bruichladdichs still to be found that holds the exact character that for many years made this the island's favoured dram. Available from only Royal Mile Whiskies, Edinburgh.

Scott's Selection Bruichladdich 1986 bott 01 **(71)** n19 t18 f17 b17. Slightly too unevenly developed for its age. **55%**. *Robert Scott & Co.*

BUNNAHABHAIN
Islay, 1881. Burn Stewart. Working.

Bunnahabhain Aged 12 Years db **(87)** n21 soft hint of sultana and sea-breeze, even a vague waft of smoke – something new; t22 mouth-filling and mouth-watering fruit had takes a lead role then a gradual build-up of intense malt, flanked by salt; f22 remains salty and dries as vanilla approaches and sweetens for a short burst of malt. Dries for a second, final time as the oak and salt move back in; **b22** a greatly improved dram in recent years thanks to better quality casks and a slight toning down of the sherry. But still not a patch on 20 years ago when it was Scotland's most bracing, provocative dram. Hopefully the new owners will be able to restore it to its former superstar (though little-known) glory. **40%**

Bunnahabhain 1968 Family Silver Vintage Reserve db **(85)** n21 gentle sherry pepped up by a salty breeze; t22 fat and malt-lush with the sherry and oak fighting for second spot; f21 dries towards oak and cocoa; **b21** just about hanging on in there, but the sherry is a delight. **40%**

Berrys' Own Selection Bunnahabhain 1980 bott 02 **(88)** n22 stupendous fresh salt breeze: pure Bunna! t23 silky, honied start, more brine and barley; f21 doesn't quite pan out in terms of complexity as one might have hoped, but the oak behaves well and offers limited vanilla; **b22** a big honied, high-quality version that is just so Bunna. **55.6%**. *Berry Bros & Rudd.*

Dun Bheagan Bunnahabhain 22 Year Old cask 5899 **(87)** n21 lots of honey and salted butter; t23 chewy and spicy with a massive malt surge; f21 signs of liquorice and mocha amid the salt and spice; **b22** genuine quality and a cask emptied just at the right time. **58%**

Hart Brothers Bunnahabhain Aged 35 Years dist Mar 67, bott Sep 02 **(87)** n23 dank fruitcake: just beautiful; t22 mouthwatering and surprisingly malty and fresh, lovely toasty notes and grape juice; f21 the oak is a bit on the tired side but still sits well with the barley and fruit; **b21** a dram to be savoured. **40.5%**

The MacPhail's Collection Bunnahabhain 1988 (78) n19 t21 f19 b19. Exceptionally light even for a Bunna, with moderate salty intervention **40%**. *Gordon & MacPhail.*

The MacPhail's Collection Bunnahabhain 1989 (83) n20 t22 f20 b21. Salty and biting, a fierce dram for its strength. **40%**. *Gordon & MacPhail.*

Murray McDavid Bunnahabhain 1979 Bourbon cask MM 2080, dist Mar 79, bott Apr 99 **(53)** n5 t17 f16 b15. A curry-nosed entirely flawed disaster. **46%. nc ncf sc.**

Murray McDavid Bunnahabhain 1979 Sherry caskMM 2081, dist Mar 79, bott Apr 99 **(79)** n21 t20 f19 b19. The rich sherry papers over some cracks; great spice with the fresh, plummy fruit dominating. **46%. nc ncf sc.**

Old Malt Cask Bunnahabhain Aged 16 Years dist Mar 85, bott Mar 01 **(93)** n23 thundering mixture of salt and sea breeze with ragged malt: so complex – similar in style to a Glenmorangie; t24 Brilliant! Again the mouth explodes on impact as the salty, malty front leads the way for some sizzling spices to follow with honey calming frayed tastebuds; f23 delicate and controlled complexity, the malt and oak harmonising as cocoa kicks in; **b23** simply, unambiguously, the best Bunna I have ever found in bottled form ... though over the years I have spotted similar peaches in their warehouses. It has lashings of everything that makes the distillery tick: new owners Burn Stewart could do worse than grab a bottle of this and use it as a template for their future range. **50%. nc ncf.** *Douglas Laing. 366 bottles.*

Old Masters Bunnahabhain 1979 bott 99 **(82)** n19 t23 f20 b20. Excellent fruit on arrival; finishes like watered bitters. **57%.** *James MacArthur.*

Peerless Bunnahabhain 1966 cask 4872, dist Jun 66 **(89)** n22 salty, refreshing, mildly honied barley; t23 really intense heather-honey spruced up by salt and a hint of bourbon; f21 mildly spicy with soft oak drifting about; b23 this is a stupendous Bunna, the best at this age I have ever found. And bottled in the nick of time if the strength is anything to go by.... **40.1%.** *Duncan Taylor & Co.*

Peerless Bunnahabhain 1969 cask 6717, dist Jun 69 33-y-o **(82)** n20 t21 f21 b20. Zesty on the nose and bitter marmalade on the palate. **42.8%.** *Duncan Taylor & Co.*

Private Cellar Bunnahabhain 1988 bott Feb 03 **(84)** n20 t22 f20 b22. Bracing, fresh and gently honied. **50%**

Rare Old Bunnahabhain 1965 **(82)** n22 t21 f19 b20. The sherry starts brightly enough and then flattens with curious haste. **40%**

Single Barrel Collection Bunnahabhain 1988 dist June 88, bott Dec 01 **(79)** n20 t18 f21 b20. Brusque, islandy but quite unlike the distiller's own version. **55.93%. nc ncf.**

CAOL ILA
Islay, 1846. Diageo. Working.

Caol Ila Aged 12 Years db **(86)** n21 oily, pungent peat coats the nosebuds; t22 big sweet peat swamps the palate with some gristy, mildly green notes balancing out some rich vanilla; f21 very soft, peaty, peppery spices form alongside some toffee tones; b22 toffee on the finish apart, this is a quite beautiful dram whose power-packing peatiness does not hinder the sensual ride. **43%**

Caol Ila Aged 18 Years db **(77)** n20 t20 f18 b19. Meanders, sometimes big and spicy, sometimes dead on the palate. Very odd and overall pretty frustrating and disappointing. **43%**

Caol Ila Aged 21 Years Rare Malts Selection dist 75 db **(94)** n24 biting, searing peat on an oily bed; t22 enormous peat of the highest order battles it out with some vanilla notes; f24 spellbinding complexity: the sweet-dry ratio is entirely in sync; some enormously arousing fresh malty notes survive despite the enormous age: amazing; b24 perhaps this bottling represents the first time the owners took this distillery entirely seriously and produced arguably the definitive dram. It's off the Richter scale. **61.3%.**

Caol Ila Aged 23 Years Rare Malts Selection dist 78, bott May 02 db **(91)** n22 lively coastal attack: salty, iodine-peat; dry and decent oak presence; t23 sweet malt, then the most linear build-up of peat imaginable with little explosions all around the palate for good measure; f23 some liquorice and coffee join the peat for a really deep, chewy and very long finish; b23 less a malt and more of a saga, the flavours always going that extra chapter further. Superb. **61.7%.** *6,000 bottles.*

Caol Ila Cask Strength db **(91)** n22 pungent lead weight; atypical for this distillery; t23 massive peat attack; f23 softens, sweetens and charms; b23 this is a bruiser, enormously sweet and the phenol level is surely way over the usual 35ppms. Mysteriously, the back label instructs the drinker to drink one part Caol Ila for two parts water to "enjoy a single malt cask at its best". Bizarre: you might just as well buy it at 43%. Take it from me: for best results add one part Caol Ila to one part Caol Ila and, if in doubt, add another part Caol Ila. Then warm in the hand. If you need water, add it to some lemon squash before going to bed. **55%. ncf.**

Berrys' Own Selection Caol Ila 1983 bott 02 **(85)** n23 pretty crispish for a Caol Ila, with some oilier notes wandering leisurely through: big time peat; t21 fills the mouth with gently oiled peat and the barley does spread out to form something brittle. Pleasant fruit-tones; f20 dries with oak making some toasty notes; b21 a very decent dram with attractive complexity. **46%**

Blackadder Raw Cask Caol Ila 1992 cask 10637, dist 19 June 92, bott Apr 02 **(86)** n22 clean, young, full-bodied and slightly oily peat; t22 vibrant malt arrival on palate, dark chocolate drops in on the chewy peat; f21 cocoa and vanilla plus waves of smoke; b21 sweet and confident. A typical Caol Ila of this age. **58.6%. nc ncf sc.**

Cadenhead's Caol Ila 10 Years Old dist 93, bott 03/03 **(92)** n23 classic, unmistakable: oily, fat and phenolic; t24 superb spices hit the tastebuds in waves. The malt is sweet and peaty and beautifully clean; f22 oily but light with lots of vanilla and banana replacing the spice; b23 with minimum oak interference from a wrung-out cask Caol Ila, as a 10-year-old, is rarely found any better than this. **60.8%**

Cask Caol Ila 1980 casks 10540–3, bott 94 **(84)** n20 t22 f21 b21. Both explosive and gentle in equal measures, but just a little raw through the middle. **62.6%.** *Gordon & MacPhail.*

Cask Caol Ila 1981 casks 2081–6, bott Nov 96 **(83)** n21 t21 f20 b21. Attractively buttery and biscuity amid the very soft peat. Enormously sweet. **63.4%.** *Gordon & MacPhail.*

Cask Caol Ila 1988 casks 1084–7 (refill hogsheads), dist 4/5/88, bott 17/1/02 **(87)** n23 unambiguously Caol Ila offering a hint of grist; t22 big at first then settles down to a zingy, zesty citrus freshness among the peat; f21 soft vanilla kicks in; b21 quality Caol Ila. **57.6%.** *Gordon & MacPhail.*

Connoisseurs Choice Caol Ila 1980 **(88)** n24 a monster of a nose, peaty and beechy. Just about spot-on balance between malt and oak. It doesn't come much better than this; t22 the flavour doesn't follow through with the peat at first, more emphasis on fruit, but the smoke gathers momentum; f20 lots of vanilla and salt; b22 the closest in style to the old CC that used to accompany me around the island in the early 80s. Delicious. **40%.** *Gordon & MacPhail.*

Connoisseurs Choice Caol Ila 1981 **(73)** n19 t19 f17 b18. A bizarrely passionless Caol Ila. **40%**

Connoisseurs Choice Caol Ila 1988 **(83)** n20 t20 f23 b20. Sweet and relaxed peat encounters little resistance. The complexity arrives all on the long, quite wonderful finish. **40%.** *Gordon & MacPhail.*

Coopers Choice Caol Ila 1991 bott 03 (11 Years old) **(83)** n20 t21 f20 b22. So, now you have it – the UNPEATED! Caol Ila. From a cask that could sit undetected a mile or two along the coast at Bunnahabhain, this bottling ranks alongside the latter Ardbeg 17-y-o and the bourbon cask Macallans. Not the first time I have tasted Caol Ila in this form, but the first time I can ever remember seeing it bottled. A really fascinating dram in which a softly salty character thrives but suffers slightly for some so-so fruit influence which probably masks the higher complexity. Anyway, well done for bringing this one to us: a must for every Islay-phile. **43%.** *The Vintage Malt Whisky Co.*

Dun Bheagan Caol Ila Aged 10 Years dist 90, bott 00 **(91)** n24 one of the most complex and expressive Caol Ila noses on the market: enormous complexity with the light gristy style of the malt allowing a seaweed character to develop, totally sensational; t23 sweet malt with just a touch of soft oil to help stick it to the roof of the mouth: simmering spices and good oak complete the picture; f21 good bitter-sweet malty-oaky character: quite hard; b23 ladies and gentleman, we have a genuine classic on our hands. It really amazes me when the actual distillery bottling described Caol Ila as less pungent than some other Islays. This is pungent enough. **43%.** *William Maxwell.*

Hart Brothers Caol Ila Aged 23 Years dist 75, bott 98 **(79)** n*19* t*20* f*21* b*19*. A noble, attractive, complex if rather tired version of one of the first-ever makes of the new-style Caol Ila after its rebuilding in 1974. **43%**

Milroy's Caol Ila Over 10 Years Old (89) n*23* absolutely typical Caol Ila: a flat-ish oily aroma lifted by sweet peat and more jolting salty, coastal notes. Unmistakably from this distillery: could be used as a blueprint for any 10-y-o Caol Ila! t*22* real sweetie, in every sense. The oaky vanilla holds out for only a matter of seconds before being swept away by a majestic wave of chunky peat. Softens back to its oily norm for the chewy middle; f*21* lingering peat and dark chocolate echo around the palate for an impressively long period. Dries delightfully at the very end, as a delicate spiciness emerges; b*23* what a cracker! Caol Ila at probably its best age and from a well-used cask which allows the massive peat free rein to do its, sweet, oily best. This is Caol Ila at its most bruising and confident. **43%**. *UK.*

Murray McDavid Caol Ila 1989 bourbon cask 2107, dist Dec 89, bott Dec 01 **(85)** n*22* oily, gristy; t*21* big spice kick from start; f*21* gentle oak follow-through and a hint of something citrussy; b*21* complex sweet-dry character: oily and big. **46%. nc ncf sc.**

Old Malt Cask Caol Ila Aged 17 Years dist Nov 84 **(88)** n*22* vanilla and peat; t*24* peat and peat; f*22* peat ... errr ... and vanilla; b*20* the peat level is way above the norm for a Caol Ila, but the complexity has been lost. A sweet, oily, rambling, rumbling dram that is sheer bliss for those who love to chew peat. **50%. nc ncf.** *Douglas Laing. 408 bottles.*

Old Malt Cask Caol Ila Aged 19 Years (Sherry) dist Feb 81, bott Jun 00 **(85)** n*21* fruit pudding and hints of peat; t*22* silky, malty then a vanilla surge. Smoke wafts around in the background; f*21* signs of age but the complexity is impressive; b*21* lots of sultanas to go with the subdued peat. **50%. nc ncf.** *Douglas Laing. 793 bottles.*

Old Malt Cask Caol Ila 26 Years Old dist Dec 74, bott Apr 01 **(88)** n*23* heaps of oranges amid suble peat-reek; t*22* spicy and smoky from first sip, the oiliness helping to spread a brown sugar sweetness with it; f*21* oaky, but well-controlled and forms pleasant layers with the fading peat and developing chocolate; b*22* really tastebud-rattling stuff with a kick far greater than the alcohol strength suggests. Beautiful. **50%. nc ncf.** *Douglas Laing. 294 bottles.*

Private Collection Caol Ila 1965 (79) n*21* t*18* f*20* b*20*. Lovely nose, but then a big oaky dive on the palate. Recovers beautifully, though. **45.6%.** *Gordon & MacPhail.*

Private Collection Caol Ila Calvados Finish 1988 (85) n*22* sharp burst of flighty peat and etheric apple-based fruits; t*20* refreshing; f*22* spicy and fruity with the peat unable to decide whether to stay or go; b*21* a malt I have warmed to over the years in a big way. Certainly shows more complexity and charm than I first thought and a revitalising dram when drunk chilled. **40%.** *Gordon & MacPhail.*

Private Collection Caol Ila Claret 1988 (83) n*18* t*22* f*22* b*21*. That most unique of beasts: a light, fruity, mouthwatering thirst-slaking Caol Ila. Yes, such a thing exists and allows a hefty degree of peat to filter through for good measure. The nose is a bit of a challenge for old-fashioned Islay-philes like me, but worth a place in any collection or simply for a unique experience. Didn't originally think much of it: has grown on me. **40%.** *Gordon & MacPhail.*

Private Collection Caol Ila Cognac Finish 1988 (83) n*22* t*20* f*21* b*20*. Very odd: hard as nails, flinty and green. Great nose. **40%.** *Gordon & MacPhail.*

Private Collection Caol Ila Cognac Finish 1990 (74) n*16* t*20* f*19* b*19*. Almost the complete opposite of the '88: nose apart, too soft and shapeless. **40%.** *Gordon & MacPhail.*

Private Collection Caol Ila Port Wood Finish 1990 (77) n*20* t*20* f*19* b*18*. Some juicy, fruity moments, but doesn't quite cling together. **40%.** *Gordon & MacPhail.*

Private Collection Caol Ila Sherry 1988 (76) n20 t19 f18 b19. Sherry and peat out of step. **40%.** *Gordon & MacPhail.*

Shieldaig Caol Ila Aged 17 Years dist 83 **(78) n**20 t21 f18 b19. A steady, dram: lightly peated by CI standards. **43%.** *William Maxwell France.*

Signatory Caol Ila 11 Years Old Cask Strength sherry butt 5360, dist 1/12/89, bott 24/11/01 **(83) n**23 t21 f19 b20. Superb nose, but the soft sherry is tying one hand behind the malt's back and you feel it could do so much more **58.1%.** *586 bottles.*

Ultimate Selection Caol Ila 1994 cask 10836, dist 6/9/94, bott 19/9/02 **(88) n**22 clean unrestricted peat balancing out grassy barley; **t**23 refreshing, crisp dram, mouthwatering with a beautiful build-up of oily peat; **f**22 a minor incursion of vanilla as the salty peat drifts off; **b**21 there is not a blender in Scotland who won't recognise this young-ish Caol Ila for its gristy-peaty-grassy yet slightly oily quality from a cask on its second or, more likely, third time around the block. Fabulous to get the chance to buy in bottled form. **43%.** *Van Wees NL.*

Usquebaugh Society Caol Ila 1989 dist 2/5/98, bott Sep 99 **(85) n**23 classic Caol Ila: at once oily and punchy; **t**22 big peat arrival, spices then quick oak.; **f**20 the peat hangs on by its finger nails as the oak gains control. Slick honey adds a soothing touch; **b**20 a curiously oak-advanced Caol Ila for its age. **45%.** *NL.*

Whisky Galore Caol Ila 1989 (88) n22 peaty and oily; **t**22 sweet peat; more oil; **f**22 soft vanilla on the peat. Gentle and simplistic; **b**22 Caol Ila at 12 years in a nutshell: all delicious effect, little complexity. **46%.** *Duncan Taylor & Co*

CAPERDONICH
Speyside, 1898. Chivas. Silent.

Caledonian Selection Caperdonich 1970 cask 3337 bott (in decanter) 01 **(78) n**20 t20 f20 b18. Oaky, pleasant but perhaps lacking guile. **46%. nc ncf.** *Liquid Gold Enterprises. From hogshead.*

Connoisseurs Choice Caperdonich 1968 (77) n21 t20 f17 b19. Clean malt, but a little thin and hot. **40%.** *Gordon & MacPhail.*

Connoisseurs Choice Caperdonich 1980 bottl 2000 **(73) n**20 t19 f17 b17. Ordinary fare. **40%.** *Gordon and MacPhail.*

Hart Brothers Caperdonich Aged 32 Years dist 1968 **(85) n**21 apples and bananas; **t**22 very tasty, mouthwatering malt, at times sweet; **f**21 quite long with the barley keeping the oak at arm's length and even some peat drifts in at the death; **b**21 a quite juicy Caper, thankfully displaying little of its great age. **44.5%**

Lombard Caperdonich 1968 (59) n12 t17 f15 b15. A fleeting moment of rich malt fruit on the palate, but otherwise soapy. **46%**

The Old Malt Cask Caperdonich Aged 27 Years dist Oct 74 **(88) n**23 exquisitely delicate, floral, rose petals with hints of cinnamon and cucumber. Honestly, folks! Some good old-fashioned spice and honey also on standby. The oak is weaving one of the most complicated patterns of 2002's releases; **t**22 beautifully sweet and gently honied, the barley has a minor role but it is the complexity of the oak that astonishes: really pleasing build-up of rumbling spices; **f**21 classic soft cocoa notes as you might expect from an oak-dominated malt, and a lick of liquorice gives some extra length; **b**22 Old Masters don't come more delicate than this. The brilliant nose is no way let down by what follows. Fabulous and one of the great Caperdonichs of all time. **50%.** *Douglas Laing.*

Old Malt Cask Caperdonich Aged 30 Years dist May 70, bott Jun 00 **(74) n**20 t19 f17 b18. Displays the usual Caperdonich butteriness, but also its fragility. A touch too oaky, especially at the finish. **50%.** *Dougls Laing. nc ncf. 180 bottles.*

Scotch Malt Whisky Society Cask 38.11 Aged 32 Years (91) n24 unquestionably the most complex Caperdonich I have nosed. Shy and retiring, you seriously have to hunt the aromas: not unlike your eyes acclimatising to the night sky to realise just how many stars are visible. The most subtle of floral and citrus notes combine with a faintly bourbony oak: spiced yet sweet, dry yet fruity, Caperdonich but fantastic; t23 now we are in the realms of Kentucky: slightly more bourbon signs here than Scotch, but with a lightweight 32-y-o what do you expect? Lovely oils coat the mouth, slapping on the last malt traces; f21 slightly creosote-ish (yes, I have drunk creosote...) with the oak now in total control, still sweet against the odds; b23 this Scotch has turned bourbon in pursuit of brilliance, and who cares? Great whisky is great whisky. And this is great whisky. Believe me: for a Caperdonich, it's better than great! **53.6%. nc ncf sc.**

CARDHU (see Cardow)

CARDOW
Speyside, 1824. Diageo. Working.
Cardhu 12 Years Old db **(90) n**23 just about the cleanest, most uncluttered, pure, sweet malt you will ever find, a touch of apple, perhaps, giving an extra dimension; t24 again the malt is pure and rich, just a thread of oak adding some dryness and depth; f21 vanilla and malt; b22 I remember at a tasting in America once being asked to define "malt whisky". I answered with one word: Cardhu. Because no whisky, even the exceptional Glen Moray, is quite as intensely malty as this and, although it may lack overall complexity, the sheer beauty of this malt has been one I have savoured for over 20 years and never once seen a drop in quality or been disappointed by it. I don't think there's a blender in the land, including myself, who would not give his left little pinky for unlimited supplies of this astonishing malt. Johnnie Walker use the distillery as their home base: hardly any surprise there. The bad news is that for the foreseeable future this is the last bottling of Cardhu as a single malt in a bid to preserve stock. The distillery has been given back its original name of Cardow and there are no plans to bottle under this title. Future Cardhu will be in vatted form. **40%**
(see also Cardhu Pure Malt)

CLYNELISH
Highlands (Northern), 1968. Diageo. Working.
Clynelish 14 Years Old (old Flora and Fauna label) db **(86) n**22 weighty, toasty malt with some rich fruity notes and a three-quarters-strangled smokiness; t20 light yet very sweet malts, then an assertive spiciness; f22 enormous emphasis on the malt still, with the sweetness becoming heavier as oak intervenes; b22 a lovely dram with a sweet malt dependency rather than the usual Clynelish complexity. **43%**
Clynelish 14 Years Old (new "Coastal Highland" label) db **(88) n**22 weighty, toasty malt with some rich fruity notes and a half-strangled smokiness; t21 sweet, absorbing, mildly gristy malt, coated lightly with muscovado sugar; f22 slightly more fruity, yet bitter. Some delicate (perhaps peaty?) spices see out the late brittle barley notes; b23 a high-quality dram that is firmer than most Clynelish on the market and is not afraid to throw its weight round. **46%**
Clynelish 24 Years Old Rare Malts Slection db dist 72 **(84) n**21 t22 f20 b21. Lots of toasted barley but a tad to much oak. Has some lovely honey moments, though. **61.3%**
Adelphi Clynelish 11 Years Old cask 1698, dist 88, bott 99 **(79) n**21 t21 f18 b19. Bananas and malt but thin and hot on the finish. **59.8%**
Adelphi Clynelish 12 Years Old cask 3280, dist 89, bott 01 **(64) n**17 t16 f15 b16. Something not right about this one at all. **57.2%**

Adelphi Clynelish 13 Years Old cask 3281, dist 89, bott 02 **(81) n**19 **t**21 **f**20 **b**21. Intense malt with some honey threads. At times oddly thin and wispish, but an enormous improvement on the cask 3280. **56.%**

Adelphi Clynelish 16 Years Old cask 3077, bott 00 **(83) n**20 **t**22 **f**20 **b**21. Impressively malty, delicate for its age. **54%**

Adelphi Clynelish 27 Years Old cask 2565, dist 74, bott 01 **(89) n**23 slightly peated plus some clean-as-you-like malt as a secondary layer; **t**22 big, sturdy, fully-oaked but cushioned by soft peat; **f**22 some bitter-ish oak, but lovely fresh malt survives the years; **b**22. **56.3%**. A collector's item to some as the distillery is spelled "Clynelsh" on the label.

Adelphi Clynelish 28 Years Old cask 14264, dist 72, bott 00 **(92) n**24 fresh, grassy malt, clean beyond belief for its age. The subtlety of the peat is beguiling.; **t**24 shimmering, salivating malt that is faultlessly fresh and chewy. Spices and a touch of smoke guaranee complexity; **f**22 spice, and soft oak and peat, **b**22 I'm a sucker for this kind of grassy yet peaty conundrum. Brilliant. **57.3%**

Berrys' Own Selection Clynelish 1972 bott 02 **(92) n**23 subtle, suety and salty; **t**23 a soft smoke drifts through a procession of passing tones of malt. A gradual build-up of soft, sugary notes makes it more edible still; **f**23 still hints of smoke as a little oak gains a toe-hold; **b**23 a dream: a malt that just floats round the tastebuds like a hostess in a ballgown. **43%**. *Berry Bros & Rudd.*

Blackadder Raw Cask Clynelish 1976 sherry cask 6501, dist 5/8/76, bott Apr 02 **(94) n**23 tangy, zesty orange amid layers of oak, malt and peat, bunches of succulent white grapes, too. **t**24 sensational. Absolutely astonishing depth which you can chew until your jaws ache. Aided by some sweet peat, the fruit and malt melt into one. There is even some wonderful nip and bite to keep you on your toes; **f**23 long, with some fruit chocolate and smoke; **b**24 here you have it, folks: arguably the best single cask bottled in 2002, certainly one to rival Macallan's ESC IV. A true masterpiece and one which reveals Clynelish to the unitiated as one of the great Scottish distilleries. **59%. nc ncf sc.**

Blackadder Raw Cask Clynelish 1989 bourbon barrel 6088, dist 26 Sep 89, bott Mar 03 **(89) n**22 bracing sea air, a salty bite to sweet malt; **t**23 beautiful and fresh with buzzing spices against the wall of salty malt; **f**22 long, vanilla and malt; **b**22 really excellent malt thrust, complexity and bitter-sweet balance. **60.6%. nc ncf sc.**

Connoisseurs Choice Clynelish 1984 (79) n19 **t**21 **f**19 **b**20. Chewy and rich, big hickory-oak finale **40%**

Connoisseurs Choice Clynelish 1990 (80) n22 **t**20 **f**19 **b**19. Great nose and early riches. **40%**. *Gordon & MacPhail.*

Coopers Choice Clynelish 1990 bott 02 (12 Years Old) **(84) n**23 **t**20 **f**20 **b**21. Amazingly light and malty. A beautifully soft dram. **43%**. *The Vintage Malt Whisky Co.*

Coopers Choice Clynelish 1990 Port Finish bott 02 (12 Years old) **(91) n**23 lovely peppers and spices on top of a malt-fruit marriage; **t**22 an immediate array of invigorating fruit, pretty sweet but with some comforting vanilla, pounds around the palate; **f**23 spices return for a subtle fade-out: majestically complex; **b**23 my hat is off for a job well done: one of the best wine finishes to have come on the market in the last few years. A sensational achievement – congrats to all concerned. **46%**. *The Vintage Malt Whisky Co.*

Coopers Choice Clynelish Aged 16 Years dist 83, bott 00 **(85) n**22 green, grassy malt and crushed pine nuts; **t**22 succulent, salivating grassiness; **f**21 oaky-cocoa, smoky notes; **b**20 a dram that grows on you. **43%. sc.**

Gordon & MacPhail Clynelish 1989 Cask Strength (77) n19 **t**19 **f**20 **b**19. Not quite the cleanest sherry you could ask for. **57.9%**

Hart Brothers Clynelish Aged 14 Years dist Mar 88, bott Sep 02 **(79) n**21 **t**21 **f**18 **b**19. Some very decent honey. **53.3%**

James MacArthur Clynelish 10 Year Old **(88) n**21 lively and complex: pure Clynelish for its age; **t**23 so sensuous: the mouthfeel is lush and has clinging to it stupendous toasted honey malt and soft oak; **f**22 the spicy oak intensifies the age, but the dryness counters the early sweet tones; **b**22 a real monster for a 10-y-o: the tastebuds are swamped with goodies. **43%**

Mission Range Clynelish 1972 **(92) n**22 elegantly aged with just the right amount of oak dryness; **t**23 absolutely stunning: the malt-barley fit is just about perfect and spices evolve early on; **f**23 thins out slightly with the oak now in the ascendency but still shows class and compensating silky sweetness; **b**23 a real gem. The mouthfeel is textbook. **46%. nc ncf.** Murray McDavid.

Old Malt Cask Clynelish Aged 30 Years dist Sep 70, bott Apr 01 **(90) n**23 slivers of peat are sandwiched between delicate oak and toasty malt. Yummy; **t**23 this is unfair: you think the taste at this age can't get past the nose, but it does. Astonishing. So much sugared malt, but it's never too sweet thanks to the tangy oak. The oiliness and mouthfeel is just about perfect; **f**22 fades, but does so while injecting glorious spices and re-introducing that shadowy wisp of peat; **b**22 this is how you dream a 30-y-o should be, but so rarely is. **42%. nc ncf.** Douglas Laing.

Old Malt Cask Clynelish Aged 31 Years Sherry Finish dist Sep 70, bott Sep 01 **(89) n**23 coal-gas and malt, ripe figs and raisins; **t**23 sensuously long and refined, syrupy yet enough oak for some rough patches; **f**21 a hint of smoke breaks through, lovely coffee finish, pretty dry, bordering on bitter; **b**22 quality malt with a few hidden extras that need searching for. **48.4% nc ncf sc.** Douglas Laing. 186 bottles.

Old Masters Clynelish Aged 10 Years **(89) n**22 gentle smoke and citrus tones: very refreshing; **t**23 massive malt, beautifully shiny and honied on palate; **f**22 gentle smoke and vanilla; **b**22 near faultless for its age. **59.8%**

Old Masters Clynelish 1989 **(88) n**22 chocolate lime and smoke: superb; **t**22 trademark Clynelish silkiness and ultra-intense malt; **f**22 hints of smoke; **b**22 a superb all-round single malt. **59.1%.** James MacArthur.

Provenance Summer Distillation Clynelish Over 11 Years dist Summer 89, bott Autumn 00 **(89) n**22 slightly fiery: kumquats and diced apple soften it. The grassy maltiness adds to the attraction; **t**23 fabulously complex delivery with the malt nothing short of enormous. The sweetness is muted thanks to some very gentle but effective vanilla. The effect is a palate that can barely cope with subtlety; **f**21 some saltiness arrives as the whisky dries, but cannot stem the flow of malt. Very long; **b**23 no colouring, not chill filtered: you can see why blenders love this stuff. It doesn't half make a bad single malt, either! This bottling shows just what complexity it can muster from apparently nowhere. **43%. nc ncf.** Douglas McGibbon & Co.

Signatory Clynelish 12 Years South African Sherry Butt cask 3239, dist 17/05/89, bott 05/11/01 **(81) n**19 **t**21 **f**20 **b**21. Interesting, unquestionably fruity and sweet with a spicy background. **43%.** 868 bottles.

Ultimate Selection Clynelish 1992 **(73)** dist 5/11/92, bott 15/8/02 **n**16 **t**19 **f**20 **b**18. Fails to gel early on but the middle and early finish are fine. **43%.** Van Wees NL.

COLEBURN
Speyside, 1897–1985. Diageo. Closed.

Connoisseurs Choice Coleburn 1972 **(72) n**17 **t**20 **f**18 **b**17. A strange, off-balanced, rather sweet malt. One for collectors rather than purists. **40%.** Gordon & MacPhail.

Old Malt Cask Coleburn Aged 20 Years (Sherry) dist Sep 80, dist Jan 01 **(71) n**16 **t**21 **f**17 **b**17. Big mouth arrival, but little else works. **50%.** 648 bottles.

CONVALMORE
Speyside, 1894–1985. Closed.

Connoisseurs Choice Convalmore 1969 **(86) n**21 suet pudding with diced fruit, a slight hint of smoke; **t**22 beautifully silky, sweet malt-rich but succulent fruit; **f**22 attractive vanilla, a touch of spice and trailing peat; **b**21 a wonderful old Convalmore from a bottling from the 90s still doing the rounds in Europe. **40%.** *Gordon & MacPhail.*

Dun Bheagan Convalmore Aged 16 Years dist 84, bott 00 **(78) n**20 **t**19 **f**20 **b**19. Spicy and oaky, no shortage of character. **43%.** *William Maxwell.*

Rare Old Convalmore 1960 **(86) n**22 violets and muted cloves with light honey and a touch of bourbon; **t**22 soft malt and honeycomb with restrained oak. More bourbon towards the end of the middle as the oak digs in; **f**21 long, oily with some liquorice and chicory for extra effect; **b**21 takes some studying to get to the bottom of this one: take your time. **40%.** *Gordon & MacPhail.*

Old Malt Cask Convalmore Aged 22 Years dist Jan 78, bott Jun 00 **(80) n**19 **t**20 **f**21 **b**20. Threatened on the nose by oak, but boasts sufficient barley intensity to make an impressively chewy-tofffee dram of it. **50%. nc ncf.** *Douglas Laing. 336 bottles.*

Signatory Convalmore 1981 dist 18/3/81, bott 8/1/02 **(86) n**21 gristy, fresh and clean; **t**21 direct translation onto the tastebuds: rich textured and signs of good copper involvement; **f**22 highly complex with some subtle spices playing against the intense barley; **b**22 a well-used cask has thankfully preserved this malt so it retains a grassy, mildly honey shape. **43%.** *462 bottles.*

CRAGGANMORE
Speyside, 1870. Diageo. Working.

Cragganmore 12 Years Old db **(85) n**21 a layer of crushed sultana overlooked by coke smoke; **t**22 soft, extremely sweet and fruit-influenced; **f**21 long, the smoke returns with a degree of buzzing spice; **b**21 I admit it has been a couple of years since I last tasted Cragganmore, and this is not what I expected to find: those, like me, who remember the dry, crusty malty-oaky complex dram are in for a sherried surprise. **40%**

Cragganmore Distillers Edition Double Matured 1988 bott 2002, port-wine cask wood finish, db **(88) n**23 genuinely different to anything else around: the heaviness of the fruit does not contain the usual spice from port but rather a strange diffused mixture of unripened gooseberry juice and elderberry, genuinely odd, but very attractive; **t**22 the spice arrives now, but softly so with some bitterness creeping in to counter an instant malt-sweetness; **f**20 throat grabbingly dry with bitter almonds popping up; **b**23 this is one very weird whisky, the like of which cannot be found outside this bottling. Sit back and marvel. **40%**

Blackadder Raw Cask Cragganmore 1989 cask 1966, dist 13 Sep 89, bott Jun 00 **(89) n**22 malt and spice combine; **t**23 raw malt: grassy yet firm and chewy; **f**22 long, sweet malt, hints of Costa Rica coffee; **b**22 absolutely cracking Cragganmore. **59.6%. nc ncf sc.**

Cask Cragganmore 1978 cask 4959, dist 13/9/78, bott Nov 96 **(92) n**23 deep fruity tones amalgamate with the most intense malt imaginable: clean and astounding; **t**24 the taste is a mirror image of the nose with the malt being nothing short of seismic in its enormity and faultless in its grassy beauty; **f**22 hints of vanilla amid the magnificent malt; **b**23 one of those little pieces of genius that G&M has a tendency to unleash on us every now and again. **60.1%.** *Gordon & MacPhail.*

Connoisseurs Choice Cragganmore 1976 **(81) n**20 **t**21 **f**19 **b**21. Chocolate fruit and nut. Sweet and chewy. **40%.** *Gordon & MacPhail.*

Connoisseurs Choice Cragganmore 1978 (70) n19 **t**18 **f**16 **b**17. Pretty boring stuff: never gets even close to getting off the ground. **40%.** *Gordon & MacPhail.*

Murray McDavid Cragganmore 1990 bourbon cask MM9833, dist Apr 90, bott Oct 01 **(87) n**22 grassy malt and clean vanilla., very fresh, even with soft oak surround; **t**23 juicy arrival on palate: sweet sugared biscuits with vanilla development; **f**21 light and lazy, vanilla dominates; **b**21 simply a good Speyside cask: blender's fodder. **46%. nc ncf sc.**

Murray McDavid Cragganmore 1990 bourbon cask MM1410, dist April 90, bott Nov 01 **(88) n**22 an old bourbon barrel has done little to blunt the sharpness of the malt; **t**23 juicy, mouthwatering and palate-overloading stuff: just a distant hint of vanilla joins the clean, young maltiness; **f**22 longer follow-through of fresh malt and late spice; **b**21 a re-run of cask MM9833 except the finish has more spice and malt on the finale. **46% nc ncf sc.**

Signatory Cragganmore 13 Years Old dist 89, bott 02 **(89) n**22 clean, fresh, mouthwatering malt; **t**23 brilliant sharp barley arrival with young grass, fabulously juicy; **f**22 some spice and soft vanilla; **b**22 frankly, this is how the official Classic Malt Cragganmore should be: screaming undisguised Speyside at you.

Ultimate Selection Cragganmore 1989 cask 96, dist 18/4/89, bott 14/1/03 **(79) n**21 **t**21 **f**18 **b**19. Big malt start, but becomes furry and chalky. Just 1000 casks before the Blackadder Cragganmore, but they are poles apart. **sc.** *Van Wees NL.*

CRAIGELLACHIE
Speyside, 1891. Dewar's. Working.

Connoisseurs Choice Craigellachie 1982 (76) n20 **t**20 **f**17 **b**19. You get the feeling that disruptive caramel has crept in from somewhere. **40%.** *Gordon & MacPhail.*

Connoisseurs Choice Craigellachie 1987 (87) n21 floral, violets; hint of smoke, confident oak; **t**22 succulent, juicy, oily malt with no mean dash of low-profile peat to weight things down and spice things up; **f**22 pretty long and sweet with decent oak fade; **b**22 a really punchy Speysider that's no shrinking violet. **40%**

Old Malt Cask Craigellachie Aged 12 Years dist Oct 88 **(79) n**20 **t**21 **f**18 **b**20. Beautifully fresh with a very lively personality. **50%. nc ncf.** *Douglas Laing.*

Scott's Selection Craigellachie 1982 bott 99 **(81) n**19 **t**23 **f**19 **b**20. Craigellachie can sometimes be the bruiser of Speyside and here it takes no prisoners with its sweetness. **62.3%.** *Robert Scott & Co.*

DAILUAINE
Speyside, 1854. Diageo. Working.

Dailuaine Aged 16 Years db **(83) n**19 **t**22 **f**21 **b**21. Checking through my old tasting notes, I see I have scored this higher than any previous Flora and Fauna bottling from this distillery. Mildly lighter, yet more smoked than some, it offers a charming, mouthwatering freshness. Solid and delicious. **43%**

Adelphi Dailuaine 22 Years Old cask 4151, dist 80, bott 02 **(93) n**24 one of the all-time-great Dailuaine noses: honied with just about bang on malt-oak balance and very, very faintest hint of peat; **t**24 sensational! Fabulous sweet malt is wrapped in a softly oiled body and then more manuka honey and soft spice; **f**22 slightly bitter by comparison as oak makes a stand, but the malt remains superb; **b**23 I have waited many years for a really premier Dailuaine to turn up and here it is. A superb blend of weighty Highland style and grassy Speyside. **55.2%**

Connoisseurs Choice Dailuaine 1974 (84) n21 **t**22 **f**20 **b**21. Sweet, sensuously silky and malty. A lovely dram. **40%.** *Gordon & MacPhail.*

Connoisseurs Choice Dailuaine 1975 (81) n20 **t**22 **f**19 **b**20. Rhubarb on the nose and a lot to say for itself on the extremely malt-rich middle palate. **40%.** *Gordon & MacPhail.*

Old Malt Cask Dailuaine Aged 20 Years dist Feb 80, bott Feb 00 (83) n21 t21 f20 b21. A linear, clean, peachy malt that is a blender's dream. 50%. nc ncf. Douglas Laing. 368 bottles.

Old Malt Cask Dailuaine Aged 23 Years Sherry Finish dist Sep 78, bott Sep 01 (83) n19 t22 f21 b21. Dull nose, but plenty to compensate in a lively mouth-explosion. 50%. nc ncf. Douglas Laing. 276 bottles.

DALLAS DHU
Speyside, 1899–1983. Closed. Now a museum.

Dallas Dhu 21 Years Old Rare Malts Selection (83) n21 t21 f20 b21. An uncompromising barley-rich effort as one might expect, but otherwise a bit thin and lacking that usual extra depth. 61.9%. United Distillers/Diageo.

Cadenhead's Dallas Dhu 23 Years Old dist 79, bott 03/03 (89) n20 pleasant, but a bit lazy; t23 trademark rich honey that was always so apparent from 10–12 years old has been preserved and improved upon; f23 enormously long with deft fingers of smoke stimulating the honey; b23 a true gem from one of the most-missed distilleries in the world. 60.8%

Connoisseurs Choice Dallas Dhu 1971 (87) n23 smoky and honied, quite weighty; t22 soft, chewy malt and a hint of peat; f21 vanilla, cocoa, soft and silky; b21 a really clean, rich Dallas Dhu with quite beautiful smoke. 40%

Gordon & MacPhail Dallas Dhu 1980 (85) n23 hot cross buns, doughy, icing sugar: genuinely beautiful; t21 early oak surrounds the barley, but is just in balance; f20 sugared almonds and oak; b21 the oak has done some damage, but the charisma of a great malt still shimmers through. 40%

Mission Range Dallas Dhu 1979 (90) n23 beautiful raisiny, resiny oak: rich: t22 wave upon wave of barley with a little more oak as each one lands; f23 the most tender, sweet oak imaginable, a wisp of peat at the death; b22 this is such a classy, classic whisky. Age cannot dim its shafts of gold. 46%. Murray McDavid.

Old Malt Cask Dallas Dhu Aged 20 Year dist Nov 79, bott Apr 00 (76) n19 t21 f18 b18. Pretty rich middle, but a little hot and splutters about a bit. 50%. nc ncf. Douglas Laing. 324 bottles.

Old Malt Cask Dallas Dhu Aged 21 Years dist Mar 80, bott May 01 (79) n20 t20 f19 b20. Soft and malty. 50%. nc ncf. Douglas Laing. 348 bottles.

Old Malt Cask Dallas Dhu Aged 24 Years dist Oct 76, bott Jan 01 (76) n20 t20 f19 b17. Attractively powerful early arrival but otherwise uninspiring. 50%. nc ncf. Douglas Laing. 630 bottles.

Old Malt Cask Dallas Dhu 31 Years Old dist Dec 68, bott May 00 (88) n21 toasty, oaky; t23 sweet oak and biting spices. The chocolate honeycomb is beautiful; f22 lengthy, graceful, excellent bitter-sweet finish; b22 bliss. 50%. Douglas Laing. 253 bottles.

Signatory Rare Reserve Dallas Dhu 30 Years Old refill sherry butt 673, dist 6/3/70, bott 25/7/00 (84) n20 t23 f20 b21. The oak does little damage at first, offering lavender to the nose and a jagged spicy counter to the lush sweet malt in the fabulous middle. But it catches up in the end. 56.5%. 378 bottles.

DALMORE
Highand (northern), 1839. Kyndal. Working.

Dalmore 12 Years Old db (91) n22 big, fruity, firm, a threat of smoke, weighty; t24 well-muscled malt surge followed by clean fruity tones, immaculate mouth-presence and bitter-sweet balance; f22 long, tapering fruit-malt residue, some brown sugar coating and uncomplicated oak; b23 simply one of the great Highland malt whiskies at just about the perfect age: what I would do to see this unplugged at 46% minimum and no bottling hall interference. 40%

The Dalmore 21 Years Old db (87) n22 just how many citrus notes can we find here? Answers on a postcard ... on second thoughts, don't. Just beautifully light and effervescent for its age: a genuine delight; **t**23 again, wonderfully fruity though this time the malt pushes through confidently to create its own chewy island: fabulous texture; **f**20 simplifies towards toffee slightly too much in the interests of great balance. But a lovely coffee flourish late on; **b**22 bottled elegance. **43%**

The Dalmore 30 Years Old Stillman's Dram (89) n23 nuts and oranges in a rich fruitcake, lime marmalade adds to the fruit cocktail: seductive; **t**22 enormous fruit explosion, silky malt then an injection of bitter oak; **f**22 medium length, but the emphasis is on the malt as the oakiness burns off. The complexity levels rise as the fruit recedes and some spices arrive late; **b**22 in some ways the ultimate bitter-sweet dram, with the burnt-toast oak fighting against the sweet fruit and malt. It's a battle royale. **45%**

The Dalmore 50 Years Old db **(88) n**21 buxom and bourbony, the oak makes no secret of the antiquity; **t**19 again the oak arrives first and without apology, some salty malt creaking in later. Ripe cherries offer a mouthwatering backdrop; **f**25 comes into its own as harmony is achieved as the oak quietens to allow a beautiful malt-cherry interplay. Spices arrive for good measure in an absolutely has-it-all, faultless finish: really as much a privilege to taste as a delight; **b**23 takes a little while to warm up, but when it does becomes a genuinely classy and memorable dram befitting one of the world's great and undervalued distilleries. **52%**

The Dalmore 62 Years Old db **(95) n**23 PM or REV marked demerara pot-still rum, surely? Massive coffee presence, clean and enormous, stunning, top-drawer peat just to round things off; **t**25 this is brilliant: pure silk wrapping fabulous moist fruitcake soaked in finest oloroso sherry and then weighed with peat which somehow has defied nature and survived in cask all these years. I really cannot fault this: I sit here stunned and in awe; **f**24 perfect spices with flecks of ginger and lemon rind; **b**24 if I am just half as beautiful, elegant and fascinating as this by the time I reach 62, I'll be a happy man. Somehow I doubt it. A once-in-a-lifetime whisky – something that comes around every 62 years, in fact. Forget Dalmore Cigar Malt – even I might be tempted to start smoking just to get a full bottle of this. **40.5%**

The Dalmore 1966 db **(86) n**23 marzipan-orange, apple and malt; **t**22 clean, lush mouth arrival with superb, sparky spice; **f**20 flattens considerably as the vanilla kicks in; **b**21 a remakable dram for the years that it has kept its fruity integrity despite the big age. **44.6%**

The Dalmore 1973 Gonzalez Byass Sherry Cask Finish db **(93) n**24 outstanding fruit-spice: one of the cleaner sherry butts you are likely to find. This is dry and as delicate as an eighteenth-century Wedgewood figurine. Grapes, a touch of banana and very distant coal smoke. Don't sniff too hard: you might break it; **t**23 clean, almost Speyside light by Dalmore standards then a slow rolling in of crisp, dry sherry. The body is lightly oiled; **f**22 takes on an entirely new phase as oak arrives and the malt begins to vanish. Hints of cocoa and distant peat. Everything unravels in slow motion; **b**24 What happens when you get one of Scotland's greatest – if entirely undervalued – drams and fill it into what what was obviously a special, hand-picked, clean and flawless sherry butt? You get this. **52.3%**

The Dalmore Black Isle db **(77) n**19 **t**20 **f**19 **b**19. Very little of the complexity I automatically associate with Dalmore; slightly furry and a little drab. **40%**

The Dalmore Cigar Malt db **(71) n**17 **t**20 **f**16 **b**18. For me, flat and un-Dalmore-like. But there again I have never smoked as much as a cigarette in all my life – so what do I know? **43%**

Adelphi Dalmore 11 Years Old cask 998, dist 89, bott 00 **(69) n**16 **t**19 **f**17 **b**17. Sulphur to the fore, pure demerara sugar to the middle and sour, bitter notes aft. Some people will love this: for me this is not in the usual sure-footed mould of either the distillery or the bottlers. **57.2%. sc.**

Provenance Dalmore Over 11 Years Winter Distillation dist Winter 88, bott Autumn 00 **(89)** n*22* green, grassy and young; most unlike Dalmore as usually bottled; t*24* massive: the malt explores every single crevice in the palate, offering young malt and a hint of smoke; f*22* sweet malt fades with aplomb, allowing just a hint of oak to intervene. Lovely spices and cocoa bid adeau; b*21* Oh, if only more malt were bottled with this zest and youthfulness! Some may say it's undercooked: rather raw than burnt to a crisp, I say. **43%. nc ncf**. *Douglas McGibbon & Co.*

DALWHINNIE
Highlands (central), 1898. Diageo. Working.
Dalwhinnie 15 Years Old db **(94)** n*23* sublime stuff: a curious mixture of coke smoke and peat-reek wafts teasingly over the gently honied malt. A hint of melon offers some fruit but the caressing malt stars; t*24* that rarest of combinations: at once silky and malt intense, yet at the same time peppery and tin-hat time for the tastebuds, but the silk wins out and a sheen of barley sugar coats everything, soft peat included; f*23* some cocoa and coffee notes, yet the pervading slightly honied sweetness means that there is no bitterness that cannot be controlled; b*24* a malt it is hard to decide whether to drink or bath in: I suggest you do both. One of the most complete mainland malts of them all. Know anyone who reckons they don't like whisky? Give them a glass of this – that's them cured. Oh, if only the average masterpiece could be this good. **43%**

Dalwhinnie Distillers Edition 1986 Double Matured oloroso finish, bott 02 db **(87)** n*23* exceptionally clean sherry freshens up the nose without too much cost to the honey; t*23* beautiful mouth arrival and then radiating out of fruit, the malt regroups but is outnumbered; f*20* quite dry and oak rich; b*21* good sherry butt, but if anything goes to prove how sherry influence can reduce the all-round complexity of a great malt. **43%**

Dalwhinnie 36 Years Old db **(92)** n*23* well-peated and weird for a Highlander: there is something distinctly coastal for a whisky matured up a mountain, though the heather is quite fitting; t*24* brilliant oak and salt seep into the tastebuds leaving a honey stain wherever they go. Soft peats are also very evident; f*22* much drier, with a soft, oaky-peaty buzz; b*23* rarely does a Dalwhinnie of this antiquity make it to market. Even rarer is it for a Perthshire-style whisky to retain its smoky-heather-honey shape to this degree. Brilliant. **47.2%**

DEANSTON
Highlands (Perthshire), 1966. Burn Stewart. Working.
Deanston 12 Year Old db **(66)** n*15* t*18* f*16* b*17*. Butyric and thin. **40%**
Deanston 17 Year Old db **(68)** n*17* t*17* f*17* b*17*. A 17-year-old anorexic with agoraphobia: painfully thin and goes nowhere. **40%**

DUFFTOWN
Speyside, 1898. Diageo. Silent.
Dufftown Aged 15 Years db **(69)** n*16* t*19* f*17* b*17*. Rubbery, syrupy and sickly sweet: Dufftown in a nutshell. **43%**. *Flora and Fauna range*.
Dufftown Rare Malts Aged 21 Years db dist 1975 **(59)** n*14* t*17* f*14* b*14*. Not rare enough. **54.8%**
Berrys' Own Selection Dufftown 1984 bott 02 **(86)** n*22* very attractive spice amid ... well, something (being Dufftown, you are never quite sure what); t*22* I don't believe it: the landing on the palate is superb, concentrated malt with a dash of molassed sugar tipped in for good measure; f*21* a slight rubberyness dissolves into the gristy-sugary malt, but decent oak helps to counter; b*21* well, it had to happen one day: a Dufftown under 20 years old I can actually offer to people without the use of a brown paper bag. Hats off to that other prince of St James's Dougie McIvor at Berrys', owner of the best nose of Scotch never to find

its way into a blending lab. Never did I ever expect to heap such lavish praise on a Charlton supporter... or this particular distillery. **56.8%** Berry Bros & Rudd.

Coopers Choice Dufftown 1982 bott 01 sherry cask (19 Years Old) **(72)** n19 t18 f16 b19. Whenever I see a sherry cask Dufftown pour into a glass I shudder ... Pavlov, dogs, that kind of thing. However that strange tinned-tomatoes-meets-demerara-rum nose wasn't too bad and this is pretty drinkable. **46%**

Old Malt Cask Dufftown Aged 20 Years Sherry dist Feb 80, bott Jun 00 **(82)** n19 t22 f21 b20. A collector's item: a very drinkable post-'60s Dufftown. Big-chested and brazen, this is one for big boys. Hefty and edible. **50%. nc ncf.** Douglas Laing.

Old Malt Cask Dufftown Aged 20 Years dist Oct 81 **(69)** n15 t18 f19 b17. Trademark dirty nose, but has some big moments afterwards. **50%. nc ncf.** Douglas Laing.

Old Malt Cask Dufftown Aged 35 Years Sherry dist Oct 62, bott Apr 01 **(88)** n23 soft toffee and tannins with a hint of small grain: are we on the right continent here? t22 beautifully rich and mouthfilling with just the right weight of alcohol kick to intensify the natural oaky spices amid the malt. Again there is a Kentuckian feel to it; f21 enormous vanilla: sweet but never sappy; b22 forget sherry: what we are talking here is fine quality bourbon! **49.6%. nc ncf sc.** Douglas Laing. 228 bottles.

Provenance Spring Distillation Dufftown Over 11 Years (50) dist Spring 90, bott Autumn 01 n10 t15 f13 b12. Proof in a bottle as to why this distillery closed. **43%. nc ncf.** Douglas McGibbon & Co.

Royal Mile Whiskies Dufftown 17 Years Old dist Dec 79, bott Nov 97 **(69)** n15 t18 f19 b17. Run-a-mile whisky from the normally dependable Royal Mile. Bottled in the days before they knew better. **sc.** Edinburgh UK.

Ultimate Collection Dufftown 17 Years Old sherry butt 6030, dist 27/11/85 **(69)** n17 t18 f18 b16. Tinned tomatoes meets golden syrup. **sc.** Van Wees NL.

Whisky Galore Dufftown 1987 15-y-o (85) n20 sparkling, light malt despite the usual slightly dirty off-notes; t22 mouthwatering, fresh and, for a Dufftown, remarkably clean; f21 the rich malt continues; b22 not the most complex of whiskies, but perhaps the use of a round-the-block cask or two has helped settle this whisky down. Truly outstanding for a Dufftown. **46%.** Duncan Taylor & Co.

DUNGLASS (see Littlemill)

EDRADOUR
Highland (Perthshire), 1837. Signatory. Working.

Edradour 10 Years Old db **(86)** n21 charmingly heathery with soft citrus and a glimmer of honey; t22 unusual sweet malt and saccharine with very soft oak; f22 nodules of honey on the encroaching oak and oil; b21 too rarely do you get bottlings from this distillery particularly close and this one is very different, though the honey is a constant. Some of you may have tasted a feinty disaster of a bottling from 2002 – I experienced it while giving a tasting in Stockholm: hopefully that was a one-off and you can return to this brand with a degree of confidence. **40%**

Signatory Edradour 10 Years Old Un-chillfiltered dist 92, bott 02 db **(81)** n20 t21 f20 b20. Some pleasant honey flits around. **46%**

Signatory Edradour 1989 Glass Decanter Collection cask 354, dist 26/09/89, bott 22/01/03 db **(74)** n17 t20 f18 b19. A very disappointing, below-average cask. **57.2%.** 608 bottles.

Old Masters Edradour 1976 bott 02 **(81)** n21 f22 f18 b20. As one might expect, a very distinctive and different dram: heavy with unusual spices but some honey to see off some slightly bitter notes on the finish. **49%.** James MacArthur.

Signatory Edradour 24 Years Old dist 76, bott 01 **(63)** n15 t17 f15 b16. Soapy. Flawed. **50.8%.** 432 bottles.

FETTERCAIRN
Highland (Eastern), 1824. Kyndal. Working.

Fettercairn 1824 db **(69) n**17 **t**19 **f**16 **b**17 By Fettercairn standards, not a bad offering. Relatively free from its inherent sulphury and rubbery qualities, this displays a sweet nutty character not altogther unattractive – though I think caramel plays a calming role here. Still need my arm twisting for a second glass, though. **40%**

Old Fettercairn Stillman's Dram 26 Years Old db **(88) n**22 beauty and the beast ... there are some strange off-notes but they are rendered completely irrelevant by the most gorgeous fruity fanfare you could wish for. Anyone who has ever plucked over-ripe figs off the tree will know where I am coming from here, **t**23 charismatic and playful, the malt offers an astonishingly rich theme for even more fruit to develop; **f**22 a hint of spice and a few thickening oaky tones amid the rebuilding rubber. But it's a joy;. **b**21 OK folks time to lie down: I am about to say it. It's Fettercairn. And I love it. A flawed gem maybe, but a gem nonetheless. **45%** *(Note to readers: I have just counted and discovered this is the 888th distillery-recognised Scotch single malt I have tasted for this book. And it gets a mark of 88 ... what's the chances of that happening, eh?)*

Old Fettercairn Stillman's Dram 30 Years Old db **(84) n**21 **t**22 **f**20 **b**21. To celebrate my 1,000th named distillery Scotch single malt tasted specially for this book I turned to my old nemesis, Fettercairn. And I celebrated in style: a chunky, clean dram with plenty of orangey notes on the nose and deep malt on the palate. **45%**

James MacArthur Fettercairn 1992 bott 02 **(63) n**16 **t**16 **f**15 **b**16. Ah! Pure Fettercairn! **60.5%**

GLEN ALBYN
Highland (Northern) 1846–1983. Demolished.

Glen Albyn Aged 26 Years Rare Malts Collection dist 75 db **(88) n**22 fruity and floral there is still some surprising gristy freshness; **t**23 big kick, but not from the alcohol. The spices seem to have a sugary coating to which the malt is attached. A very unusual mouthfeel but wholly delicious; **f**21 yet more spice with oak massaging and nibbling the tastebuds **b**22 quite a sensual whisky, full of clout but the sweetness disguises the collosal nature of the beast. **54.8%.** *6,000 bottles.*

Connoisseurs Choice Glen Albyn 1972 (85) n23 very softly peated, dreamy; **t**21 malty and sweet with some drying oak; **f**20 sugar-coated soft peat; **b**21 a complex, delicate dram. **40%.** *Gordon & MacPail.*

Connoisseurs Choice Glen Albyn 1974 (83) n19 **t**23 **f**20 **b**21. Skip the nose and finish and concentrate directly on the sugar-barley palate. **40%**

Old Malt Cask Glen Albyn 26 Years Old dist Apr 74, bott Jun 00 **(69) n**18 **t**19 **f**15 **b**17. Thin, overly or sickly sweet, one-dimensional. The finish is a bit grim. **50%.** *Douglas Laing. 264 bottles.*

Old Malt Cask Glen Albyn Aged 34 Years dist Dec 66, bott May 01 **(79) n**21 **t**20 **f**19 **b**19. Toasty, burny honeycomb. Just slightly too aged. But single casks don't come any rarer than this! **42%. nc ncf.** *Douglas Laing. 66 bottles.*

GLENALLACHIE
Speyside, 1968. Chivas. Working.

Usquebaugh Society Glenallachie 1991 dist 5/3/91, bott 16/3/01 **(76) n**19 **t**21 **f**18 **b**18. Rock-hard and barley-sharp; pleasant, refreshing blending fodder. **46%. ncf.** *NL.*

GLENBURGIE
Speyside, 1810. Allied. Working.

Cask Glenburgie 1984 (87) n22 clean malt: grassy, rich, oak-toffee; **t**23 mouthwatering, clean, exemplary Speyside; **f**20 shortish with some vanilla driving home; **b**22 Glenburgie at its most illustrious. **62.3%.** *Gordon & MacPhail.*

Gordon & MacPhail Glenburgie Aged 10 Years **(77)** n*19* t*20* f*19* b*19*. Chewy, with curious coal-smoke weight. **40%**

Hart Brothers Glenburgie aged 35 Years **(84)** n*21* t*22* f*20* b*21*. Like a prim Edwardian village maid, it exudes old fashioned grace, subtle scents and a dry, dusty charm.

GLENCADAM
Highland (Eastern), 1825. Angus Dundee. To be re-opened late 2003.

Cadenhead's Glencadam 13 Years Old dist 89, bott 03/03 **(80)** n*19* t*22* f*20* b*19*. Syrupy stuff: sweet, sugar-coated malt that's more candy than whisky. **59.4%**

Connoisseurs Choice Glencadam 1974 **(75)** n*20* t*19* f*18* b*18*. Pleasant, middle-of-the-road. **40%**. *Gordon & MacPhail.*

Connoisseurs Choice Glencadam 1987 **(80)** n*21* t*22* f*18* b*19*. An abrupt finish to something that promised much on nose and early malt start. **40%**. *Gordon & MacPhail.*

Old Malt Cask Glencadam 28 Year Old dist Dec 71. bott July 00 **(72)** n*16* t*21* f*19* b*16*. Massively sweet and intense middle, otherwise all over the place. Not, I suspect, from the world's greatest cask. **50%**. *Douglas Laing. 268 bottles.*

GLENCRAIG
Speyside, 1958. Allied. Two Lomond stills operating within the Glenburgie plant. Now silent.

Connoisseurs Choice Glencraig 1970 **(90)** n*22* oily, malty notes of considerable weight and brilliant bitter-sweet balance. The fruit is ripe and salivating; t*22* big malt, with deft oiliness that gives weight to the body. Silky and sits perfectly on the palate. A touch of smoke is an added bonus; f*22* vanilla and sweet malt; b*24* this is absolutely brilliant malt: why it was discontinued I'll never know. Few Speysiders achieve such harmony in weight and balance. If you ever see a bottle, grab it if it's the last thing you do. And heartfelt congrats to G&M for preserving posterity: and priceless posterity at that. A company way ahead of its time. **40%**. *Gordon & MacPhail.*

Connoisseurs Choice Glencraig 1975 **(85)** n*21* crushed bananas in milk sprinkled with brown sugar. Oily malts filter through for company; t*22* the oak is doing its best to dry out the enormous malt kick and to an extent succeeds; f*21* slightly bitter thanks to the oak, but that sugared malt refuses to give up the fight, sticking grimly to the roof of the mouth, offering a brief flicker of peat into the bargain; b*21* a once great whisky that has seen better days and trying for all its worth to maintain dignity. It suceeds this time, but for how much longer only later bottlings will reveal. **40%**. *Gordon & MacPhail.*

GLENDRONACH
Speyside, 1826. Allied. Working.

Glendronach 15 Years Old db **(83)** n*20* t*22* f*20* b*21*. Chocolate fudge and grape juice to start then tails off towards a slightly bitter, dry finish. **40%**

Old Malt Cask Glendronach Aged 22 Years **(87)** n*21* malty, clean but thin; t*23* complex: sweet yet spicy ,fruity yet malty; f*22* the spice continues and gathers sweetness; b*21* a confused and confusing dram that can't make its mind up where it wants to go: superb nonetheless. **50%. nc ncf.** *Douglas Laing. 252 bottles.*

Old Malt Cask Glendronach Aged 24 Years dist Nov 76, bott Sept 01 **(91)** n*22* marmalade and peated malt; t*24* intense malt, then an orgasmic meeting of subtle oak and subtler smoke; slightly hot; f*22* long, buttery, sweet with a waft of peat; b*23* better than anything bottled so far by the distillery. Possibly the ultimate Glendronach. **50%. nc ncf.** *Douglas Laing. 228 bottles.*

Old Malt Cask Aged 26 Years dist Dec 74, bott Aug 01 **(86)** n23 smoky with good oak weight; t22 light, delicate malt but with some oaky provenance; f20 sweet and malty but the oak takes charge at finale; b21 a malt on the edge. **47.5%. nc ncf.** *Douglas Laing.* 198 bottles.

GLENDULLAN (see also below)
Speyside, 1898–1985. Closed.
Platinum Old and Rare Glendullan Aged 34 Years dist Mar 72, bott Jan 03 **(78)** n20 t22 f18 b18. Big malty mouth arrival but the balance suffers later. **46.8%. nc ncf.**

Platinum Old and Rare Glendullan 36 Years Old **(89)** n20 the oak is in the vanguard followed by a train of marginally sweeter elements. Malt and vanilla intertwine plus spice and sultanas. A dash of peat is in there for extra weight; t23 outstanding arrival of beautifully textured and sweetened malt – almost gristy in the way it dissolves in the mouth. The oak is much less pronounced on the nose except for the very initial impact. Wonderfully spiced; f23 long, very subtly smoked with a bombardment of peppers giving way to cocoa; b23 a whisky of brilliance from the original old stills of this little-known but reliable Speysider. **55.1%. nc ncf.** *Douglas Laing.*

GLENDULLAN (see also above)
Speyside, 1972. Diageo. Working.
Glendullan Aged 8 Years db **(89)** n20 fresh, gingery, zesty; t22 distinctly mealy and malty. f24 brilliant – really stunning grassy malt powers through. Speyside in a glass – and a nutshell; b23 this is just how I like my Speysiders: young fresh and uplifting. A charming malt.

Glendullan Aged 12 Years (old stock circa 99, bottling mark – on reverse of label – LLJB0461179, light green print) db **(90)** n22 lively, fresh malt with a distinctive waft of shy peat; t23 mouthwatering, clean and a sublime build-up of intense and sweet malt. The most delicate hint of smoke on the horizon; f22 beautiful texture and slight fruity outline; b23 this is a great Speyside dram: big, strong yet never muscular. Superb. **43%.** *Flora and Fauna range.*

Glendullan Aged 12 Years (new stock circa 03, bottling mark – on reverse of label – L19R01457997, dark green print) db **(77)** n19 t20 f19 b19. Oily, flat and bitter towards the finish. Really disappointing. **43%.** *Flora and Fauna range.*

GLEN ELGIN
Speyside, 1900. Diageo. Working.
Glen Elgin Aged 12 Years db **(89)** n23 blistering, mouthwatering fruit of unspecified origin. The intensity of the malt is breathtaking; t24 stunning fresh malt arrival, salivating barley that is both crisp and lush: then a big round of spice amid some squashed, over-ripe plums. Faultless mouthfeel; f20 the spice continues as does the intense malt but is devalued dramatically by a bitter-toffee effect; b22 absolutely murders Cragganmore as Diageo's top dog bottled Speysider. The marks would be several points further north if one – rightly or wrongly – didn't get the feeling that some caramel was weaving a derogatory spell. Brilliant stuff nonetheless. States Pot Still on label – not to be confused with Irish Pot Still. This is 100% malt... and it shows! **43%**

Adelphi Glen Elgin 26 Years Old cask 3, dist 74, bott 00 **(82)** n21 t20 f20 b21. Plenty of quality about this dram, but I would love to have tasted it as a 10-year-old! **57.3%**

Connoisseurs Choice Glen Elgin 1968 **(77)** n20 t19 f19 b19. Big chewy, sweet malt, but totters very slightly under some unwieldy oak. **40%**

GLENESK
Highland (Eastern), 1897–1985. Closed.

Hillside 25 Years Old Rare Malts Selection db **(83)** n20 t23 f20 b20. Hot as Hades, but for a Glenesk this gets off to a cracking start and is let down only by the paucity of the finale. Plenty to enjoy, though, with some really top-rate malt-honey notes. **62%**

Connoisseurs Choice Glenesk 1982 **(68)** n17 t18 f16 b17. Poorly made whisky. Not at all pleasant. **40%.** *Gordon & MacPhail.*

Connoisseurs Choice Glenesk 1984 **(77)** n19 t20 f19 b19. Sticky and syrupy. **40%.** *Gordon & MacPhail.*

Connoisseurs Choice Glenesk 1985 bott 00 **(67)** n19 t17 f15 b16. Attractive nose, goes downhill rapidly. **40%.** *Gordon & MacPhail.*

GLENFARCLAS
Speyside, 1844. J&G Grant. Working.

Glenfarclas 8 Years Old db **(76)** n18 t20 f19 b19. Fresh, tangy, fruity and chewy. **40%.** *J&G Grant.*

Glenfarclas 10 Years Old db **(77)** n15 t21 f21 b20. Great honey notes. **40%.** *J&G Grant.*

Glenfarclas 12 Years Old db **(90)** n22 honeycomb and barley concentrate; t23 just about perfect mouthfeel: a touch oily but gloriously sweet barley, a dash of fruit and drying vanilla; f23 much less demonstrative, but the oak is sublime, the length eternal; b22 it is unlikely Speyside offers a much better 12-year-old. **43%.** *J&G Grant.*

Glenfarclas 15 Years Old db **(74)** n17 t20 f19 b18. Never quite gets going. **46%.** *J&G Grant.*

Glenfarclas 21 Years Old db **(89)** n24 a touch of peat adds weight to a stunning, nigh-on faultless aroma; t22 honey and oak form parallel layers, with something smoky in between; f21 vanilla and honey plus some grape-juice sweetness. The smoke also hangs on; b22 what genuinely top quality malt this is. **43%.** *J&G Grant.*

Glenfarclas 25 Years Old db **(91)** n22 beautifully developed oak, yet remains light and malty; t23 the complexity on the mouth-arrival is glorious: fruit and malt abound, honey confirms the age; f23 some wonderful spices percolate, firm oak finale. b23 this is just great whisky. Absolutely top class. **43%.** *J&G Grant.*

Glenfarclas 30 Years Old db **(82)** n22 t20 f21 b19. Delicious, but a few wrinkles. **43%.** *J&G Grant.*

Glenfarclas 40 Years Old Millennium Edition db **(92)** n23 beautifully defined oak which has taken on a handsomely sweet bourbon character. This is almost chestnut sweet, very softly peated and enticingly gentle. Steps up a gear when warmed in the hand with tantalising spices keeping in harmony with waxy malt and ultra-clean sherry. The way the old oak behaves itself and toes the line is nothing short of wonderful; t23 the oak is again first to show but remains soft and laid back and teasingly spicy. The initial burst of oak does suggest a worn dryness, but this is soon counterbalanced by a demerara sweetness. This blends effortlessly with some heavy, intense malt and a lingering but quite unmistakable hint of liquorice which emerges from the refined sherry-trifle middle; f23 long, chewy, smoky and initially sweet with the liquorice continuing, but dries very slowly to deliver an oaky encore. Stays just the right side of being vanilla rich to ensure continuing charm and quality; b23 an almost immaculate portrayal of an old-fashioned, high-quality malt with unblemished sherry freshness and depth. The hallmark of quality is the sherry's refusal to dominate the spicy, softly peated malt. The oak offers a bourbony sweetness but ensures a rich depth throughout. Quite outstanding for its age. **nc ncf.** *J&G Grant.*

Glenfarclas 105 Cask Strength db **(75)** n18 t19 f20 b18. Sweet and raw. **60%** *J&G Grant.*

Glenfarclas 1968 db **(82)** n20 t22 f19 b21. Initially hot and spicy, but some wonderful natural toffee and honey in there. Another effortless beauty from a great distillery. **54.1%. nc ncf.** J&G Grant.

Glenfarclas 1968 Cask 684 db bott 00 **(90)** n24 toffee apple, molasses and so much more. Close on perfect for sherry genre. Outrageous oak but, thanks to the sherry, it stays in balance; t21 an outbreak of oak-induced spices followed by intense ultra-clean, toffeed oloroso and big-age bourbon; f23 more rum-type demerara, burnt honeycomb, melting oak and liquorice; b22 if you ever wonder why I mark down so many latter-day sherry casks, just try this for size. An almost lost style of sherry: one of flawless intensity. Only a touch of deliciously OTT oak prevents this from being a masterpiece. **54.2%. nc ncf.** J&G Grant.

Glenfarclas 1968 Vintage (88) n24 an exhibition of subtlety. slightly nutty with no more than a hint of oak and a coating of sherry: refined and sophisticated; t21 sweet barley and soft vanillins; f21 a succesion of soft oak tones, with vanilla dominant; b22 never quite lives up to the mercurial nose, but sheer quality nonetheless. **43%.** J & G Grant.

Glenfarclas 1970 db **(83)** n20 t20 f22 b21. Rich and spicy. **50.1%. nc ncf.** J&G Grant.

Glenfarclas 1973 Sherry 1st Fill db **(88)** n21 a massive nose with even some gentle smoke escaping through the sherry and oak; t23 intense, sweet, gloriously fruity; f22 soft oak that dries at a very slow pace; b22 a mountain of a whisky to start with significant oak presence, but quietens into a delicate thing by the finish. Great stuff. **51.4%. nc ncf.** J&G Grant.

Glenfarclas 1974 Vintage (89) n22 light, fino-style sherry influence with the malt its usual subtle self; t22 dry oak arrival vanished quickly to allow the sweetest malt: great spice; f22 lashings of rich malt and very late cocoa; b23 for all the sweetness, this is just so delicate. **43%. nc ncf.** J&G Grant.

Glenfarclas 1978 db **(83)** n22 t21 f20 b20. Sweet chestnuts and malt to nose; hot, sweet and malty to taste. **53.3%.nc ncf.** J&G Grant.

Glenfarclas 1979 db **(89)** n22 big, sweet, chocolate pudding and fruit; t23 spicy from the off and a lovely fanning out of chewy malt and burnt fudge; f22 very long with some toasted honeycomb in there; b22 a big, bruising, full-flavoured malt that takes no prisoners. **51.8%. nc ncf.** J&G Grant.

Glenfarclas 1980 db **(69)** n16 t19 f17 b17 . Rich but sulphur-stained. **55%.** J&G Grant.

Glenfarclas 1983 db dist 9/3/83, bott 16/12/02 **(78)** n18 t21 f20 b19. Punchy fruit and some bite. **43%.** J&G Grant.

Glenfarclas 1988 Vintage 12 Years Old Oloroso sherry bott 2000 db **(84)** n21 t22 f20 b21. Subtle, with lovely natural toffee and above-average oak for its age. **43%.** J&G Grant.

Glenfarclas 1986 Fino Sherry Cask db **(90)** n22 appears thin by Glenfarclas standards but genuinely complex with dry oak and sweeter toffeed malt; t22 an explosion of very sweet malt followed rapidly by something much drier; f23 very dry and mildly salty with some bitter cocoa; b23 an eye-closing, think-about-it dram. A laid-back classic. **43%.** J&G Grant.

Glenfarclas 1989 Oloroso Sherry Cask 1st Fill db **(90)** n24 cream toffee, mocha, brown sugar – and not an off-note in sight; t23 mouthwatering sweet malt despite the forming dry notes. The oak is quite chunky for its age, but the malt and sherry are wonderfully sure-footed. Not dissimilar to a demerara pot-still rum in mouthfeel; f21 the oak gathers pace to offer liquorice and soft oils; b22 it says "1st fill Sherry" on the label. A waste of ink. Just one sniff will tell you! **43%. nc ncf.** J&G Grant.

Glenfarclas 1990 Family Malt Collection db **(79)** n18 t20 f22 b19. Rich, chewy, salty with big finish. **43%.** J&G Grant.

Blackadder Raw Cask Blairfindy Aged 40 Years first-fill sherry cask 5, dist 9 Jan 1963, bott Mar 03 **(89) n**23 salty, pulsating sherry and heavy roast Brazilian coffee; **t**24 ridiculously clean and beautifully defined fruit, lush and sensuously spiced with a hint of something a tad smoky; **f**20 rather hard and bitter as the oak kicks in without remorse. Just enough fruit to hold shape; **b**22 even the severe finish cannot take away from the joy of the nose and mouth arrival. **52.3%.** The label doesn't mention Glenfarclas. Blackadder won't confirm or deny, but didn't the Grant family have a farm called by some similar name? Anyway, sheer Glenfarclas in character: it is hard to think of many other distilleries quite capable of producing something this good.

Blackadder Raw Cask Blairfindy 1990 cask 5983, dist 6 Jun 80, bott May 02 **(91) n**22 thick sherry: wild blackcurrants and peppery spices about; **t**24 a dry oaky edge to a pulsing, peppery start then sweetness with malt and fruit: massive; **f**22 quite long with a good malt flow-through that softens the big oak impact. Rich sherry holds its ground; **b**23 enormous whisky of unquestionable quality. **57.6%**

Cadenhead's Glenfarclas 31 Years Old dist 70, bott 06/02 **(88) n**21 big, weighty fruit – diced apple, banana, plums and grape. And some malt squeezes in while a bourbony character develops to show the oak; **t**23 clean as a whistle. The fruit and malt combine with soft caresses for a wonderfully rich, chewy middle. Still a little bourbony in style; **f**22 long, natural toffee joining the lingering fruit and malt; **b**22 an elegant and refined non-distillery version of a fine, rich malt. **54.4%**

Craigellachie Hotel of Speyside Glenfarclas 1972 Single Cask Bottling 2001 cask 3540, dist 30/05/72, bott 7/12/01 **(87) n**22 very firm with citrus on grape and a vague smokiness in the distant background, mildly salty; **t**22 now the age really does ram itself home! An immediate oak impact again with a sharp, bristling saltiness which acts as seasoning to the calmer, sweeter malt. The fruit also offers a softening buffer; **f**21 gentle spices mix well in the company of cocoa, fruit and vanilla; **b**22 a bracing dram for chilly midwinters beside a roaring fire and for those who like oak in the glass as well as the panelling around them. **51.2%.** UK. 602 bottles.

MacLeod's Speyside Aged 8 Years (86) n21 slightly nutty, crisp barley with some distinctive tangerine notes. Some digestive biscuit saltiness combines with soft oak trace: delicate and complex; **t**22 fresh, sharp, mildly green arrival on palate with some silky barley playing off against subtle citrus. Lovely sheen offering an oily coating to the roof of the mouth from which some oaky weight hangs; **f**21 amazingly clean and uncluttered with some coffee hanging on to the barley, quite chewy but always fresh; **b**22 a real delight of a dram: busy and fresh on the tastebuds. Just love the soft coffee tones as the first oak notes kick in. **40%.** Ian MacLeod (Glenfarclas malt used, though not stated).

Peerless Glenfarclas 1967 cask 5811, dist Oct 67 **(69) n**21 **t**17 **f**16 **b**15. Several summers too old. **42.9%.** Duncan Taylor & Co. Ltd.

GLENFIDDICH
Speyside, 1887. William Grant & Sons. Working.

Glenfiddich Special Reserve (no age statement) db **(88) n**21 fresh, grassy, clean, salivating; **t**23 perhaps the crispest, freshest most mouthwatering malts known to mankind: young yet energetic clean beyond measure and a waft of gentle peat for a hint of weight; **f**22 such wonderful, unequalled grassy malt with a touch of vanilla; **b**22 no longer produced and now a malt for collectors: one that brings a tear to the eye of us 40-somethings. This is malt that kept us going when none others were obtainable. Never has the term "familiarity breeds contempt" ever been more apposite to any whisky as this. It's become de rigueur in recent years for connoisseurs to rubbish this whisky (though, it has to be said, never by me) as a poor man's malt. A brilliant, effervescent whisky missed more sorely than words can describe. I never thought I would find myself writing those words, but there you have it. I believe in honesty: I have built my reputation on it. And in all honesty, the whisky world is poorer without this unpretentious, landmark malt. The official "Bring Back The No-Age Statement Glenfiddich Special Reserve" campaign starts here. **40%**

Glenfiddich Aged 12 Years Caoran Reserve db **(84)** n*19* t*23* f*21* b*21*. Juicy, lively, deliciously spiced, crisp malt, mildly smoky. **40%**

Glenfiddich Aged 12 Years Special Reserve db **(80)** n*20* t*22* f*19* b*19*. Delicious malt but perhaps a touch too much caramel subtracts from the otherwise juicy maltfest. Just not the same as the old (younger) version. Much flatter and less fun than its predecessor. **40%**

Glenfiddich Aged 15 Years Cask Strength db **(80)** n*21* t*21* f*19* b*19* Very toffeed: is it the oak or possibly caramel? Big dram, all the same. **51%**

Glenfiddich Aged 15 Years Solera Reserve db **(93)** n*24* a marriage of citrus notes (especially oranges) subtle spices and oak; t*23* honey leads the way with balancing spices and oak. The malt remains fresh and refreshing; f*23* medium to long with soft sherry and gently building cocoa; b*23* this is one of my regular drams, and the one I immediately display to people who rubbish Glenfiddich. Over the years I have noticed a shift in quality in both directions, the best being two marks higher, the worst cropping six points, mainly due to traces of sulphur on the sherry. However, this sample is pretty representative of a quite brilliant Speyside malt of awesome complexity. Just wish they'd up the strength and make it nonchillfiltered and noncoloured. **40%**

Glenfiddich Aged 18 Years Ancient Reserve db **(92)** n*24* blood oranges, apples, the most gentle of smoke and oaky saltiness: delicate, complex and enormously sexy; t*23* those oranges are there again as the malt melts in the mouth. Quite salty still but sherry and sultanas to fatten things up, brown sugar sweetens things a little; f*22* a dry finale of medium length with unsweetened mocha: clean, chewy and well-defined; b*23* another nail in the coffin of those who sniffilly insist that Glenfiddich can't make good whisky. Taste this – and Solera Reserve – then find me two distillery-bottled malts of this age anywhere on Speyside that offers this enormity of complexity and sheer élan.

Glenfiddich Aged 21 Years Havana Reserve db **(75)** n*19* t*20* f*18* b*18*. I know a lot of people are jumping up and down about this one in excitement. But, sorry, I just don't get the picture. Cuban rums tend to be light in character, so in theory it should marry with the distillery's elegant character. However, we seem to have everything cancelling each other out leaving a pleasant experience with a decent cream coffee-toffee middle/finish, but little else besides to really get the pulses racing. **40%**

Glenfiddich Aged 21 Years Millennium Reserve db **(86)** n*22* spritely barley; vaguely doughy and suet-like, a wisp of smoke; t*22* refreshing barley juice with lovely build-up in sweetness; f*21* a move towads a bourbon/Canadian style but intervention by toffee; b*21* a very shy, delicate dram best at full strength and not quite fully warmed. **43%**

Glenfiddich 30 Years Old db **(85)** n*22* the sweetness is so similar to when you open up a tin of "Quality Street" chocolates: cocoa and nuts, marzipan, coconut, plastic wrappers ... well, maybe not the wrappers; t*22* delicate malt notes, a swift wave of peaty spice and then a slight menthol oakiness; f*20* very light, clean and gently toffeed. Dry oak gathers momentum for the finale; b*21* comes through just about unscathed by time, or at least the scars don't show too badly. **40%**

Glenfiddich Rare Collection 40 Years Old db **(92)** n*23* curiously and attractively smoked, lots of sweet vanilla and stunning spices: remarkable and beautiful; t*24* brimming with oaky, toasty vanilla, malt punching through for silky, rich and mildly honied middle. Signs of oaky wear and tear, but do not detract from the overall beauty; **f**22 remains silky with a return of peat, mixed with cocoa; **b**23 quite brilliant for a Glenfiddich of this antiquity: rarely does it survive to this age. In fact, brilliant for any distillery. **43.6%. 600 bottles.**

Glenfiddich 1937 db **(94) n**24 smoky, almost agricultural farmyardy, with kippers spitting on the range, salted butter melting into them. Quite beautiful, the peat almost hitting perfection. Truly unique; **t**23 sweet malt that just dissolves around the mouth but leaving traces of the most elegant oak, almost too soft to be true. Again the smoke is just stunning in its elegance; **f**23 long, silky, soft oak and – amazingly – clean barley; **b**24 when this was distilled my football team, Millwall, reached the FA Cup semi final. My late dad went to the game in my old mate Michael Jackson's country, 'uddersfield. We lost 2–1. They haven't reached the FA Cup semi finals since. I'll taste this again the next time we do ... it could be a long wait. From a sheer whisky perspective, proof – alongside some older Macallans – that Speyside once made a much peatier dram, one which perhaps only Ardmore can today match. How this whisky has remained this truly fabulous for so long has been entirely in the lap of the Gods. To whoever, whatever, is responsible: thank you!! **40%.** 61 bottles only (going for in the region of £10,000 each).

Glenfiddich 1961 Vintage Reserve db **(75) n**20 lots of toffee-fudge and barley; **t**19 honied and soft with a wave of gentle peat that is not evident on the nose and various oaky notes; **f**18 a bit flat and oaky-dimensional; **b**18 hasn't withstood the test of time quite as well as might be hoped. **43.2%. sc.**

Glenfiddich 1967 Vintage Reserve db **(87) n**23 sensuous, softly spiced and boasting a maple sweetness to counter the mouthwatering barley sharpness, beautifully fruity and balanced; **t**22 early oak then a surge of sweet, deliciously textured malt, soft, peppery and a hint of fudge; **f**21 dry and slightly oaky but with barley-richness, late hints of milk chocolate and liquorice; **b**21 an unusually refreshing dram for such age. **43.6%. sc.**

Glenfiddich 1973 Vintage Reserve db **(88) n**23 fresh, fruity, tangy, enormously live and a hint of peat; **t**23 heaps of oak arrive first, but the malt is intense and crisp and spices chase anything that moves: an enormous mouthful; **f**21 dies slightly as some vanilla and toffee-fudge arrive; **b**21 great to find a Glenfiddich at natural strength. **49.2% sc**

GLENFLAGLER
Lowland, 1965–1982. Demolished.

Glenflagler 29 Years Old db **(88) n**22 pretty ripe tangerines on vanilla ice cream. The oak makes for just about perfect bitter-sweet balance; **t**23 massive fresh fruity to start – citrus again – then an astounding intense and clean malty follow-through; **f**21 a quiet finale with the malt remaining confident, the oak adding a slight bitterness, but all under control; **b**22 I've tasted some Glenflagler over the years, but nothing quite as accomplished as this. Lowlander it might be, but this has seen off the years with the grace and élan of the noblest Highlander. Forget about collector's item: eminently drinkable in its own right. **46%.** A unique malt, as it was run through a Kentucky-type beer still before entering a pot still: a Lowlander made the American way.

Killyloch 35 Years Old db **(80) n**20 thin, malty nose, but strong enough to see off the oak; **t**20 again a thin, wispy start wth the malt offering sweetness but always in the shadow of something oaky; **f**20 holds together reasonably well: the oak does play the major role but behaves itself while again the malt makes a valiant stand; **b**20 only the fourth Killyloch I have ever tasted – even including lab sample form – and, I admit, a lot better than I thought it might be. It doesn't have either the muscle or complexity to guarantee a great malt, but very few faults, either. Rather, it hangs on in there proudly – like a frail old lady successfully crossing a busy road – so you can relax and enjoy it for the pretty decent dram it is. **40%**

GLEN GARIOCH
Highland (Eastern), 1798. Suntory. Working.

Glen Garioch 10 Years Old db **(80) n**19 **t**22 **f**19 **b**20. Chunky and charming, this is a malt that once would have ripped your tonsils out. Much more sedate and even a touch of honey to the rich body. Toffeed at the finish. **40%**

Glen Garioch 15 Years Old db **(79) n**20 **t**21 **f**19 **b**19, The proud owner of a distinctive Glen Garioch character, a hint of rubber on nose and taste (once common here) but compensated by some brown sugar sweetness. A really characterful dram. **40%**

Glen Garioch 16 Years Old db **(88) n**20 fruity and spiced: a real heavyweight with a hint of peat thrown in; **t**23 clean, fresh oloroso character massively chewy with a fine malt thread; **f**22 lengthy, sweetening malt, a hint of peat and spice returns; **b**23 lovely whisky, setting off a bit like a Dufftown but heading into a galaxy that poor old Speysider can only dream of. Really high grade malt with bags of character and attitude. **55.4%**

Glen Garioch 21 Years Old db **(83) n**18 **t**21 **f**23 **b**21. For a start, the nose is truly weird. I mean, cuckooland nuts. An entirely one-off. By no means unpleasant, but so hard to know exactly what it is trying to say, or just who or what, rather, is saying it. It could be some strange hybrid between peat and sherry. The slightly peaty mouthfeel is silky and the all-round experience is quite lovely. The elegance of the finish in particular is impressive: one that grows on you. Whisky Club alert: worth buying just to fathom the nose. **43%**

Glen Garioch Highland Tradition db **(80) n**19 **t**21 **f**20 **b**20. Light and fresh, there is an effervescent complexity that is always enjoyable. **40%**

Glen Garioch National Trust db **(77) n**18 **t**21 d19 **b**19. Mouthwatering, and would be even more so but for a toffeed intrusion. **43%**

Cadenhead's Glengarioch 11 Years Old dist 90, bott 07/01 **(72) n**15 **t**20 **f**19 **b**18. The feinty nose is compensated – to a point – by the big, rich body, as one might expect. **56.6%**

GLENGLASSAUGH
Speyside, 1875. Edrington. Silent since 1986.

Glenglassaugh 1973 Family Silver db **(95) n**23 fruity and exceptionally complex: quite coastal with something vaguely citrussy, orange in particular; **t**24 melt-in-the-mouth malt that intensifies by the second. Never becomes either too sweet or vaguely woody. There is a soft hint of peat around the spices; **f**24 virtually without a blemish as the malt continues on its rich and merry way. Some sublime marmalade follows through on the spice; **b**24 from first to last this whisky caresses and teases. It is old but shows no over-ageing. It offers what appears a malt veneer but is complexity itself. Brilliant. And now, sadly, almost impossible to find. Except, possibly, at the Mansefield Hotel, Elgin. **40%**

Cadenhead's Glenglassaugh 25 Years Old dist 78, bott 03/03 **(93) n**23 fresh oloroso, salt, light oak, yet sweet and deep as well. **t**24 soft, melting fruit that leads into lilting malt. Almost too clean and perfectly sweet to be true; **f**22 relatively short, but perfectly formed. Loads of natural toffee-apple richness and the most friendly oak of all time; **b**24 this is just one of those bottlings never to be forgotten. I have tasted perhaps more individual casks from this distillery than anyone outside the old Highland Distillers company. And oloroso versions of this style from there are rarer than 20-something, know-nothing whisky ambassadors not on an ego trip. Trust those magnificent lifetime-of-whisky-in-their-blood stalwarts at Cadenhead to come up with a gem like this. A bottling that will rightly become a legend, mark my words. **45.2%**

Connoisseurs Choice Glenglassaugh 1983 **(81) n**20 **t**22 **f**20 **b**19. Quite rich, rounded, buttery and sweet. Thin towards the finish. **40%**. Gordon & MacPhail.

GLENGOYNE
Highlands (Southwest), 1833. Peter Russell. Working.

Glengoyne 10 Years Old db **(88)** n21 beautifully clean despite coal-gas bite. The barley is almost in concentrate form with a marmalade sweetness adding richness; t22 crisp, firm arrival with massive barley surge, seriously chewy and textbook bitter-sweet balance; f22 incredibly long and refined for such a light malt. The oak, which made soft noises in the middle now intensifies, but harmonises with the intense barley; b23 proof that to create balance you do not have to have peat at work. The secret is the intensity of barley intermingling with oak. Not a single negative note from first to last. A little beauty. **43%**

Glengoyne 17 Years Old db **(76)** n19 t22 f17 d18. Elegant and charming at first, but the malt is too light to hold the oak. **43%**

Glengoyne 21 Years Old db **(79)** n17 t22 f20 b20. The middle is honied, waxy and fabulous, but caramel flattens the fun. **43%**

Glengoyne 2000 AD 30 Years Old db **(91)** n23 big age, no shortage of ripe, grapey fruit and, dare I say it, a hint of smoke...! t23 fat, full and fruity, mouthwateringly ripe, superb spices and drifting peat; f22 sweet, long, very attactive vanilla, toffee and raisins; b23 top-of-the-range, chewy malt that sets the pulse racing. **51.3%**

Glengoyne 1985 Cask 103 dist Feb 85, bott 97 **(93)** n23 heavy sherry, the oloroso should drown out most complexity but allows in roast Java coffee and salt and the spices are superb; t23 big, busty fruit with full-bodied spice and a continuation of the coffee theme, this time mocha holding fort; f23 massive, salty, fruit-rich and yet more coffee; b24 just so complex and rewarding. Masterful malt. Why did Highland stop producing such one-off drams? The new owners have a near flawless template: let the hunt begin for 12-y-o of such magnitude and magnificence. **57.8%**

Glengoyne 1985 Cask 104 dist Feb 85, bott 97 **(91)** n24 subtle sherry (possibly fino), raisin fruitcake; just magnificent fruit control, complexity and balance from a cask of rare quality; t23 cocoa, vanilla and remnants of very intense malt; f22 light, grape juice and crispy barley; b22 a very unusual malt offering a shape on the palate that is highly distinctive and far from the norm. **59.1%**

GLEN GRANT
Speyside, 1840. Chivas. Working.

Glen Grant db **(89)** n22 young, clean malt doesn't come much cleaner, maltier – or even younger than this: drooling stuff; t23 crisp, brittle grain nibbling at the tastebuds, lovely and mouthwatering; f22 more of the same: the intensity of the malt is stunning, yet it remains delicate throughout; b22 little oak, so not much complexity, but the balance and quality is nothing short of superb. **40%. nc.** *France.*

Glen Grant 5 Years Old db **(84)** n21 t21 f21 b21. Enormous malt, much more oily than the non-age-statement version with an unusual lack of crispness for a Glen Grant. Still mouthwateringly delicious, though! **40%. nc.** *Italy.*

Glen Grant 10 Years Old db **(87)** n21 fine, flinty grain, quite hard and with limited oak interference; t23 really mouthwatering, clean and fresh: not an off-note in sight; f21 gentle, almost half sleeping, just malt and a faint buzz of oak; b22 a relaxed, confident malt from a distillery that makes great whisky with effortless charm and each mouthful seems to show that it knows it. **43%. nc.**

Adelphi Glen Grant 27 Years Old cask 7638, dist 74, bott 01 **(92)** n22 classic GG fresh sherry cask, some light spice also entertains; t23 enormously clean oloroso fits hand in glove with some pulsating malt; f23 remains malty and cultured with gentle fruit keeping out any sign of oak; b24 stunning whisky, its beauty underlined by the crispness of outline. Fine old whisky of umblemished quality. **56.9%**

Adelphi Glen Grant 31 Years Old cask 1706, bott 99 **(94)** n23 bourbony with grape and lime for extra zest; **t**24 sherry at its most shaggable. The sweetness borders on OTT, but just enough oak and malt intervene to make the middle some kind of whisky Utopia; **f**23 the fruit – and a hint of smoke – are now background noise as soft oak and cocoa dominate; **b**24 if the man behind Adelphi, Jamie Walker ever has an off day, he can take this bottle in hand and say: "Well, at least I gave the world this ... !" By the way, boys and girls: consume at full strength for maximum effect. A sweet masterpiece. **57.7%. sc.**

Adelphi Glen Grant 31 Years Old cask 1772, bott 99 **(87) n**22 a more dour sherry aroma: straight oloroso and no fussing; **t**23 again the sherry is exemplary, quite dry and shipping oak; **f**21 oak and liquorice; **b**21 dry and weighty like an American news anchorman who loses himself very seriously indeed. **53.9%. sc.**

Berrys' Own Selection Glen Grant 1970 bott 01 **(86) n**20 quite heavy, muscular sherry with a barely detectable taint; **t**23 massive, chewy and pretty dry despite the assembled sweet malt; **f**22 long, hints of black liquorice and red candy liquorice; **b**21 I would love to have seen the sherry butt this came from: an interesting history, I'd say. A few blemishes on this one, like foxing on a rare first edition. But readable all the same. **55%.** Berry Bros & Rudd.

Berrys' Own Selection Glen Grant 30 Years Old bott 02 **(82) n**21 **t**20 **f**21 **b**20. A pervasive bitterness creeps in and undermines the sherried bliss. **43%.** Berry Bros & Rudd.

Berrys' Own Selection Glen Grant 31 Year Old cask 1041, bott 01 **(88) n**22 dry, old wall plaster and ripe plums with a touch of something Kentucky; **t**22 enormously spiced: chilli on fruit and malt extract; **f**23 remains bitingly spiced and chewy; the tongue cannot help but attack the roof of the mouth to extract the last salty, fruity morsel; **b**21 massive whisky that shoots prisoners on sight. **55.6%.** Berry Bros & Rudd.

Gordon & MacPhail Glen Grant 21 Year Old (76) n22 **t**19 **f** 17 **b**18. The weakest of the Glen Grants bottled by G&M. Caramel-flattened and lifeless. **40%.** Gordon & MacPhail.

Gordon & MacPhail Glen Grant 1948 (90) n23 big oranges, oak and smoke; **t**24 massive malt intensity, with the oak being nothing like as threatening as the nose suggests. Some peat drifts around, filling in some age-cracks, but the malt is quite overwhelming; **f**21 lots of toffee-vanilla; **b**22 a real cracker of a malt displaying controlled power and aggression. Stunning. **40%**

Gordon & MacPhail Glen Grant 1950 (90) n23 remarkable: the oak, presumably, takes the form of newly opened horsechestnuts while soft grapey notes waft around: highly unusual and very enticing; **t**23 massively sweet: both malt and sultana concentrate congregate for a whisky version of the noble rot; **f**22 some smoke and cocoa take a bow; **b**22 no spitting out this one: this has to be one of the world's most extraordinary bottlings. Not only is it of enormous age, but it remains entirely intact and revelling in its sweet glory. Defiant and utterly delightful. **40%**

Gordon & MacPhail Glen Grant 1952 (85) n24 Arbroath smokies, sweet and malty: stunning; **t**21 some early oak creates a chalky field in which the fruit and grassy malt works; **f**19 tiring rapidly, the oak is really giving the malt a hard time. Some very late smoke helps cushion the attack; **b**21 in 1992 I bought a bottle of this to mark my wife's 40th birthday. Seven months later we were no longer an item: obviously she didn't like the whisky, so I kept it... **40%**

Hart Brothers Glen Grant Aged 29 Years dist Oct 72 **(96) n**24 slightly smoky, seeing off the heavy grape. The malt is compacted and forms banks on either side of the fruit. Just so sensuous; **t**24 unbelievably nubile sherry: deft grapes happily give way to the most fabulous malt arrival imaginable: enormous; **f**24 longer than War and Peace. And a lot easier going, too. Fruity and fresh, it defies age and challenges your tastebuds. Massively thick malt is meeting the demarara-sugared fruit head on; **b**24 if only my sex life was this good. Possibly one of the top twenty whiskies I have ever tasted: certainly one of the greatest moments in my (not inconsiderable) whisky life. It has everything. If you can find it, life will take on a slightly different dimension. October 72: I had just set a personal record for 1,500 metres: 4 mins 46 seconds. Meanwhile, someone in Speyside was filling a cask.... **53.6%.** *Matured in sherry wood.*

Hart Brothers Glen Grant Aged 33 Years dist Oct 69, bott Jan 03 **(83)** **n**21 **t**22 **f**20 **b**20. A sweet, uncomplicated malty dram with a buttery sheen. **51.5%**

Murray McDavid Glen Grant 1989 bourbon cask MM2105, dist Oct 89, bott Dec 01 **(79) n**20 **t**20 **f**19 **b**20. A thinnish, buttery dram, a bit on the warm side.

Old Malt Cask Glen Grant Aged 27 Years dist Sep 72, bott Jul 02 **(76)** **n**17 **t**23 **f**17 **b**19. I'm speechless: just not what you expect from an OMC. The nose is off-key and confirmation that all is not right in the world comes with the bitter finish. But the arrival on the palate is awesome.

Old Masters Glen Grant 1969 bott 01 **(94) n**23 spicy with an injection of heavy roast Blue Mountain Jamaican coffee. The sherry is sure-footed and ripe; **t**25 more coffee, but softened by enormous malt presence. In fact, this has to be about the maltiest dram on the market today. With the spices thrown in for good measure, I can't fault this; **f**23 lots of natural toffee and vanilla; **b**23 if only the finish could have kept pace with the unbelievable start, we would have had something to battle the monumental Hart Brothers 29-y-o. As it is, the initial flavour and thrust goes down in the book as perfection. **57.1%.** *James Macarthur.*

Peerless Glen Grant 1970 cask 811, dist Feb 70 32-y-o **(89) n**22 a forest of oak but such is the quality of oloroso the splinters are absorbed by the fruit and soft spices: hints of bourbon, cocoa and orange complete the romp in the woods; **t**23 a thick marriage of sherry, oaky and orange with some malt still being heard; **f**22 slightly bitter oak but the malt now does have a say: gentle spices still play around; **b**22 this is big, macho stuff that retains a fabulous sense of theatre. **46.6%.** *Duncan Taylor & Co.*

Peerless Glen Grant 1972 cask 1640, dist Feb 72 30-y-o **(89) n**21 spiced, a hint of stem ginger; **t**23 big, oily, honied and unbelievably intense: a real mouthful; **f**22 vanilla and honey combine while the malt intensifies without the oil: the oak offers cocoa; **b**23 a wonderfully controlled dram where the oak stays in the background. The sweetness is of almost perfect intensity. Excellent.

Peerless Glen Grant 1972 cask 1643, dist Feb 72 **(85) n**20 some worrying partly hidden signs of tired oak, but there is enough apple and cream to offer hope; **t**22 an intensely malty start that sweetens impressively. A lovely oiliness also develops and all is surprisingly well-balanced. There is even a touch of honey to improve and enrich things further. Truly massive and complex; **f**22 long and vanilla-rich but the oak, though hinting slightly of burnt toast, behaves itself. The oily, honied malt lasts the distance; **b**21 a turn up for the book, this. The nose, though quite sweet and full, shows tell-tale signs of tiredness which is not confirmed on the very characterful palate. A really enjoyable old dram offering much class. **60.6%.** *Duncan Taylor & Co.*

Peerless Glen Grant 1974 cask 16584, dist Nov 74 28-y-o **(93) n**23 Speyside it may be, but salty it is; **t**23 massive salt-malt arrival encompasses the firm, chewy oak: amazingly complex; **f**24 very softly smoked with an amazingly long barley fade-out. Brilliant; **b**23 man, this is whisky! **55.1%.** *Duncan Taylor & Co.*

Private Collection Glen Grant 1953 (95) n24 mountainous oloroso. Pretty crisp and shapely for the great age, though some salt has crept in; **t**24 salty and spicy, the oloroso develops a life of its own. Loads of coffee notes and excellent bitter-sweet ratio; **f**23 a silky coating of salty sherry encrusts the tastebuds guaranteeing an amazingly long and deep finale; **b**24 What can be said? Except that this malt has no right whatsoever to be anything close to this good. G&M have their detractors, and sometimes they do make life hard for themselves. But when it comes to delivering golden treasures from the past they are the Lord Caernarvon of the whisky world. A dry masterpiece. **45%.** *Gordon & MacPhail.*

Scotch Malt Whisky Society 18th Anniversary Special Bottling Cask No. 9.30 dist Oct 72, bott Sep 01 **(93) n**24 beautifully sculpted: slightly nutty but any sherry-oaky dryness is countered by extraordinary fruits, including (honestly!) strawberries! **t**23 incredible arrival of natural toffee, glutinous in character, carrying with it oak, liquorice and salt; **f** 23 the curtain is brought down gently with a little more salt, toffee and spice. The vanilla treads softly; **b**23 a massive whisky with a strangely coastal resonance for a Speysider and always triumphalist about coming from such a wonderfully clean sherry cask. Tasted blind I would have sworn this to be top-notch Springbank! **56.6%**

Scotch Malt Whisky Society Cask 9.32 Aged 30 Years (85) n23 weighty sweet oak and cream coffee, burnt raisins on top, roasty and rich, almost demerara rum in style; **t**22 dry, massive spice attack with a pinch of salt, fruity, plum jam on burnt toast; **f**19 long, the sweetness increasing at first but a lot of tannin in there still and becoming bitter to the point of off-key; **b**21 big, chewy and challenging. The oak contributes much but becomes rather over-excited on the finish. **56.2%. nc ncf sc.**

Scott's Selection Glen Grant 1977 bott Jun 03 **(89) n**21 slightly mean, with the oak offering the lion's share; **t**23 opens up towards enormous bitter-sweet, almost crunchy malt with a surging wave of honied spice and then darker oak tones; **f**22 pretty long, a distant hint of smoke but the oak slowly begins to take command from the rigid malt; **b**23 really impressive malt from a great distillery and holds off the oak brilliantly. **55.4%.** *Robert Scott & Co.*

GLEN KEITH
Speyside, 1957. Chivas. Silent.

Glen Keith 10 Years Old db **(80) n**22 **t**21 **f**18 **b**19. A malty if thin dram that finishes with a whimper after an impressively refreshing, grassy start. **43%**

Glen Keith Distilled Before 1983 db **(79) n**21 **t**21 **f**18 **b**19. Lemon-drop nose of concentrated malt in palate; pleasant but fades just too much towards oaky bitterness. **43%**

Cadenhead's Glen Keith 16 Years Old dist 85, bott 07/01 **(72) n**17 **t**19 **f**18 **b**18. Hot as hell and mildly off-key. **59.2%**

Connoisseurs Choice Glen Keith 1967 (86) n23 the best nose to any Glen Keith I have found in over 20 years. Total complexity as rival factions of sweet/dry malty/oaky fruity/spicy battle it out with feathers; **t**20 starts almost too softly to register, then builds up sweetly, then some telling spice; **f**22 long vanilla and malty notes take an age to fade; **b**21 an unusually fine example of a pretty rare malt these days. **40%.** *Gordon & MacPhail.*

Scotch Malt Whisky Society Cask 81.3 Aged 33 Years (83) n21 **t**22 **f**20 **b**20. Low-ester Jamaica rum for the nose and a superb honey-malt middle. This is really attractive whisky. Sweet and warming. **58.3%. nc ncf sc.**

GLENKINCHIE
Lowland, 1837. Diageo. Working.

Glenkinchie 10 Years Old db **(80) n**20 **t**21 **f**19 **b**20. This has been more jazzed up in recent years; certainly much more robust on nose and palate with fruit and toffee replacing malt as the main theme. **43%**

Glenkinchie Distillers Edition Glenkinchie 1989 Double Matured amontillado cask finish, bott 02 db **(83) n**21 **t**22 **f**20 **b**20. A strange thing happened: I opened this bottle absent-mindedly without realising what it was. Suddenly I thought I had opened up a bottle of sherry by mistake, such was the power of the wine on popping the cork. Now that may be good news to some, but I come from that strange old school of wanting to drink light Lowland whisky when I have it in my hand ... having said that, the nose is lovely, but the amontillado wipes the floor with the usual subtleties of a Glenkinchie aroma. Clean, enjoyable, near faultless stuff in many ways: from a technical point of view one of the best Double Matured I have tasted from there and the casks must have been quite superb. **43%**

THE GLENLIVET
Speyside 1824. Chivas. Working.

The Glenlivet Aged 12 Years db **(83)** n20 t22 f20 b21. A surfeit of apples on both nose and body. The malt is quite rich at first but thins out for the vanilla at the death. **40%**

The Glenlivet Aged 12 Years American Oak Finish db **(86)** n21 light malt and delicate oak; t22 lush, mildly oily body, the malt coming through in small waves with soft pear-like fruit just behind with a lovely spice sub-stratum; f22 long and chewy; the fruit remains clean and harmonised with the budding vanilla and spice; b21 stylish and under-stated in every department. **40%**

The Glenlivet Aged 12 Years French Oak Finished db **(83)** n21 t22 f20 b20. The oak is extraordinary and offers an unusual style of spiciness, though the finish is flatter than might be expected. Good bitter-sweet sync. **40%**. *Finished in French Limousin oak.*

The Glenlivet Aged 15 Years db **(84)** n22 t21 f20 b21. Good spice and complexity. Very well-weighted throughout. **43%**

The Glenlivet Aged 18 Years db **(87)** n22 fresh for its age and mildly smoked; t23 attractive fruity complexity adds to the busy malt; f21 quietens and dries rapidly, lots of vanilla; b21 another Glenlivet that starts beautifully but lacks stamina. **43%**

The Glenlivet Archive Aged 21 Years db **(77)** n21 t20 f18 b18. The more I have got to know this whisky, the more I despair of it. After a lovely fruity start, way too much toffee-caramel, I'm afraid. **43%**

The Glenlivet Cellar Collection 1959 bott 02 db **(90)** n22 diced apples and raisins, a hint of allspice; t23 enormously silky and spicy then a wave of concentrated malt and hints of cocoa; f22 light smatterings of vanilla and liquorice, beautifully bitter-sweet with more than a bit of the old bourbon about it; b23 no malt has any right to be this good at this kind of age. Oak has done very little damage, apart from giving a mildly bourbony feel amid some indulgent liquorice, and that can hardly be construed as damage at all. It is the élan of the fruitiness jousting with the rich malt that impresses most. If anyone was born in 1959, this is the bottle you must buy: a 2cl nip every birthday should be enough to see you through to the end in style. **42.28%**

The Glenlivet Cellar Collection 1967 bott 00 db **(88)** n23 fabulously delicate: soft vanilla, flickering malt with smoke/oak combo; t23 very even, none-specific fruitiness with attitude, sensual spices; f20 light and softly oaked and smoked, but dulled by caramel; b22 marks would be higher if I didn't detect caramel on the finish. But distillery manager Jim Cryle did a great job selecting these casks. **46%**

The Glenlivet Cellar Collection 1983 Finished in French Oak bott 03 db **(88)** n22 busy and bubbly: lots of vanillins pepper the big malt, quite unusual; t23 the mouth is gripped by a mini malty-oak battle with lots of spicy sub plots. Lovely fruity richness, too; f21 more spice lingering with the oak, slightly Jamaica rum-like in its fade; b22 sophistication and attitude rolled into one. **46%**

The Glenlivet Cellar Collection 30 Years Old American Oak Finish bott 01 db **(93)** n23 well, whaddya know? Bourbon – with a lingering fruity-malt-rye side-dish. Very odd, indeed; t24 big oak arrival, slightly Kentucky-like except for a real rollerball of ultra-intense malt that kicks and screams its way around the palate; f23 more sedate and sane but the oaky, spicy intensity still takes some getting used to; b23 Love quiet old whiskies? You know, the sort that nose of leather chairs and taste of toasty, oaky malt and then die quietly on the finish? If so, don't get this, for this is the dram that flew over the cuckoo's nest, needing several straitjackets to keep it in control. There is more than a touch of bourbon about this one; hardly surprising seeing the kind of oak it ended up in. But what has surprised – nay, shocked, readers – is the bucking bronco violence of the malt in retaliation at being treated this way. Anyone who seriously adores whisky has to stump up for this one. See if you can ride it. **48%**

The Glenlivet Vintage 1967 db **(85)** n21 hints of old leather and smoke; t22 oily wave of sweet sherry-malt; f21 chocolate and a hard-metallic tang; b21 excellent complexity and no over-ageing.

The Glenlivet Vintage 1968 db **(82)** n20 t22 20 b20. Firm oak, interesting bite.

The Glenlivet Vintage 1969 db **(89)** n22 fabulously clean and precise sherry, deftly smoked; t24 Dry oak to begin then salt and fruitcake; f21 soft oak and bitter-sweet chewy finale; b22 brilliant whisky with great but controlled age.

The Glenlivet Vintage 1970 db **(93)** n24 honey replaces sherry: tangerine, salty oak and coconut milk; t23 oiled and intense honey richness, perfectly balanced with roast oak and malt; f22 brilliant, bitter-sweet, oaky dry with some lingering honey; b24 outstanding. The finest and probably most delicate distillery-bottled Glenlivet I have tasted.

The Glenlivet Vintage 1972 db **(84)** n21 t22 f20 b21. Very dry sherry ensures complexity and maximum spice.

Adelphi Glenlivet 27 Years Old dist 75 bott 02 **(87)** n21 a hint of peat and marzipan amid powering malt; t22 fat and oily with a touch of smoke; f22 long vanilla and malty strands offer some late honey and then drier oak; b22 effortlessly elegant. **55.4%**

Berrys' Own Selection Glenlivet 1975 bott 02 **(93)** n24 this is a baby: soft honey and the cleanest of rich malt. Aaaaah! t24 the silk honey dissolves around the tastebuds leaving oaky strands and flighty malt; f22 slighly bitter as the oak kicks in, but plenty of silk still to go around; b23 you know Lawson's 12-y-o, the blend? Well, this seems to be the honey section of it in single malt form. A real treat that seduces without any shame whatsoever. **43%**. *Berry Bros & Rudd.*

Blackadder Raw Cask Glenlivet 1966 sherry cask 3898, dist 30 Nov 66, bott Apr 02 **(77)** n19 t20 f19 b19. Faded despite some serious malt incursions in the late middle of the palate. **64.2%. nc ncf.**

Cask Glenlivet 1973 refill American hogshead 8847, 8850, dist 16/11/73, bott 7/6/02 **(92)** n21 crisp malt, almost brick-hard and impenetrable; t25 for those of you who love intense, silky concentrated malt just take a mouthful of this: multi-orgasmic; f23 more of the same but with a gentle letting-in of some guest oak; b23 made in the days when The Glenlivet distillery produced the finest malt in Speyside. I still remember them – just. **55.9%**. *Gordon & MacPhail.*

Cask Glenlivet 1978 casks 16419–16423, dist 13/10/78, bott Nov 96 **(91)** n22 grassy and crisp malt; t24 mouthwatering, fresh malt: flavour development barely moves beyond the barley; f22 an introduction of vanilla calms down the rampaging malt. Good, lively spice, too; b23 this, clearly, is what Gordon & MacPhail do best. **60.2%**

Craigellachie Hotel of Speyside Glenlivet 1980 Single Cask Bottling 2002 cask 1520, dist 22/01/80, bott 17/12/02 **(89)** n23 beautifully clean and spicy fruit, egg custard pie and rich malt: impressive; t23 a real mouthful of a dram: amazingly clean fruit combining with sweet, mouthwatering malt, beautifully textured. Just so Speyside; f21 a buzz of spice and some oak working its way into the fruity fray; b22 for all its age there is still a wonderful freshness to this dram. The crescendo of spice is a classy touch. **59.1%**. *222 bottles.*

George & J.G Smith's 15 Year Old Glenlivet 40% (81) n20 t21 f20 b20. A veritable maltfest, but perhaps lacking complexity. *Gordon & MacPhail.*

George & J G Smith's 15 Year Old Glenlivet 46% (84) n19 t22 f22 b21. Dustier nose, but the extra intensity makes for happier malt. *Gordon & MacPhail.*

Hart Brothers Glenlivet Aged 34 Years dist Oct 68, bott Jan 03 **(81)** n*20* t*22* f*19* b*20*. A few grey hairs, as one might expect from an old smoothie. **50.6%**

Mission Range Glenlivet 1974 (89) n*22* honey and golden syrup with a sprinkling of malt; t*23* even more honey this time with vanilla in tandem; f*22* deft malt, a touch of salt and some cocoa; b*22* stupendous mouthfeel. A wonderful non-peated nightcap. **46%. nc ncf.** *Murray McDavid.*

Old Malt Cask Glenlivet Aged 20 Years dist Dec 81, bott Feb 02 **(87)** n*22* honey, malt and spice; r*22* typical high-octane malt with a sweet edge; f*22* very easy-going and relaxed malt-oak marriage; b*21* don't bother with complexity here: it just tastes good. **46.7%. nc ncf sc.** *Douglas Laing. 108 bottles.*

Old Malt Cask Glenlivet Aged 26 Years dist May 74, bott Jan 01 **(84)** n*20* t*22* f*22* b*20*. Molten toffee, delicious, though. **50%. nc ncf.** *Douglas Laing. 306 bottles*

Old Malt Cask Glenlivet Aged 29 Years dist Aug 71, bott Jan 01 **(82)** n*22* t*21* f*19* b*20*. For all the coffee and toffee apples, can't really make my mind up here. Sometimes I mark very high when tasting this, but on the weight of evidence I'd say bottled on its way down, probably five or six years after being brilliant. You missed this one, boys!! First time for everything, I suppose... **50%. nc ncf.** *Douglas Laing. 558 bottles.*

Old Masters Glenlivet 1976 (69) n*15* t*21* f*17* b*16*. I am sure there are those who will swoon at this. But it is one of those with which I have problems with the sherry cask. It does have some gloriously rich moments in the middle. But... **59.9%. nc ncf.** *James MacArthur.*

Peerless Glenlivet 1968 cask 5254, dist Sep 68 34-y-o **(75)** n*19* t*19* f*18* b*19*. Sharp, malty, spicy middle but it never escapes the big oak. **50%.** *Duncan Taylor & Co.*

Private Collection Smith's Glenlivet 1943 (87) n*21* an astonishing mixture of understated oaky notes intertwined with clean, distinctive malt and the most distant aroma of peat: a gentleman of an aroma; t*20* maintains a malty integrity despite the accompaniment of oak; f*23* for its age, quite astounding: no over-the-top oak or dryness, just soothing waves of malty-oak which are neither bitter nor sweet; b*23* remarkable. How a whisky remains this enjoyable after so many years is what makes spending a lifetime investigating the world's greatest drink such a great profession! No off-notes and, whilst it is not the greatest dram you will ever find, it is certainly the finest wartime relic you can find to keep you company whilst watching Whisky Galore. **40%.** *Gordon & MacPhail.*

Scotch Malt Whisky Society Cask 2.46 Aged 13 Years (83) n*21* t*22* f*19* b*21*. Natural toffee sweetens it, but quite chalky from the oak. Plenty to chew on. **60.3%. nc ncf sc.**

Scott's Selection Glenlivet Sherry Wood 1976 bott 01 **(88)** n*23* treacle toffee intermingles with red-hot peppers. Beneath this explosive mixture is something fresh and fruity; not unlike freshly bitten toffee-apple. Some malt also sings softly. There really is some complexity here; t*22* a busy introduction fair takes the breath away! The fruit is mouthwatering but the spices are to be respected. The oak thrusts some bitter notes into the chewy cauldron but it balances quite well with the sweeter malt; f*21* perhaps a little exhausted after such a massive start. The vanillas calm the wilder aspects of the oak somewhat and at last the malt shows with some freedom; lingering and moreish; b*22* Oh that all Glenlivets were like this! Fifteen years ago I came across samples like this quite regularly. Not now. How often will we see its like again? **56.9%.** *Robert Scott & Co.*

Smith's Glenlivet 1948 (85) n*21* marmalade and toast; t*22* really intense malt with lovely fruity edge; f*21* slighly biting oak, dry with some peat softening things a little; b*21* good whisky which is impressive on its own merits, let alone the great age.

Smith's Glenlivet 1951 (82) n*19* a touch on the oaky side; t*21* sweet malts dominate. and a hint of smoke registers in the background; f*21* light, delicate oak and malt; **b**21 silky and sweet with delicious milky, malty depth. Not half as oaky as the nose threatens. **40%**. *Gordon & MacPhail*.

Smith's Glenlivet 1955 **(87) n**23 big ripe fruit, sensuously clean within a frame of oak and malt; **t**20 oak immediately asserts itself, then a follow-through of fruit and soft peat, fruitcake rich; **f**22 much more sensible and structured with some mouthwatering malt adding complexity; **b**22 absolutely hypnotic whisky. **40%**. *Gordon & MacPhail*.

Smith's Glenlivet 21 Years Old **(88) n**21 teasing malts ranging from grassy to very mildly smoked; **t**23 silky, malt-rich with exceptional balance; **f**22 long, lightly spiced rich vanilla dulled by caramel; **b**22 what a cracking dram this is. There is a caramel effect which could be natural that prevents this from hitting the 90s. Superb nonetheless. *Gordon & MacPhail*.

GLENLOCHY
Highland (Western), 1898–1983. Closed.

Connoisseurs Choice Glenlochy 1977 **(77) n**20 **t**21 **f**18 **b**18. Decent malt and texture, a shade too much caramel. **40%**. *Gordon & MacPhail*.

Gordon & MacPhail Glenlochy 1965 **(87) n**22 a hint of smoke; **t**22 beautifully fruity, really lovely honey and complexity; **f**21 lip-smacking honey and oak; **b**22 brilliant stuff. **40%**

Old Malt Cask Glenlochy Aged 26 Years dist Mar 75, bott Jun 01 **(91) n**24 textbook: words cannot really describe or pigeon-hole the complexity here. The oak offers almost perfect dryness to the sweeter honied malt. Just sniff for yourself! **t**23 almost equally as stunning: the malt shimmers on the palate. The natural caramels from the oak offer toffee riches, but really it is the depth of the juicy barley that impresses most; **f**21 some spice hangs on to the oak, as does a little smoke; **b**23 yet another bottle that begs the question: why the hell was this distillery closed? **50%. nc ncf**. *Douglas Laing. 258 bottles.*

GLENLOSSIE
Speyside, 1876. Diageo. Working.

Glenlossie Aged 10 Years db **(91) n**23 brilliant: big, big malt with a distant glazed stem ginger echo; **t**23 so rich-textured and beatifully lush, the malt is mega intense with soft spice, a touch of salt and oak; **f**22 sweet malt with mounting vanilla and a rumble of distant smoke; **b**23 first-class Speyside malt with excellent weight and good distance on the palate. Easily one of the best Flora and Fauna bottlings of them all. **43%**

Adelphi Glenlossie 17 Years Old cask 1679, dist 81, bott 98 **(89) n**23 a sherried heavyweight that wallows in its oaky resonance and fruity, malty sweetness: really pleasing; **t**23 magnificent display of toffee apple and chocolate fudge plus demerara sugar and ripe figs; **f**21 sweet vanilla, late wisp of peat and drier, grinding oak; **b**22 Glenlossie peaks a lot younger than this: rare to find one from this distillery in such good sherry form and of such unspoiled antiquity.

Connoisseurs Choice Glenlossie 1974 **(78)** 20 **t**22 **f**17 **b**19. The finish is bitter and twisted, the build-up beautiful. **40%**. *Gordon & MacPhail*.

Connoisseurs Choice Glenlossie 1975 **(79) n**19 **t**21 **f**19 **b**20. Molassed and well-oaked. **40%**. *Gordon & MacPhail*.

Coopers Choice Glenlossie 1978 bott 01 (22 Years Old) **(69) n**17 **t**18 **f**17 **b**17. Sorry, just not the kind of sherry butt I get along with. **43%**. *The Vintage Malt Co.*

Gordon & MacPhail Glenlossie 1961 bott 02 **(87) n**22 toasted brown bread, soft vanilla and honey. A dab of smoke hangs in there; **t**22 fabulous mouth-arrival, at first sweet malt then the toastiness arrives with, again, a subtle hint of honey; **f**21 cocoa, burnt fudge and a late waft of peat; **b**22 a really lovely old dram that has seen off the years with some style. **40%**

Provenance Autumn distillation Glenlossie Over 10 Years dist Autumn 89, bott Spring 00 **(79)** n20 t21 b18 f20. A light, refreshing grassy malt that charms rather than seduces. **43%**. *Douglas McGibbon & Co.*

GLEN MHOR
Highland (Northern), 1892–1983. Demolished.

Cask Glen Mhor 1979 cask 2376, dist 25/5/79, bott May 94 **(85)** n19 a vague off-note is swamped by apple; t23 quite enormous, sheened arrival of solid, clean malt retaining just a degree of grassiness; f21 heaps of toffee and vanilla; b22 worth checking a few labels for: won't see it at this relative youth again. **66.7%**. *Gordon & MacPhail.*

Cask Glen Mhor 1979 cask 2379, dist 25/5/79, bott Sep 99 **(80)** n18 t22 f20 b20. Big, biscuity malt, beautifully structured though mildly flawed. **66.3%**. *Gordon & MacPhail.*

Coopers Choice Glen Mhor 1980 bott 01 (20 Years Old) **(90)** n23 a celebration of honey and crushed digestive biscuit; t23 spellbindingly intense malt with that wonderful tinge of honey suggested in the nose; f21 the oak works its way in to offer a burnt toasty diversion from the sweet malt; b23 just wonderful whisky from a lost source: unlikely we shall see quality like this too often from Glen Mhor. A must buy.

Gordon & MacPhail Glen Mhor 1965 (74) n19 t20 f18 b17. Somewhat bitty and unbalanced. **40%**

Gordon & MacPhail Glen Mhor 1979 (74) n17 t19 f19 b19. A long way from their best-ever bottling from this distillery. **40%**

Hart Brothers Glen Mhor Aged 21 Years dist 76 **(81)** n19 t21 f20 b21. Glossy and attractively weighted with heavy malt. Lovely bitter-sweet balance **43%**

Old Malt Cask Glen Mhor Aged 24 Years dist Jul 75, bott Apr 00 **(92)** n22 softly smoked, sweet and rich, not unlike a light Jamaican pot-still rum; t23 honey-enriched fireworks explode to reveal varying shades of pure barley and smoke; f23 long, brilliantly textured and boasting exquisite mouthfeel to the very end; b24 the stuff of legend. 5**0%. nc ncf**. *Douglas Laing. 263 bottles.*

Old Malt Cask Glen Mhor Aged 25 Years dist Dec 75, bott Apr 01 **(88)** n22 a bit of nip and bite amid the lavender; t23 hot but sweet; f21 healthy oak and honey: lovely spice; b22 a busy, fascinating and delicious dram. **50%. nc ncf**. *Douglas Laing. 270 bottles.*

Old Malt Cask Glen Mhor Aged 34 Years dist Feb 66, bott Jul 00 **(89)** n24 lush, spotless and faultless sherry with a sub-stratum of oak; t23 mouth-coatingly sweet and spicy: the spices tingle but the fruitcake middle is awesome; f21 dies quickly but leaves remnants of medium roast Java coffee and oak; b21 fantastic sherry – to blow your mind, vat a tiny amount with some OMC Glen Mhor 24-y-o.... **50%. nc ncf**. *Douglas Laing. 396 bottles.*

GLENMORANGIE
Highland (Northern), 1843. Glenmorangie plc. Working.

Glenmorangie 10 Years Old db **(94)** n24 perhaps the most enigmatic aroma of them all: delicate yet assertive, sweet yet dry, young yet oaky: a malty tone poem; t22 flaky oakiness throughout but there is an impossibly complex toastiness to the barley which seems to suggest the lightest hint of smoke; f24 amazingly long for such a light dram, drying from the initial sweetness but with flaked almonds amid the oakier, rich cocoa notes; b24 remains one of the great single malts: a whisky of uncompromising aesthetic beauty from the first enigmatic whiff to the last teasing and tantalising gulp. Complexity at its most complex. **40%**

Glenmorangie 15 Years Old db **(89)** n23 fruitier with dense grapey tones, malty yet not as complex as the 10; t23 the most silky mouthfeel then delicious, controlled explosion of malty, peppery notes around the palate. Clean fruit, including the juiciest of plums, balances nicely; **f**21 remains warm and lingering with more emphasis on simple vanilla and malt; **b**22 rich by Glenmorangie standards and very warming. **43%**

Glenmorangie 18 Years Old **(87) n**23 big citrus presence: fresh and sparkling; **t**22 big, yet somehow subdued, as though on best behaviour. The sweet fruit dominates through a silky sheen, though the malt recovers; **f**21 the oak battles grimly for control, but the malt holds fast, supported by the fruit. The finale is pure custard tart. Lovely! **b**21 a real sweet, smoothie. **43%**

Glenmorangie 25 Years Old db **(84) n**21 **t**22 **f**20 **b**21. Soft as a baby's bum, but for all its clean tones needs an injection of complexity. **43%**

Glenmorangie 25 Year Old Malaga Wood db **(89) n**23 delicious infusion of sweet, highly perfumed notes of the candy shop: toasted mallows, lemon drops, perhaps, and fruity boiled sweets, all dusted with a sprinkling of oak; **t**22 that sweetness is evident early on, but soon diminishes as a fruity lustre gives way to a significant build-up of spices; **f**22 extremely long, peppery at first then fine malt interacts with oak and just a little smoke; **b**22 of all the many finishes Glenmorangie have provided over the last five years this is perhaps the most arresting: complex and downright deliciously unusual. **43%**

Glenmorangie 1977 db **(84) n**22 **t**22 **f**20 **b**20. Complex and tasty, but feels an oaky pinch at the finish. **43%**

Glenmorangie Bergundy Wood Finish db **(78) n**17 **t**21 **f**20 **b**20. The nose is a curious and less than wonderful mix of pepper and sweaty armpits and the spice really does go for it on mouth arrival. A wave of fresh fruit and barley sugar cushions the blows and though the finish is shortish it has an attractive chewability. **43%**

Glenmorangie Cognac Matured db **(83) n**21 **t**21 **f**20 **b**21. Complex, but the famous Glenmorangie top notes have been flattened slightly. About as soft a Glenmorangie you are likely to find. **43%**

Glenmorangie Cote de Beaune db **(63) n**10 **t**18 **f**19 **b**16. Hard to get past the disastrous nose. Improves towards the end, but too little, too late. **46%**

Glenmorangie Cote de Nuits db **(77) n**19 **t**20 **f**19 **b**19. One of those whiskies where things never quite fall into place, though a second mouthful is no chore whatsoever. Fruity and dry. **43%**

Glenmorangie Fino Sherry Wood Finish db **(85) n**22 crisp, dry with some hiding smoke. It's all very delicate and striking; **t**21 remains clean and dry and understated; **f**21 It's all about delicacy and sweet-dry balance; **b**21 rather lovely and unusual stuff. They don't come more delicate and reserved than this. **43%**

Glenmorangie Distillery Manager's Choice 1983 db bott 00 **(91) n**22 fresh, complex, particularly well-structured with the oak offering superb zest; **t**24 brilliant. Glenmorangie nutshelled: gloriously intense medium-sweet malt punctured by busy oak. So amazingly complex; **f**22 slightly brittle and oaky but some wonderful natural toffee that suggests extremely high-quality Canadian; **b**23 an exhibition of complexity. **53.2%**

Glenmorangie Distillery Manager's Choice 2001 db **(93) n**23 fresh fruit, almost cut-glass clarity; **t**24 Oh, you little beauty! The arrival in the mouth is just so charismatic: spicy, fruity, malty, oaky, all at different levels but at some stage touching; **f**22 relaxed, end-of-season kick-about with emphasis on technical ability rather than thrills, but each goal scored is a stunner; **b**24 What can you say? Don't have the label to hand, but the effect is similar to extremely fresh port pipes. Astonishing whisky: every whisky club should try and get a bottle of this to share. **57.2%**

Glenmorangie Madeira Wood Finish db **(82) n**17 **t**22 **f**22 **b**21. Like all the Glenmorangie wood finishes the quality can vary dramatically. It's all part of the fun. Here a poor nose is rescued by a wonderful fruit-pastel, candy, mouthwatering arrival. Succulent and sweet. **43%**

Glenmorangie Missouri Oak db **(88)** n*21* well I'll be darned tootin': this is Scotch, ain't it? Had me goin' for a minute it were one of them thar bourbons; t*23* a tornado of tannins and sweet sap. The barley recovers, but it's some shoot-out; f*23* fabulous spices sit brilliantly with the simmering oak. The barley is a just a side-kick; b*21* Yes-siree. This is one hell of a bourbon for a Scotch ... technically; appears slightly too butyric ever to be a classic. But this ain't no one-horse whisky. Howdy stranger! Welcome into town. **56.2%**

Glenmorangie Port Wood Finish db **(84)** n*22* t*23* f*19* b*20*. Perhaps because of the nature of the beast – finishing the whisky for a while in port pipes – this can be a variable dram. Not at its best here, it still shows an early complexity that defies belief, then superb spices. Just too sweet and toffee-rich on the finish in this bottling. **43%**

Glenmorangie Sauternes Wood Finish db **(89)** n*21* spices and dark chocolate; t*22* at first falls apart, but quickly regains composure for the intense grapeyness to hold the malt in place for good weight; f*24* just so long and deft: the fruit-malt-oak ratio is brilliant – liquid Manor House cake. b*22* one of the success stories of the wood-finishing programme: superb.

Glenmorangie Sherry Wood Finish **(80)** n*21* t*23* f*17* b*19*. The finish here is more cream toffee than sherry: somewhat disappointing, knowing how good it can be. The initial mouth arrival is superb, though. **43%**

Glenmorangie 3 Cask Matured db **(77)** n*20* t*20* f*18* f*19*. Chalky and dry with fleeting fruit. **40%**

GLEN MORAY

Speyside, 1897. Glenmorangie plc. Working.

Glen Moray (no age statement) db **(82)** n*19* t*22* f*21* b*20*. Young, vibrant, fresh malt, beautifully made. Has the feeling of a young blend – without the grain! **40%**

Glen Moray 12 Years Old db **(91)** n*23* a comfortable straddle between very light, teasing malt and soft vanilla; t*22* lazy flavour entry: the malt saunters round the palate as if it owns the place, perfect harmony between sweet malt and drier oak; f*23* here's where we get to business with the delicate complexity between malt and oak which is simply sublime. Some minor bourbony notes make a subdued approach; b*23* one of my favourite Speyside malts for the last 17 years simply because it is so unfailingly consistent and the delicate nature of the whisky has to be experienced to be believed. **40%**

Glen Moray 12 Years Old Chenin Blanc db **(87)** n*22* big, over-ripe sultanas and some unusual oaky tones; t*23* oily and lush. The malt and grape go hand in glove; f*21* lots of vanilla, dries, becomes a little flakey; b*21* a malt that feels good about itself in this slightly exotic form. **40%**

Glen Moray 16 Years Old **(79)** n*21* t*21* f*18* b*19*. A heavier, fruitier expression but one that could come from any Speyside distillery and lacks the unambiguous characteristics of Glen Moray. **43%**

Glen Moray 16 Years Old Chenin Blanc db **(85)** n*20* apples and sultanas sit well with the intense malt and a hint of smoke; t*22* the oak makes for fuller mouthfeel on the oil and lush malt and fruit; f*22* complex and medium dry with hints of coffee breaking through the chalky oak and softer fruit; b*21* a dram just brimming with complexity. **40%**

Glen Moray 1959 Rare Vintage db **(91)** n*25* various orangey-tangerine notes amid a waft of smoke and a touch of bourbon keeps the nose intrigued. Probably the best nose of a malt this age you'll ever find; t*23* beautiful mouthfeel then a wave of clear, clean oak and then sweeter, surprisingly gristy malt; f*21* fades, as might be expected but there is no bitterness as one might expect from this age, just lots of sweet toffee; b*22* they must have been keeping their eyes on this one for a long time: a stunning malt that just about defies nature. The nose reaches absolute perfection. **50.9%**

Glen Moray 1971 db bott 99 **(83)** n*22* t*21* f*20* b*20*. Fruity yet a little dry and chalky. **43%**. *(bott 99)*

Glen Moray 1974 Distillery Manager's Choice bott 02 db **(88)** n*23* this is all about just how subtle oak can be: the malt has a walk-on part but tannin-induced spices abound; t*23* fabulous natural cream toffee. You can just chew and chew: the malt has come to life but still it's about controlled oak; f*21* dries and loses some of its earlier pliability. The spice – and dab of smoke that one suspects on the nose – offers a third dimension; b*21* this is brinkmanship of the highest level: this shows just how far a malt can be stretched by oak without snapping. **53.4%. ncf.**

Glen Moray 1981 Distillery Manager's Choice db **(92)** n*25* classic sherry nose: tomatoes, figs, crushed raisins, bitter chocolate, coffee etc. Entirely faultless – a freak; t*23* exceptionally well-balanced in terms of mouthfeel and bitter-sweet ratio, but the oak gets just a little too assertive too early; f*22* lots of spices and dancing oak; b*22* always said my old mate Ed at Glen Moray was a bit of a whisky genius. He should be struck a medal for finding this stunner.

Glen Moray Vallée du Rhône (75) n*17* t*20* f*19* b*19*. C'est comme ci comme ça. **46%**

MacLeod's Highland Aged 8 Years (89) n*22* stunning honey, so beautifully clean that the mouth salivates! Crisp barley concentrate that is firm and full and hardly troubled by oak, quite sensuous and very, very delicately smoked; t*21* really malty with a highly accentuated barley thrust that offers brilliant sweet/dry ratio. Hardly complex by way of invading flavours, but the shape of the whisky is so delicious! f*23* lots of bitter cocoa that perfectly counters the hinted sweetness of the barley. Some smoke simmers through; b*23* Wow! This may be a Highlander by name on the label, though the source of the whisky is Speyside. But it is Highland by nature with some enormous earthy, resonance. Absolutely top-class stuff that bites and teases deliciously. Love to have seen this at 46% nonchillfiltered: might have had a minor classic on our hands. Glen Moray, though not stated on label. **40%**

Signatory Glen Moray Aged 9 Years sherry butt 4670, dist 29/06/89, bott 5/10/98, **(81)** n*21* t*21* f*19* b*20*. The fruit influence appears to nullify the malt; the stand-off results in a peppery dram with more grape and oak than barley. **59.2%**

GLEN ORD
Highland (Northern) 1838. Diageo. Working.

Glen Ord Aged 12 Years db **(88)** n*23* busy spices fail to interrupt the fruity malt flow; t*22* more spice, then wave upon wave of quite brittle malt before a hint of smoke and vanilla appears; f*21* a tad lazy as the malts luxuriate in a soft, sweet glow; b*22* enormously improved on the boring old bottling with the trademark spices re-introduced and the malt spanning several layers of complexity. Much closer to how I remember it 20 years ago: the sherry style has been dropped and the malts reign. A very well-made malt ... welcome back! **43%**

Glen Ord Aged 23 Years db dist 1974, bott Oct 98 Rare Malts Selection **(84)** n*21* t*21* f*21* b*21*. Big, chewy, fat, oaky, some honey and smoke. **60.8%**

Cadenhead's Ord 19 Years Old dist 83, bott 03/03 **(85)** n*22* a hint of coal smoke against brittle malt; t*21* biting, irrascible, nippy but the malt is crisp and constant; f*22* superb softening of malt alongside some natural cream toffee-fudge; b*20* a mouthwatering dram that was born to blend. **57%**

Signatory Glen Ord 18 Years Old refill sherry butt 377, dist 02/02/83, bott 24/08/01 **(84)** n*19* t*22* f*21* b*22*. Cream toffee, raisin. **58.3%**. *226 bottles.*

GLENROTHES
Speyside, 1878. Edrington. Working.

The Glenrothes 1966 cask 1437, bott 02 db **(87)** n*24* rich, heady toffee apple and demerara pot-still rum, beautifully clean with fruity red liquorice candy; **t**21 massive oak and grape hand in hand, but the oak has the harder, more bitter grip; **f**21 more liquorice and molassed sugar and the malt snaps and snarls at the marginally sappy, salty oak; **b**21 really lovely stuff, but the oak punishes just a little too hard for this to be a true classic. **52.8%. nc.** 216 bottles.

The Glenrothes 1967 cask 6998, bott 02 db **(94)** **n**24 amiable malt blunders into vanilla: this relaxed, seriously laid-back yet ultra-complex malt keeps you sniffing until your nose bleeds; **t**24 glorious. Just a celebration of all things malty yet softly spiced, fruity yet grained, sweet yet at times slightly dry; **f**23 a slight hint of something smoky as the peppers tone down to something softer amid the sweet vanilla; **b**23 Glenrothes at its most seductive and complex. Now this is a classic: not just as a Speysider but among all Scotland malts. Almost Sprinbankesque in sheer, unfettered élan. **46.3%. nc.** 180 bottles.

The Glenrothes 1971 db bott 99 **(89)** **n**23 lovely malt concentrate tempered with intense bourbony oak and plummy fruit; **t**22 delicious amalgam of rich barley and richer toffee and ripe fruit. Controlled sweetness counters a natural dryness; **f**21 long, drying with a hint of liquorice, spice and honey; **b**23 big age on this, but kept in shape by firm malt and rich fruit. **43%**

The Glenrothes 1973 db bott 00 **(91)** **n**22 just brilliant fruit: apples and tangerine in particular; **t**24 dazzling malt arrival with outstanding complexity thanks to the most delicate yet occasionally vicious spices; **f**23 the fruit and spice hang on in for a while, the complexity gathering momentum towards the end; **b**22 great malt from a Speysider that dares to offer something big and bruising yet somehow complex and sophisticated. **43%**

The Glenrothes 1979 db bott 02 **(92)** **n**22 a complex, grainy nose with bite: not unlike a very good blend; **t**24 just love this: fresh, crisp, clean then honied; **f**23 back to that grainy crispness and a soft, floating smokiness; **b**23 a very unusual Glenrothes of alluring and memorable complexity. A must for us blend lovers! **43%**

The Glenrothes 1987 db bott 99 **(84)** **n**21 **t**22 **f**20. **b**21 Soft cream-toffee-caramel checks the development of an otherwise lovely-weighted and fruity malt. **43%**

The Glenrothes 1989 db bott 01 **(75)** **n**19 **t**20 **f**18 **b**18. Disappointingly dull and caramel rich. **43%**

The Glenrothes 1989 db bott 00 **(76)** **n**19 **t**21 **f**18 **b**18. Cloakroomy, musty rainjackets, dusty churches. Makes for an interesting nose, shame it's nothing like as curious to taste. I think '89, with the odd exception here and there, must have been a sub-standard vintage for this usually impeccable distillery. **43%**

Adelphi Glenrothes 10 Years Old cask 10965, dist 92, bott 02 **(79)** **n**20 **t**19 **f**20 **b**20. Toasty and dry for the most part; hot and malty in others. **57.1%**

Adelphi Glenrothes 24 Years Old cask 2711, dist 76 bott 00 **(78)** **n**19 **t**21 **f**19 **b**19. Mildly feinty and enormously oily. **52.7%. sc.**

Cadenhead's Glenrothes 12 Years Old dist 90, bott 10/02 **(69)** **n**17 **t**19 **f**17 **b**16. Sulphur-tainted throughout. **46%**

Coopers Choice Glenrothes 1985 dist 01 (15 Years Old) **(89)** **n**22 stem ginger and molasses; **t**22 big, chewy, malty; **f**22 tufts of liquorice amid dry oak and sweet sugars; **b**23 an absolute little cracker. **56%.** The Vintage Malt Whisky Co.

Coopers Choice Glenrothes 1975 dist 02 (26 Years old) **(87)** **n**22 fresh fruit and spices with just a hint of something smoky; **t**21 big mouthfeel, wave upon wave of buttery sherry; **f**22 soft, sultanas and raisins and some spices; **b**22 a fine sherry cask without an off-note. In some ways too perfect! **51%.** The Vintage Malt Whisky Co.

Gordon & MacPhail Glenrothes 1961 **(82)** **n**20 **t**21 **f**21 **b**20. Gooseberries on the nose and malty-silk on the palate. No off-notes or oak deterioration whatsoever. **40%**

Hart Brothers Glenrothes Aged 33 Years dist Oct 69, bott Jan 03 **(80)** n21 t21 f19 b19. Chalky but cheerful. **46.8%**

James MacArthur Glenrothes 12 Year Old (85) n21 firm, wth a mixture of tangerine and nicotine; t22 fresh and fruity at first then a wave of grassy malt and spice. f21 busy oak; b21 very big and weighty. **43%**

The MacPhail's Collection Glenrothes 8 Years Old (80) n19 t22 f20 b19. Really complex middle stars. **40%**

Old Malt Cask Glenrothes Aged 31 Years dist Jun 69, bott Feb 01 **(72)** n18 t19 f17 b18. Off the pace. **50%. nc ncf.** Douglas Laing. 174 bottles.

Old Masters Glenrothes 1989 bott 01 **(86)** n21 buttery, cream toffee; t22 uncomplicated malt: clean, intense and naturally toffeed; f22 long with some soft oaks intruding on the malt; b21 a real mouthful. Blenders die for this stuff. **64.7%.** James MacArthur.

Peerless Glenrothes 1967 cask 8389, dist May 67 **(74)** n20 t18 f18 b18, Some honied moments, but pretty tired. **40.9%.** Duncan Taylor & Co.

Peerless Glenrothes 1968 cask 13481, dist Nov 68 34-y-o **(80)** n19 t21 f20 b20. An oaky, substantial beast. **57%.** Duncan Taylor & Co.

Peerless Glenrothes 1969 cask 382, dist Jan 69 **(86)** n20 light and just a little shy for its great age, the oak strikes an impressively delicate balance with the malt but insists on a degree of superiority. Some spice does bite hard but the toffee softens it all down; t23 Wow! Piledriving spices hammer home but are consumed by the most extraordinary sweetness. This takes an oily form that coats the mouth with an unusual mixture of coffee-cocoa and honey. Excellent; f21 long and fat with many variations on a drying oaky theme. Perhaps just a little too bitter at the death, but that can be forgiven; b22 an impressive bottling. **50.7%.** Duncan Taylor & Co Ltd.

Scott's Selection Glenrothes 1973 bott May 03 **(92)** n23 this is glorious: the malt and oak have combined for golden shafts of honey to fall on some delicate smoky tones: light and heavy, sweet and dry; t24 carries on from the nose with a shimmering, concentrated honied maltiness; f22 heaps of spice, with that softly spoken peat on the nose making another murmur; b23 I know those who regard Glenrothes as the finest of all Speyside distilleries: on the evidence of this it is hard to offer too much of an argument. **50.2%.** Robert Scott & Co.

Ultimate Selection Glenrothes 1994 sherry butt 6882, dist 10/6/94, bott 4/3/02 **(89)** n21 fresh, young, youthful malt with just enough oak; t24 beautiful malt: grassy, crystal clear in flavour and wonderfully bitter-sweet; f23 slightly short but the malt persists and some late dark chocolate suggests some oak involvement; b21 if this were any cleaner you could wash yourself with it. Delicious: the sherry butt has obviously done the rounds as it plays no part in the malt's development. Everybody should have a bottle of this. **43%.** Van Wees NL.

GLEN SCOTIA
Campbeltown, 1832. Glen Catrine. Working.

Glen Scotia 14 Years Old db **(90)** n23 complex, with darting malty notes nipping around, almost like the small grains in a bourbon: really top-quality stuff; t22 busy, light maltiness with flickering intensity. The malty sweetness is never more than a passing illumination amid the gathering cocoa oakiness; f22 gristy malt and soft oak intertwine; b23 if Glen Scotia had been this good in the past it wouldn't have suffered such a chequered career. Absolutely engrossing malt with fabulous complexity. **40%**

The MacPhail's Collection Glen Scotia 1990 (86) n21 peat and honey; t22 peat and honey f22 guess what? ... peat and honey ... and oak; b21 for those in search of a softly peated and honied dram. A real collector's item for Glen Scotia – the peatiest I have ever come across bottled by some margin. Simple, but delicious. **40%.** Gordon & MacPhail.

Milroy's Glen Scotia Aged Over 10 Years (75) n19 t17 f20 b19. Big whisky with power and bite, but hard as nails and a little spirity. **43%**

Scotch Malt Whisky Society Cask 93.10 Aged 11 Years (94) n23 for something so rich and honied there is no shortage of weight: such an enticing mildly peaty dram; t24 a raucous arrival of sweet malt and thumping oak, a punch-up in which much honey is spilt; f23 some smoke lingers with the spices and lush, rich malty notes; b24 like a top-rate Talisker ... with honey! If you have a friend who is a member of the society, let him have your wife for the weekend in exchange for a miniature of this distillery's finest in bottled form. For the entire bottle, it might be worth allowing him to keep her. (For the PC – only joking (yeah, right!)) **63.8%. nc ncf sc.**

GLEN SPEY
Speyside, 1885. Diageo. Working.

Glen Spey Aged 12 Years db **(85)** n21 a soothing, softly malted aroma, hints of toffee maybe but definite oak; t22 refreshing and grassy malt battles through some toffee-heaviness most uncharacteristic of Glen Spey. Vague hints of something molassed and oaky; f21 quite long with some bitter cocoa and distant peppers; b21 for those of us brought up on Glen Spey being light, crystalline and grassy, this is a strange bottling to get to grips with. The heaviest Glen Spey I've come across in 20 years which, though not quite representative of the distillery's character, offers an acceptably intriguing and complex dram. **43%**

GLENTAUCHERS
Speyside, 1898. Allied. Working.

Gordon & MacPhail Glentauchers 1990 (86) n21 a tantalising mixture of soft malts and oaks with just a sprinkling of peat for good measure; t22 stupendous mouthfeel with again subtle nuances found of the three major contributors; f21 moves towards oaky vanilla with a hint of spice; b22 this is an unspectacular malt that somehow contrives to be quite charming. Everything is delicate and understated, but the journey is wonderful. **40%**

The Master of Malt Glentauchers 11 Years Old (84) n21 t22 f21 b21. Really impressive chewing malt with a healthy streak of peat and a little nip. **43%**

GLENTURRET
Highlands (Perthshire), 1775. Edrington. Working.

Glenturret 10 Years Old db **(86)** n21 firm honey thread, exceptionally clean malt with the most teasing hint of ginger; t22 rich Glenturret mouthfeel, as if lots of copper has been used in the process. Again the malts are clean and slick; f21 mild hints of something spicy enlivens the malt-honey processsion; b22 those of you into Lochnagar will recognise this style of rich, intense whisky. Amazing coppery mouthfeel, softened by the trademark honey: very well-made whisky, indeed. **40%**

The Glenturret Aged 15 Years db **(87)** n21 honey and cherry tomato: rich yet clean; t22 highly intense malt that sweetens, mildly oily with a hint of oak; f22 honey returns, vaguely waxy with a mild spice finale; b22 a beautifully clean, small-still style dram that would have benefitted from being bottled at a fuller strength. A discontinued bottling now: if you see it, it is worth the small investment. **40%**

The Glenturret Aged 18 Years db **(86)** n21 floral and herbal: a gardener's dram; t22 good grip in the palate with acacia honey booming in; f21 cream toffee and marmalade. Just a faint hint of honey battles through; b22 very delicate and holds its age well. Discontinued. If you see it, it's the last of the line. **40%**

The Glenturret Aged 21 Years db **(85)** n20 fruity, honied but a tad soapy; t22 beautifully oiled with the honey going into orbit and even a hint of peat; f21 lots of cream toffee with cocoa, then the soapiness returns; **b**21 a soft, honied dram that is way understrength for its age and style. **40%**

Glenturret 1972 bott Dec 02 db **(87) n**22 I don't think I've come across so much vanilla on a nose, especially one that is already overflowing with honey; **t**21 slightly soapy, but acceptably so, then a wave of intense malt and honey; **f**22 back to the massive vanilla wall: those long strands of honey just keep on going; **b**22 a really unusual dram, a bit on the soapy side, but such is the enormity of honey/vanilla mix, wholly acceptable. **47%**. *Four hogsheads producing just 522 bottles.*

Blackadder Glenturret 17 Years Old cask 4906, dist 7 April 80, bott May 97 **(93) n**23 damp millet and budgie seed! Who's a pretty boy? **t**23 Glenturret honey by the spoonful. Classic; **f**23 enormous malt richness that keeps oak at bay; **b**24 saw this in a bar in Hamburg recently, so delighted to include it here. This is a Glenturret classic, not so much for the complexity, which is limited, but simply because few Perthshire malts come this honied and sweet without making you gag. A perfect dram for budgies, too, as my son's one, Borat, will testify. He loves to nose it... and with very good reason! **53.7%. sc.**

Cadenhead's Glenturret 15 Years Old dist 86, bott 10/02 **(89) n**21 lively and a tad soapy, but slowly some very piercing malt notes appear; **t**22 sublime texture of yielding yet biting malt – excellent complexity; **f**24 now the honey arives for Glenturret overdrive. Few other distilleries have this kind of flourish to their signature: cocoa mixes brilliantly with the soft honey; **b**22 for all its playful bite and nip, a dram you can sink into. **54%**

Hart Brothers Glenturret Aged 11 Years dist Jun 91, bott Sep 02 **(83) n**19 **t**22 **f**21 **b**21. Slightly dusty, but the palate arrival is pure Perthshire! **55.5%**

MacPhail's Collection Glenturret 1990 Vintage **(84) n**21 **t**22 **f**20 **b**21. Beautiful honey, dry on finish. **40%**. *Gordon & MacPhail.*

Old Malt Cask Glenturret Aged 15 Years dist 86, bott 02 **(84) n**21 **t**22 **f**19 **b**22. A whisky of beguiling enormity that reeks of rich Perthshire honey. There are one or two minor flaws here, almost certainly cask-related, but so lush and sweet is this whisky that a blind eye can be turned. **50%. nc ncf.** *Douglas Laing.*

Old Masters Glenturret 1986 bott 02 **(88) n**21 standard mildly oily Glenturret aroma; **t**23 rich oils fill the mouth: sweet yet sharp malt rules the roost; **f**22 a hint of honey as the vanilla arrives; **b**22 this is a very good cask selection. **51.3%.** *James MacArthur.*

Ultimate Selection Glenturret 1985 cask 119, dist 12/7/85, bott 4/3/02 **(90) n**23 honey and diced raw carrots; **t**23 perfect mouthfeel and wonderful marriage of sweet malt and toffee bonbons; **f**22 soft, chalky oak; **b**22 ask to be shown a first-class cask of 16-y-o Glenturret, and you'll get this. **43%. sc.** *Van Wees NL.*

GLENUGIE
Highland (Eastern). 1834–1983. Closed.

Connoisseurs Choice Glenugie 1967 **(89) n**23 tangerines, grist and vanilla: a wonderful combination; **t**23 softly oiled and massive, sweet malt. The barley just revels. A touch of peat, too; **f**21 soft vanilla and lingering malt; **b**22 the first Glenugie I ever tasted: has never been bettered in bottle. **40%**. *Gordon & MacPhail.*

Gordon & MacPhail Glenugie 1968 **(86) n**22 oaky and a little starchy, big, big malt; **t**22 oak first again, but levels out to let in very sweet, biscuity barley; **f**21 lovely balance here as the oak recedes to allow in figs and vanilla; **b**21 incredibly sweet and malty. Really lovely stuff, with fine oak. **40%**

Old Malt Cask Glenugie Aged 26 Years dist March 76 **(76) n**22 **t**20 **f**16 **b**18. Brilliant fruit and custard nose, but the palate – after the initial malty burst – shows inevitable signs of wear and tear. **50%**. *Douglas Laing.*

GLENURY ROYAL
Highland (Eastern), 1868–1985. Demolished.

Connoisseurs Choice Glenury Royal 1976 **(83)** n*21* t*22* f*20*. b*20*. Malt and clean with lovely citrus freshness. **40%**

Gordon & MacPhail Glenury Royal 1972 **(70)** n*18* t*19* f*16* b*17*. Decent early show, then dies. **40%**

Old Malt Cask Glenury Aged 21 Years (sherry) dist March 80, bott May 01 **(83)** n*21* t*22* f*20* b*20*. Big, chewy, oaky. Lots of natural toffee. **50%. nc ncf.** Douglas Laing. 504 bottles.

Old Malt Cask Glenury Aged 32 Years dist Nov 68, bott Feb 01 **(89)** n*22* massive oak and sherry mix; t*23* enormous mouth arrival with liquorice and malt outgunning the spice; f*22* elegant, natural toffee and raisins; b*22* a strappingly big laddie. **49.4%. nc ncf.** Douglas Laing. 258 bottles.

Platinum Glenury 34 Years Old dist Nov 68, bott Jan 03 **(72)** n*18* T*19* f*17* b*18*. Honey but too aged. **43.4%.** Douglas Laing.

HIGHLAND PARK
Highland (Island–Orkney), 1795. Edrington. Working.

Highland Park 8 Years Old db **(87)** n*22* firm young, honied malt with food coke/peat smoke; t*22* silky honey and excellent complexity for a malt so young; f*22* complex layers of vanilla and soft peat at first then caramel grabs hold: shame; b*21* a journey back in time for some of us: this is the orginal distillery bottling of the 70s and 80s, bottles of which are still doing the rounds in obscure Japanese bars and specialist outlets such as the Whisky Exchange. **40%**

Highland Park Aged 12 Years db **(92)** n*24* sublime: the peat is almost sprinkled on by hand in exact measures, the honey and vague molasses guaranteeing contolled sweetness, salt, old leather and apples in there, too; t*22* moderately weighty mouth arrival, sweet yet enough oak to offer some bitter complexity. This fabulour bitter-sweet balance pans out in favour of the honey though there is enough peat around to add extra weight; f*22* long, spicy, some earthy heather and more oak than usual. Excellent cocoa hangs about with the peat; b*24* it defies belief that an international brand can maintain this quality, more or less, year in year out. Few drams are as silkily enveloped as this gem. **40%**

Highland Park Aged 15 Years db **(83)** n*20* t*22* f*21* b*20*. The new kid on the block has yet to show the voluptuous expansiveness of its brothers. The nose is surprisingly closed and the flavours never fully open on the palate, either. Good smoke and spice, though. **40%. For Sainsbury UK.**

Highland Park Aged 18 Years db **(95)** n*24* an empty honey jar which once held peaty embers. An enormous nose of excellent consistency, with salty butter and burnt honeycomb is always present; t*23* beautifully sweet, in some ways sweeter than even the 12-y-o thanks to some manuka honey, which is accentuated against the drier oaky tones and rumbling peat towards the back of the palate: beautifully chewy, a touch oily and wholly substantial; f*24* some citrus, heathery notes, controlled oak and outstanding cocoa and peat: long and rewarding; b*24* a consistent dram of enormous weight and complexity, bottle after bottle, and never short of breathtakingly brilliant: the ace in the Highland Park pack. **43%**

Highland Park Aged 25 Years db **(94)** n*23* enormous sherry, but enough spice and peat battles through to guarantee balance. A zesty, honied maltiness can also be found; the oak is also loud and clear; t*24* seriously rich and weighty; oily textured, fruity but a really gripping spiciness buzzes around the palate. The crescendo is silk-textured and honey sweet with some grape and cocoa; f*23* long, with the cocoa taking its time to clear. Late heather but the oak is restrained by comparison with the nose and the esters remain fat and sparkling; b*24* since the launch of the 18 and 25, for me there has always been a wide gap in quality with the 18 always on top. This latest bottling suggests the gap is closing fast. Brilliant use of some sherry, it seems, has calmed the former excesses of the oak and we are left with an aged whisky that is an essay in balance and sophistication. **50.7%**

Highland Park Aged 25 Years db **(89) n**23 emphasis on the heather-honey though significant fruit – apple especially – abounds. Some pulsating oak, but the theme is sweetish and gently spiced. No more than a hint of smoke; **t**23 firm bodied with soft, smoky spices forming a guard around the burnt honey and barley; much more rigid and crisp than normal HP but this doesn't detract from the radiating complexity; **f**21 layers of vanilla and rich honey. Pretty short, though; **b**22 a very different animal to the 50.7% version with less expansion, depth and expression. Not a bad dram, though... **51.5%**

Highland Park Bicentenary Vintage 1977 Reserve db **(93) n**24 herbal and salty. The heather is in full bloom; **t**25 the early peat dissolves in the mouth allowing the honey and vanilla the stage. Lovely greengages and salt add to the complexity: truly fantastic, to the point of faultless; **f**21 cocoa and Jamaican coffee compensate for an otherwise lazy though lightly spiced finale; **b**23 should have been bottled at 46–50% for full effect: they were making great whisky at this time at HP and this is a pretty peaty version. **40%**

Adelphi Highland Park 20 Years Old cask 1286, dist 82, bott 02 **(90) n**21 quite sharp malt, honied of course; **t**23 so rich ... enormous malt-honey start but some peat sneaks in slowly; **f**23 touches of cocoa make for a brilliant counter-dryness and some salt in there, too; **b**23 the cocoa at the end adds an extra supreme dimension to an already fabulous whisky. Brilliant. **56.4%**

Adelphi Highland Park 21 Years Old cask 4146, dist 79, bott 00 **(84) n**21 **t**23 **f**20 **b**20. A strangely listless malt from Adelphi. The fore and middle are big and long, offering lots of sweetness. But the smoke and complexity just isn't there all round and is replaced by toffee. **51.7%. sc.**

Blackadder Highland Park 10 Years Old refill sherry cask 20569, dist 11 Nov 92, bott Mar 03 **(80) n**19 **t**22 **f**20 **b**19. Very sweet and refreshing. **45%**

Blackadder Old Man of Hoy db **(89) n**22 winey and rich, softly oaked with an oily peatiness. Flower-scented sweetness and heather: the kind of malt that would send bees into a frenzy; **t**23 fat and oily; a wave of intensely sweet malt upon successive waves of gentle peat. Thick, intense and chewy; **f**22 a long strand of peat compliments the heather and oak; **b**22 the label doesn't say which Orkney distillery this hails from, but two seconds alone with a glass of it leaves no doubt whatsoever. **58%**

Blackadder Raw Cask Highland Park 1989 sherry hogshead cask 10042, dist 1 March 89, bott April 02 **(88) n**21 lively, spicy, heathery; **t**23 usual honey tang and delicious sweetness with some vanilla balancing the middle out a bit; **f**22 very long with vanilla and busy spices; **b**22 a relatively light HP with limited smoke inclusion but the soft honey complexity is quite lovely.

Cadenhead's Highland Park 22 Years Old dist 79, bott 10/02 **(79) n**19 **t**22 **f**18 **b**20. Honied, but a little hidden soapiness just takes it down a peg or two. **50.4%**

Cask Highland Park 1989 (79) n20 **t**22 **f**18 **b**19. The usual honey and stuff and some berry chewy moments, but otherwise not firing on all cylinders. **58.4%.** *Gordon & MacPhail.*

Gordon & MacPhail Highland Park 1970 (78) n22 **t**20 **f**18 **b**18. Honied nose (surprise, surprise) but the body is just a fraction too thin and oaky. **40%**

Hart Brothers Highland Park Aged 10 Years dist 89 bott 00 **(82) n**20 **t**22 **f**20 **b**20. Lots of soft vanilla douses the usual honey. The spices are excellent, though. **43%**

Hart Brothers Highland Park 20 Years Old dist 77 **(83) n**20 **t**22 **f**21 **b**20. The malt has thinned and soft vanilla holds sway. Delightfully delicate all the same. **43%**

Hart Brothers Highland Park 25 Years Old dist 75 **(89)** n*23* ripping honey and oak balance with glorious peaty side-dish. The oak threatens towards big age, but so what! t*22* heather-honey and leather Winchesters and soft oak: it's like drinking a library; f*22* dries with a honied sheen; b*22* this is just one hell of a Highland Park. Thinks about going over the woody edge, but stays the right side of the warning line. **43%**

Lombard Highland Park 1989 (86) n*20* coal smoke and a hint of lime; t*24* the gradual arrival of honey amid the intense malt is a sheer delight. Couched in equally increasing smoke, this is so soft it is almost unreal. A great whisky moment! f*20* what follows is a relative let-down as the malt-honey growth stops and drier, more toffeed tones appear; b*22* one of the better bottlings by some distance from Lombard. **50%**

The MacPhail's Collection Highland Park 8 Years Old (86) n 21 honey and smoke; t*22* velvety malt and the heather honey makes its guest appearance; f*22* long with hints of delicious cocoa; b*21* straight as a die: smoke and honey all the way with no hesitation or deviation. **40%**

Mission Range Highland Park 1979 (94) n*22* coke and seaweed, quite salty plus soft oak; t*24* just an amazing infusion of varying honey tones with the most delicate peat; f*24* complexity goes into overdrive here as the heathery, earthy tones gain a healthy foothold and rock with the smoke and oak: sweet massive and long. Great spices kick in, too; b*24* just wicked whisky: simple as that. Another extraordinary dram that helps put the Mission Range among the most impossibly brilliant in world bottlings. **46%.** *Murray McDavid.*

Murray McDavid Highland Park 1979 cask 7749 dist May 79, bott Jun 97 **(89)** n*22* a big, slightly brawny, oaky nose with diffused peaty notes; t*24* early hint of dryness then an immediate peat and honey of the very highest order counters with tradional Orcadean riches; f*21* longish with vanilla and fruit, soft peat lingers to the end; b*22* one of the better independent bottlings at non-cask strength you will ever find. **46%. nc ncf sc.**

Old Malt Cask Highland Park Aged 17 Years sherry dist May 84, bott May 01 **(72)** n*17* t*20* f*18* b*17*. Cloyingly sweet, poor balanced, less than impressive cask. Apart from that... **50%. nc ncf.** *Douglas Laing. 786 bottles.*

Old Malt Cask Highland Park Aged 23 Years dist Feb 78, bott Apr 01 **(77)** n*19* t*20* f*19* b*19*. Decent, quite rich but not classic. **50%. nc ncf.** *Douglas Laing. 606 bottles.*

Old Malt Cask Highland Park Aged 25 Years dist Nov 75, bott May 01 **(93)** n*23* dry oak, sea shore saltiness, formidable complexity; t*24* awash with honey; beautifully textured, chewy and perfectly smoked; f*23* light smoke forms a lovely spicy affair with the vanilla; b*23* the nose may be less than promising, but all else afterwards is sheer bliss. Truly mind-blowing and tastebud-raping. **50%.** *Douglas Laing. 288 bottles.*

Old Malt Cask Highland Park Aged 30 Years dist Nov 70, bott Apr 01 **(83)** n*20* t*20* f*23* b*20*. Too much oak and sherry early on, perhaps, but the finish is Highland Park heaven. **50%. nc ncf.** *Douglas Laing. 570 bottles.*

Peerless Highland Park 1966 cask 4627, dist May 66 36-y-o **(89)** n*21* certainly some oak around, but the honey sings; t*23* silky with soft peaty spices and burgeoning honey; f*22* excellent follow-through of complex heather-honey and oak; b*23* this really is a charming malt: it has held its head high over the years. **43.4%.** *Duncan Taylor & Co.*

Private Cellar Highland Park 1985 bott Feb 03 **(88)** n*21* beautiful citrus-honey tones; t*23* rich, honied malt with just a soft fade of peat. More fruit gathers towards the middle; f*22* curvaceous to the very end with the malt still sparkling and offering gentle honey/brown sugar sweetness; b*22* I have always said that 18 years is the optimum age for this distillery, and while there are more complex versions around this is a little stunner. **43%**

Provenance Winter Distillation Highland Park Over 10 Years cask DI Ref 726*, dist Spring 92, bott Winter 02 **(82) n**19 **t**22 **f**21 **b**20. Slightly raw and un-refined but, as usual, the honey notes are a delight. **46%. nc ncf sc.** *Douglas McGibbon & Co.*

Rare Old Highland Park 1964 (92) n24 peaty, but in a diffused, fruity way. Cocoa and chocolate mingles with the malt: so very complex; **t**24 heather-honey, HP trademark, then a rush of peat and spices with more softening cocoa; **f**21 the Achilles heel: is it natural or unnatural toffee that flattens out the high points of this great malt? Loads of fruit, either way; **b**23 one of the great Gordon & MacPhail bottlings of all time still found on Japanese shelves at mortgage requiring prices **40%.** *Gordon & MacPhail.*

Scotch Malt Whisky Society Cask 4.73 (91) n24 toffee apple and cocoa, clean oloroso at its most luxuriant; **t**23 natural toffee bedding down with intense malt. Some bitter chocolate battles it out with the sweet fruit puree; **f**22 myriad oak notes, most of them sweet and lingering malt; **b**22 a handsome whisky by any standards, the only problem being that the sherry butt is so good the character of the distillery is lost somewhat. Still, not a bad price to pay if it is effect you are after.

Scott's Selection Highland Park 1975 bott 00 **(87) n**24 archetypal Highland Park with lashings of heather, very sweet honey and soft, swirling smoke: a template for 25-y-o Highland Parks! **t**22 rich, melting honey and then a big surge of chewy peat leading to some liquorice notes. The peppers are busy but refrained; **f**20 tires a little with toast and vanilla edging out the honey, but very long and remains chewy and intriguing. Perhaps a little over-oaked on the finale, but this whisky has given its all! **b**21 if the middle and finish were as good as the nose and entry on the palate, we would be in for something amazing. As it is, this is big, sweet, lively and pretty delicious. **52%.** *Robert Scott & Co.*

Scott's Selection Highland Park 1977 bott 98 **(89) n**21 a relatively heavily smoked number for Highland Park, with the honey there but slightly masked. A tad salty and some drying vanilla displays encroaching age; **t**24 there is enormous honey-brown sugar sweetness on the arrival, made all the more effective for the sheer silkiness of body. The peat plays hide and seek, showing early then vanishing until towards the finish: Highland Park at its shimmering best; **f**22 excellent, peppery spices abound and interlock with the ripples of peat. The oak is muted, restricting itself to some drying, dusty vanilla notes. The honey isn't entirely dormant, either; **b**22 the complexity is sheer Highland Park, the arrival in the palate is sheer theatre. Keep this one in the mouth for longer than normal before swallowing. **52.9%.** *Robert Scott & Co.*

Single Barrel Collection Highland Park 1988 cask 10001, dist Mar 88, bott Dec 01 **(83) n**18 **t**22 **f**22 **b**21. A confrontational HP with the honey upfront to the point of rudeness. Oddly, more like a Jamaican pot-still rum long in the bottle than a typical Highland Park. Quite a shock on first meeting, this is a dram that grows and grows on you big time. **59.39%. sc nc ncf.** *Germany.*

Usquebaugh Society Highland Park 1992 dist 11/11/92, bott 12/3/02 **(86) n**21 gristy, slightly smoked malt; **t**23 clean, fresh, vaguely honied; **f**21 delicate oak and fine cocoa; **b**21 an understated and refined dram. **46%.** *NL.*

Whisky Galore Highland Park 1989 (58) n18 **t**15 **f**12 **b**13. If the whisky was attached to a cardiograph, there would be a straight line. **40%.** *Duncan Taylor & Co Ltd.*

HILLSIDE (see Glenesk)

IMPERIAL
Speyside, 1897. Allied. Silent.

Cadenhead's Imperial-Glenlivet 24 Years Old dist 77, bott 10/02 **(87) n**22 very beautifully shaped oak but it is the integrity of the enormous malt that really impresses; **t**22 a re-run of the nose. The enormity of the malt on landing is immense, with a few orangey notes too; **f**21 soft malt and vanilla; **b**22 you could almost shed a tear when realising the likely fate of this distillery. **57.6%**

Gordon & MacPhail Imperial 1979 **(87) n**22 grassy and smoky; **t**22 mouthwatering, clean, refreshing: fresh, soft malt all the way; **f**22 very light vanilla but still the sweet malt dominates; **b**21 a very simple, light and enjoyable Speysider. **40%**. *Gordon & MacPhail*.

Gordon & MacPhail Imperial 1990 **(82) n**20 **t**22 **f**19 **b**21. Very good example of clean, light, mouthwatering Speyside blending malt. Delicious. **40%**

Private Collection Imperial Calvados Finish 1990 **(56) n**14 **t**15 **f**14 **b**13. Just doesn't work. A disaster that should have been tipped (with care) into a blend. **40%**. *Gordon & MacPhail*.

Private Collection Imperial Claret Finish 1990 **(83) n**22 **t**21 **f**20 **b**20. Superb stuff with a glorious, concentrated Turkish-delight nose and start. Trails slightly at end.

Private Collection Imperial Cognac Finish 1990 **(88) n**21 malty, fruity, elegant, simple and one-dimensional – but delightfully so; **t**23 beautifully complex from start with delighful interplay between malt and oak, quite malty and mealy; **f**22 charmingly bitter-sweet with soft vanilla and spice; **b**22 great stuff. **40%**. *Gordon & MacPhail*.

Private Collection Imperial Cognac Finish 1991 **(79) n**18 **t**21 **f**19 **b**21. Enjoyable, but missing much of the élan of the '90. **40%**. *Gordon & MacPhail*.

Private Collection Imperial Port Wood Finish 1991 **(83) n**20 **t**22 **f**20 **f**21. Very sweet and maybe short on complexity but deliciously chewy with good spice. **40%**. *Gordon & McPhail*.

Private Collection Imperial Sherry Wood Finish 1990 **(72) n**19 **t**19 **f**18 **b**16. Not very exciting and slightly off-key, towards the finish especially. **40%**. *Gordon & MacPhail*.

Provenance Imperial Winter Distillation Over 11 Years dist Winter 89, bott Winter 20 **(68) n**15 **t**19 **f**17 **b**17. Half-hearted. Doesn't sit right at all. **43%. nc ncf**. *Douglas McGibbon & Co*.

INCHGOWER
Speyside, 1872. Diageo. Working.

Inchgower Aged 14 Years db **(77) n**19 **t**20 **f**19 **b**19. A vague hint of peat and a sprinkling of spice lifts the dram above something treacly and over-sweet. **43%**. *Flora and Fauna*.

Hart Brothers Inchgower Aged 26 Years dist Aug 76, bott Sep 02 **(89) n**21 slightly sharp, but the malt is crisp; **t**23 liquid honey, lightly oiled and with some spices to pep it up; **f**23 long malt fade, soft vanilla; **b**22 this is exactly how I remember tasting Inchgower at the distillery 20-odd years ago. A magnificent malt for any collector. **49.9%**

Old Malt Cask Inchgower Aged 25 Years dist Nov 74, bott Jun 00 **(88) n**20 big malt, hint of peat; **t**22 full-bodied, the malt still retains a grassy freshness; **f**24 massive spice kicks in then a slow unravelling of the richest honey you could dream of; **b**22 glorious whisky from an under-stated distillery. **50%**. *Douglas Laing. 234 bottles*.

INCHMURRIN (see Loch Lomond)

INVERLEVEN
Lowland, 1938–1991. Closed.

Gordon & MacPhail Inverleven 1986 **(89) n**22 scrumptious apples and pears, feather light, malty and enticing; **t**23 mouth-filling malt, excellent body and more soft fruit; **f**22 gentle coating of vanilla, sprinkled with barley sugar; **b**22 this is just the most simplistic, but sexy dram you could wish for. Easily the best expression by G&M of this distillery to date. **40%**

ISLE OF ARRAN

Highland (Island–Arran), 1995. Isle of Arran Distillers. Working.

Arran db **(87)** n*21* fat and massively malty, not as fruity as some bottlings; t*22* unbelievably oily with a subtle malt sweetness that also offers the faintest trace of oak. The voluptuous viscosity is unique; f*22* long and sensuous with the thickest coating of malt you will ever find; b*22* there is not enough oak interference here to get the complexity going, but putting on my blending hat for a minute I must say that it occurs to me that a little Arran goes a long, long way. This is great malt that is one of a kind. **40%**

The Arran Malt Non Chill Filtered db **(84)** n*18* t*23* f*22* b*21*. A young, raw nose is an ingeniously false lead to the magnificent story that unfolds on the palate. Mouthwatering and intense, a subtle oiliness holds gathering spices to the roof of the mouth. What a cracking wee dram. **46%. ncf.**

The Arran Malt db **(87)** n*22* buttery, fresh, soft, a pinch of coke-smoke, very complex, with some apples thrown in; t*22* sweet, silky, natural cream-toffee and vanilla: the malt intensity is phenomenal, the weight on the palate confident and rewarding; f*21* remains gentle with further vanilla which is chewy and long. Some really tantalising spices make a late extra addition; b*22* an immensely soft and soothing dram showing rich creamy style. I have tasted the last two bottlings, the last of which was in March 2003. And I have to say it is getting better and better. For all its relatively tender years, this is unambiguously great whisky – and one must now ask: a classic in the making? **43%**

The Arran Malt Limited Edition 1996 db dist 12/8/96, bott 14/4/03 **(88)** n*22* intense malt with a hint of spearmint and heavy oak for its age; t*23* big and softly spiced, with the trademark oiliness clinging to the roof of the mouth along with some charming citrus; f*21* subtle stuff: the malt remains massive and chewy. The contrast between bitter and sweet is minimal and the oak input is telling with some chewy toffee rounding things off; b*22* when Arran whisky was little more than an embryo, I predicted rapid maturation. Even I didn't expect something quite like this from a six-year-old. Astonishing and massively drinkable. **57%.** *175 bottles.*

The Arran Malt Limited Edition 1997 db dist 18/7/97, bott 15/10/02 from hogshead **(82)** n*21* t*21* f*20* b*20*. Decent single cask but falling between fruit or oak influence. **58.3%.** *341 bottles.*

Robert Burns World Federation Arran Single Island Malt db **(84)** n*19* t*22* f*22* b*21*. Fat, creamy, full-bodied. The malt sweetens by the second to become something like a good old-fashioned American malt milkshake: amazing but there is enough oak for a drying balance. One of the most intense young malts on the market, only the naivety of the nose preventing it from hitting the heights. A delightful, tastebud-massaging malt experience. **40%.** *Isle of Arran.*

Blackadder Raw Cask Lochranza 1996 dist 24/1/96, bott Apr 02 **(90)** n*22* charismatic and rich, the malt is thick, with no hint of sweetness; t*23* absolutely beautifully shaped with the most lovely cream-toffee imaginable. The spices arrive hand-in-hand with the sweeter malt tones; f*23* spicy oak, long, lovely and oily; b*22* there is no other six-year-old single malt that compares to this: in giving my speech at the opening ceremony of the distillery I stuck my neck out and predicted this would become a fast-maturing malt. Isn't it just!!!! **56.8%. nc ncf.**

ISLE OF JURA

Highland (Island–Jura), 1810. Kyndal. Working.

Isle of Jura 10 Years Old db **(77)** n*18* t*19* f*21* b*19*. A tangy malt that seems younger than its 10 years. The finish is long and offers the faintest hint of smoke on the rich malt. **40%**

Isle of Jura 16 Years Old db **(80)** 18 t*22* f*20* b*20*. Some lovely, mildly salty honey thorugh the middle. But an indefinable something is missing. A variable dram at the best of times, this expression is pleasant but ... variable. **40%**

Isle of Jura Aged 21 Years db **(78)** n*20* t*21* f*19* b*18*. Pleasant enough, but surprisingly short of charisma. **40%**

Isle of Jura 21 Years Old Cask Strength db **(92)** n*22* something hard and grainy against the ultra-clean fruit; t*24* fabulous mouth arrival, just such a brilliant fruit-spice combo held together in a malty soup; f*23* long and intensely malty; b*23* every mouthful exudes class and quality. A must-have for Scottish Island collector ... or those who know how to appreciate a damn fine malt **58.1%**

Isle of Jura Aged 36 Years (dist 1965) db **(96)** n*25* bloody hell's bells! I didn't expect to be thumped by peat quite like that: light and tangy phenols, offering something quite different in character to anything offered across the other side of the Port Askaig ferry; t*25* honey at its honiest meets peat at its peatiest. It's like a bee trapped in a smoke chamber; a Perthshire distillery dumped on Islay. Unique in style in all my experience and something to tell the grandchildren about or, preferably, give them some to be weaned on. f*23* becomes so soft you feel your teeth dissolve into it ... I'm now down to the gums. The smoke is now more subdued and a few tannins break sweat for an oaky intervention; b*23* I remember 20-odd years ago being taken into a corner of Jura's warehouse and tasting a cask of something big and smoky. It was different to all the other Juras around, but had none of this honey. Is this the same cask, a generation on? Most probably. I then returned to the hotel opposite for a dram (and a bottle) of their own Jura and wondered what would become of that peaty one-off. Now I know. **44%**

Isle of Jura 1973 Vintage db bott 23/2/03 **(93)** n*25* Aaaaahhhhh!!! A sherry butt from heaven sent: clean, full of big, ripe cherries and fruitcake and, of its type, faultless; t*23* the oak shows signs of deterioration, but the complete brilliance of sherry plugs the holes: chewy, spicy, burnt raisins and, of course, big oak; f*21* long, with the remaining malt hard and flinty. Stays fruity and offers majestic bitter-sweet balance to the very end; b*24* if you want to know what a truly great sherry nose is like, start here. The balance isn't bad, either. Brilliant! **55.6%**

Isle of Jura 1984 db **(69)** n*15* t*18* f*18* b*18*. Big brother ... with sulphur. All whiskies are equal, but some are more equal than others. Oops, wrong book. **42%.** *Bottled to commemorate George Orwell who wrote the book 1984 while on the island.*

Isle of Jura 1989 db bott 23/2/03 **(66)** n*16* t*17* f*17* b*16*. Wrong kind of sherry influence: off-key. Not my cup of tea at all. **57.2%**

Isle of Jura Legacy db **(82)** n*19* t*22* f*20* b*21*. Some very chewy honeycomb on the middle. Pretty big stuff. **40%**

Isle of Jura Stillman's Dram Limited Edition Aged 27 Years db **(90)** n*24* a single thread of peat holds together a toasty-honeycomb malt and oak combination: outstanding; t*23* the zesty middle follows a honied start, some buttery notes, too; f*21* medium length with roast malt and budding oak, very discreet peat at the death; b*22* one of the most complex Juras yet bottled. **45%**

Isle of Jura Superstition db **(86)** n*21* busy, peat and spice-led. Seems young despite some distinguished oak: very unusual; t*22* a beguiling array of soft barley and oak tones pinned to the tastebuds by green peat; f*20* much thinner and more relaxed than the intense mouth arrival; b*23* a rare case of where the whole is better than the parts. A malt that wins through because of a superb balance between peat and sweeter barley. Distinctive to the point of being almost unique. **45%**

Adelphi Isle of Jura 6 Years Old cask 1917, dist 96, bott 02 **(82)** n*21* t*22* f*19* b*20*. A lush and magnificent malt-honey nose and mouthfeel is undone slightly by a build-up of toffee on the finish. **60.5%**

Blackadder Raw Cask Jura 1988 cask 1639, dist Oct 88, bott Apr 02, **(75)** n18 t20 f19 b18. A bit on the thin side despite a quick maltburst on arrival. **59.4%. nc ncf.** *Hogshead.*

Connoisseurs Choice Jura 1989 (72) n19 t19 f17 b17. Little impact. **40%.** *Gordon & MacPhail.*

Dun Bheagan Isle of Jura Aged 14 Years dist 86, bott 01 **(67)** n16 t18 f17 b16. Sulphur-tainted sherry butt. **43%.** *William Maxwell.*

Old Malt Cask Isle of Jura Aged 35 Years dist Apr 66, bott May 01 **(75)** n19 t20 f18 b18. Some tangy, sweet fruit, but the oak is a little too loud. **47.8%. nc ncf.** *Douglas Laing. 204 bottles.*

Scotch Malt Whisky Society Cask 31.10 Aged 18 Years (84) n22 t22 f20 b20. Salty nose and mouth arrival with brimming spices. Quick toffee-fudge fade. **59.9%. nc ncf sc.**

Ultimate Selection Isle of Jura 1988 dist 12/10/88, bott 19/9/02 **(73)** n17 t18 f 20 b18. Chewy finish, but an early struggle. **43%.** *Van Wees NL.*

KNOCKANDO
Speyside, 1898. Diageo. Working.

Knockando 1990 bott 23 db **(83)** n21 t22 f20 b20. The most fruity Knockando I've come across with some attractive salty notes. Dry, but a little extra malty sweetness these days. **40%**

KNOCKDHU
Speyside, 1894. Inver House. Working.

AnCnoc 12 Year Old db (90) n22 massive aroma with a grassy maltiness enriching a grapey-juicy fruitiness, lovely coal smoke for good measure; t23 absolutely fabulous, near-perfect, malt arrival, perhaps the most clean, yet intense of any in Scotland. The complexity is staggering with not only multi-layers of malt but a distant peat and oak infusion; f22 deliciously spicy; b23 if there is a more complete 12-year-old Speyside malt on the market, I have yet to find it. A malt that should adorn a shelf in every whisky-drinking home.

AnCnoc 13 Year Old Highland Selection db **(85)** n21 usual coal smoke with ripe pears and oak for company; t23 rich, juicy, spicy and then so, so malty! f20 flattens rather unexpectedly; b21 a big Knockdhu, but something is dulling the complexity. **46%**

AnCnoc 26 Years Old Highland Selection db **(89)** n23 profound. Everything is big, but perfectly proportioned: massive grapey fruit and malt concentrate; t22 pure Knockdhu: intense malt carrying some beautiful spices and an obscure but refreshing fruit; f23 the lull after a minor storm: rich vanilla and echoes of malt; b21 there is a little flat moment between the middle and finish for which I have chipped off a point or two. That apart, superb. **48.2%**

Knockdhu 23 Years Old db **(94)** n23 coal gas and fruit (getting the pattern?): telling oak, but wonderfully crafted with the malt untarnished and rich beyond your wildest dreams; t24 the spiced malt makes violent love to your tastebuds. It's no-holds-barred, bodice-ripping stuff. Toasty honey tries to play a more gentle role, but gets caught up in the taste orgy: really hot stuff; f23 spent passion and a bewildering afterglow of malt, honey and fading spice; b24 pass the smelling salts. This is whisky to knock you out. A malt that confirms Knockdhu as simply one of the great Speysiders, but unquestionably among the world's elite. **57.4%.** *Limited edition.*

LADYBURN
Lowland, 1966–1974. Closed.

Ladyburn 1973 db **(60)** n15 varying shades of light oak have not entirely ...med the m... a tad spirity but pleasant with minimum complexity; t15 oak, oak and more (spicy) oak; f17 oak; b13 this has lost all trace of shape and form. Pretty one-dimensional yet easily drinkable thanks to a singular malty sweetness, especially towards the very end. Don't bother opening.

Old Rare Malt Ayrshire Distillery 1970 (71) n16 t17 f21 b17. A mildly soapy nose, uncomfortably hot on the palate but redeemed by a superb, clean malt surge at the end that is deliciously out of character. 40%. Gordon & MacPhail.

LAGAVULIN
Islay, 1816. Diageo. Working.

Lagavulin 12 Years Old db (92) n24 clean sea-brine and peat: first class; t23 explosive peat and soft barley make delicious bedfellows; f22 cocoa and smoke. The barley hangs sweetly around; b23 really charming Islay with a frisky peatiness that is sweet and lingering. One to savour and reminisce for those of us who were hooked on the Lagavulin in pre-Classic Malt era. 58%

Lagavulin 15 Years Old db (in ceramic decanter from late 80s) (89) n22 weighty, meaty malt, oak has healthy presence and the peat forms only a sweet backdrop; t23 old-fashioned light Lagavulin with a biting, salty style that has changed in recent years: superb spices; f22 the spices continue and some dark chocolate arrives; b22 this reminds me of how I discovered Lagavulin nearly a quarter of a century ago: proof indeed that styles within distilleries change. A real belter, nonetheless. 45%

Lagavulin Aged 16 Years db (88) n23 the peat, though full, is also unusually linear and lacking its trademark complexity: much more gristy than normal; t22 exceedingly soft with a quick surge of vanilla followed by some fruity notes. The sweet peat, of course, is everywhere; f21 slightly oilier than usual and bitter, too; b22 a bit unfair to pass judgement on this bottling: looking at my notes since year 2000, the average mark runs out at a fraction under 92 ... !!

Lagavulin 25 Years Old db bott 2002 (78) n19 t 21 f19 b19. Apart from the early mouth arrival, blunt and disappointing. Lagavulin, says Jim, but not as we know it. 57.2%. 9,000 bottles.

Lagavulin 1986 Distillers Edition Double Matured bott 02 Pedro-Ximenez finish db (86) n22 big peat and crushed ripe cherries, sweet pipe tobacco smoke; t22 fresh wine gives a bitter-sweet but glass-like countenance that seems to keep the peat at bay, though it does sneak up impressively whilst you're not watching; f21 juicy, boiled-sweet fruitiness and virtually peatless; b21 I really can't believe what I'm reading on the back label: "This is the definitive Islay Malt – untameable with the strongest peat flavour of any of the malt whiskies from this wild island shore." Well, sorry. But someone's had a bottle too many there. Big peat on the nose, sure, but then after that a whimper. It doesn't even begin to compare with the 12 and 16-y.o. Still, a good 'un for the juicy ones amongst us. 43%

Aom 11 Years Old Single Islay Cask (89) n22 oily and spicy, really very rich – very atypical of the distillery in bottled form; t23 exceptionally sweet peat syrup, incredibly oily – very Caol Ila-ish in style, but the phenolic intensity must be around the 50ppm – hence Lagavulin; f21 fades surpisingly to allow in some vanilla. But the peat stays the course, as does that amazing sweetness; b23 this is one hell of a Lagavulin and it is from that famed distillery that my dear friend Tatsuya Minagawa personally selected it for the now defunct M's bar in Edinburgh. The bottles have now re-surfaced in Japan. 46%

Mission Range Lagavulin 1979 in oak casks for 23 years (90) n22 sturdy and stimulating, the peat is aggressive and very oily for this distillery. Shows no wear or tear for such great age; t23 sweet and glossy with the peat forming varying layers of intensity; f22 brilliant oak arrival which is flakey and surprisingly light; b23 it's hardly possible that a malt of this age can maintain an almost youthful lightness and dexterity at the same time as offering thumping peat! Fabulous. 46%. Murray McDavid. 600 bottles.

...od's Islay 8 Years Old **(90) n**24 an astonishing array of citrus (lime a... ...e) battles with some success against the crashing waves of clean peat th... ...dine-rich and enticingly green. Something that no true whisky lover sh... ...l to experience; **t**22 fresh-faced and tender, there is an enveloping sw... ...t that is like liquid peat. The peat almost pings around the mouth, so cri... Only on the middle does the lack of age seem to offer an unfilled hole; **f**2... ...y and luscious, it is still spritely and fun and boasts massive liquoricey ch... ...y, but so very green and immature – fabulous all the same! **b**23 the no... ...y, pure Islay. At half the age of what you would normally taste Lagavulin this... ...scent malt helps you learn so much more about this great distillery. No Isla... ...on the market comes cleaner than this: only the old Bowmore 5-y-o use... ...now such childish abandon. This dram should be in every serious col... ...r Islay-phile's home. I'm 100% certain this is Lagavulin. **40%**

S...ry Vintage Islay Malt (Lagavulin 5 Years Old) **(85) n**20 raw yet qui... ...tiful, powering peat; **t**23 fruity, oranges in particular, with rich, velvety pea... **f**21 quietens a little and the youth returns; **b**21 an advanced Lagavulin for... ...er years but still hasn't quite reached puberty. A stupendous blending ma... ...state and a fascinating singleton. **58.4%**

LA...AIG

Isla... . Allied. Working.

L...ig 10 Years Old db **(90) n**24 impossible not to nose this and think of I... ...other aroma so perfectly encapsulates the island – clean despite the ram... ...peat-reek and soft oak, raggy coast-scapes and screeching gulls – all in a... 23 one of the crispiest, peaty malts of them all, the barley standing out... ...brittle and unbowed, before the peat comes rushing in like the tide: iodi... soft salty tones; **f**21 the peat now takes control for a sweet, disti... ...d finish; **b**22 quite light compared to of old with the peat taking a more sub... ...rmonious stance. But it is every bit as good if not better simply because there... ...clearer definition and shape. This, undisputably, is classic whisky. The favou... Prince Charles, apparently: he will make a wise king ... **40%**

La...ig 10 Years Old Original Cask Strength db **(93) n**23 explosive peat,... ...malts as well and no shortage of dry vanilla; **t**24 a mouthful of this is on... ...s little treasures: a stunning unravelling of peat at various levels of inten... ...netimes accompanied by brine, other times by subtle oils or vanilla; **f**23 g... ...d sweet, with long, pounding waves of soft smoke and iodine. Salty to the... ...and that end is a long time in coming; **b**23 a home without one of these... ...is barely worth visiting. This is Laphroaig nutshelled: wild and winds... ...t calm and controlled. Marvellous malt. **57.3%**

Lap...g Aged 15 Years db **(79) n**20 **t**20 **f**19 **b**20. A hugely disapp... ...lacklustre dram that is oily and woefully short on complexity. Not what o... ...es to expect from either this distillery or age. **43%**

Lap... Aged 30 Years db **(94) n**24 subtle, sweet peat-reek from distant... ...coupled with pungent sea spray: outstanding; **t**23 ultra-delicate peat tip... ...er the tastebuds. The malt and oak combine effortlessly to create a swe... ...lla-toffee package; **f**23 long, vanilla-peat echoes; **b**24 the best La... ...of all time? Nope, because the 40-y-o is perhaps better still... just. H... Laphroaig of this subtlety and charm gives even the very finest A... a run for its money. A sheer treat that should be bottled at greater... . **43%**

Laph... Aged 40 Years db **(94) n**23 smoky oranges, salty kippers: can this real... ...ch a gigantic age? **t**24 clean, precise peated malt at first, almost soft and... ...ning, then a slow procession of oak halting as it reaches bitter cocoa m... ...th the smoke; **f**23 more fruit and some developing oils that guarante... ...eet and fabulously long finish; **b**24 mind-blowing. This is a malt that defies all logic and theory to be in this kind of shape at such enormous age. The Jane Fonda of Islay whisky. **43%**

Limited Editions Laphroaig 1979 dist July 79, bott Sep 97 **(92) n**23 lemon and peat in thick, smoky form; **t**24 sweet, melt-in-the-mouth peaty malt, gristy and clean. Younger than the age suggests with no oak apparent; **f**23 long with some developing vanilla. The smoke swirls around failing to dim the sweet malty tail; **b**22 grab yourself a standard 14–15 year old cask of Laphroaig that has been faultlessly made and contains all its briny, smoky hallmarks... and you get this. Except this is a couple of years older and still unblemished. I have spotted the odd bottle of this still around. Grab it – even if it is just a couple of cls in a Scandinavian bar. **54.5%. nc ncf sc.** *Blackadder.*

Murray McDavid Laphroaig 1988 bourbon cask 2108, dist July 88, bott Dec 01 **(90) n**23 green, gristy, under-ripe malt with dazzling unbowed peat; **t**23 enormously sweet, wort-like. The peat is thick, chewy and entirely untainted; **f**22 lots of the softest vanilla imaginable, coupling with that gristy peaty malt; **b**22 Laphroaig in its purest form: if ever you want to know what happens to a Laphroaig when put into a tired cask offering limited year-on-year development, here's your chance to find out. Lacks the obvious complexity gained from oak but at the same time the youthful edges have been rounded for the most brilliant natural hybrid. I'd have this over porridge for breakfast any day. **46%**

Murray McDavid Leapfrog 1987 bourbon cask MM2868, dist Mar 87, bott Apr 99 **(91) n**23 soft and aloof then reveals a complex array of iodiney-salty smoky notes, sweet malt and drier oak: classically laid back; **t**23 sweet malt then waves of firm peat. Toffee-vanilla oak intervenes between waves; **f**22 a toasty dryness cannot deter the lip-smacking, smokey spiciness with some cocoa at the death; **b**23 due to legal action by Allied the bottlers were not allowed to state the distillery of origin. So they simply called it "Leapfrog". A folklore collector's item for what is in and outside of the bottle. **46%**

The Old Malt Cask Laphroaig Aged 15 Years dist Feb 87, bott Apr 02 **(86) n**21 yieldingly pungent and very young in style for age with crisp iodine, very delicate despite the obvious peat; **t**21 lively and lovely with big spice arrival to complement the peaty surround. The malt is especially sweet and clean; **f**22 long with ever-increasing soft-oaked vanilla blending with the malt. But it is the clarity of the spiky malt that wins through: enormously spicy towards the end; **b**22 an immense whisky that is among the sweetest Laphroaigs to have been bottled in recent years. The spicy fizz adds fun. A genuine joy. **50%. nc ncf.** *Douglas Laing. 336 bottles.*

Old Malt Cask Laphroaig Aged 17 Years dist Feb 85, bott Apr 02 **(75) n**19 **t**20 **f**18 **b**18. One bloody weird whisky. The aroma took me back over 30 years to the peculiar, carbolic aroma of the Morris Minor driven by Miss Nora Bavin, the spinster school secretary of the Grammar I attended. I never thought of that aroma in many decades: why should I? But there it is, in bottled form, in the guise of a Laphroaig. Life – whisky – never ceases to amaze... **50%. nc ncf.** *Douglas Laing. 306 bottles.*

Premier Malts Laphroaig 12 Years Old dist 30/10/90, bott Nov 02 **(80) n**20 **t**21 **f**19 **b**20. Begins with bite and nip but settles as a silky dram. **56.2%.** *Malcolm Pride.*

Signatory Laphroaig 15 Years Old Un-chillfiltered Collection refill sherry butt 3600, dist 16/3/88, bott 22/3/03 **(79) n**21 **t**20 **f**19 **b**19, Has its pretty chewy moments. But you are left feeling disappointed at the lack of overall development and complexity: a bit like lusting after the village beauty for a couple of years and, when the passionless deed is done, thinking: "Was that it... ?" **46%. 625 bottles.**

Ultimate Selection Laphroaig 1988 refill sherry butt 3598, dist 16/3/88, bott 25/3/03 **(88) n**23 clean, utterly faultless. The peat is sweet, salty and coastal;

sp malt pretty young in style, grassy for all the peat; f21 soft vanilla
the peat; b21 a cask refilled more than once on the evidence of this. Very
or its age and about the cleanest Laphroaig you'll ever find. A minor treat:
nt bottling for those trying to find every character in the Laphroaig
lity. **43%.** *Van Wees NL.*

(see Tobermory)

HGOW (see St. Magdalene)

OOD
e, 1820. Diageo. Working.

wood 12 Years Old db **(90) n**22 custard pie and crispy malt; **t**23
s: a blistering arrival of among the cleanest malt you will find,
weet and enormously chewy – any cleaner and you could wash yourself
hints of smoke keep the vanilla in check. Still the malt carries on and on
b23 this is one hell of a Speysider. Being part of the Flora and
nge, the bottle depicts a swan on the label. Nothing could have been
43%

ood Aged 26 Years Rare Malts Selection dist 75 bott, May 02 db
hints of bourbon plus lavender and tangerine, but all so very subtle; **t**22
f bourbony, start at first with sweet malt overcoming an oily wave...; **f**24
ow, does this baby take off! Not in a big way, but in the must delicate
with orange on vanilla, all spread around the palate by this amazing
ocoa and further bourbon notes go that extra yard on a seemingly
ing finale. One of the longest finishes in the whisky world! **b**22 a great
by Speyside standards especially, takes an eternity to complete each
e mouthful. **56.1%**

i Linkwood 17 Years Old cask 4592, dist 82, bott 99 **(91) n**22
hly ground malt and the deftest oak imaginable, brilliantly fresh for its
nind-blowing mouth arrival with the malt in concentrated form, then a
tion of sweet, vaguely honied notes and even something a little smoky.
e of oiliness is exemplary; **f**23 beautiful ground cocoa beans; **b**23
ou find light, grassy-style Speysiders this age: the total lack
rference is the key. A must if you can still find it. **64.2%**

dder Raw Cask Linkwood 1989 sherry butt 5624, dist Oct 89, bott
n20 **t**22 **f**20 **b**21. Solid malt, clean sherry and spicy. Blackadder with
. **nc ncf sc.**

dder Raw Cask Linkwood 1989 first-fill sherry butt 5624, dist Oct
r 03 **(84) n**20 **t**22 **f**21 **b**21. Just a little extra salt and depth on the
mparison with the earlier bottling from this cask. **59.3%. nc ncf sc.**

nkwood 1989 dist 3/10/89, bott 29/3/01 **(76) n**19 **t**20 **f**18 **b**19. A bit
lty for all the strength. **61%.** *Gordon & MacPhail.*

egends Single Cask Linkwood 1989 hogshead 3193, bott 01 **(75)**
0 **b**19. A complex and delicious dram that does its best to make up
nose. **46%. ncf.** *Liquid Gold.*

Choice Linkwood 1990 bott 03 (12 Years Old) **(79) n**18 **t**21 **f**20
y syrupy, but decent spices. **43%.** *The Vintage Malt Whisky Co.*

& MacPhail Linkwood 1954 (69) n18 vanilla and cream-coffee;
malty thrust can be felt amid the oak; **f**17 very salty and oaky; **b**18
ndays and anniversaries only. **40%**

& MacPhail Linkwood 1969 (69) n17 **t**18 **f**16 **b**18. Old, tired and
grim reaper. **40%.** *Gordon & MacPhail.*

& MacPhail Linkwood 1972 (72) n20 **t**18 **f**17 **b**17. Decent
ust a shade too heavily oaked. **40%.** *Gordon & MacPhail.*

Hart Brothers Linkwood Aged 12 Years Sherry Cask dist May 90, bott Jan 03 **(68)** n*17* t*17* f*17* b*17*. Some blenders at the distiller's parent company don't like working with their sherry casks. You can see why. Just not my type at all. **46%**

Murray McDavid Linkwood 1989 fresh sherry cask MM5117, bott 01 **(83)** n*20* t*22* f*20* b*21*. Very fruity but slightly cramped for complexity. **46%. nc ncf sc.**

Old Malt Cask Linkwood Aged 20 Years Sherry dist Jul 79, bott Apr 00 **(76)** n*17* t*21* f*19* b*19*. Some sulphur has crept in to spoil a very malty party. **50%. nc ncf.** Douglas Laing.

Old Masters Linkwood 1990 bott 01 **(72)** n*16* t*20* f*18* b*18*. Some off-notes ruin what would have been a rich dram. **59.2%.** James MacArthur.

Signatory Decanter Collection Linkwood 1987 dist 12/11/87, bott 21/11/02 cask 4132 **(84)** n*19* t*22* f*21* b*22*. A better malt than it noses being rich-textured, young and mouthwatering for its age. **43%.** 928 bottles.

Usquebaugh Society Linkwood 1988 dist 31/5/88, bott Nov 97 **(85)** n*21* clean and malty; t*22* a real beauty with a light, refreshing malty sweetness that coats the mouth; f*21* more of the same with some lazily arriving oak; b*21* everything one might expect from a decent cask of Linkwood at this age. **43%.** NL.

Whisky Galore Linkwood 1987 15-y-o (81) n*20* t*22* f*19* b*20*. A decent Speysider, biscuity and malty. **46%.** Duncan Taylor & Co.

LITTLEMILL
Lowland, 1772. Glen Catrine Now closed awaiting demolition.

Littlemill 8 Years Old db **(81)** n*20* t*20* f*21* b*20*. This malt has moved on a lot since its days as the byword for paintstripper. The malt in here is not eight but at least 13 or so and the oak absorbed into the system has had a calming and sweetening effect. Now a fruity, mouthwatering Lowlander of no little charm and finesse. A real shock to the system. **40%**

Littlemill 1964 db **(82)** n*21* t*20* f*21* b*20*. A soft-natured, bourbony chap that shows little of the manic tendencies that made this one of Scotland's most-feared malts. Talk about mellowing with age ... **40%**

Connoisseurs Choice Littlemill 1985 (86) n*22* gristy, young intense malt; t*22* beautifully sweet with ultra-clean barley dissolving on the tongue; f*20* thin but clean; b*22* I'd like this distillery to be remembered for this charming and, to be frank, unrepresentative bottling. Clean as a whistle, there is a wonderful barley grist air about the nose and palate arrival. Limited complexity and troubled even less by oak, this is a delightful little version which everybody should try and get hold of. Had its whisky always been this good the distillery would never have closed. **40%.** Gordon & MacPhail.

Dunglas (17) n*6* classic butyric (baby sick) qualities and something else besides: soapy beyond belief; t*7* malty, but the off-key oils suggest a still out of control f*0* oak fails to save an impossible situation: it might even be adding to it. The soapiness will be with you for days. I had to stop tasting for the day after this one; b*4* the stills at Littlemill often caused problems at the best of times. When they experimented with the rectifier to produce Dunglas it was as if they were trying to perfect the art of making bad whisky. This is one of the rarest whisky bottlings in the world and worth being in any collection. Buy it for the experience and to learn. But don't expect to enjoy that experience. Interestingly, and in fairness to Littlemill, I have discovered these same faults with some casks in Scotland and beyond. An educated guess is that the stillman had major problems keeping the still under control and used large chunks of soap to calm down the frothing wash. There was probably a soap shortage in the area for some months after. **46%.** Bravely bottled by The Whisky Exchange, London. (www.thewhiskyexchange.com). 102 bottles. For serious whisky devotees or people with a serious grudge against their tastebuds.

Malt Cask Littlemill Aged 35 Years dist Oct 65, bott Jan 01 **(81) n**18
0 **b**21. A hot and fruity old chap that radiates lush, sweet malt in its really
moments. **47.4%. nc ncf.** Douglas Laing.

LOMOND

nd (Southwestern), 1966. Glen Catrine. Working.

murrin 10 Years Old db **(81) n**21 **t**21 **f**19 **b**20. A sturdy, sweet and
ntly complex malt that struggles very slightly on the mildly bitter finale. **40%**
Lomond db **(80) n**20 **t**22 **f**19 **b**19. Bold, fruity start. Big, silky body
in its prime presumably by caramel. **40%.** No age mentioned but
between five and eight years.

enhead's Inchmurrin 29 Years Old dist 74, bott 03/03 **(84) n**20 **t**23
0. Lots of vanilla and tangerines amid the malt and muscovado sugar.
elicious. **54.4%**

on & MacPhail Inchmurrin 1973 **(78) n**20 **t**19 **f**20 **b**19. Curiously very
some oily old corn whiskies I used to find in the States 20 years ago. **40%**

IDE

and (Eastern), 1957–1992. Closed.

oisseurs Choice Lochside 1981 **(77) n**18 **t**21 **f**19 **b**19. Light, chalky
ty. **40%.** Gordon & MacPhail.

s' Own Selection Lochside 1981 bott 02 **(76) n**19 **t**20 **f**18 **b**19.
weet malt but lacking staying power and depth. **43%.** Berry Bros & Rudd.
on & MacPhail Lochside 1981 bott 00 **(61) n**15 **t**17 **f**14 **b**15.
isky. **40%**

ard Lochside 1981 **(85) n**21 beautiful marmalade; **t**23 fresh fruit,
atering in style, clean malt, exemplary Lochside style; **f**20 bit too much
the finish; **b**21 a lovely dram marred perhaps by too much either natural
ural caramel. **50%**

ay-McDavid Lochside 1981 cask MM 2106, dist May 81, bottled Dec
n23 **t**20 **f**19 **b**20. The nose stars and nothing quite lives up to it. Pretty
umber, nonetheless.

Malt Cask Lochside Aged 21 Years dist May 79, bott June 00 **(87)**
ly excellent oak-barley balance, big and toasty; **t**22 much sweeter than
says with the malt really whipping up a storm; **f**22 very long with an
slow build-up of oak and spice; **b**21 quality malt. **50%. nc ncf.** Douglas
06 bottles.

Malt Cask Lochside Aged 35 Years dist Dec 66, bott Jan 02 **(74)**
f18 **b**18. Hot whisky. **50%. nc ncf.** Douglas Laing. 216 bottles.

h Malt Whisky Society Cask 92.9 Aged 30 Years dist May 81,
1 **(85) n**21 bourbony with no shortage of citrus fruit and ripe banana; **t**22
urbon oakiness to the fore, sweet malts abound; **f**21 long and very well-
he oak softens out; **b**21 still mothwaterng after all these years. **61.2%**

L   ORN
S   e, 1895. Chivas. Working.

norn 15 Years Old db **(93) n**23 curiously salty and coastal for a
really beautifully structured oak but the malt offers both African violets
y sugar; **t**24 your mouth aches from the enormity of the complexity,
r tongue wipes grooves into the roof of your mouth. Just about flawless
et balance, the intensity of the malt is enormous, yet – even after 15
maintains a cut-grass Speyside character; **f**22 long, acceptably sappy
with chewy malt and oak. Just refuses to end; **b**24 this latest bottling
st yet: previous ones had shown just a little too much oak but this has
ect compromise. An all-time Speyside great. **45%**

Blackadder Raw Cask 1973 sherry cask 3974, dist 8 May 73, bott May 02 **(91) n**23 intense, thick oloroso oozes some hefty oak: a 16-ton weight in a glass; **t**24 sweet, over-ripe figs and plums sprinkled with brown sugar, nutmeg and pepper, stunningly lush and chewy; **f**22 something has to crack and the oak comes out on top; **b**22 a dram that takes no prisoners: wimpy tastebuds should stand well clear. Glorious! **56.9%. nc ncf sc.**

Cask Longmorn 1969 (92) n24 supreme sherry: ripe cherries and zesty; **t**24 magnificent: an explosion of spices, scattering with it intense malt and soft oak. Loads of natural toffee; **f**22 surprisingly light; **b**22 this is one of those give-away classics that can still be bought relatively cheaply. Find it! **61.2%.** Gordon & MacPhail.

Cask Longmorn 1973 cask 3235, dist 13/4/73, bott Jul 00 **(94) n**23 quite brilliant sherry character: perfectly spiced to counter encroaching oak; **t**24 Yes!!! A stunner: sweet sherry notes fill the mouth but the intensity of malt and spice is superb: a chewing whisky; **f**23 age makes itself felt, but elegantly so. The oak dryness is in keeping with the initial fruit intensity. The spices towards the end are nothing short of magnificent; **b**24 good old Gordon & MacPhail. Longmorn has long been one of their mainstays and here they have done each other proud. Probably the pick of the entire G&M range. **55.7%.** Gordon & MacPhail.

Gordon & MacPhail Longmorn-Glenlivet Age 12 Years (75) n18 **t**20 **f**19 **b**18. Been drinking (as opposed to tasting!) this chap regularly for some 20 years: it's normally a lot better than this. Too much age and fruit – just doesn't hang right. **40%**

Gordon & MacPhail Longmorn 25 Years Old (81) n20 **t**22 **f**19 **b**20. Fruit biscuit, with dry finish. **40%**

Gordon & MacPhail Longmorn 1970 (85) n22 salt and honey and harmony, especially with that wisp of smoke; **t**22 more honey with a lovely malt and cucumber middle (really!); **f**20 the oak kicks in with a chalky dryness; **b**21 just enough all-round weight and complexity to make into a very decent dram. **40%**

Old Malt Cask Longmorn Aged 20 Years Sherry dist Nov 81, bott Nov 01 **(87) n**21 quite molassed and rummy. Yummy! **t**22 so, so sweet: again more Caribbean than Caledonian; **f**22 very long, varying fruit and sugar flavours tempered by oak; **b**22 I shall start blending some malt with pot-still Jamaican to see if I can recreate this one. **50%. nc ncf.** Douglas Laing. 570 bottles.

Old Malt Cask Longmorn Aged 31 Years dist May 69, bott Feb 01 **(91) n**23 hefty, chunky malt captures just the right amount of oak with some citrus notes early on; **t**24 spices enter the malt-honey fray as some hidden peat reveals itself. The mouthfeel almost makes you purr; **f**22 uncomplicated vanilla and barley that dries a little; **b**22 an ambiguous quality. **45.6%. nc ncf.** Douglas Laing. 210 bottles.

Old Masters Longmorn 1967 bott 2002 **(90) n**21 exceptionally firm malt and oak softened only by grapey fruit and a vague hint of smoke; **t**23 multi-layered oak, all of the softest, most yielding character. The sweet malt can be chewed, the soft fruits offering mouthwatering complexity; **f**23 chocolate fruit and nut bar in liquid form; **b**23 this is wonderful whisky: warm it in the hand and see it come alive. **57.1%.** James MacArthur.

Peerless Longmorn 1969 cask 2948, dist May 69 **(90) n**23 rich honey and a barely perceptible stratum of menthyl. Fruity physalis stars amid the barley concentrate: beautiful; **t**22 silky and soft, the honey and fruit dovetail brilliantly. A wonderful breeze of smoke wafts elegantly through the palate, barely distracting from the busy, popping malt notes in the middle; **f**21 smoky with plenty of oaky, toasty notes to balance the sweeter malt: terrific style and balance; **b**24 a supreme old whisky from a truly great distillery. Few Speysiders show such poise, grace and complexity at this age. A must. **44.1%.** Duncan Taylor & Co Ltd.

Private Cellar Longmorn-Glenlivet 1970 bott 03 **(93) n**23 oranges and ripe physalis combine with juicy pears and malt. Some oak offers weight; **t**24 an astonishing mixture of fresh fruit and weighty, oaky depth, unusual and delicious; **f**22 spicy but wave upon wave of succulent, fruity malt; **b**24 some say there is no such thing as vintages: let's just say that in the late 60s and early 70s God smiled benevolently on Longmorn. **43%.** *Forbes Ross Co.*

Scotch Malt Whisky Society Cask 7.21 Aged 33 Years (82) n19 **t**22 **f**21 **b**20. Malty and spiced but heading south. **60.3%. nc ncf sc.**

Scott´s Selection Longmorn-Glenlivet 1971 bott 99 **(95) n**24 this is an essay in clean sherry, almost certainly oloroso. Take time here and find the subtle spices that infiltrate the Melton Mowbray-type fruitcake. High-roast Java coffee is also to be found plus a little peat smoke, tar and creosote. Sounds awful – noses like a dream; **t**24 Wow!! Hold on to your hats as you are taken on a helter-skelter ride of fruit (plum and over-ripe cherry) concentrate and a beguiling mixture of herbs, spices and salt. Loads of thick oak – you can almost feel the splinters – but completely tamed by the fruit and massive ultra-sweet malt; **f**23 amazingly long and thins by the second. The blue skies after the storm reveal fields of sweet barley and charming vanilla. Remains mouthwatering to the very end; **b**24 my indifference to over-sherried whiskies is well-documented. But if they were all like this absolute gem then you wouldn't hear a word of complaint from me. This is nothing short of stupendous. It is how every distiller dreams his whisky will taste 28 years after filling the cask ... but believes it to be impossible. A classic among classics. **57.8%.** *Robert Scott & Co.*

Whisky Galore Longmorn 1990 12-y-o (86) n21 coal-smoky; **t**23 bright, clean and a little nutty: the intensity of the malt is startling; **f**20 malty but becomes just a little bitter; **b**22 a really big Speysider. **46%.** *Duncan Taylor & Co.*

LONGROW (see Springbank)

MACALLAN
Speyside, 1824. Edrington. Working.
The Macallan 7 Years Old db **(87) n**22 beautifully clean sherry, lively, salty, gentle peppers; **t**21 mouth-filling and slightly oily. Some coffee tones intertwine with deep barley and fruit; **f**22 unravels to reveal very soft oak and lingering fruity spice; **b**22 an outstanding dram that underlines just how good young malts can be. Fun and fabulous. **40%**

The Macallan 10 Years Old db **(81) n**20 **t**21 **f**21 **b**19. Delicious, but perhaps a little too slick to allow for full complexity **40%**

The Macallan 10 Years Old Cask Strength db **(87) n**20 aggressive but beautifully clean and sweet oloroso; **t**23 outstanding sherry-barley balance with a biscuity chewiness; **f**22 long, clean sherry, molassed and silky; **b**22 everything the standard 10-y-o wants to be. Stunning, controlled aggression. **58.8%.** *Duty free.*

The Macallan 12 Years Old db **(77) n**17 **t**20 **f**21 **b**19. A slightly bitter, off-key bottling with some lingering, mouthwatering, sherry-rich moments – but usually much better than this. **40%**

The Macallan 18 Years Old 1982 db **(83) n**21 **t**20 **f**21 **b**21. An intense malt with excellent barley core. **43%**

The Macallan 18 Years Old 1983 db **(85) n**21 a thick, punchy sherried aroma of enormous weight; **t**22 fat, mouth-filling starting softly then building a caramel-biscuit middle; **f**21 lightens in body but spices evolve pleasantly; **b**21 sparkling sherry-barley on the palate. Good oils. **43%**

The Macallan 18 Years Old 1984 db **(88) n**21 controlled oak showing a hint of smoke amid the plums and apples; **t**22 beautifully sweet and intense barley and very clean fruit; **f**21 excellent sherry-barley balance; **b**24 exceptionally well-balanced, revealing some lingering youth on the barley and fruit with older, oaky notes. Impressive. **43%**

The Macallan 25 Years Old db **(80) n**20 **t**22 **f**19 **b**19. Decent, but a much thinner, oak-dominant expression than usual. The quality of this Macallan can vary dramatically. **43%**

The Macallan 30 Years Old db **(92) n**24 orange pith and oak, really charming and incredibly sexy and complex; **t**23 mouth-filling with a mixture of full fruits and beguiling spices, brilliant layer of honied barley; **f**22 slightly medium to short after the brilliance of the palate, but lovely vanilla and lingering, silky sweet malt; **b**23 a greatly improved dram than a few years back. An astounding mixture of age and beauty. **43%**

The Macallan 1841 Replica db **(83) n**21 **t**21 **f**20 **b**21. Cultured, classy, well-balanced malt, fresh with a lovely whiff of smoke. **41.7%**

The Macallan 1861 Replica db **(82) n**19 **t**21 **f**22 **b**20. The nose is a miss, the rest is bliss. A pageant of honey and spice. **42.7%**

The Macallan 1946 Select Reserve db **(93) n**25 does peat arrive any more delicately than this? The sherry, barley and oak offer perfect harmony, perfect and faultless; **t**23 teasingly mouthwatering and fruity. Crushed sultanas cruise with the peat; **f**22 the oak makes inroads at the expense of the barley. Remains chewy and tantalisingly smoky, though; **b**23 I have never found a finer nose to any whisky. Once-in-a-lifetime whisky. **40%**

The Macallan 1948 Select Reserve db **(75) n**22 **t**19 **f**17 **b**17. What a fabulous nose! Sadly the package trails behind the '46. **40%**

The Macallan 1972 29 Years Old cask 4043, bott 02 db **(93) n**25 well, it has to be said: a quite faultless nose. The spices are entirely in true with the perfect sherry-oak balance. This is big stuff, but perfectly proportioned: it almost seems a shame to drink it...; **t**24 stupendous spice-plum-giant-boiled-Italian-tomato: enormous with a waft of smoke through the middle; **f**21 slightly bitter as the oak nibbles but still lots of complexity; **b**23 the sherry butt used for this was a classic: the intensity of the whisky memorable. If, as Macallan claim, the sherry accounts for only 5% of the flavour, I'd like to know what happened to the other 95.... **58.4%**

The Macallan Distillers Choice db **(80) n**21 **t**22 **f**18 **b**19. Seems like young stuff, lively, mouthwatering and good, clean sherry influence. Something wild, raw and different amongst Macallans. Great fun.

The Macallan Cask Strength **(78) n**18 **t**21 **f**20 **b**19. A straight-up-and-down malt with few surprises. **58.6%**. *USA*.

The Macallan Gran Reserva 1981 db **(90) n**23 fully ripe wild cherries, a thin stratum of smoke, luxuriant grape plus barley, spice and oak. Pretty damn good! **t**22 succulent, mouthwatering grape and barley with a lovely rumble of deeper oak and smoke; **f**22 long, oaky, toast and marmalade; **b**23 Macallan in a nutshell. Brilliant. But could do with being at 46% for full effect. **40%**

The Macallan Gran Reserva 1982 db **(82) n**21 **t**22 **f**20 **b**19. Big, clean, sweet sherry influence from first to last but doesn't open up and sing like the '81 vintage. **40%**

The Macallan Elegancia 1990 db **(70) n**16 **t**19 **f**17 **b**18. Struggles to get past the sulphur. Ironic, considering this is the only Macallan bottled by the distillery that contains bourbon as well as sherry casks. **40%**

The Macallan ESC IV 1990 cask 24690 db **(95) n**24 the cleanest sherry cask you can find: spices intermingle with crisp barley and cut-glass grape: extraordinary; **t**24 the tastebuds are completely over-run by an intense infusion of salivating barley and succulent fruit with some spice and a hint of peat to round off the show; **f**23 hints of cocoa as the curtain comes down on an almost unbelievable choreography of bitter-sweet dexterity. The oak, though present, plays the perfect background role; **b**24. What can you say? These notes are just a sketch of something that words cannot adequately describe. ESC stands for Extra Special Cask. They are not kidding. For this, unquestionably, is the greatest Macallan of them all. Not an off-note. No domination by any character in the drama. Not too sweet. Not too dry. Not too smooth. Savour at full strength. Do not add water. Do not add ice. Just drink something that approaches an absolutely perfect whisky. **57.2%**

The Macallan Millenium 50 Years Old (1949) decanter db **(90)** n23 toffee and sherry hand in hand, alongside ripe apples and grape: sweet and sexy; t22 mouth-filling and malt, sandwiched by some fine and extremely clean sherry notes and intense oak; f22 lingering oloroso and liquorice, good age but light enough for the malt, spice and smoke to appear; b23 magnificent finesse and charm despite some big oak makes this a Macallan to die for. **40%**

The Macallan Travel 1920s db **(67)** n17 t18 f15 b17. Does absolutely nothing for me at all. Totally off-key, no finish. Nothing roaring about this one. **40%**

The Macallan Travel 1930s db **(91)** n22 beautiful peat and sherry combo; t23 the cleanest, most mouthwatering sherry you could pray for; f23 soft vanilla and lingering, lazy smoke; b23 an essay in complexity and balance. Clean sherry at its finest. You little darling! **40%**

The Macallan Travel 1940s db **(81)** n21 t22 f17 b21. Lovely smoke and complexity, but let down by the sherry and a faltering finish. **40%**

The Macallan Travel 1950s db **(92)** n24 intense, immaculate sherry and blood orange with playful spices adding nose prickle; t22 massive but voluptuous sherry, then a wave of malt concentrate; f23 more barley, a touch of smoke and then juicy sultanas and lingering spice; b23 sit back, take a deep, mouth-filling draught, close your eyes and listen to Hogie Carmichael's "Stardust", for this is just what this whisky is. **40%**

Adelphi Macallan 12 Years Old **(83)** n20 t22 f21 b20. An unusually honied and sweet Macallan, almost malt syrup, with no sherry influence whatsoever considering it is from bourbon cask. But plenty of spices to go round. **57.4%**. For Michael Skurnik Wines New York.

Adelphi Macallan 12 Years Old dist 88, bott 00 **(66)** n15 t19 f16 b16. Ooops. Sul-phar, sul-bad. Least said the better. **57.5%**

"As We Get It" Macallan-Glenlivet dist 90, bott 02 **(80)** n18 t22 f20 b20. Unusually sweet Macallan: tastes and finishes a lot better than it noses. **55.6%**. Kirsch-Import Skye.

Blackadder Raw Cask Macallan 1990 bourbon hogshead 1051 dist 23, Jan 90 bott Apr 03 **(79)** n20 t21 f19 b19. Sweet and malty. **55%**

Cadenhead's Macallan-Glenlivet 12 Years Old dist 89, bott 10/01 **(73)** n17 t20 f18 b18. Blemished by sulphur, though from the colour doesn't look like a sherry cask bottling. Strange! Decent malt middle. **46%**

Coopers Choice Macallan 1988 bott 01 (12 Years Old) **(86)** n20 clean, intense sherry, a spice prickle and a vague waft of smoke; t22 big, salty and fruit intense with an immediate arrival of zingy spice; f22 a more even fruitcake follow-through. Lots of chewing to do; b22 a big, lumbering malt, sometimes a little off-balance yet somehow completes the job it set out to do: entertain. **55.5%**. The Vintage Malt Whisky Co.

Hart Brothers Macallan Aged 12 Years Sherry Cask dist Jun 90, bott Feb 03 **(75)** n18 t20 f18 b19. Brilliant mouth entry but a hint of something sulphury undermines the dram. **46%**

Murray McDavid Macallan-Glenlivet 1974 cask MM 6024, fresh sherry wood, dist Dec 74, bott Nov 96 **(92)** n24 lots of marmalade and vanilla with a dab of smoke. Stick your nose in this for half an hour; t23 a kaleidoscope of dovetailing spice and honey notes with rich, grapey sherry tossed in: massive; f22 more subtle oak and some smoke; b23 a minor classic among independently bottled Macallans, bottles of which can still be found, I hear. **46%**

Murray McDavid Macallan 1990 cask MM 10242, fresh sherry, dist Dec 90, bott March 01 **(85)** n*19* the Achilles heel: decent toffee but green and a slight, heavily-disguised off-note; t*23* now it comes alive with magnificent intensity on the palate: just about perfect mouthfeel incorporates stunning barley brilliance with an oily, sherry, mildly smoky background; f*21* lots of vanilla and decent depth; b*22* if it wasn't for the nose, this would be right up there. **46%. ncf nc.**

Old Masters Macallan 1979 Cask Strength Selection bott 2001 **(82)** n*21* t*22* f*20* b*19*. Without a sherry shield, the oak is slightly dominant. But some lovely, honey-sweet charm. **55.5%.** *James MacArthur.*

Peerless Macallan 1967 cask 7678, dist Sep 67 35-y-o **(89)** n*22* quite dry for all the spice, malt and honey; t*23* massively intense and rich with a sublime chocolate-lime and rich copper-estery middle; f*22* pretty long with the malt expanding in every direction; b*22* a brilliant non-sherried Macallan of a very rare richness. **45.1%.** *Duncan Taylor & Co.*

Peerless Macallan 1969 cask 5390, dist May 69 33-y-o **(75)** n*20* t*19* f*18* b*18*. Malty and soufflé light. **40.3%.** *Duncan Taylor & Co.*

Private Cellar Macallan 1971 bott Feb 03 **(79)** n*20* t*21* f*19* b*19*. A very odd whisky; almost green with being under-ripe. There is a stunning malt surge early on in the palate but while generally pleasant something doesn't shape up right. **43%.** *Forbes Ross Co.*

Provenance Summer Distillation Macallan Over 10 Years dist Summer 1990, bott Winter 2001 **(75)** n*17* t*19* f*20* b*19*. Very slightly flawed nose; brilliant recovering finish. **43%.** *Douglas McGibbon & Co.*

Scott's Selection Macallan 1973 bott 99 **(85)** n*23* suet pudding and sultanas plus a touch of allspice, even a hint of something vaguely smoky. Tangy, fruity, malty and fabulously complex; t*23* an all-embracing arrival of concentrated malty notes carries rich acacia honey and cocoa, with holes punched through it by hot, piercing spices; f*19* perhaps just a little too oak-dominated, drying too briskly and comprehensively; b*20* forget the finish: just enjoy the unfettered brilliance of its arrival on the palate. One of the most honied Macallans around, enjoying its freedom from sherry. **50.9%.** *Robert Scott & Co.*

Single Barrel Collection Macallan 1989 cask 18072, dist Oct 89, bott 01 **(74)** n*18* t*19* f*18* b*19*. A Macallan shorn of its sherried skin that is much lighter than the norm from ex-bourbon cask and one never ascending great heights. **58.14%. nc ncf sc.** *Germany.*

Speymalt from Macallan 1966 (92) n*24* pantheon of oak, but still displays lovely, soft peat and cracking barley: dreamy; t*23* silky oak and then a build-up of burnt honeycomb and smoke; f*22* softer vanillas and lingering barley; b*23* an absolutely outstanding bottling from the Speyside specialists. **40%.** *Gordon & MacPhail.*

Speymalt from Macallan 1978 (79) n*22* t*20* f*19* b*18*. Lovely butterscotch nose, but a shade too dry and oaked. **40%.** *Gordon & MacPhail.*

Speymalt from Macallan 1990 (76) n*17* t*20* f*20* b*19*. A big Speysider, but some sulphur notes spoil it. **40%.** *Gordon & MacPhail.*

Speymalt from Macallan 1994 (88) n*24* too beautifully honied to be true; t*22* clean-cut sweet barley and simple vanillas; f*21* long, deftly oaked and big, clean barley; b*21* little sherry evidence. Worth getting for the nose alone. **40%.** *Gordon and MacPhail.*

Whisky Galore Macallan 1989 40% **(58)** n*17* t*15* f*13* b*13*. One of the most boring Macallans I have happened across in over 25 years. I hope someone didn't just add caramel to make up for the lack of sherry. **40%.** *Duncan Taylor & Co.*

Whisky Galore Macallan 1989 46% **(71)** n*17* t*18* f*18* b*18*. Big improvement on the earlier, coloured version. But still unimpressive. **46%.** *Duncan Taylor & Co.*

MACDUFF
Speyside, 1963. Dewar's. Working

Glen Deveron Aged 10 Years dist 1992 db **(72)** n*19* t*18* f*17* **b***18*. A peculiar, oily, softly smoked nose of a hot-running model train engine, but like the remainder of the malt off-key and altogether odd. **40%**

Glen Deveron Aged 12 Years dist 1984 db **(86)** n*21* rich, biscuity malt, well-balanced; t*21* really big barley which sweetens; f*22* softest wisps of honey on vanilla; **b***22* a clean absolutely delicious malt that is honied but never overly sweet. **40%**

Coinnoisseurs Choice Macduff 1980 **(83)** n*20* t*23* f*21* **b***19*. A pot of light honey: quintessential Macduff – make a bee-line for it. **40%**. *Gordon & MacPhail.*

Connoisseurs Choice Macduff 1988 **(79)** n*19* t*21* f*19* **b***20*. Honied and charming, but a little thin for a usual MacDuff. **40%**

Peerless Macduff 1969 cask 3672, dist Apr 69 33-y-o **(78)** n*19* t*21* f*19* **b***19*. Sweet, a touch oily but rich. **40.3%**. *Duncan Taylor & Co.*

Platinum Old and Rare Macduff 36 Years old **(84)** n*23* t*22* f*18* **b***21*. Forget the exhausted finale. With a whisky of such improbable age, that is forgivable. The nose and arrival on the palate are moments to genuinely savour. **49.2%**. *From Douglas Laing and Co.*

MANNOCHMORE
Speyside, 1971. Diageo. Working.

Mannochmore Aged 12 Years db **(84)** n*22* t*21* f*20* **b***21*. As usual the mouth arrival fails to live up to the great nose. Quite a greasy dram with sweet malt and bitter oak. **43%**. *Flora and Fauna.*

Mannochmore 22 Years Old Rare Malts Selection db dist 74 **(87)** n*22* hazelnut and malt; t*22* silky oils offer a superb richness to the malt; f*21* vanilla kicks in, sweetens and becomes quite chewy with late cocoa; **b***22* lively, warming dram with a big malt character. **60.1%**

Connoisseurs Choice Mannochmore 1984 **(79)** n*22* t*20* f*18* **b***19*. What a tragedy the flat palate no way matches the fruity exuberance of the nose. **40%**. *Gordon & MacPhail.*

Old Masters Mannochmore 1990 bott 01 **(86)** n*22* malt-oak and spice: complex; t*22* mouth-filling, nippy, textbook ultra-malty Speyside style; f*21* some burnt honeycomb; **b***21* honeycomb malt with attitude. Delicious. **59.8%**. *James MacArthur.*

MILLBURN
Highland (Northern), 1807–1985. Closed.

Connoisseurs Choice Millburn 1972 **(80)** n*20* t*22* f*18* **b***20* A hint of something sulphury on the nose is adequately countered by peat. It's a gentle, malty chew, though. **40%**

Connoisseurs Choice Millburn 1976 **(75)** n*21* t*20* f*18* **b***16*. Pleasant, but lacks direction or depth. **40%**. *Gordon & MacPhail.*

Gordon & MacPhail Millburn 1978 cask 3166, cask dist 9/8/78, bott June 97 **(83)** n*20* t*22* f*21* **b***20*. Silky, ultra-sweet and malty. **65.6%**

The Old Malt Cask Millburn Aged 34 Years dist Nov 67, bott Dec 01 **(94)** n*23* clean sherry mingles with cherry-tomatoes. Fabulously deft spices are a triumphant fanfare to controlled oakiness: big, muscular and superbly balanced, almost too complex to be true! t*23* the sherry influence from the very outset is a triumph. Meticulously clean and a touch smoky, the richness is subtle and understated. Sweet and chewy at first like a raisin-fruit biscuit, then the spices arrive to add peppery intrigue. The silkiness on the palate is touching perfection. Truly superb! f*24* long and spicy, the malt makes a belated entrance only when the intensity of oak and sherry fades. Some cocoa and medium-roast coffee and even a hint of peat ignite at the finish. Very sweet vanilla has the final word; **b***24*

What a way for this long-lost distillery to be remembered! One of the finest sherry-cask bottlings you will ever find, this casts a shadow over the quality of present sherry butts. Though Millburn`s character has been lost somewhat amid the splendour of the wood, it still had to have sufficient depth to add to the complexity and balance, both of which are near faultless. One of the whiskies of a lifetime, just buy and savour it if you ever see it around. **50%.** *Douglas Laing. 552 bottles.*

Signatory Silent Stills Millburn 20 Years Old sherry butt 3632A, dist 11/12/80, bott 7/3/01 **(77) n**17 **t**22 **f**19 **b**19. Disappointing, sulphur-tainted sherry but it does hit a delicious, though short-lived high on the palate. **58.7%.** *240 bottles.*

The Whisky Shop Millburn 1976 **(89) n**23 heather-honey with a hint of spice ... is it HP in disguise? Reassuring oak for the age; **t**23 dense malt that is wonderfully rich and chewy accompanied by some pretty busy spices; **f**21 the oak is more confident and towards the end becomes a little loud. But the malt retains its shape to add to the cream-toffee effect; **b**22 lost distilleries like these don't die: they just fade on the palate. **58.9%.** *The Whisky Shop, Scotland. 276 bottles.*

MILTONDUFF
Speyside, 1824. Allied. Working.

Gordon & MacPhail Miltonduff 10 Years Old **(73) n**19 **t**21 **f**16 **b**17. A steady, rich middleweight but a slack finish. **40%**

Gordon & MacPhail Miltonduff 1968 **(79) n**20 **t**21 **f**19 **b**19. A bit sappy and dry for all the fruit. **40%**

Hart Brothers Miltonduff 10 Years Old **(73) n**16 **t**21 **f**17 **b**19. Good spice and a hint of honey but slightly cask tainted. **40%**

Peerless Miltonduff 1966 cask 1014, dist Feb 66 36-y-o **(83) n**21 **t**20 **f**21 **b**21. The Speyside character remains intact on the nose, amazingly for its age. Dies on entry but resurfaces later with some splendid malt-oak complexity and spice. **42.7%.** *Duncan Taylor & Co.*

Single Barrel Collection Miltonduff 1989 bott 01 **(74) n**17 **t**20 **f**18 **b**19. Not a dram for the faint- – or feint – hearted. Big, bustling stuff that for all its obvious flaws offers massive compensation when sampled at full strength. **65.28%. nc ncf sc.** *Germany.*

Ultimate Selection Miltonduff 1989 bourbon barrel 67180, dist 3/9/89, bott 28/11/02 **(76) n**19 **t**21 **f**17 **b**19. The fresh, malty intensity is up front. **43%.** *Van Wees NL.*

MORTLACH
Speyside, 1824. Diageo. Working.

Mortlach Aged 16 Years db **(87) n**20 big, big sherry, but not exactly without a blemish or two; **t**23 sumptuous fruit and then a really outstanding malt and melon mouthwatering rush; **f**22 returns to heavier duty with a touch of spice, too; **b**22 once it gets past the bold if very mildly sulphured nose, the rest of the journey is superb. Earlier Mortlachs in this range had a slightly unclean feel to them and the nose here doesn't inspire confidence. But from arrival on the palate onwards, it's sure-footed, fruity and even refreshing ... and always delicious. **43%.** *Flora and Fauna range.*

Mortlach 1980 Limited Bottling bott 97 db **(66) n**16 **t**18 **f**16 **b**16. A sulphur-ridden disaster. A bit like the hilarious tasting notes on the bottle. **63.1%**

Adelphi Mortlach 13 Years Old **(83) n**19 **t**23 **f**20 **b**21. A big whisky with ripe cherries with the massive malt middle. Toffeed finish.

Adelphi Mortlach 19 Years Old cask 2166, dist 1980, bott 99 **(74) n**20 **t**20 **f**17 **b**17. Should come complete with fire extinguisher.... **59.3%. sc.**

Adelphi Mortlach 1990 **(86) n**23 supreme sherry, clean and faultless enough, but maybe needs more input from the malt; **t**22 hot and spicy with enormous sherry bite, sweet, fruity middle; **f**21 some toffee and oak with some late malt; **b**20 delicious but could be integrated better.

Blackadder Raw Cask Mortlach 1989 sherry butt 5149, dist Oct 89, bott Apr 02 **(73) n**16 **t**18 **f**21 **b**18. Big, juicy-sweet and fruity, but tainted by sulphur. **59.4%. nc ncf sc.**

Blackadder Raw Cask Mortlach 1989 first-fill sherry butt 5149, dist Oct 89, bott Mar 03 **(74) n**17 **t**18 **f**20 **b**19. Still slightly sulphured but a little more comfortable. **59.9%. nc ncf sc.**

Chieftain's Choice Mortlach Aged 10 Years dist 1988 **(79) n**21 **t**21 **f**18 **b**19. Starts well but falters. **43%**

Coopers Choice Mortlach 1989 first-fill sherry, bott 00 **(77) n**20 **t**21 **f**18 **b**18. Never quite gets out of bed, for all the sherry. **43%. nc sc.**

Coopers Choice Mortlach 1989 sherry ask bott 02 (aged 12 Years) **(79) n**20 **t**21 **f**19 **b**19. A sweeter version of a previous Coopers Choice Mortlach, with plenty of attractive tones, including a touch of peat, but none that quicken the pulse. **43%.** *The Vintage Malt Whisky Co.*

Gordon & MacPhail Mortlach 1954 (78) n20 very soft, gentle toffee apple; **t**20 the oak chokes the barley slightly but enough juice makes its way through; **f**18 big oak, but just enough sweetness to see out the balance, good late spice; **b**20 survived the oak attack well – enough character to enjoy on a cold night

Gordon & MacPhail Mortlach 1959 (82) n22 deep, sweet oak to the point of bourbon: lovely, though; **t**20 trademark, mildly honied bourbon style with some malt arriving in the vanilla middle; **f**21 surprisingly graceful and soft; **b**19 what it lacks in complexity it makes up for in effortless charm. **40%**

Gordon & MacPhail Mortlach 1980 Cask Strength (90) n23 glorious mix of raisins and spice, penetrating oak, but beautifully balanced; **t**23 a massive outbreak of mouthwatering fruit with undertones of the softest peat, liquorice and honey; **f**22 medium to long with some cocoa amid lingering, silky malt; **b**22 sit back, close your eyes and bask in sheer beauty. **63.8%**

Gordon & MacPhail Mortlach 15 Years Old (79) n21 **t** 23 **f**16 **b**19. The stupendously sweet and complex taste is failed by the blandest of finishes. **40%**

Hart Brothers Mortlach Aged 12 Years dist May 90, bott Jan 03 **(69) n**15 **t**18 **f**18 **b**18. United Distiller's sherry wood policy of the early 90s leaves a little to be desired. **46%**

James MacArthur's Mortlach 1989 (87) n22 oily, fat malt, clean and intense with a sweet development; **t**22 chewy, intense malt; **f**22 a welcome arrival of some spicy notes as the malt clings to the roof of the mouth; **b**21 forget about complexity: this is like alcoholic malt extract. **43%**

Lombard Mortlach 1990 (83) n20 **t**23 **f**20 **b**20. Astonishing degree of malt throughout with a very sweet edge. Not much complexity, but a superb ride. **50%**

Milroys Mortlach Over 12 Years Old dist 88, bott 00 **(71) n**15 **t**18 **f**19 **b**19. A whisky that improves the further it travels from the sulphured nose and early mouth arrival. **43%.** *UK.*

Murray McDavid Mortlach 1989 dist Aug 89, bott 01 **(73) n**13 **t**19 **f**23 **b**18. A moody and magnificent finale works heroically to make up for earlier failings. Just try and ignore the sulphur-ruined nose: it is worth tasting just for the fabulous finish alone. **46%. nc ncf sc.**

The Old Malt Cask Mortlach Aged 10 Years dist Nov 90 **(74) n**17 **t**21 **f**18 **b**18. Green and barley-rich. **50%**

Old Masters Mortlach 14 Year Old (85) n22 sheer joy! A delicate array of oak and barley; **t**22 barley-rich, green for its age and mouthwatering, lovely spices and a hint of honey; **f**20 soft oak that dries slowly; **b**21 an attractive expression of Mortlach at this age. **43%.** *James MacArthur.*

Old Masters Mortlach 1990 (87) n21 lovely signs of sherry influence: deep, clean and spiced; **t**23 incredible arrival of intense young barley and succulent grape. The tastebuds are almost overwhelmed; f21 dissipates quickly to leave a warming, fruity, oaky finish; **b**22 excellent.

Usquebaugh Society Mortlach 1988 dist 26/5/88, bott 6/98 **(75)** n18 t20 f19 b18. Rich middle. **43%.** NL.

The Wee Dram Mortlach Aged 12 Years (77) matured in a sherry butt n17 t21 f20 b19. Fresh, grassy middle for all the sherry. Lovely spice and sweetness. **43%.** *Exclusive to The Wee Dram, Bakewell, UK.*

Whisky Galore Mortlach 1990 40% (60) n18 t18 f13 b11. Grinds to a halt with caramel digging deep. Dull as ditchwater **40%.** *Duncan Taylor & Co Ltd.*

Whisky Galore Mortlach 1990 46% (84) n21 t21 f21 b21. Good grief! Same brand name, same distillery and year ... yet. If this is not proof enough of what damage caramel does to a whisky, nothing is. This is fresh, light, mouthwatering – the unfettered essence of Speyside. Even some smoke on the finish. A little treat. **46%.** *Duncan Taylor & Co.*

MOSSTOWIE
Speyside, 1964–1981. Two Lomond stills located within Miltonduff Distillery. Now dismantled.

Connoisseurs Choice Mosstowie 1975 (85) n22 fat and fruity, surprisingly clean and malty in style despite the body; t21 spicy from the off then a flowering of varied malty tones; f20 very light for Mosstowie wth the malt dominating; **b**22 a busy dram with massive malt influence. **40%**

Connoisseurs Choice Mosstowie 1979 (86) n20 oily enough to fry chips in, malty and sweet, too, with surprisingly little oak restraint; t23 still unbelievably fat and malt-rich after all these years: few whiskies boast such a shimmering, intense maltiness as this. What a joy! f22 buttery yet remains sweet and clean; **b**21 not the most complex of drams, but the weight of the malt is amazing: not entirely unlike an old-fashioned Scottish heavy ale but in sweeter form.

NORTH PORT
Highland (Eastern), 1820–1983. Demolished.

Adelphi Brechin 24 Years Old cask 3897, dist 76, bott 00 **(83)** n22 t21 f20 b20. The nose doesn't warn you about the firewater about to come, but experience should have. This takes me back to when it was a young make incinerating my youthful tastebuds. Still has some malty, sweet moments. **60.4%**

Connoisseurs Choice North Port-Brechin 1974 (84) n19 t21 f23 b21. A seriously good dram, about as clean as you are likely to find from this distillery. Just gets better as it stays on the palate, thanks to some fruit pudding and peaty ingredients. One to find. **40%**

Connoisseurs Choice North Port-Brechin 1981 (74) n18 t19 f19 b18. Gristy, oaty. **40%.** *Gordon & MacPhail.*

Old Malt Cask North Port Aged 35 Years dist Mar 66, bott Jul 01 **(84)** n21 t20 f22 b21. Lots of marmalade and oak. Deliciously chewy, with some smoke thrown in for extra ballast. **50%. nc ncf sc.** *Douglas Laing. 186 bottles.*

Old Malt Cask North Port Aged 36 Years (75) n19 t21 f19 b16. Big sherry number with powerful palate presence but never quite gets into balance. **50%.** *Douglas Laing.*

OBAN
Highland (Western), 1794. Diageo. Working.

Oban 14 db **(84)** n20 t22 f21 b21. Slick and fruity, you can close your eyes and think of Jerez. Oban seems a long way away. A very decent dram, I grant you. But I want my old, bracing, mildly smoky, fruitless Oban back!! Those who prefer malts with a sheen, sweet and with enormous fruit depth won't be disappointed. **43%**

Oban The Distillers Edition Double Matured 1987 bott 02, montillo mino finish, db **(80)** n*22* t*20* f*18* **b**20. Dry despite the apricot and tinned tangerine edge on the nose; the body seems frustratingly flat, especially on the finish. Pleasant in parts but disappointing overall. **43%**

Oban Bicentenary Manager's Dram 16 Years Old 1794–1994 db **(93)** n*24* oloroso at its finest: fruit and a slight hint of peat but the malt remains enormous; **t***23* an explosion of spices: the grapey fruit leads the way but the malt remains steadfast and crunchy; **f***23* smoky, sherried and late, late malt; **b***23* when you get a distillery manager, such as Ian Williams, so in touch with the distillery in which he worked, there is little surprise that he comes up with something quite as enormous and enriching as this. Massive and magnificent: a true collector's dram not to sit on a shelf but to be savoured in the glass. **64%**

PITTYVAICH
Speyside 1975–1993. Closed.

Pittyvaich Aged 12 Years (new stock circa 99 – no bottling mark, light brown print) db **(70)** n*17* t*20* f*16* **b***17*. The nose is scuffed in classic neighbouring Dufftown distillery style, but the simmering malts are kept in check by the same brute forces. Grim going. **43%**. *Flora and Fauna range.*

Pittyvaich Aged 12 Years (new stock circa 03 – bottling number L19R01941144, dark brown print) db **(84)** n*22* t*21* f*20* **b***21*. For a dram that will tear your throat out as soon as look at you, this has been tempered dramatically by the use of some exceptionally clean sherry casks which show to their best on the nose. Pittyvaich in a form I thought I'd never see it in my lifetime ... drinkable! And deliciously so. **43%**. *Flora and Fauna range.*

PORT ELLEN
Islay, 1825–1983. Closed.

Port Ellen Aged 20 Years Rare Malts Collection dist 78 db **(89)** n*22* a crisp, lively nose with gentle spice to the peat-reek, salty and nutty, chunky iodine, ripe pears; **t***23* explosive stuff with heavy, chewy peat, nothing like as complex as the nose but the vanilla does offer a calming diversion; **f***22* good age with intense vanilla lingering on a higher layer than the deeper yet sweeter peat; **b***22* a big whisky that has successfully withstood the test of time. Top rate and memorable. **60.9%**

Port Ellen Aged 24 Years Distilled 1978 second year release db **(86)** n*21* light, floral, smoked kippers; **t***23* explosive, sweet peat and chewable until your tongue drops off; **f***22* delicate, subtle and suave; **b***20* a really fine malt, though not if you have a sweet tooth. **59.3%**

Adelphi Port Ellen 24 Years Old cask 1765, dist 75, bott 99 **(94)** n*23* rolls back the years: young, pastel-shaded and gristy; **t***24* you really can't ask for more than this: the integrity of the malt is unblemished, the peat soft and alluring in the unique Port Ellen manner: liquid grist; **f***23* slightly drier as some oak apologetically makes an entrance but the peat merges into cocoa; **b***24* a must-buy malt. Despite the age of the whisky, it acts very much like a Port Ellen of half those years. One of the all-time Adelphi – and Port Ellen – greats. **56%**

Cask Port Ellen 1980 casks 5090, 5101–4, dist 19/11/80, bott Jun 96 **(95)** n*24* fresh malt and lively, gristy peat; **t***24* the sweetest, most intense bottled Port Ellen of all time. The malt arrives in many layers, each one offering a degree of unique complexity; **f***23* enormously long with the peat burning off and leaving fresh, sweet malt. The oak is there but no more than adjudicates; **b***24* a Port Ellen that is more like a 12-y-o than the 16 you must ransack every wine and spirit merchants to find. A piece of Port Ellen folklore. For me the greatest Port Ellen bottling of all time, eclipsing even the Adelphi offering. A Gordon and MacPhail legend. **63.9%**. *Gordon & MacPhail.*

Connoisseurs Choice Port Ellen 1980 (88) n24 just so gristy, you could eat it. Allow to warm in glass, unwatered, for maximum effect; **t**22 sweet and uncomplicated: soft malted peat; **f**21some vanilla gets a toe-hold but the peat remains at two levels: calm yet increasingly spicy; **b**21 a gentle giant, bottled in the 90s when still relatively youthful. **40%.** *Gordon & MacPhail.*

Connoisseurs Choice Port Ellen 1982 (90) n23 totally classic, clean, smoky grist, uniquely Port Ellen; **t**23 melt-in-the-mouth peat that allows in just enough oak for balance; **f**22 sweet with lingering gristy barley; **b**22 if anyone asked me to describe Port Ellen, I would hold up this bottle and say: "It tastes exactly like this." Truly classic and representative of how it was at its peak as a 12-year-old. Time has stood still. Spooky. **40%.** *Gordon & MacPhail.*

Islay Whisky Shop Port Ellen 18 Years Old dist 1982 **(91) n**23 a really raw medium betwixt massive peat and rich sherry: big and boisterous; **t**24 a fantastic arrival of peat dovetails with the cleanest sherry available. This is the stuff of dreams; **f**22 hard and uncompromising malt with equally big peat; **b**22 if you are ever on the Isle of Islay, you have only yourself to blame for not grabbing a bottle of something very different and absolutely superb. **50%.** *Islay UK.*

Old Malt Cask Port Ellen Aged 18 Years (sherry) dist Sep 82, bott Aug 01 **(82) n**22 **t**22 **f**18 **b**20. Very salty with the sherry outweighing the peat. **50%. nc ncf.** *Douglas Laing. 777 bottles.*

Old Malt Cask Port Ellen Aged 18 Years cask 2740, dist Nov 82, **(85) n**22 clean sherry, coffee but little peat; **t**22 silky grape notes, big malt middle; **f**21 more ripe plums; **b**20 delicious Port Ellen but curious because the peat has all but vanished under the weight of the sherry. **50%. nc ncf.** *Douglas Laing.*

Old Malt Cask Port Ellen Aged 19 Years (sherry) dist Feb 82, bott Sep 01 **(77) n**20 **t**20 **f**18 **b**19. 50% The nose has a curious, though not entirely unattractive, coal-dust effect. The remainder is central heating. **50%. nc ncf.** *Douglas Laing. 720 bottles.*

Old Malt Cask Port Ellen Aged 21 Years (sherry) dist Sep 79, bott Feb 01 **(87) n**22 sherry and peat that works together. Hurrah! **t**22 pounding, gutsy peat floating in a sea of ripe grapes; **f**21 the oak says hullo after the massive peat-malt-sherry orgy; **b**22 big whisky: pure fun. **50%.** *Douglas Laing. 546 bottles.*

Old Malt Cask Port Ellen Aged 21 Years dist Jan 79, bott Jul 00 **(79) n**23 **t**21 **f**17 **b**18. Very peculiar: very bitty-flavoured with a winey finish. Do not drink cold. The gristy nose, though, is extraordinary. **50%. nc ncf.** *Douglas Laing. 336 bottles.*

Old Malt Cask Port Ellen Aged 22 Years dist Mar 78, bott Feb 01 **(82) n**21 **t**21 **f**20 **b**20. Fruity malt and subdued peat. **50%. nc ncf.** *Douglas Laing. 352 bottles.*

Old Malt Cask Port Ellen Aged 23 Years Sherry Finished dist Jan 78, bott Sep 01 Years **(68) n**16 **t**19 **f**17 **b**16. Massive peat but spoiled by sulphur from six months in sherry cask. A shame. **50%. nc ncf.** *Douglas Laing. 764 bottles.*

Old Malt Cask Port Ellen Aged 25 Years bott Mar 76, bott Apr 01 **(82) n**22 **t**22 **f**18 **b**20. Salty and peaty and delicious, but a little unsympathetic oak. **50%. nc ncf.** *Douglas Laing. 522 bottles.*

Provenance Winter Distillation Port Ellen Over 18 Years dist Winter 81, bott Spring 00 **(81) n**20 **t**21 **f**20 **b**20. This is Port Ellen, reader, but not as we know it. Not the very best sherry butt ever to be delivered to the island, but one with enough about it to ensure complexity and not a little intrigue. **43%. nc ncf.** *Douglas McGibbon & Co.*

Scott's Selection Port Ellen 1981 bott 00 **(80) n**19 **t**21 **f**20 **b**20. This must have started as an only fairly peated Port Ellen and age has softened it further still. Even so, chewy and attractive stuff, though maybe a little world-weary at times. **56.3%.** *Robert Scott & Co.*

Scott's Selection Port Ellen 1982 bott May 03 **(90)** n22 massive peat with soft fruits to calm it down slightly; one of the bigger Port Ellen noses in recent years; t23 the enormity of the peat-reek translates directly onto the massively spiced palate: quite dry and chewy for its type; f23 some gristy malt offers a soothing sweetness before deep, sensual oak intervenes; b22 go for it folks: this will be among the last bottlings of Port Ellen in this kind of mega and irresistible form. **56.5%.** *Robert Scott & Co.*

Signatory Port Ellen 23 Years Old Cask Strength sherry butt 464, dist 5/9/78, bott 18/2/02 **(85)** n23 a ravishing nose: the cleanest sherry mixed with some punchy peat; t21 starts brilliantly with a thick wave of spicy peat then starts to go all toffee-fied: odd; f20 more vaguely faint peat with lots of toffee; b21 comes out the blocks like a champ but limps lamely to the finish. **60.9%.** 464 bottles.

Signatory Port Ellen 1979 dist 28 Aug 79, bott 5 Mar 02 **(76)** n21 t19 f18 b18. The peat is striking on the nose but wear and tear takes its toll as the experience continues. **43%**

Signatory Silent Stills Port Ellen 1979 sherry refill butt 6792, dist 16/11/79, bott 9/11/02 **(87)** n20 pretty crisp peat even now, quite kippery; t22 a bit of the rough stuff early on then settles towards melt-in-the-mouth gristy malt; f23 here it comes into its own as the sweet peat heads towards liquorice and vanilla: highly complex; b22 a very decent Port Ellen that shows some of its youth in old age. **50.3%.** *Switzerland.* 518 bottles.

The Whisky Shop Port Ellen 1978 **(93)** n25 very young and fresh for its age, the famous Port Ellen grist is back, outrageously beautiful: for Port Ellen, perfection; t23 sweet peated malt, very light in style with lovely early vanilla balance; f23 typically simplistic, clean.and peaty; b22 this doesn't blow your mind like an Ardbeg and complexity is at a premium. It's as naturally beautiful, though, as a proud, naked woman in the prime of her life. And equally as enjoyable. **57.9%.** *The Whisky Shop Scotland 10th anniversary bottling.* 602 bottles.

PULTENEY
Highland (Northern), 1826. Inver House. Working.

Old Pulteney 12 Years Old db **(83)** n21 t22 f20 b20. The nose is floral; malty; polished floorboards; to taste razor-sharp malt, firm and brittle; stays hard despite softening oak; wonderfully energetic malt. **40%**

Old Pulteney 18 Years Old Cask 546 db **(83)** n22 t21 f20 b20. Fresh and zesty despite the age. Chalky finale. **40%**

Old Pulteney Aged 26 Years Limited Bourbon Cask Edition **(82)** n23 t17 f22 b20. A lovely northern Highland malt to be enjoyed by those who love straight Glenmorangie. Suffers a little early in palate development from a lack of character and direction, but this is redeemed by the busy and entertaining finale. The tangerine-led nose, though, is to die for. **46%.** 1,600 bottles.

Old Pulteney 1983 Cask No. 6181 db **(91)** n22 tangerines and malt in massive quantities and of unimpeachable quality; t24 faultlessly clean, intense barley with the usual citric suspects hanging around with a touch of peat to complete the picture; f23 long, with lovely malty tones now hand in glove with delicate oak; b22 a whisky for late night, when you've had a tough day and you need something to take your mind off everything except what is occupying your tastebuds. Gloriously indulgent. **57.5%.**

Adelphi Pulteney 19 Years Old cask 2610, dist 84 bott 03 **(84)** n23 t22 f19 b20. Nose to die for and taste absolutely mercurial, but let down by the short, thin finish. **51.9%**

Blackadder Raw Cask Pulteney 1990 bourbon barrel 3952, dist 13 Aug 90, bott Mar 03 **(87)** n21 quite hard, fruity and yet not unlike a young bourbon;

t_23_ usual Pulteney lift-off on the palate, massive malty sweetness, almost "Malteser"-like, with a chocolate hint; **f**_21_ vanilla and more very sweet malt; **b**_22_ a cracking example of a fine malt at an age that suits it. Ripe for drinking. **62.7%**

Cadenhead's Pulteney 12 Years Old dist 90, bott 10/02 **(90)** **n**_22_ a firm malt aroma softened by something vaguely orangey; **t**_23_ stupendous mouth arrival: silky, mildly gristy malt and accompanying spices flushed with a very vague fruitiness; **f**_22_ that wonderful oily body remains, this time with some cold-coffee notes clinging to it; **b**_23_ you can't ask much more of any 12-y-o than this. **59%**

Gordon & MacPhail Old Pulteney Aged 8 Years **(85)** **n**_22_ kumquats and malt; **t**_22_ more orangey fruit with teeming barley, **f**_20_ quietens rapidly with caramel; **b**_21_ a fine dram. **40%**

Gordon & MacPhail Old Pulteney 1966 **(87)** **n**_23_ switched-on oak; massive orangey, pithy presence; **t**_21_ malt then tangerines and soft oak; **f**_22_ a hint of smoke adds weight to the fruit; **b**_21_ remarkable whisky for its age, perfect for vitamin C lovers. **40%**

Gordon & MacPhail Old Pulteney 1990 Cask first-fill sherry butt cask 5471, dist 5/10/90, bott 31/12/02 **(85)** **n**_21_ almost immaculate butt: irritating sulphur distant echo apart, sherry clean to the point of squeaking and spices pinging all over the nose; **t**_22_ consumes the mouth and tastebuds with neat sherry, dry and chewy; **f**_21_ some malt has the temerity to show its face; **b**_21_ the most apologetic trace of sulphur prevents this from being a minor classic. Impressive all the same. **59.4%**

Hart Brothers Pulteney 10 Years Old **(87)** **n**_20_ hint of young bourbon; **t**_22_ malty, oily; **f**_23_ big, impressive finish with honey and smoke; **b**_22_ seriously good quality malt. **55.6%**

Ultimate Selection Old Pulteney 1990 bourbon barrel 25005, dist 26/4/90, bott 6/11/02 **(89)** **n**_22_ soft peat frames some wonderfully crisp malt; **t**_22_ mouthwatering, refreshing. The malt plays lead role with some vanilla ganging up in the middle; **f**_23_ very complex with tangerines mingling with soft smoke and relaxed, sweet malt; **b**_22_ this is, quite simply, first-class malt whisky. **43%**. *Van Wees NL.*

ROSEBANK

Lowland 1840–1993. Closed. (But if there is a God will surely one day re-open.)

Rosebank Aged 12 Years db **(87)** **n**_21_ sawdusty and dry; **t**_23_ supreme complex maltiness, rich tea biscuit and spice; **f**_22_ a soft diffusion of those busy malty tones, surprising sweetness; **b**_21_ a few years past its best, but still offers a malt of awesome natural beauty. The soft, malty sweetness is remarkable; **43%**. *Flora and Fauna range.*

Rosebank Aged 19 Years Rare Malts Selection db dist 79 **(85)** **n**_22_ peppery, bristling malt; **t**_22_ excellent mouthfeel but the early intense barley loses shape slightly; **f**_20_ bitter vanilla saved by good malt follow-through; **b**_21_ pleasant enough but bottled 10 years too late. **60.2%**

Rosebank Aged 20 Years Rare Malts Selection dist 81, bott May 02 db **(94)** **n**_23_ a volley of peppery spices are fired across the nosebuds: oak is present but takes shelter from the fire. Does some of that smoke contain peat? **t**_24_ f*** my old boots. This is a Rosebank? At 20 Years? Incredible. This is tin-hat whisky, explosive and just so brilliantly balanced with sweet and sour running hand in hand. There are some vague fruits, but it's the malt that stars until a coffee-laden oakiness begins to assert itself; **f**_23_ long, long, long with the oak trying to take control but complex malt notes fighting a rearguard action. Even a tad of peat adds to the mayhem; **b**_24_ well I had always said that the best Rosebank should be tasted at eight years old. Time to rip up my notebook: this one has re-written the rules. For Christ's sake re-open this distillery! How many can make a malt that sends us to heaven and back from eight to 20 years? **62.3%**. *6,000 bottles.*

Adelphi Rosebank 9 Years Old cask no. 1447 (92) n23 amazing dry marzipan and delicate malts. So complex! **t**24 celery and sweet malt combine with a touch of salt and an outline of oak; **f**22 vanilla and natural toffee represents the oak, myriad hits on the tatsebuds, and even a tiny degree of smoke is there for the malts; **b**23 a Lowlander? A closed distillery? Shurely shome mishtake ... this is nothing short of sensational. **61%**

Blackadder Raw Cask Rosebank 1992 hogshead cask no. 1452 distilled 25/3/92, bott Apr 02 **(87) n**22 beautiful malt, dry and touched by oak.; **t**22 full-bodied malt, fleetingly sweet and intense but reverts to a more languid dry and spicy posture; **f**21 soft oaks and straggling malt; **b**22 solidly good whisky with loads to keep the tastebuds amused. **61%. nc ncf sc.**

Cadenhead's Rosebank 12 Years Old dist 89, bott 07/01 **(88) n**22 about as naturally weighty a Lowlander as you are likely to find; **t**23 complex malts and fruits intertwine with oak gathering momentum; **f**21 flattens towards a toffeed finish; **b**22 12 years is a bit old for this distillery but the complexity is still superb. **56.4%**

Connoisseurs Choice Rosebank 1984 (90) n22 diced almonds and cherry cake; **t**23 supreme mouth texture: medium sweetness with rich malt and such sexy oaky interventions. A touch of smoke lends weight; **f**22 dries to bitter chocolate; **b**23 quite excellent **40%**. *Gordon & MacPhail.*

Connoisseurs Choice Rosebank 1988 (82) n24 **t**21 **f**18 **b**19. A stunning whisky until it all goes flat at the finish. The smoke and marzipan nose is stupendous, though. **40%**. *Gordon & MacPhail.*

Connoisseurs Choice Rosebank 1989 (89) n23 dovetailing of sandalwood and marzipan; **t**23 really beautiful context that seems to accentuate the clever malt-oak complexity. Lovely spices abound; **f**21 quiet and sweet with vanilla; **b**22 sophisticated stuff. *Gordon & MacPhail.*

Coopers Choice Rosebank 1992 bott 00 **(93) n**24 complex maltiness punctuated by series of grassy, spicy, honied, coal-smoky notes: fabulously delicate; **t**24 mouthwatering at first, then a honeydew melon and ginger attack; **f**22 dries quickly but leaves behind the spice; **b**23 flawless example of the most luscious and complex Lowlander of them all, bottled at exactly the right time. Pity it wasn't at a purer strength. **40%**

Lombard Rosebank 1989 (85) n21 green 'n' grassy; **t**22 lovely weight on the palate: malt zings around, no more of a hint of vanilla amid some spices; **f**21 very malty; **b**21 an old cask fails to provide depth, but the fresh richness of the malt is reward enough. **50%**

Milroy's Rosebank Over 13 Years Old dist 89, bott 02 **(89) n**22 intriguing and mouthwatering, the freshness of the aroma matches the extraordinary paleness of the whisky and is remarkable for a whisky of such age. The barley is fresh and flitting: coal-gas notes tweak the nose as does a very soft peat and barely a hint of oak is detectable. Absolutely charming! **t**22 exactly how it noses and looks! A beautiful, subtle sweetness becomes ultra-malty and grassy. Clean, refreshing, youthful with an arrival of cocoa powder reminding us that it has, after all, spent a long time in a cask; **f**22 surprisingly long and teasing with an incredible barley fade that lasts forever. Even a hint of peat can be found: for something so light, the chewiness is superb! **b**23 a one-off classic. From perhaps a third- or even fourth-filled cask, the whisky is all but colourless. But the charisma and charm of a whisky from one of the great distilleries unfolds tantalisingly and deliciously on the palate. For those, like me, who love a great blend this has absolutely everything you will ever need and more.

Murray McDavid Rosebank 1990 bourbon cask MM 517, dist Feb 90, bott May 98 **(76) n**15 **t**22 **f**20 **b**19. The label quotes from one of my books, referring to Rosebank: "If you ever find one aged 8, re-mortgage the house for it." What I had in mind was the distillery bottling or one like Coopers Choice 1992, launched a few years after I typed those words. What I didn't have in mind was this: the cask must have been around the warehouses a few times; having said that, this dram does have a fresh, irresistible middle. I do actually like it: but not as a Rosebank 8-year-old! **46%**

Murray McDavid Rosebank 1990 cask MM 2113, dist Mar 90, bott Dec 01 **(72)** n*17* t*17* f*20* b*18*. Another slightly odd Rosebank from MM: some years back they produced a young-un that never quite got off the ground. That mysterious, lurking juniper is an attractive tease, though. **46%. nc ncf sc.**

Murray McDavid Rosebank 1992 cask MM 1413, dist Mar 92, bott May 02 **(88)** n*21* clean with big barley; t*23* the arrival on the palate is like so many butterflies landing on the tastebuds. Spices accentuate its delicate nature; f*22* long, remains fresh, sparkling and fizzy; b*22* a real little cracker. **46%**

Old Malt Cask Rosebank Aged 12 Years dist Feb 89 **(86)** n*21* primroses lead the way in a very floral aroma, lovely sweet sub-stratum of honey, the oak is softly seasoned: about as delicate as it gets; t*23* light, flitting malt becomes increasingly more intense, hints of coffee towards the middle, but with plenty of lumps of brown sugar. The complexity and balance is exemplary; f*21* very long and sweet for what appears at first as a lightweight. Excellent oak retention that offers superb balance; b*21* a gilded malt that could crack under the oak if the intensity and complexity of spirit was not so powerful. Magnificent stuff. **50%. nc ncf sc.** *Douglas Laing.*

Old Malt Cask Rosebank Aged 20 Years dist Feb 81, bott May 01 **(82)** n*20* t*21* f*21* b*20*. A lively, clean dram with a wisp of late smoke. But age has eroded slightly the unique Rosebank style. **50%.** *Douglas Laing. 828 bottles.*

Old Malt Cask Rosebank Aged 22 Years dist Sept 78, bott May 01 **(80)** n*19* t*21* f*20* b*20*. Bright and refreshing with some lovely cocoa. **50%. nc ncf.** *Douglas Laing. 444 bottles.*

Provenance Spring Distillation Rosebank Over 11 Years dist Spring 89, bott Autumn 00 **(82)** n*22* t*21* f*19* b*20*. Fabulous whisky from a fabulous distillery. Can't help wondering what this would have been like if bottled three years earlier – even more complex and beautiful I suspect. **43%. nc ncf.** *Douglas McGibbon & Co.*

Scotch Malt Whisky Society Cask 25.30 Aged 13 Years **(93)** n*22* old lavender and spiced oak; t*24* a tidal wave of peppered honey and rich malt. salty and spiced: enormous; f*23* fades to a degree, but slowly and not without upping the complexity, the length is almost immeasurable; b*24* Rosebank in younger years offers something remarkable: this is the best sample yet of something much older and confirming just what a top-of-the-line malt this is. The oak is bold, but the depth of the malt – plus the stunning sweet-sour balance – is up to the challenge. A distillery milestone. **59.7%. nc ncf sc.**

Ultimate Dram Rosebank 1991 dist 18/2/91, bott 6/11/02 **(85)** n*22* soft vanilla, almost like soft ice cream cone; t*22* refreshing malt, clean and lip-smacking delicious early entry; f*20* a touch of salt gives it a life; b*21* clean and chewy. *Van Wees NL*

ROYAL BRACKLA
Speyside, 1812. Dewar's. Working.

Royal Brackla db **(80)** n*21* t*20* f*19* b*20*. A very soft, young and steady dram. **40%**

Royal Brackla Aged 10 Years db **(72)** n*18* t*19* f*17* b*18*. Malty, but unusually hot and nippy. **43%.** *Flora and Fauna range.*

Royal Brackla Rare Malts Selection Aged 20 Years dist 78 db **(78)** n*19* t*22* f*18* b*19*. Apart from a rousing early chorus of malt on the tastebuds, pretty tired stuff. **59.8%**

Royal Brackla Aged 25 Years dist 78, bott Mar 03 db **(88)** n*23* old walnuts, tangerines and slightly green melon; t*22* firm-bodied, curiously grainy at first then the slow evolution of creamy pulped fruit and chewy malt; **f**21 much drier despite a hint of toasted raisin; **b**22 a very complex malt that for a light Speysider has survived the passing summers much better than can be expected and is bold enough to display its own richness of style. Some excellent cask selection has gone into this one. **43%**

Connoisseurs Choice Royal Brackla 1974 (76) n19 **t**20 **f**18 **b**19. Somewhat thin despite some distant peat. **40%**

Coopers Choice Royal Brackla 1975 bott 01 (25 Years Old) **(79) n**20 **t**22 **f**18 **b**19. You know, it crossed my mind to do two sets of scores for this one. On the one hand I like it a lot, on the other I'm just not sure about it at all. The scores fall between two stools, although the strange flavour on the finish tends to confirm the suspicions aroused by the weirdly peated nose. Yet, on the other hand ... **43%**. *The Vintage Malt Whisky Co.*

Coopers Choice Royal Brackla 1984 (13 Years Old) bott 98 **(85) n**22 orange and marmalade notes; **t**22 complex malt and tangy fruit; **f**21 a spicy flourish; **b**20 a decent dram better served slightly cold. **43%. sc.**

"Green" Brackla 1975 27 Years Old cask 5471, bott 28 Oct 02 **(93) n**24 intense floral and citrus combined with some sweet demerara notes – rum not sugar: beautifully weighted; **t**24 imperious malt-sugar notes then a big arrival of intact oak, Mouth-coating and gloriously crisp and precise; **f**22 fabulously long with outstanding barley-sugar characteristics and spice; **b**23 the cask type says "unknown" on the label, but this is almost certainly ex-rum, most probably a demerara wooden column still. The type of whisky where one glass can last you an hour: complexity of extraordinary rarity. Moments like this make my job more rewarding. www.thewhiskyexchange.com *204 bottles.*

Mission Range Royal Brackla 1975 (92) n22 unripened kumquats and seven-year-old bourbon. **t**24 Sssssh! Don't make a sound: listen to the extraordinary subtlety and deftness as the fruit and malt dovetails. The weight and mouthfeel is near enough perfect; **f**22 hints of smoke, but the oak-malt interplay intrigues; **b**24 this is a whisky that is essentially all about complexity and secret messages. Find a silent room, save for a ticking clock or the crackle of the fire, lights dimmed to twilight, and just concentrate on something rather special. **46%**

Provenance Winter Distillation Brackla Over 6 Years dist Winter 94, bott Winter 00 **(84) n**20 **b**22 **t**21 **f**21. What a treat to find a delicate Speysider bottled at an age that suits the whisky rather than a marketing department. Also reveals why young blended Scotch can be so satisfying. One of the most refreshing, thirst-quenching drams you´ll find. **43%. nc ncf.** *Douglas McGibbon & Co.*

Scott's Selection Royal Brackla 1976 bott May 03 **(83) n**20 **t**23 **f**19 **b**21. Wonderful, clean, sweet malt through the middle. **57.2%.** *Robert Scott & Co.*

ROYAL LOCHNAGAR
Highland (Eastern), 1826. Diageo. Working.

Royal Lochnagar Aged 12 Years db **(79) n**20 **t**21 19 **f**19. Disappointing: a bit on the hot side with toffee where the malt should be. **40%**

Royal Lochnagar Aged 23 Years Rare Malts Selection db **(94) n**23 toasted honeycomb and nougat, slightly nutty; **t**24 magnificent richness, with some early tired oakiness repaired by the sheer enormity of the malt: a dram for grown-ups; **f**23 now the oak gets in with liquorice but some demerara sugar keeps the balance; **b**24 This is great whisky: seems at times over the edge, but some invisible force of greatness is holding it back. About as good a Lochnagar you will ever find. **59.7%**

Royal Lochnagar Selected Reserve db **(89) n**23 superb oloroso, clean and spicy with apples and pears; **t**23 stupendous spice lift-off which really starts showing the malts to great effect; **f**21 the malts fade as the toffee progresses; **b**22 quite brilliant sherry influence. The spices are a treat. **43%**

Old Malt Cask Lochnagar Aged 28 Years dist May 73, bott 01 **(76)** n*20* t*20* f*17* b*19*. Beginning to fall apart. **50%. nc ncf.** *Douglas Laing. 252 bottles.*

Platinum Old And Rare Lochnagar 30 Years Old (72) n*22* t*17* f*16* b*17*. Stunning sherry nose, but a little aged. **57.6%.** *Douglas Laing.*

Scotch Malt Whisky Society Cask 103.8 Aged 34 Years (79) n*19* t*21* f*20* b*19*. An old, big-oaked malt, not unlike some old Irish pot still that turns up now and again. The ageing process has left scars across the malt. But a hint of molassed sugar fills some of the holes though not all. A dram for those who like their malt sweet but with warts and all. **66.1%. nc ncf sc.**

ST MAGDALENE
Lowland, 1798–1983. Closed.

St Magdalene Aged 19 Years Rare Malts Selection db dist 79, bott Oct 98 **(87)** n*19* coal gas, clean malt; t*23* honied and unbelievably rich with a fabulous texture of silky, complex malts; f*23* long, oily with outstanding build-up of caramel biscuit sweetness and coffee; b*22* quite outstanding Lowland malt. As good as this distillery gets. **63.8%**

Blackadder Raw Cask Linlithgow 1975 hogshead 30012, dist 2/6/75, bott Apr 02 **(86)** n*22* exceptionally clean and intense malt with layers of oaky complexity; t*21* the malt arrives softly at first, then there is a massive second wave, gentle smoke is also there: pleasingly oiled; f*21* drier oak; b*22* an exceptional quality Linlithgow, displaying massive malt. **59.3%. nc ncf sc.**

Connoisseurs Choice St Magdalene 1966 (83) n*20* t*22* f*21* b*20*. Chewy toffee and sweet. Fabulous mouthfeel but perhaps too much caramel chips at the complexity? **40%.** *Gordon & MacPhail.*

Gordon & MacPhail St Magdalene 1982 (90) n*21* greengages and cream with just a dab of oak; t*23* perfect sweetness: the barley is all guns blazing and cleaner than a freshly scrubbed nun; f*23* lovely spice drifts with the vanilla oak, longer than a Sunday sermon. b*23* a minor miracle from G&M: a classic, sweet-velvet dram from a malt that in its youth would have burnt your throat out. **40%**

Old Malt Cask Linlithgow Aged 26 Years dist Jun 75, bott Dec 01 **(79)** n*21* t*20* f*19* b*19*. Very malty sweet, but overall thin and warming. **50%. nc ncf sc.** *Douglas Laing. 288 bottles*

Scott's Selection Linlithgow 1975 bott 99 **(77)** n*18* t*20* f*19* b*20*. Has withstood the test of time to present an attractive Lowland, sweet and rich in charm. **56.3%.** *Robert Scott & Co.*

SCAPA
Highland (Island–Orkney), 1885. Allied. Working intermittently.

Scapa 12 Years Old db **(88)** n*23* honeydew melon, soft salt and myriad styles of barley: really complex with a sprinkling of coal dust on the fruit; t*22* truly brilliant mouth arrival: the most complex display of malt and cocoa, the fruit is ripe figs with a thread of honey; f*21* a slight bitterness with some developing toffee, but the malt stays the distance; b*22* always a joy. **40%**

Gordon & MacPhail Scapa 1984 (79) n*23* t*20* f*17* b*19*. Great – no, brilliant! – nose, then the Viking ship depicted on the label just sinks without trace. **40%.** *Gordon & MacPhail.*

Gordon & MacPhail Scapa 1985 (83) n 22 t*22* f*19* b*20*. Fresh, lemon-zesty nose and alluring maltiness on the palate but the toffee-fudge gets greedy. **40%**

Gordon & MacPhail Scapa 1987 (75) n*22* t*18* f*18* b*17*. Rather simplistic and lacking its usual cocoa depth. **40%**

Gordon & MacPhail Scapa 1988 (76) n*21* t*20* f*17* b*18*. Fine malt, but some numbing caramel bites deep from somewhere. **40%**

Gordon & MacPhail Scapa 1990 (89) n*22* coal dust, timber and exceptionally clean malt: quite lovely; t*22* mouthwatering entry with the malt just zooming off in all directions; **f**23 brilliant fall-out with a touch of smoke clinging to the cocoa and malt; **b**22 immeasurably better than recent bottlings, the subtle character of the distillery sketched beautifully in an awesome dram.

Old Malt Cask Scapa Aged 25 Years dist Nov 74, bott May 00 **(94) n**22 slightly smoky, big malt presence, almost a sly complexity; **t**23 tangerines, honey and malt extract, some smoke thrown in for good measure; **f**25 almost too long and sophisticated to be true. The tapering finale holds something peaty to add as dead weight alongside the cocoa. With spices bordering on the sensual, the oak is perfectly proportioned to the much lighter, sweeter malt. I have to say, this is a faultless finish; **b**24 there are times you have to hold your hands up and say: words alone cannot do this justice. Except to say that every member of Allied should taste this so they can get the distillery back into full-time operation. **50%. nc ncf.** Douglas Laing. 524 bottles.

Old Malt Cask Scapa Aged 25 Years dist Aug 75, bott Feb 01 **(92) n**23 coke smoke and malt. The fruit is ripe for picking. If it wasn't already marmalade.... **t**24 busy and spicy from the start, loads of crisp, initially sweet barley to chew on; **f**23 medium length with fruitier notes taking hold; **b**22 spicy and lively, this is a whisky that defines complexity. **50%. nc ncf.** Douglas Laing. 438 bottles.

Old Malt Cask Scapa Aged 25 Years Sherry dist Aug 75, bott Jun 01 **(91) n**22 slightly sooty, dry but excellent malt with big grape digging in; **t**23 you chew this one until your ears ache: just enormous malt of varying shades and complexity; **f**23 long and touching as only stars can...; **b**23 apologies for the retro lyrics but once again words fail as we see just what truly great whisky is all about. This is obviously a relation to OMC's previous bottling, but do twins come more beautiful than this? **50%. nc ncf.** Douglas Laing.

SPEYBURN

Speyside, 1897. Inver House. Working.

Speyburn 10 Years Old db **(81) n**19 **t**21 **f**21 **b**20. Soft, slightly smoked, sweet, syrupy, simple: Speyburn so stylish. **40%**

Speyburn 21 Years Old Single Malt db cask 2711 **(84) n**20 **t**22 **f**21 **b**21. Sherried, sultana-sweet, smoky, spiced. **40%**

Speyburn 21 Year Old Single Cask cask 1811, dist 77, bott 99 db **(83) n**23 **t**20 **f**20 **b**20. A very rare specimen of an old-fashioned Speyside type. The original lightness of the make means that the malt struggles to be heard amid the fruit and oak. But despite a degree of tiredness and some ragged edges towards the finish, it holds together impressively. **61.9%**

Speyburn 25 Years Old db cask 1810 **(88) n**19 pulped and slightly burnt raisins, about as heavy as sherry gets (with a slight crack) so the malt barely troubles the aroma, if at all; **t**22 total sherry saturation but there are plenty of soft spices to kick life into the fruity onslaught; **f**24 fat gooseberries lighten it a little while heavy roast, dry cocoa heads towards the finale. Becomes salty as the oak really kicks in and then – some malt has the temerity to make itself heard; **b**23 I know there are those who will mark this a lot higher. But I can't say I'm a great lover of the nose and the mouth arrival is just too one-dimensional. It is only on the very long, absolutely outstanding and extraordinary finish that the tangled web is unwoven and much-needed lightening of body complexity arrives. Love it or otherwise, not a dram you forget in a hurry. **61.6%**

Connoisseurs Choice Speyburn 1971 (87) n22 fruit and smoke in same, moderate proportions; **t**22 refreshing, grassy, Speysidey malt with tinned fruit but bolstering spices **f**21 quite long, smoky, zesty with lingering malt; **b**22 really a complex, lingering dram of some serious quality. A minor classic in terms of the distillery. One I used to drink a lot of many years back and worth hunting today. **40%. Gordon & MacPhail.**

Connoisseurs Choice Speyburn 1974 **(72)** n*17* t*19* f*18* **b***18*. Sweet, malty and silky. But not quite hanging together. **40%**. *Gordon & MacPhail.*

SPEYSIDE
Speyside, 1990. Working.

Drumguish db **(78)** n*18* t*21* f*19* **b***20*. A very fruity and malty young Speysider (three years old, to be precise) that is hard and intense. This bottling is pretty sweet, though hot. Some, though, are on the feinty side. **40%**

Speyside 10 Years Old db **(81)** n*19* t*21* f*20* **b***21*. Plenty of sharp oranges around; the malt is towering and the bite is deep. A weighty Speysider with no shortage of mouth prickle. **40%**

Cu Dhub **(66)** n*15* **b***18* t*16* **b***17*. A whisky bottled exclusively by Danish whisky importers Mac Y for their home market after requests to find a "Black Whisky". This is, basically, young malt from the Speyside distillery with lashings of caramel colouring. It does have one all too brief golden moment a few seconds after hitting the palate. But don't expect anything too much beyond the novelty. One for ice and coke. **40%**

SPRINGBANK
Campbeltown, 1828. J&A Mitchell & Co. Working.

Longrow 10 Years Old 1993 db **(89)** n*22* deft peat flies sweetly around. There is something young and alluring about this; t*23* mouthfilling, sweet malt offers limited complexity but the peat makes it a dram to savour; f*22* clean, sweet, gristy, **b***22* not unlike a Port Ellen at about the same age. Certainly the closest we'll ever get to it again. **46%**

Longrow 10 Years Old Bourbon Cask db bott 00 **(88)** n*22* mealy and slightly farmyardy; t*23* enormously sweet with the peat being pretty relaxed to the point of laziness; f*22* vanilla and young malt intertwine; **b***21* a very simple malt, beautifully made, though the peating level is lower than previous distillations. That said, it's just glorious. **46%**

Longrow 10 Years Old Sherry Cask db bott 00 **(82)** n*20* t*22* f*20* **b***20*. Technically, beautifully made, clean and flawless. Talking from the heart, the peat and sherry seem to rub each other out leaving an attractive dram but one short of those special Longrow moments **46%**

Longrow 13 Years Old Sherry Cask db bott 02 **(91)** n*23* clever peat-fruit interplay, traces of oak as a third dimension; t*23* fat and full mouthfeel, brilliant sweet peat-dry sherry balance with a spicy side-dish; f*22* sweetens towards the malt as the sherry thins out; **b***23* glorious whisky which just goes to show how malt from this distillery takes a few years to get cracking **53.2%**

Springbank 10 Year Old db **(90)** n*22* fresh, unusual complexity with remarkable barley-oak jousting; t*23* massive: an Etna of an arrival with the main explosion being pure malt then a descending pyroclastic of salty vanilla notes and amazing spice; f*22* medium length but the malt remains indescribably lucid; **b***23* I am in my third decade as a Springbank devotee. Never, though, has their 10-year-old been even close to being quite this good. Masterful. **46%. nc ncf.**

Springbank 12 Years Old 175th Anniversary db **(86)** n*20* gentle; t*24* malt, malt, malt and malt. Oh, and some malt; f*21* long, oily and very velvety, displaying – guess what? – with the oak...; **b***21* an unusually soft Springbank with less complexity than usual but displaying amazing intensity. **46%**. *12,000 bottles worldwide from Apr 03. The age may not be stated.*

Springbank 15 Year Old db **(85)** n*22* punchy, lively malt which remains fresh despite some salty age with a surprising degree of oak; t*22* very intense malt concentrate that starts sweet then dries spectacularly; f*20* pretty dry oak, cocoa and marmalade; **b***21* a decent but not great Springbank. **46%. nc ncf.**

Springbank Aged 25 Years (91) n24 sherry oak was made for this: the cleanest, fruitiest, crushed grape aroma imaginable dovetailing with rich, salty, malty waves; t22 really deep malt, like layers of an onion: the inherent malty sweetness is always lurking despite the oak; f22 long, chewy and deep: late hints of citrus burst from nowhere; b23 I think complex is the word. **46%**

Springbank FFF 25 Year Old db (90) n23 salty with the usual complex oaky-malty battles raging; t22 lovely oils bring out the richness of the oak, malt bounces around the tastebuds with hints of some citrus; f22 long finale with the accent on oaky-malty things: a real jaw-acher in its chewiness; b23 the words Springbank and complexity seem conjoined: they are again here. **46%**

Springbank Aged 35 Years limited edition, bott 99 db (95) n24 ultra-ripe cherries, massive clean sherry aroma. Melton Mowbray Hunting Cake at its most raisiny: spicy, complex and just about perfect; t24 massively clean with spices and grape plus a spoonful of demerara sugar. Some big oak which doesn't even make a scratch on the sherry: sweet, yet oaky; f23 long, outrageously clean and grapey; b24 no whisky of this age should be quite this faultless or good. One of the great sherry casks of recent times. **46%. nc ncf.**

Springbank Wood Expression 12 Year Old Rum Wood (93) db n22 quiet yet complex; t25 Bloody hell! One is given the impression that one's tastebuds have just exploded. It's a bit of a mess: there is no rhyme nor reason to what is happening, it just happens ...; f23 heavy shades of cocoa and high roast Java; b23 uncontrolled, unstable, explosive Springbank at its most deadly ... and for a while too delicious to be true. **54.6%.** *Seven years in bourbon cask. Five years in demerara barrel. 25 years minimum in the memory bank.*

Springbank 1966 cask 500, dist Feb 66, bott Aug 98 db (92) n23 big oak influence offering enormous complexity: soft, sweet bourbon notes with heavy muscovado sugar sprinkled delicately over barley. A little salt brings the aromas out further, including some covert fruit: excellent; t23 massive, massive malt followed by big oak and thudding spices. Hardly subtle: it's all about power and beauty; f23 now we do have subtlety. The spices caress the tastebuds, there is no nipping and biting and the oak is dry but perfectly counterbalanced by nagging sweet malt; b23 this is sublime, complex whisky. It is entirely typical of the distillery style of the mid-60s from bourbon. **54.2%**

Springbank Wood Expression 1989 Port Wood 13 Years Old db (90) n20 very clean and fresh port wood influence – but at the cost of some complexity, though spice is not in short supply; t23 astonishing, succulent fruit with the most wonderful peppery attack, the most mouthwatering Springbank bottled in the last 25 years; f23 absolutely top-class chocolate and malt finale; b24 yet another piece of freaky genius from Springbank. **54.2%.** *10 years refill bourbon, three years port pipes. Mainland Europe only.*

Blackadder Raw Cask Springbank 1991 hogshead 04, dist Jun 91, bott Apr 02 (93) n22 light, complex but mainly coal-gas; t25 trademark malt explosion carried along with some rich oils, and spice: pretty hot but unmistakably brilliant. The malt starts sweet then settles: truly faultless; f23 digestive biscuit, complete with salt but with lashings of malt on top; b23 there is a certain burn to this whisky that has nothing to do with the alcohol content. The specific flavour of the malt is about as good as it ever gets in whisky. Had I owned this cask it would never have seen the light of day. It would have been mine, I tell you ... all mine!!! If you ever spot a bottle, knock yourself out. **57.4%. nc ncf sc.**

Chieftain's Springbank 1972 (30 years old) (88) n20 initially showing some signs of tiredness, a fraction too much oak leading to a slight bourbony character, but the fruit here is massive for all that: orange concentrate with big, big toffee; t23 silky with the most intense natural caramel you can imagine: again the bitter-sweetness is absolutely spot on, buttery and chewy with the most intense barley richness imaginable; f23 deep, the slightest hint of liquorice and some sweet malts until a much drier oakiness kicks in. Some spice in there, too; **b**22 a whisky you have to get to know – you will be rewarded. **57.8%**

Chieftain's Springbank 1974 (27 years old) **(84) n**21 **t**21 **f**21 **b**21. Fat, oily and resounding. This is big, big whisky – again not of a character that one immediately associates with Springbank. But the raw quality will not be denied. **56.6%**

Chieftain's Springbank 1974 (28 years old) **(81) n**21 **t**22 **f**18 **b**20. Light and amazingly delicate for a Springbank, but missing the usual saline intensity. **46%**

Da Mhile Organic Springbank 1992 Aged 7 Years dist June 92, bott Sept 99 **(74) n**17 **t**20 **f**19 **b**18. Really big, oily and chewy. Also a bit feinty, but a real one-off. The only organic whisky around. **46%.** *Made for organic farmer John Savage-Onstwedder.*

Juul's Private Bottling Springbank Vintage 1966 Aged 34 Years (93) n23 a rich fruitcake nose not without some bourbony-style oakiness; **t**24 a mind-blowing array of salty, oaky notes neatly wrapped in lush fruit: outstanding mouthfeel; **f**22 the salty theme continues, with some pepper for company plus hickory, liquorice and Blue Mountain coffee; **b**24 a stupendous cask which marked Copenhagen's landmark whisky shop's 75th anniversary in 2001 in awesome style. **47.1%.** *190 bottles.*

Lombard Jewels of Scotland Springbank Distilled 1991 bott 2001 **(72) n**17 **t**21 **f**17 **b**17. Disappointing due to a pervading natural caramel effect. Unfortunate. Flat nose and finish but delicious mouth arrival. **50%**

Murray McDavid Springbank 1965 bott 99 **(93) n**24 mildly sawdusty but enriched by a beguiling array of spicy, faintly smoked, fruity notes; **t**24 an outstanding tidal wave of spicy, oaky tones level out to reveal multi-layered richness of malt and a sherry butt beyond criticism; **f**22 long, toasty and dries to expose the great age; **b**23 truly brilliant whisky, once tasted never forgotten. Classic, classy stuff. **46%. nc ncf sc.**

Old Malt Cask Springbank Aged 33 Years dist May 67, bott Feb 01 **(78) n**23 dried dates and malt extract; **t**20 starts indulgently then suddenly dies on the spot; **f**17 dry, chalky and characterless; **b**18 I started the full tasting notes on this because the nose suggested we were in for a classic. It was not to be. **41.4%. nc ncf sc.** *Douglas Laing. 204 bottles.*

Open Championship 2000 Bottling Campbeltown Single Malt cask 600R, dist 93 **(88) n**22 meaty oloroso. The malt chimes in but the oak stays quiet: very clean with some wonderful coffee notes; **t**23 massive. The sherry is dripping off the tastebuds with a malt-extracty sweetness adding to the weight. The spices are almost alarming; **f**21 charming and slightly reserved, with neither the youthful malt nor sherry quite having the confidence to take the lead; **b**22 sheer class. I'd be tempted to buy a bottle, shove the contents into a tiny oak barrel and let it reach brilliance. **59.2%.** *Available from only Luvians Bottleshop of Cupar, Scotland. States 300 bottles – there were only 258 produced. This is Springbank, though not stated on bottle.*

Peerless Springbank 1967 cask 1940, dist May 67 36-y-o **(86) n**22 lemon drops, very sharp malt and some heavier oak; **t**19 some over-weighty oak at first but complex malts gather; **f**23 enormously long, the complexity levels going off the scales: bitter-sweet balance just about perfect despite the persistent oak; **b**22 takes time to settle but well worth the wait. **41.1%.** *Duncan Taylor & Co.*

Scotch Malt Whisky Society Millennium Malt Nine Years Old First Release Distillery 114 (Longrow) **(87) n**21 delicately peaty and curiously gristy; **t**22 now the peat arives big time, fruity and malty-sweet; **f**23 chewy, vanilla-rich, kippery, buttery, still gristy and young but very long; **b**21 a cask culled in its youth. A joyous dram, but one that still has a long way to go before maturity. **58.1%**

Scotch Malt Whisky Society "27.49" 12 Years Old dist Dec 89, bott Aug 02 **(86) n**23 salty, sea-swept and malty: archetypal Springbank; **t**22 youthful, exuberant, zesty, malty; **f**20 slightly green and tart, but no shortage of complexity; **b**21 it may not say Springbank on the label, but there's just no mistaking it. **54.7%**

Signatory Springbank 9 Years Old sherry cask, dist 90, bott 00 **(85) n**21 salt and pepper, quite sweet malt; **t**22 rich and mouth-filling with a surge of clean, intense malt; **f**21 long with some gathering oils and spices; **b**21 a really enjoyable dram with plenty going on, though you feel that, given time, there could have been so much more. **46%**. 215 bottles.

STRATHISLA
Speyside, 1786. Chivas. Working.

Strathisla 12 Years Old db **(87) n**21 a dab of distant peat adds even more weight to something that is malt-heavy already; **t**22 pleasant, sultana-fruity with a very rich malt follow-through; **f**22 some almost apologetic oak breaks into the rich maltiness. Some hints of cocoa and more smoke elongate the finish; **b**22 an infinitely better dram than a few years back that was a bit oily and shapeless. Today the heavily-weighted, full-bodied malt engages the tastebuds from first to last with a complexity and richness of genuine class. **43%**

Blackadder Raw Cask 1989 sherry cask 9411, dist 6 Nov 89, bott Apr 02 **(87) n**22 big grassy malts, a waft of smoke; **t**23 massive malt gangs up and thumps the tastebuds mercilessly, hints of oak and smoke; **f**21 medium length, vanilla and bitter chocolate; **b**21 sherry cask, but the influence is non-existent. **61.3%**

Cask Strathisla 1974 casks 2206–7, dist 25/3/74, bott Jul 92 **(93) n**24 pungent, spicy sherry with roast chestnuts: seriously scrummy; **t**24 massive sherry sweetens the fizzing oak. **f**22 some malt and vanilla attempt to calm the spice and fruit; **b**23 one of G&M's masterpieces still (amazingly) available in places like Vintage House, London. Close your eyes and go for the ride. **57.8%**. Gordon & MacPhail.

Gordon & MacPhail Strathisla 25 Year Old **(89) n**24 Oh my word! A sprinkling of everything, except OTT oak. It seems almost a shame to drink it; **t**23 sweet, sugary malt. The subtle smoke on the nose doesn't filter down, though; 20 just a little flat and vanilla-bound; **b**22 a quite remarkable malt, never quite living up to the nose in terms of complexity – but that would have been asking bit too much. **40%**

Gordon & MacPhail Strathisla 1953 **(90) n**22 heavy duty and dense, ery big vanilla oak but enough fruit for balance; **t**22 Well done! The oak is kept bay as massively intense malt and rich sultanas take centre stage. Some spices ver as does a welcome hint of smoke; **f**23 more grapes just melt in the mouth does the malt; **b**23 whisky of this antiquity has no right to be this good or an. An undisputed classic of its type. **40%**

Gordon & MacPhail Strathisla 1963 **(90) n**23 ripened wild cherries and shy greengages. Some nose! **t**23 a malt extravaganza, at once both uthwatering and dry – always chewy; **f**22 some bitterness creeps in as the arrives, but the malt continues to the end; **b**22 good old Gordon & MacPhail nearth a little cracker. **40%**

Gordon & MacPhail Strathisla 1982 **(83) n**22 **t**21 **f**20 **b**20. Solid, juicy, -made malt that runs out of steam slightly at the finish. **40%**

Gordon & MacPhail Strathisla 1987 **(76) n**19 **t**20 **f**18 **b**19. Regulation yside. **40%**

eerless Strathisla 1967 cask 1533, dist Feb 67 35-y-o **(92) n**22 a fraction ky; honied and rich; **t**24 spellbinding series of crystal-clear, powering urs starting with sweet butterscotch through avocado to honied malt; **f**22 rice and muscovado sugar: the peat-smoke returns slightly at the death; **b**24 is dreamy stuff with balance and complexity by the bucketful. **51.1%**. an Taylor & Co.

Scotch Malt Whisky Society "58.5" 32 Years Old dist Nov 69, bott Aug 02 **(85)** n23 enormous clean oloroso (one suspects through the oaky haze), sprinkled with spice and generously topped with top-rate old bourbon; t24 an exhibition of clean fruit and punchy spice with chewy burnt toffee for good measure; f18 threatens to fall off the tracks age-wise and does so, spectacularly: slightly sappy and bitter; b20 fun at the beginning while it lasted. **56.4%**

Signatory Rare Reserve Strathisla 33 Years Old cask 2372, dist 11/04/68, bott 23/07/01 **(88)** n23 coffee and walnut cake; t22 sweet muscovado sugar sprinkled on the gathering oak; f21 at last the oak that has been threatening since the nose arrives but with it a delicious oily malt that softens the landing; b22 a pretty tired dram, but one with enough character and complexity to ensure a long and enjoyable mouthful. **50.2%**. 148 bottles.

Ultimate Selection Strathisla 1989 dist 7/6/89, bott 14/1/03 **(79)** n19 t21 f19 b20. Pleasant, sweet and malty. **43%**. Van Wees NL.

STRATHMILL
Speyside, 1891. Diageo. Working.

Strathmill Aged 12 Years db **(79)** n21 t21 f18 b19. A big malt for a normally light, delicate Speysider. Brilliant spice and rich mouthfeel but fatally let down by caramel-toffee. Strathmill, but not as God intended. **43%**. Flora and Fauna range.

Connoisseurs Choice Strathmill 1991 **(71)** n17 t20 f17 b17. Strangely bitter and off-key. **40%**. Gordon & MacPhail.

The Old Malt Cask Bottling Strathmill Aged 11 Years dist Oct 88, bott Jun 00 **(85)** n20 delicate with an almost guava-like spiciness; t21 firm and warming arrival on palate. The exceptionally sweet malt intertwines with soft vanillas from the oak and eventually gives way to the marauding spice; f22 long and displaying great versatility, depth and no little complexity, quite oily towards the end, coating the mouth to allow the sweetness back and then linger: very chewy and satisfying finale; b22 a real odd-ball of a Strathmill, not entirely in keeping with malt of this age from there. But its propensity for leading the tastebuds up blind alleys and into otherwise uncharted territory makes for intriguing drinking. Love it! No added colouring. **50%. nc ncf sc.** Douglas Laing. 420 bottles.

The Old Malt Cask Strathmill Aged 39 Years sherry, dist Apr 62, bott May 01 **(82)** n20 t19 f23 b20. Powerful oak and sherry dominate. Just enough sweetness and malty follow-through on the finish to make this a good 'un. **45.2%. nc ncf sc.** Douglas Laing. 270 bottles.

Old Masters Strathmill 1992 bott 03 **(81)** n19 t22 f20 b20. Real high-propane, heavy-duty Speysider at its very maltiest. **64.2%. nc ncf.** James MacArthur.

TALISKER
Highland (Island–Skye), 1832. Diageo. Working.

Talisker Ten Years Old db **(86)** n22 Cumberland sausage and kippers side by side; t21 worrying shades of toffee arrive early on; f22 the big peat explosion but muffled, dulled by caramel; b21 the natural brilliance of this whisky gets it into the high 80s, but someone has gone nuts with the caramel machine here and done their best to flatten those uniquely massive notes that set this distillery apart. As a rule, I give 25 for the finish as a matter of course as normally it is the greatest in the world. **45.8%**

Talisker Aged 20 Years db **(95)** n24 an exceptional sherry butt that brilliantly allows full scope for the spicy excesses of the distillery to spill over: sensational; t24 almost unreal marriage of ultra rich and clean sherry with explosive peat. The usual Talisker viciousness with the sherry somehow hanging on for the ride; f23 quietens to something approaching mere fireworks with the spices now being slightly subdued by the fruit ... though not quite; **b**24 I have been tasting Talisker for 28 years. This is the best bottling ever. Miss this and your life will be incomplete. **62%**

Talisker Aged 25 Years db **(83)** **n**20 **t**23 **f**20 **b**20. The 20-y-o is simply too hard an act to follow: the nose is surprisingly flat, weighted down by oak. The palate is superb with those spices gathering intensity to a brilliant crescendo. But then it all dies rapidly. By no means a bad whisky, but once you have experienced the 20-y-o... **59.9%**

Talisker 1989 Distillers Edition Double Matured Jerez Amoroso finish, bott 02 **(87)** **n**22 fruity, Turkish delight and soft smoke; **t**22 spicy and lively with good malt-fruit interplay; **f**21 winey notes replace the usual kaboom you get at this point: succulent redberries and vanilla... and toffee...; **b**22 an enjoyable dram that you wouldn't recognise as a Talisker unless you read the label. But doubtless quality, nonetheless. **45.8%**

Talisker Limited Edition For Sale Only at Distillery db **(88)** **n**23 kumquats, spices, red liquorice candy and biting peat; **t**22 searing peat and sweet malt: vanilla gangs up impressively **f**21 long, incredibly malty and sweet, almost gristy in style; **b**22 this is one heck of a dram: fresh yet explosive, sweet yet deep and chewy. The last time I tasted this I nearly died the very same day and was ill and unable to work for the next nine months. If you are reading this book, then it was only a coincidence.... **60%**

Old Malt Cask Tactical Aged 20 Years (62) **n**12 **t**18 **f**16 **b**16. Sulphured sherry butt sadly ruins it. **50%.** *Douglas Laing & Co Ltd.*

Old Malt Cask Tactical Aged 22 Years (90) **n**23 rich, spicy honey and well-aged, this aroma offers brilliant balance and magnificent character. The smoke has softened towards something like dry Darjeeling while the sweetness also carries hints of raisins: really quite lovely. Dissolve-in-the-mouth malt carries softly honied riches; **t**23 the peat forms a base layer of its own that now and again raises to intermingle with the higher malty-honey notes; **f**22 back to Darjeeling with a hint of some medium roast Costa Rica coffee; **b**22 pretty long and satisfying. Is this where Talisker meets Highland Park? Quite amazing stuff with heaps of honied character but with a disarming peatiness that has lost its younger fizz. **50%. nc ncf.**

Old Malt Cask Tactical Aged 31 Years (73) **n**19 **t**18 **f**18 **b**18. Finished in sherry cask for six months. Like watching a great old boxer, slugging it out for the very last time when clearly past it. Even so, shows a little of the old magic early on. Doesn't name distillery on label. **50%.** *Douglas Laing.*

TAMDHU

Speyside, 1897. Edrington. Working.

Tamdhu db **(87)** **n**23 grassy, fresh, juicy, youthful, boiled fruit candy, coke smoke: pure Speyside in a sniff; **t**22 very light malt, extremely clean, newly cut grass, deliciously chewy; **f**21 perhaps a hint of toffee but the malty show rumbles on with good weight and late burst of non-peated smoke; **b**21 nothing like as oily as of old, but charmingly refreshing, non-threatening and enormously enjoyable. **40%**

Adelphi Tamdhu 1967 34 Years Old cask 7 **(85)** **n**23 seductive honey, some vanilla bite; **t**21 intense malt and spice; **f**20 the oak is surprisingly shy for a Tamdhu of this age; **b**21 a warming dram with an even spread of oak. **49.9%. sc.**

Adelphi Tamdhu 12 Years Old cask 4593, dist 90, bott 02 **(89)** **n**23 I think we have found Tamdhu's nose at optimum age: so honied, clean and rich! **t**22 silky malt, a hint of smoke and honey and a little bite; **f**22 rich biscuity malt and very mildly molassed sugar; **b**22 a different Tamdhu: big but less oil and more sweet malt. **53.6%**

Adelphi Tamdhu 15 Years Old cask 9032, dist 85, bott 00 **(84)** **n**19 **t**22 **f**22 **b**21. Fabulous malty thrust at the middle, a bit ragged around the edges. **55.3%**

Gordon & MacPhail Tamdhu 1960 (85) n21 big, big oak: we are talking sap amid the sweet malt. But it works; t22 beautifully complex: sweet malt battles with very deep oak, neither quite getting the upper hand; f21 remains oaky, but a good traditional Tamdhu oiliness keeps the malt on course; b21 talk about brinkmanship. The oak is way over the top, but in this case the intensity of the oily malt is such that it leads to a really fascinating dual. Not for the purists, perhaps. But grizzly, macho entertainment. 40%

Gordon & MacPhail Tamdhu 1961 (83) n20 t22 f21 b20 The oak influence is such, we are talking very decent bourbon! 40%

The MacPhail's Collection Tamdhu 8 Years Old (80) n19 t22 f19 b20. Grassy, bright and mouthwatering. 40%. Gordon & MacPhail.

Old Malt Cask Tamdhu Aged 23 Years dist Feb 77, bott Jun 00 (89) n22 smoky, floral and no shortage of citrus; t22 intense malt with some background smoke and spice; f23 more spice and well-developed oak offset by fudge-like malt, more soft peat smoke on the finish; b22 really steady, top-quality malt. 50%. nc ncf. Douglas Laing. 301 bottles.

Old Malt Cask Tamdhu Aged 34 Years dist Oct 66, bott Oct 00 (77) n20 t20 f18 b19. Marmalade spread thinly over slightly burnt toast; some fine, delicate peat creeps in. 50%. nc ncf. Douglas Laing. 198 bottles.

Old Malt Cask Tamdhu Aged 34 Years dist Jan 67, bott Sep 01 (87) n23 10-y-o top dog bourbon from the middle of the warehouse; t22 sweet, bourbony, toffee-rich and chewy, excellent oak control; f21 drier oak; b21 the perfect malt for bourbon lovers. 50%. Douglas Laing. 186 bottles.

Peerless Tamdhu 1968 cask 4104, dist Jun 68 34-y-o (88) n22 very gently smoked and clean; t22 dissolving malt, sharp and fresh; f22 lovely malty finale with a soft wisper of peat once again; b22 a straight-down-the-line, high-quality whisky. 40.1%. Duncan Taylor & Co.

TAMNAVULIN
Speyside. 1966. Kyndal.

Tamnavulin 12 Years Old db (79) n19 t20 f21 b19. Quite weighty for a Speysider with a deliciously massive malty kick. But missing out on complexity somewhat. 40%

Tamnavulin Stillman's Dram 30 Years Old db (87) n22 subtle hints of bourbon amid a rigid malt frame; t23 again the malt is big and sweetens by the second. The soft oiliness helps the bourbony sweetness cling to the palate: really lovely; f21 short but clean; b21 a great example of when bourbon meets malt. Not enormously complex, just enjoyable. 45%

Gordon & MacPhail Tamnavulin 1988 Cask casks 4706–9, dist 6/12/88, bott May 97 (83) n20 t22 f20 b21. Buttery, soft and oily, the gentle malt spreads evenly over the palate. 58.9%

TEANINICH
Highland (Northern), 1817. Diageo. Working.

Teaninich Aged 10 Years db (84) n21 t21 f21 b21. A very even, ultra-malty, outwardly light dram with some pleasantly lurking spice. Flora and Fauna bottlings I have tasted over the years have ranged from 82–84 in marks, being similar in clean, malty style but varying in degree of oiliness. 43%. The notes above are from the latest bottling, L15N00298941.

Teaninich Aged 23 Years Rare Malts Selection dist 73 db (74) n19 t20 f17 b18. Lightly smoked and sweet, but disappointingly lacking in direction. 57.1%

Adelphi Teaninich 31 Years Old cask 3576, dist 71, bott 02 (82) n20 t22 f20 b20. Bold and oaky with firm, fruity body. 57.8%

Berrys' Own Selection Teaninich 1973 bott 02 (85) n19 subtly smoked, though a tad off balance; t22 a real flavour free-for-all. No discipline at all as fudgy, oaky, raisiny, smoky notes go on a walkabout. Some spice enters the fray; **f**22 remains busy and disorganised; **b**22 a roller-coaster malt that doesn't quite settle or decide what it wants to be. Softly smoked but the complexity seems to lead to cul-de-sacs. Even so, a real roof-of-mouth-licking dram. **43%**

Chieftain's Choice Teaninich Port Barrel aged 16 years (Double Wood Maturation) **(85) n**20 delicate fruit; incredibly light with unripe bananas; **t**23 indescribably complex with a teasing light barley being flanked by astonishing fruit and spice. A real silky mouthful that refuses to settle – as busy as any whisky gets; **f**21 much closer to a Jamaican pot-still rum than a single malt. Incredible riches! **b**21 an absolute one-off – so, so different. The port barrel has moved this malt into a weird and wonderful dimension where the port is hardly noticeable, but rum is!! This job doesn't get easier. **43%**. Ian MacLeod.

Chieftain's Choice Teaninich Aged 19 Years dist 1980 **(87) n**23 honied, rich and astonishingly sweet with a pinch of peat; **t**22 big oak arrival, more honey and beautifully silky; **f**21 big vanilla and drying oak, some late, lingering peat; **b**21 worth finding for the nose alone. **43%**. Ian Macleod.

Chieftain's Choice Teaninich Aged 21 Years dist 1979 **(73) n**18 **t**19 **f**18 **b**18. Good spice but a little dull. **43%**. Ian Macleod.

Connoisseurs Choice Teaninich 1975 (72) n22 **t**17 **f**16 **b**17. Great nose, some ginger on the finish but otherwise dead in the bottle. **40%**. Gordon & MacPhail.

Connoisseurs Choice Teaninich 1982 (90) n23 ginger, a hint of smoke, salty; **t**23 lively, salty, big malt kick and sweet; **f**22 levels out but the vanilla and malt keep going strong; **b**22 wonderfully complex and dangerously moreish. **40%**. Gordon & MacPhail.

Hart Brothers Teaninich Aged 13 Years dist 83 **(84) n**19 **t**22 **f**21 **b**22. A mildly butyric nose is the only blemish on an otherwise resounding malt, one that has a sensuous copper-rich mouthfeel and the usual hint of honey. **43%**.

Hedges & Butler Teaninich Aged 21 Years cask 13668, dist 79, bott 00 **(88) n**22 fabulously weighted and toasty, clean malt with a subtle touch of peat; **t**22 slightly oily and mouthfilling, massive honey on the oak and excellent spices; **f**21 a quiet unravelling of soft oak; **b**23 bottled just in time before the oak took hold. **43%**. Ian Macleod.

TOBERMORY
Highland (Island–Mull), 1795. Burn Stewart. Working.

Ledaig Aged 15 Years db **(90) n**23 honied, waxed floors, silky barley and even the peat has sheen: unique; **t**23 melts in the mouth and just crumbles on the tastebuds. The peat lands like snowflakes; **f**22 more gentle honey and slow development of vanilla; **b**22 beautiful whisky from one of the most temperamental distilleries – and ages. **43%**

Ledaig Aged 20 Years db **(86) n**22 thoroughly well-oaked with a trace of waxy honey, deep and softly smoked; **t**22 intensely sweet with a swelling of soft peat. The sheer intensity creeps up on you; **f**20 medium length with intense barley, layers of smoke and clean oak; **b**22 a lazy, laid-back, subtle malt that is much more heavily peated than it originally seems. **43%**

Ledaig 1979 Vintage db **(74) n**17 **t**22 **f**18 **b**17. By no means a classic Ledaig and one quite lacking in telling peatiness. Only the big arrival on the palate saves it from being really disappointing by Ledaig standards. **43%**

Ledaig Light db **(84) n**21 **t**22 **f**21 **b**20. A fabulously youthful dram, obviously with a lot of growing up to do – especially on the nose which introduces an amusing tequila note. That said, the magnitude of the peat, the oiliness and sweetness of the body and the clarity of the malt makes this one to go to Korea just to find. High-quality malt especially, us bachelors please note, for women – and great fun to boot! An idiosyncratic bottle I'd pour for anybody, anytime. **42%**. Korea.

Ledaig Sherry Malt db **(73)** n18 t19 f18 b18. There are some powerful forces here refusing to gel. A bit of a mish-mash. **42%**. *Japan/Asia Pacific.*

Cadenhead's Ledaig 10 Years Old dist 92, bott 03/03 **(84)** n19 t23 f21 **b**21. Not quite on top form: the nose has an off-beat and there hasn't been enough oak in the cask to effect sufficient complexity. That said, pretty fresh, green, chewy and more-ish stuff. **59.9%**

Connoisseurs Choice Ledaig 1990 (77) n18 t20 f20 b19. Honied and waxy, but fails to develop. **40%**. *Gordon & MacPhail.*

Gordon & MacPhail Ledaig 1975 (87) n23 absolutely glorious: trademark honey and soft peat abound while the vanilla cushions all impact; t23 honey-heather, waxy with a big surge of malt and oak; f20 thins rapidly but some gentle spices arrive; **b**21 a honied and waxy little charmer wth just the faintest hint of peat. A delight. **40%**

Tobermory Aged 10 Years db **(75)** n17 t19 f20 b19. Delightful custardy finish. **40%**

TOMATIN
Speyside, 1897. Working.

Tomatin Aged 12 Years db **(73)** n20 t18 f17 b18. Some seriously weird sherry influence has done no favours to this bottling. I can't believe it: Tomatin makes one of Speyside's most consistently brilliant drams, full of malty, grassy promise especially when matured in bourbon and then ... this!!! Drinkable, but for us Tomatin lovers just so hugely disappointing. **40%**

Connoisseurs Choice Tomatin 1968 (69) n16 t20 f16 b17. Disappointingly flat. **40%**. *Gordon & MacPhail.*

Old Malt Cask Tomatin Aged 23 Years dist Nov 76, bott Feb 00 **(80)** n20 t21 f19 b20. Big, sweet and spicy. **50%. nc ncf.** *Douglas Laing.* 293 bottles.

James Macarthur's Tomatin 12 Year Old (84) n21 t22 f20 b21. Silky, malty ultra-sweet and very typical version of a very sound Speysider. **43%**

Old Malt Cask Tomatin Aged 33 Years Sherry dist Jan 67, bott Jun 00 (72) n18 t19 f18 b17. Either too dry or syrupy: not my type of sherry. **50%. nc ncf.** *Douglas Laing.* 594 bottles.

Old Malt Cask Tomatin Aged 36 Years dist Jan 65, bott Feb 01 **(88)** n22 constrained oak with ripe bananas, succulent and sexy; t22 fabulous sweet malt, then an oaky back-up for balance; f21 quite long, a little oily; b23 beautifully complex, balanced and in improbably good condition for its great age. **49.7%. nc ncf.** *Douglas Laing.* 216 bottles.

Old Malt Cask Tomatin Aged 38 Years dist Sep 62, bott Jan 01 **(81)** n20 really lovely fruit – baked apples, mainly – and sweet oak; t22 melt-in-the-mouth barley that infuses beautifully with the custard-vanilla oak; f19 very light barley remains, lots of vanilla and a touch of warming spice. Loses Brownie points for bitterness; **b**20 a frail malt that has maintained its posture and elegance despite the passing years. **41%. nc ncf.** *Douglas Laing.* 186 bottles.

Peerless Tomatin 1965 cask 1867 dist Jan 65 (72) n20 t18 f16 b18. Big, oily and oaked, but the nose sparkles. **49.7%.** *Duncan Taylor & Co Ltd.*

Peerless Tomatin 1965 cask 1909 dist Jan 65 37-y-o (81) n20 t21 f20 **b**20. Heaps of natural toffee and vanilla: well-aged and well-behaved. Bourbony and honied. **48%.** *Duncan Taylor & Co.*

Single Barrel Collection Tomatin 1988 cask 1967, dist Jun 88, bott 01 **(90)** n23 fabulously floral and refined. The complexity of the oak is stupendous not least for its delicacy. Hints of Turkish delight help balance against the drier vanilla tones, but that is only part of the tale. An aroma to get lost in: stunning; t23 a zillion flitting notes tease the tastebuds as the early, drier oak is chased off by the sweeter, fatter barley. A little sultana-ish fruit arrives to juice things up and soft spices to guarantee extra fizz. The middle arrives as a brilliant mixture of the four camps with some cocoa bitterness just beginning to evolve; **f**21 some fruit hangs around long enough to make the cocoa work hard for its top stop: the bitter-sweet balance is exemplary. Some toast and vanilla arrive at the death, too; **b**23 this is about as good a Tomatin as you are likely to find. If you are looking for a study of balance and grace, this is it. **56.2%. sc nc ncf.** *Germany.*

TOMINTOUL
Speyside, 1965. Angus Dundee. Working.

Tomintoul Aged 10 Years db **(79)** n20 t21 f19 b19. A fresh, clean, malty dram but leading to toffee fudge simplicity. **40%**

Tomintoul Aged 16 Years db **(88)** n21 Weetabix in full fat milk with crushed raisins; **t**23 magnificent mouth arrival: as soft as you could pray for. Toffee-apple and malt melt in the mouth while some crisper, more mouthwatering barley notes filter through; **f**22 a long finale that remains chewy and soft; **b**22 "The gentle dram" claims the label, and so it is. In fact, few Scotch malts can match this whisky's uncanny ability to dissolve on contact with the tastebuds. Excellent bitter-sweet balance, though it tends towards sweetness with the oak kept at a safe distance until the very end. For all the toffee-effect, a real treat. A deadly more-ish dram with all the deftness of a Zola lob. **40%**

Adelphi Tomintoul 23 Years Old cask 7320, dist 76, bott 99 **(84)** n21 t22 f21 b20. Enormously sweet and delicious with added coal smoke. **54.3%. sc.**

Adelphi Tomintoul 34 Years Old cask 532, dist 66, bott 00 **(89)** n23 stunning oloroso with burnt raisins and liquorice candy; **t**23 almost too overpowering in sherry (though not quite): the fruit is of the richest variety, the malt the roastiest; **f**21 dries impressively after the sweet start, while some cocoa and dried dates accompany the building spice. Just a little too much bitterness at the death; **b**22 perhaps a couple of years too old for being a true classic: pretty fabulous anyway. **52.1%**

Gordon & MacPhail Tomintoul 1967 **(84)** n23 t21 f20 b20. The clean sherry nose is classically majestic, even offering stewed tomato! But after the early initial sweet and rich flavour arrival becomes rather too bitter. Shame, but a real honey for the nose alone. **40%**

Old Malt Cask Tomintoul 34 Years Old dist Feb 66, bott June 00 **(78)** n19 t21 f18 b20. A curious one, especially on the tangy nose and finish

TORMORE
Speyside, 1960. Allied. Working.

Tormore 12 Years Old db **(75)** n19 t20 f18 b18. Greatly improved on the old days: much more yielding and accessible now, even boasting a touch of honey. **40%**

Blackadder Tormore 1990 Raw Cask cask 1964, dist 2/2/90, bott Apr 02 **(79)** n19 t21 f19 b20. Marzipan and sugar. And something to chew. **65.9%. nc ncf.**

Provenance Spring Distillation Tormore Over 10 Years dist Spring 90, bott Autumn 00 **(78)** n17 t22 f20 b19. The tasting notes on the bottle state marzipan, and they are right. Not the rubbishy British variety, but the almost unsugared stuff from Lübeck. Slightly toasty and some toffee apparent. A little ragged and bitter at the finale but otherwise very good. **43%.** *Douglas McGibbon & Co.*

Ultimate Selection Tormore 1989 sherry butt 920259, dist 11/5/89, bott 13/11/00 **(72)** n17 t19 f18 b18. Sugary sweet and not quite hitting the heights. *Van Wees NL.*

TULLIBARDINE
Highland (Perthshire), 1949. Tullibardine Ltd. Silent since 1994, planned re-opening late 2003.

Tullibardine 10 Years Old db **(86)** n21 really lovely hint of Seville oranges refreshes an otherwise big malty theme; t22 voluptuous mouthfeel, clean malt and gentle spices; f21 good oak adding to the spice and upping the weight with a light dusting of cocoa; b22 a simple, superbly weighted and charming dram with a lovely malt presence. **40%**

Tullibardine Stillman's Dram Aged 30 Years db **(88)** n22 full, fat, fabulously fruity, with a tun-room aroma; t23 lush and oily; oak-induced spice topped by demerara sweetness; f21 long, intense barley lingering on with a tinge of oak and molassed raisins; b22 a complex, hearty and stylish dram. **45%**

Adelphi Tullibardine 35 Years Old cask 2122, dist 66, bott 01 **(78)** n17 t23 f19 b19. Big, massively sherried and salty. Some will flip and call this the best thing they have ever tasted. I have a slightly more reserved feel for it: for all its many highlights, the nose is poor and the balance seems to have drifted. **54.6%**

Blackadder Raw Cask Tullibardine 1966 sherry cask 2118, dist 23 April 66, bott May 02 **(73)** n19 t19 f18 b17. The pine from over-ageing makes this more like Swedish aquavit than Scotch. **52.1%. nc ncf sc.**

UNSPECIFIED SINGLE MALTS (Campbeltown)

Open Championship 2000 Bottling Campbeltown Single Malt from Luvians (see Springbank)

UNSPECIFIED SINGLE MALTS (Highland)

Asda Single Malt (see Douglas MacNiven)

Douglas MacNiven Highland Single Malt 12 Years Old **(80)** n20 t21 f19 b20. Pretty compact maltiness with some developing fruit and demerara sugar. Guess what I think about the caramel ...? **40%.** Asda UK.

Dun Bheagan Highland Aged 15 Years **(82)** n19 t22 f21 b20. Enormously sweet and malty with long toffee finish. **46%. ncf.** William Maxwell.

Glen Andrew Highland Single Malt 10 Years Old **(87)** n22 apple pie and custard; t22 wonderfully mouthfilling and chewy: great character. f22 the malty sweetness filters through and works well with developing spice; b21 what a pleasant, fun, unpretentious malt. More, please! **40%.** Highland & Islands Whisky Co.

Glenbeg Single Highland Malt **(82)** n21 t21 f20 b20. Young, tasty stuff that might be tastier still without the evident toffee. **40%**

Glenfoyle Highland Single Malt Aged 12 Years **(82)** n20 t22 f20 b20. Barley sugar on the nose; to taste clean malt, rich in texture and sweetens by the second. The finish is a bit fudgy. **40%.** Longman Distillers for Tesco UK.

Glenfoyle Highland Single Malt Aged 17 Years dist 85 **(72)** n17 t19 f18 b18. Sweet, ungainly and bitter towards the finish. I know those who love this style of malt – but not my cup of tea, so to speak. **40%.** Longman Distillers for Tesco.

Glen Gordon 1957 Single Highland Malt **(88)** n23 beautiful spices dart out from the rich sherry; t22 intense from the start, the spice bringing with it dry oak and a hint of liquorice; f21 pretty dry and tired around the edges, but still impressive; b22 that supreme Glen Grant/Glenfarclas sherry style that displays sheer class despite the age. **40%**

Inverey Single Highland Malt Aged 12 Years **(78)** n20 t20 f18 b20. Subtle and satisfying. **40%.** Marks & Spencer UK.

Majestic Wine Warehouse Mature Highland Malt Aged 8 Years **(77)** n20 t20 f19 b18. Decent malt struggles to penetrate the caramel. **40%.** Majestic UK.

McClelland's Highland Single Malt Sherry Cask **(78)** n19 t21 f19 b19. Silky and succulent but limited complexity **40%.** Morrison Bowmore.

McClelland's Highland Single Malt Aged 10 Years **(76)** n17 t21 f20 b18. A malty, spicy recovery after an indifferent start on the nose. Too sweet in places, though, and the balance suffers. **40%.** Somerfield Stores UK.

McClelland's Highland Single Malt 16 Years Old (79) n20 t21 f19 b19. A rich dram with lots of chewability. **40%.** Morrison Bowmore.

MacLeod's Highland Aged 8 Years (see Glen Moray)

Safeway Highland Single Malt 12 Years Old (89) n22 lemon, lime and kumquat softened by fresh-crushed barley; t23 massive citrus character that is clean and mouthwatering. The malt almost crackles on the palate; f22 genuinely lip-smacking and moreish with a late hint of smoke; b22 a very impressive own-label brand that has a lot to say for itself. A gem of its genre – absolutely adore it! **40%.** UK.

Sainsbury's Single Highland Malt Aged 12 Years (84) n21 t23 f19 b21. An impressively tempered dram allowing full vent to a complex range of malty-vanilla tones. Cut the finish-deadening caramel and it would be right up there. **40%.** UK.

Stronachie Single Highland Malt Aged 12 Years (82) n18 t21 f22 b21. An enjoyably busy dram with impressive soft spice follow-through. The nose is so-so, but some decent esters make for a chewy mouthful. Very slightly smoked, but seeing how this is meant to be the spirit of a malt distillery closed in 1928 a little more peat wouldn't go amiss for authenticity's sake. **43%.** A Dewar Rattray.

Tantallan 10 Years Old Highland Single Malt (89) n22 fresh figs and moist barley, a hint of clove; t23 the nose tells you what's coming and there is no disappointment: massive malt surge, mouthwatering and refreshing; f21 beautifully textured finish as the barley unites with the light oak; b23 the sheer brilliance of this whisky is its simplicity. Limited colouring interference and a severe lack of sherry means that the barley can do as it pleases. And pleases, it does. **40%.** The Vintage Malt Whisky Co.

Waitrose 12 Years Old Highland Single Malt (72) n18 t20 f17 b17. Some malty thrust, but the caramel is all-conquering. Waitrose Stores. UK.

Walker & Scott 12 Years Old Single Highland Malt (77) n19 t19 f20 b19. Citrussy, but quite hot and furry. Decent late spice and mild honey thread. **40%**

Wm Morrison Highland Single Malt Aged 10 Years (80) n21 t21 f18 b20. Really superb nose and mouth arrival but dulls as the oak and caramel combine. Overall, though, pretty good chewing whisky. Morrison Supermarkets UK.

UNSPECIFIED SINGLE MALTS (Island)

Majestic Wine Warehouses Island Single Malt 8 Years Old (88) n24 a nigh-faultless, clean, crisp peat aroma dovetails some youngish oaky notes: really fabulous; t22 complex interplay between fresh but mature sweet peat and first-class oak; f20 dies slightly and becomes a little bitter as complexity is lost; b22 although delivered to my tasting lab in May 2003, the bottler's date suggests early November 1999. Surely a malt as deliciously good as this hasn't been hanging around on the shelves that long? **40%.** Majestic Wine Warehouses UK.

Waitrose 10 Year Old Island from the Orkney Isles (87) n22 surprisingly well-peated, really delicate; t23 again the peat has a big input with some barley-sugar malt that is hard and flinty in contrast; f20 soft oak, smoke, burnt honey and caramel; b22 a seriously odd dram. Not even Highland Park is usually this peaty. Either we have a delightful, magnificent freak, or someone didn't change the filters after bottling the Islay – not! Either way, a real treat of a dram!! **40%.** Waitrose Stores UK.

UNSPECIFIED SINGLE MALTS (Islay)

Ardnave Single Islay Malt Aged 12 Years (88) n22 clean, oily, intense malt with a mildly salty edge to the sweetness; t23 glorious gathering of barley, sprinkled with light muscovado sugar, followed by delicate oak; **f**21 mildly bitter by comparison, a hint of toffee but still the buttery malt battles through; **b**22 there will be those who buy this as an Islay single malt disappointed that it is not bursting from the cork-top with peat. However true Islay-philes will recognise this as a really outstanding example of the unpeated variety: if this isn't Bruichladdich, then my name's Ricardo Patermismo. Having gone non-chill filtered, just wish they had the confidence to go non-coloured (I suspect). **41.2%. ncf.** *Grey Rodgers for Tesco UK.*

Finlaggen Islay Single Malt 17 Years Old (72) n20 **t**20 **f**15 **b**17. Sweet and chewy, but lots of toffee drowning out the complexity. Can't say I'm that impressed. **46%.** *The Vintage Malt Whisky Co.*

Finlaggen Islay Single Malt 21 Years Old (75) n20 **t**19 **f**18 **b**18. Some chewy moments, but overall strangely off-beam. **46%.** *The Vintage Malt Whisky Co.*

Finlaggen Old Reserve Islay Single Malt (94) n23 big breakfast fruitiness (Old Preserve, more like), plus nuts and chocolate. What a start! **t**23 fat mouth arrival, more chocolate and ... oh, peat, lashings of it; **f**24 back to fruit again, then a chocolate mousse; all interlocked by peat. Brilliant; **b**24 this is simply awesome. Someone has had access to one or two of the best casks the east coast of Islay has to offer. If you don't get a bottle of this, you'll regret it for the rest of your life. **40%.** *The Vintage Malt whisky Co.*

The Ileach Peaty Islay Single Malt (94) n24 a thick chunk of peat has been dissolved in my glass; **t**24 the oil-peat-barley balance is spot on, as is the bitter-sweet tone: just stunning; **f**23 the peat dissipates slowly to leave a slightly bitterish, oaky influence. But the spices compensate; **b**23 couldn't be an Islay single malt, perchance? Fabulous stuff, a bottle of which should sit in every household cabinet. A wonder dram. **40%.** *The Highlands & Islands Scotch Whisky Co.*

The Islay Whisky Shop Islay Single Malt Aged 9 Years (85) n21 clean, malty, soft vanilla; **t**22 silky texture and intense malt: dissolves in the mouth and never becomes too sweet; **f**21 vanilla and toffee; **b**21 try and convince me this isn't a Bruichladdich.... **43%.** *Islay only.*

McClelland's Islay Single Malt (87) n23 crisp, sea-breeze and kippery malt; **t**21 sweet malt and banana, softly oiled and enormous barley character. The peat drifts serenely along; **f**21 very light vanilla and fading peat; **b**22 what a really elegant and gentle whisky this is, quite unlike what the nose at first suggests. A reflective dram. **40%.** *Morrison Bowmore.*

MacLeod's Islay 8-y-o (see Lagavulin).

Majestic Wine Warehouses Islay Malt 8 Years Old ("this whisky has been aged in oak casks at the distillery") **(89) n**22 soft, creamy, clean peat; **t**22 rich, oily, smoked malt, lazy vanilla tones; **f**23 spice arrives as the textures changes from creamy to layered. With it comes a lovely bitter-sweet battle; **b**22 so refreshing to find an Islay malt at this relatively young age. The marks would be higher still but for the caramel: 46% non-coloured, non-chill filtered? The mind boggles. This is sumptuous, top-drawer whisky by any standards: truly Majestic. **40%.** *UK.*

Marks & Spencer Islay Single Malt Aged 10 Years (86) n23 the most delicate of peaty Islays: softly salted, almost crisp peat and malt, no more than a hint of oak. Just like being there; **t**21 soft and very silky malt, then an oily-oaky dryness; **f**21 remains dry at first, then sweet peat re-emerges; **b**21 doesn't quite live up to the nose, but a lovely dram all the same and a decent example of its genre. **40%.** *For Marks & Spencer UK.*

Old Masters Islay 1992 cask 3200 (89) n23 fabulous, clean, gristy and punchy peat; **t**24 young yet old enough to reveal enormous complexity amid the sparkling peat, sweet, but one or two oaky notches; **f**20 flattens slightly, toffee amid the dying embers; **b**22 no prisoners taken early on, but relents toward the end. **59.9%.** *James MacArthur.*

The Pibroch 12 Years Old Islay Single Malt (87) n22 oily and softly peated; t21 oily and sweet malt carries with it a clinging, silky smokiness; f22 softens to allow decent oak to arrive; b22 this was the name I wanted to launch my own Islay single malt brand with, some 20-odd years ago. But I have been beaten to it: damn! This is classical Caol Ila-style: oily with the peat subdued but still pretty rich. A very evocative dram in many ways. **43%**. *The Highlands & Islands Scotch Whisky Co.*

Waitrose 10 Year Old Islay (79) n20 t21 f18 b20. Velvet smooth and malt-sweet. But just about peatless. **40%**. *Waitrose Stores UK.*

UNSPECIFIED SINGLE MALTS (Lowland)

McClelland's Lowland Single Malt (85) n21 lively fruits, citrus in particular; t22 stunningly clean mouthfeel, then a tidal wave of grassy and fresh malt. The attractive sweetness is checked by a little spice; f21 remains a tad spicy with some vanilla offering ballast; b21 never spectacular, this is always just very good whisky with a steady development of complexity: in others words, a lovely dram. **40%**. *Morrison Bowmore.*

MacLeod's Lowland Single Malt Aged 8 Years (see Auchentoshan)

UNSPECIFIED SINGLE MALTS (Speyside)

Asda Speyside Single Malt 12 Years Old (83) n19 t22 f21 b21. A long, chewy malty dram that really spreads its wings for a refreshing middle. **40%**. *Douglas MacNiven. Asda UK.*

Glen Darbach Single Speyside Malt Aged 12 Years (71) n18 t19 f17 b17. Heather and honey say the label notes: oak says the nose. Just doesn't turn me on. **40%**. *Marks & Spencer UK.*

Glen Marnoch Single Speyside Aged 12 Years (77) n19 t21 f18 b19. Malty middle with impressive bite. **40%**. *Alistair Graham Aldi Stores.*

Glen Parker (see GlenParker)

Glen Parker Speyside Single Malt (77) n19 t20 f19 b19. Younger on nose and palate than the colour might suggest: good, sprightly chewing malt. Toffee on finish. **40%**. *Angus Dundee.*

Glinne Parras Single Speyside Malt Aged 12 Years (86) n22 fresh sliced cucumber and dry oak; t22 really big malt theme, richly textured; f21 long, sweet, confident with a mildly spicy counterattack; b21 solid, chewy, well-made whisky. **40%**. *Eaux de Vie.*

Hart Brothers Ballindalloch Aged 35 Years dist May 67, bott Sep 02 **(88)** n23 unreal: how can something spend this amount of time in wood and come out so fresh and malt-intense? The minty oak adds the faintest marmalade tang to the elegant complexity; t20 and it's that tart, citrussy note that shows first on the palate. The oak is weighty but not a blight, the malt firm and chewy; f23 big oak now with liquorice and cocoa taking the lead with some dashing spices in pursuit. The toasty flavours still include the stubborn malt which cling on to the oily body that forms by the second. This is now very big whisky; b22 this takes oak just about as far as I like to see it go. There is little sign of it on the nose, but it makes itself felt on arrival. But really it's the complexity of the oaky tones that gives such an enormous finish. Memorable stuff. **48.5%** *There is no such distillery as Ballindalloch. One can safely deduce that it is from the distillery in the area that takes a dim legal view of its name being used on a label it does not own: Glenfarclas. It's also a safe bet that a whisky of this enormous complexity at such an age is more likely to come from that Speyside distillery than any other.*

Lochruan Speyside Single Malt Scotch Aged 12 Years (86) n21 citrus-fresh, beautifully light with some curvaceous malty notes; t22 mouthwatering malt with more citrus sneaking in, fresh and only mildly oaked;

f21 a pinch of peat wafts in from somewhere, the malt dominates, but a Brownie point lost for the toffee; **b**22 a charming malt with good weight despite the citrus sub-stratum. I guess from the finish this has been coloured: would have been a belter in natural form. **40%.** *Leith Distillers for Tesco UK.*

McClelland's Speyside Single Malt (74) n17 **t**19 **f**20 **b**18. Heavy and oily. A good chew but somehow lacking a typical Speyside charm. **40%.** *Morrison Bowmore.*

McClelland's Speyside Single Malt Aged 10 Years (73) n19 **t**19 **f**17 **b**18. Surprisingly heavy for the region; oily and rumbustious but ultimately lacking the aplomb the region desires. **40%.** *Exclusive to Somerfeld Stores UK.*

MacLeod's Speyside Aged 8 Years (see Glenfarclas)

Safeway Speyside Single Malt 12 Years Old (77) n19 **t**19 **f**20 **b**19. Clean, malty, rich but a little bland in character. **40%.** *UK.*

Sainsbury's Single Speyside Malt Aged 12 Years (78) n18 **t**21 **f**19 **b**20. Above-average fruitiness and sweetness. **40%.** *UK.*

Sainsbury's Speyside Single Malt Matured for 15 Years Claret Finish (87) n23 a crisp fruitiness succeeds in accentuating some very clean malt: charming and stylish; **t**23 heavy-textured with the wine and grain labouring to hit a rhythm. The early mouthfeel, though, is lovely. The malts somersault around the tastebuds with abandon. The degree of sweetness is spot on; **f**20 surprisingly fresh for its age, remains confrontational but guarantees complexity; **b**21 an intriguing and on the whole pretty enjoyable dram. To be churlish and technical, could do with a little tightening up: that said, no way I'd say, "No." if offered a second one. Fun and fruity! **40%.** *UK.*

Waitrose 12 Year Old Speyside (72) n18 **t**20 **f**16 **b**18. Some lovely, sharp moments but dulled by caramel. **40%.** *Waitrose Stores UK.*

Waitrose Single Speyside Malt Whisky Matured in Port Wood for 21 Years dist 81 **(89) n**24 the malt and port just seem to fit like hand in glove, teasing spicy notes amid succulent, juice-dripping fruit notes: rare and ravishing; **t**22 impressively clean winey feel and a texture not unlike wine-gum candy, playful spices throughout and for a brief second a surge of something vaguely smoky; **f**21 at last the malt emerges from the fruit and intertwines with the vanilla; **b**22 it could be argued the port has taken too firm a grip, but to be honest I don't care ... and I actually don't think so. Very rare to find port pipes of this quality and whisky matured in it for this long – usually finishing the done thing. An almost unique whisky for which Waitrose deserve enormous credit in adding to their own-label portfolio. A real dram for real whisky lovers to learn a little more about the world's greatest spirit. I can see droves of European malt whisky lovers taking special flights just to get hold of this one ... **40%.** *William Maxwell for Waitrose UK.*

Wm Morrison Speyside Single Malt Aged 10 Years (86) n21 classic green, grassy maltiness. Some vanilla confirms the sympathetic age; **t**22 delicate, complex and pretty sophisticated stuff; **f**21 long with firm, slightly oily mouthfeel and good malt-vanilla balance, even some late spice, spoiled only by the toffee-effect from the caramel; **b**22 malts like this are in danger of getting supermarkets a good name. **40%.** *Morrison's UK.*

UNSPECIFIED SINGLE MALTS (General)

Celtic Whisky Malt Scotch 12 Years Old (89) n21 some quality oak sits comfortably with the rich barley; **t**22 crisp, clean barley which develops in a honied direction; **f**23 more honey and then a gradual increase in spicy oak; **b**23 genuinely first-rate whisky of a Highland-meets-Perthshire style, massive complexity and balance; **40%** *from the Celtic Spirit Company – that's the Celtic race: not to be confused with football club. Although doesn't say so on the label, I can confirm this is a single malt.*

The Classic Cask of The Millennium Aged 35 Years batch SW-202, dist 6/64, bott 9/99 **(87) n**22 very sweet, nutty, gathering fruit intensity; **t**22 enormously sweet and silky, almost coffee-liqueur-like in its arrival: massive sherry effect; **f**22 very long with some sensational and sensual toffee-coffee notes: pure velvet. The oak is pure sugared vanilla; **b**21 a distinctive and highly unusual malt, probably a Speysider, that has been swamped by one of the sweetest, silkiest sherry butts I've ever come across. One for the ladies. **40%.** *The Glenaden Distilling Co. 600 bottles.*

Cu Dhu (see Speyside Distillery)

Diners Club International Scotch Whisky 8 Years Malt (78) n18 **t**21 **f**19 **b**20. Lively, mouthwatering Speyside-style. **40%.** *Douglas Denham.*

Glen Shira (distillery, age unspecified) **(77) n**19 **t**21 **f**19 **b**18. A young, barely pubescent dram full of refreshing, uncomplicated but mouthwatering malt. Without the caramel, which guarantees a cream-toffee finish, it would have been a stormer. **40%.** *Exclusive to Asda UK.*

Glentromie 17 Years Old (distillery unspecified) **(68) n**19 **t**17 **f**16 **b**16. Charisma-free. **40%.** *Speyside Distillers. Not from own distillery.*

Harrod's Single Malt Aged 12 Years **(78) n**19 **t**21 **f**19 **b**19. Steady, untaxing game with a pleasant honied sheen to the finish. **40%**

Scotland Vatted Malts (also Pure Malts)

The year 2003 will probably not go down as a vintage year for the launching of great vatted malt. Even though, without question, it was one of the most promising in living memory. But, sadly, that is not a surprise. Because if Vatted Malt Vintages are declared like Port Vintages, it is unlikely we will have had one since Noah was collecting wood.

What is it about vatted malt? Just why are good ones so hard to find?

I have my suspicions. Mainly it is because they tend to be cheaper than single malts, often bin ends of parcels of malts overlooked elsewhere – often with good reason – but perfect when thrown together to hit a designated market at the right price. In those cases quality takes a back seat ... and it shows.

Really, vatted malts should be very good indeed. Because, like blends, they should offer the drinker a complexity and balance that single malts cannot achieve alone. But often it seems that they miss the cut and thrust of grain whisky, that often misunderstood, even pilloried, whisky type. The result can be something dull and lifeless, a whisky desperate for a spark of inventiveness from somewhere.

Newcomers to whisky are often unsure just what a vatted malt is. Commonly it is marketed as a "Pure Malt". Labels that tend not to make a point that the whisky inside the bottle is a single malt are likely to say "Pure Malt". Which means, quite simply, that it is a whisky made from 100% malted barley, but not necessarily from the just a single distillery. For that reason any label offering "Pure Malt" has been included in the vatted malt section, for vatted means that it is malt from more than one distillery but containing no grain.

It has to be said, though, that since January 2002 the quality at the top end of the vatted malt spectrum has risen. Standing out from the mundane has been some pretty impressive bottlings with James Martin's Pure Malt 20 Years Old among the elite, though that went only in limited supply to Japan, and more commonly The Famous Grouse Vintage Malt 1992. In 2003 we have seen the slightly controversial Cardhu Pure Malt hit the shelves and a very decent Compass Box model, this one called Eleuthera Vatted Malt. Sadly, if understandably, it wasn't quite in the same league as the now legendary Eleuthera All Malt.

But the one for me that has stood out and given the entire sector a welcome wake up call is the astonishing Six Isles Pure Island Malt. Some years back a small company I was consulting for asked me to come up with something new that would be revolutionary in theme and style if they went ahead and launched a vatted malt. I suggested a whisky comprising only malts from all Scotland's islands. My suggestion declined. And probably just as well because the stocks available to work with would never have created something quite as profound and wonderful as this most exciting of new drams.

Ian MacLeod through Six Isle has thrown down the vatted malt gauntlet. It will be interesting to see if there will be anyone out there in the next year or two willing to respond.

Baxter's Malt (88) n21 simple, clean, uncluttered fresh malt; **t**22 beautiful mouth arrival, refreshing clean malt; **f**23 outstanding development continuing on the same theme; **b**22 no great age to this but it's all about classic, soft Speyside character. Lovely stuff. **40%**. *Gordon & MacPhail for Baxter's. Found in the famous soup company's shops on Speyside and at Aberdeen Airport.*

Baxter's 8 Years Old Malt (83) n20 **t**22 **f**20 **b**21. Good weight and oil with some citrus on the malt. The oak adds a late dash of bitterness. **40%**. *Gordon & MacPhail for Baxter's. Found only in the Baxter's shops at Aberdeen Airport and at Fochabers, Speyside.*

Blackadder Smoking Islay cask 2002/01 **(86) n**21 raw, young, windswept beaches; peat-reek from a nearby lumb etc. **t**23 massive, clean, sweet peat, hardly any oak standing in the way; **f**22 big spices and continued concentrated malt. The peat is everywhere but remains raw and unrefined; **b**20 a pretty youngish Islay taking no prisoners. **55%. nc ncf sc** *(99% of one malt and 1% of something else added by the distillers to prevent it being sold as a self whisky).*

Blairmhor 8 Years Old (76) n22 **t**20 **f**16 **b**18. The citrus notes suggest. Old Pulteney on the nose, but the finish is rather half-hearted. **40%**. *Inver House.*

Cardhu Speyside Pure Malt Aged 12 Years (88) n22 superbly complex: no shortage of citrus and apple and pear notes to complement the deep malt, but there is also significant, almost dry, chalky oak – far more than the original Cardhu single malt – taking it off in a vaguely bourbony direction. Some spice buzz, too; **t**23 much more punchy and spicy than its single malt predecessor with some weighty cocoa arriving early as the oak bites. The intensity and mouthfeel of the chewy, sweet malt is exceptional, the cleanliness awesome; **f**21 the cocoa remains constant with a soft drying from the earlier sweet barley; a fraction too much oak at the death; **b**22 this is a gloriously crafted vatted malt with the signature of Cardhu – sorry, I mean Cardow – clearly at the heart. On the downside there is just too much oak for such a delicate creature as this. And the description on the carton perhaps needs a little attention: "The whisky is distilled by the Spey ..." True if it were Cardhu in single malt form. But seeing as the whole point is that it isn't and there are lot of Speyside distilleries a long way from the Spey.... **40%**

Century of Malts (94) n23 lots of malty snap and buzz, some intriguing apple-smoke tones, fresh and wonderfully complex; **t**24 mindblowing complexity on arrival: Speysiders lead the pack but some wonderful strands of honey, smoke and oak guarantee imperious complexity; **f**23 long, busy malt still beautifully weighted and textured with the oak slowly bleeding into the picture; **b**24 tragically, a brand now discontinued: certainly the most complete vatted malt I have come across in my lifetime. Having malts from 100 distilleries is one thing, vatting them in harmony for near perfect weight and texture is something else. This was probably Colin Scott and his team's finest moment: an art form and treasure. By the way, the little book that comes with it is a work of genius, too ... **40%**. *Chivas.*

Clan Campbell 10 Years Old Vatted Malt (83) n20 **t**22 **f**20 **b**21. Fruitier, less feisty than the blend, as one might expect. But much less fun! Competent as drinking malt all the same. **40%**. *Chivas.*

Compass Box Eleuthera All Malt (first bottling with star compass points and orange/brown label, called "All Malt".) **(93) n**23 something herbal, some delicate citrus notes amid the outstanding barley and hiding oak. very clean, very different. The soft peat offers the perfect frame; **t**24 the immediate arrival on the palate is awesome with the flavours enveloping the mouth. It's all about texture and complexity rather than indiviual flavours: outstanding; **f**22 sweet at first, then a slow seeping of drying oak, couched by lingering smoke; **b**24 quite simply, one of the most complex and truly magnificent vatted malts of all time. A collector's piece. **46%. ncf nc.**

Compass Box Eleuthera Vatted Malt (second bottling (2003) with mauve central illustration, called "Vatted Malt".) **(87)** n22 peat is a little crisper, the barley dry and biscuity; **t**21 silky sweet arrival of peat then a fall-out of lighter, sharper, malty tones and vanilla; **f**22 very long, with beautiful intertwining of smoke, oak and barley; **b**22 a slightly smokier, oilier version. Delicious, but lacking that previous touch of genius. **46%. ncf nc.**

Douglas MacNiven Islay Pure Malt 10 Years Old (82) n21 t21 f20 **b**20. Chunky, raw, green and young for its age but unmistakably from just one particular place in the world. **40%.** Asda UK.

Dun Bheagan Pure Malt Aged 8 Years (81) n19 t22 f20 b20. Big, malty, sweet and very full flavoured. **43%. ncf.** William Maxwell.

The Famous Grouse Vintage Malt 1987 aged 12 Years (86) n21 bananas, grapes, oranges, figs: they are all there if you hunt for them, very clean and crystalline with a hint of peat; **t**22 teasing malt, lush fruit and soft smoke; **f**22 fruity, with soft oak and vanilla intermingling; **b**21 when this was released in 1999 you have no idea what a relief it was to find a well-mixed vatted malt. Re-visiting it for the first time in a couple of years, I can see why I was so pleased to see it. **40%**

The Famous Grouse Vintage Malt 1989 aged 12 Years (73) n19 t20 17 **b**17. A marked disappointment on the original '87. You get the feeling that extra sherry and perhaps caramel have combined to create something as hilly as a witch's chest. **40%**

The Famous Grouse Vintage Malt 1990 bottled 03 **(78)** n17 t21 f20 b20. Pity about the poor sherry nose. The mouth arrival is scrummy. **40%**

The Famous Grouse Vintage Malt 1992 bottled 02 **(89)** n21 complex: seems weighty at first but has plenty of air, too. Some crisp malt in there; **t**23 superb mouth arrival with a velvety floor of juicy malt. The fruitiness keeps in harmony. Overall, superbly mouthwatering; **f**22 touches of vanilla reveal some oak, but still it's the malt, with a little fizzing spice for company, that stars; **b**23 a joyously harmonious affair, boasting supreme complexity and confidence. A classic vintage and a classic vatting. **40%**

Fortnum & Mason Highland Malt 12 Years Old (74) n19 t20 f17 b18. A bland dram floored, it seems, by caramel and perhaps (though impossible to tell) sherry in tandem. **40%.** UK.

Glenalmond Highland Malt dist 94, bott 02 **(83)** n21 t21 f20 b21. Above-average vatted malt, cleverly using the relative youth of the barley to form refreshing waves around the mouth. Impressive. **40%.** The Vintage Malt Whisky Co.

Glencoe Aged 8 Years (see MacDonald's Glencoe)

Glen Nicol (80) n20 t20 f20 b20. An honest Joe of a malt: lots of lively character and straight as a die. **40%.** Inver House.

Glen Roger's Pure Malt Aged 8 Years Old Reserve (63) n18 t17 f13 b15. About as dead as a whisky gets. For French market.

Glen Rosa Pure Malt (83) n21 t22 f20 b20. Young, oily, fruity with massive Arran influence. Sweet, malty and easily drinkable. **40%.** Isle of Arran.

Glen Rosa Pure Malt 8 Years Old (81) n20 t22 f19 b20. Quite a bitter finish to the sweet malt. Quite light but chewy. **40%.** Isle of Arran.

Glenstone (71) n17 t19 f17 b18. Raw and full on. **40%.** Kyndal.

Hedges & Butler Special Pure Malt (76) n18 t19 f20 b19. Very evenly weighted and juicy. **40%**

Highland Fusilier 8 Years Old (78) n19 t20 f19 b20. Well-balanced and plenty of body. **40%.** *Gordon & MacPhail.*

Inverarity Islay 10 Years Old (85) n22 laid-back, clean peat, gristy and dry; t21 woollen-textured and delicately peated; f21 quite chalky and dryish on one level, some peat offers something a little sweeter on another; b21 almost a teasing dram, so soft the flavours barely make it round the mouth. Something delightfully different. **40%**

The Jacobite Highland Malt (84) n20 t21 f22 b21. A mouthwatering, fresh, effervescent and complex malt, especially towards the finish. **40%.** *Malt House Vintners.*

James Martin 8 Year Old Malt (87) n21 complex and quite toasty: drier and oakier than the average 8-y-o; t22 stylish mouthfeel, malty and a build-up of subtle sweet, citrus notes; f22 long, remains slightly chalky but the malts are inscrutable; b22 a discreet, thoughful vatting quite beautifully constructed. **40%.** *Glenmorangie for Oddbins UK.*

James Martin's Pure Malt 20 Years Old bott 02 (89) n22 honey and very soft smoke, sweetish but some pleasant oak, too; t23 big honey surge with the malt bubbling through in almost syrupy form but without the usual over sweetness from a similar texture: something to really savour; f22 dries slightly towards bitter chocolate with a dash of smoke wafting around for good measure; b22 what an extraordinary whisky: it poured like a liquor and, when tasted, offered the creamiest body I can ever remember coming across in nearly 30 years. Just amazing. A way above-average vatted malt with a touch of everything. **46%.** *Glenmorangie. 500 bottles Japan.*

Johnnie Walker Green Label 15 Years Old (92) n24 this is one of the best vatted noses on the market: superb complexity, relatively peatless but still boasting big weight amid some fresher Speyside notes; t23 bingo! Serious flavour explosion which leans towards malty sweetness with a gradual fade-in of drier oak; f22 now some oils arrive, plus a little mint suggesting good age; b23 this is easily one of the best vatted malts in the market, pretty sweet, too. **43%**

Label 5 Pure Malt Matured for 12 Years (77) n20 t21 f17 b19. Competent and initially attractive. **40%.** *First Blending Co.*

The Living Cask (91) n22 spicy and lively; thick-textured malt and reasonable oak; t22 mouthwatering, sweet malt notes with a developing fruity edge and smoke; f24 remains chunky and intense and there are signs of the sweetness of the malt abating. Very soft signs of peat towards the outstanding and cocoa-laced finale; b23 just one of those drams you can chew forever. The complexity is awesome. **56%.** *Probably the most pointless tasting notes I'll ever write, as the whole point of the vatting is that it changes constantly as defined by George Saintsbury in his Notes On A Cellar Book of the 1920s. There he suggests topping up a cask of whisky on a solera basis, which is what they have been doing for a few years now at Loch Fyne Whiskies at Inveraray. Shifting sands, with very few bottlings the same, but fun anyway! This sample was drawn in June 2003.*

Lochinvar Pure Malt (84) n19 t22 f22 b21. A very good dram indeed showing no shortage of honey-smoke notes in the chorus. Rich, full-bodied and clearly one of the better ones to be found around Europe's supermarkets. *Roscow Greig (Somerfield) UK.*

MacDonald's Glencoe Aged 8 Years (82) n20 t22 f20 b20. Mouthwatering in parts; lots of cereal, spice and kick. **58%. nc.** *Ben Nevis Distillery.*

Matisse Pure Malt Over 12 Years (73) n16 t21 f18 b18. Explosive on the palate, but too much caramel. **40%**

Old Elgin 8 Years Old (82) n21 t20 f21 b20. Lush, lengthy, honied and a little spicy. A good anytime, anywhere whisky. **40%.** *Gordon & MacPhail.*

Old Elgin 15 Years Old (71) n17 t19 f17 b18. A tad sulphury and off-key **40%.** *Gordon & MacPhail.*

Poit Dhubh 8 Bliadhna (81) n20 **t**22 **f**19 **b**20. Generously peated and rich in the middle but foiled by very un-Gaelic toffee. **43%**. *Praban Na Linne. Conduct their business, whenever possible, in Gaelic: bliadhna means "years old".*

Poit Dhubh 12 Bliadhna (82) n22 **t**21 **f**19 **b**20. Big, fruity and complex but rather bitter. **40%**. *Praban Na Linne.*

Poit Dhubh 12 Bliadhna Unchillfiltered (88) n23 oranges and juicy pears combine spectacularly wth a peat sub-stratum; **t**21 a mildly flat, toffeed arrival but then an eruption of smoky spices; **f**22 more spice, sweetening malt and then vanilla; **b**22 an exceptionally fine vatted malt with considerable attitude, complexity and personality to get over the low-key mouth arrival. Great stuff. **46%. ncf.** *Praban Na Linne.*

Poit Dhubh 21 Bliadhna (85) n22 fruity and spicy; **t**22 big, juicy malt arrival with spices and a touch of smoke; **f**20 rich toffee but some salty compromise; **b**21 a mouthwatering vatting with a distinctly coastal saltiness. **43%. ncf.** *Praban Na Linne.*

Pride of Islay 12 Years Old (88) n22 real hospital antiseptic stuff here, oily, too; **t**22 comes to life with a soft upping of peaty intensity after some original fruity notes wear thin; **f**23 quite long and enjoys fine integration between peat and oak; **b**21 I love the gentle but firm nature of the peat with this one. Unusual as an Islay but then, as a vatted version, so it should be. **40%**. *Gordon & MacPhail.*

Pride of the Lowlands 12 Years Old (77) n20 **t**18 **f**20 **b**19. Lively and the character of a certain distillery shines clearly through. **40%**. *Gordon & MacPhail.*

Pride of Orkney 12 Years Old (72) n18 **t**19 **f**18 **b**17. A vatting from Orkney … now I wonder which distilleries they used? As it happens, there is a very slight soapiness to this one. **40%**. *Gordon & MacPhail.*

Pride of Speyside 12 Years Old (87) n21 really deep malt, a touch of citrus and raw carrot! **t**22 beautiful mouthfeel. There is a sheen to the malt which intensifies as the oak encroaches; **f**22 stylish cocoa-touched finish: not the most complex, but elegant and shapely; **b**22 well if good ol' G&M can't get it right with a vatted Speysider, no-one can. A lovely dram. **40%**. *Gordon & MacPhail.*

Prince Lordon Old Malt (79) n21 **t**20 **f**19 **b**19. Clean, lively energetic malt, sharp grassy notes, refreshing on the nose, with enormous cream-toffee body and finish. **40%**. *VDB Spirit. A specially prepared kosher whisky, in which no sherry is used barrels are cleaned and so on. For US market.*

Royal Swan 10 Years Old Pure Malt (70) n18 **t**19 **f**16 **b**17. Fun at first, let down by dodgy finish. **40%**. *Quality Spirits International.*

Sainsbury's Malt Whisky Finished in Sherry Casks (69) n17 **t**20 **f**16 **b**16. Back to the drawing board on this one: balance is at a premium. Some better quality butts wouldn't go amiss. **40%**. *UK.*

Sainsbury's Pure Islay Malt Aged 10 Years (90) n23 oily, tarry, heavy … and peaty; **t**23 outstanding oak and oil weight to guide the complex peat around the tastebuds; **f**22 softens, lots of vegetation; **b**22 you could not expect to find better from an own-label brand. One for Islay-philes to savour (except for evidence of caramel, which has docked points off the finish). Otherwise, pure Islay malt, indeed. **40%**. *UK.*

Safeway Islay Pure Malt 10 Years Old (94) n24 just stupendous salty, iodine peat character. The complexity is enormous; **t**23 gently oiled but otherwise a supreme mixture of gristy malt and a harder, firm barley juiciness; **f**23 about as long a finish as you could wish for with the gristiness continuing and at last some oak giving drection; **b**24 one of those stupendous drams that carries you back to the island wherever you may be sitting or standing at the time of drinking. Forget the fact this is from a supermarket, or is most probably vatted. This is Islay: an eye-wetting gem! Whisky you pray for. **40%**. *UK.*

Safeway Vatted Malt Aged 8 Years (70) n17 **t**18 **f**18 **b**17. Feinty and flawed on the nose but otherwise rich-textured and intensely malty. **40%**. *UK.*

Scottish Pride 12 Years Old Pure Malt (80) n20 **t**21 **f**19 **b**20. A lively, lovely and busy vatted malt of some character. **40%**

Sheep Dip (84) n19 **t**22 **f**22 **b**21. Young and sprightly like a new-born lamb, this enjoys a fresh, mouthwatering grassy style wth a touch of spice. Maligned by some, but to me a clever, accomplished vatting of alluring complexity. **40%**

The Six Isles Pure Island Malt Uisge Beatha (943) n24 fresh, alluring, sensuously smoked with an underlying intense barley charisma; **t**23 a gentle massaging of young peat malt never becomes overly sweet, beautifully oily and lush; **f**23 long, increasingly spicy: a glorious array of vanilla and barley; **b**24 Wow! For all the peat, the strength of the whisky is its masterful balance: never sweet, never dry. About as charming and charismatic a vatted malt as you are likely to find. Contains malt from Islay, Jura, Skye, Mull, Orkney and Arran. Together they make unquestionably the best standard, non-deluxe vatted malt I have found in my lifetime. **43%.** *William Maxwell.*

Stewarts Pure Malt (68) n16 **t**18 **f**17 **b**17. Loads of flavour but, for me, just doesn't gel **40%.** *Kyndal.*

Tambowie Highland Pure Malt (75) n18 **t**20 **f**19 **b**18. Don't think that this is the old Tambowie distillery come back to life. Just a vatted malt put together to bring the old name back to life? It's claimed that this is what they think the old distillery (built in 1885 – great year: that's when Millwall FC were founded) would have produced. My own feeling is that this is a degree too light in character. **40%.** *The Vintage Malt Whisky Co.*

Tambowie Highland Pure Malt 12 Years Old (73) n18 **t**18 **f**19 **b**18. Slightly fusty; has some bright fruity moments but fades too quickly. **40%.** *The Highlands & Islands Scotch Whisky Co.*

Tulchan Lodge 12 Year Old Speyside Malt (80) n19 **t**20 **f**21 **b**20. Pretty rich and builds up well; the toffee dictates at the last. **40%.** *Tulchan Estate.*

Vintner's Choice Highland Aged 10 Years (60) n18 **t**15 **f**13 **b**14. Staggeringly flat and unimpressive. **40%**

Vintner's Choice Speyside Aged 10 Years (73) n16 **t**19 **f**19 **b**19. Malty with some fruit. **40%**

Vintner's Choice Speyside Pure Malt Aged 10 years Finished in Port Wood dist 1991, bott Nov 2001 **(82) n**20 **t**22 **f**21 **b**19. Highly enjoyable, but lacking a little balance. **43%**

Waitrose Highland Malt Sherry Finished (80) n20 **t**21 **f**20 **b**19, Rich fruitcake with bite and spice to counter the softness of the sherry. **40%.** *Waitrose Stores UK.*

Waitrose Pure Highland Malt (78) n20 **t**21 **f**18 **b**19. Highly intense, delicious malt with some spice. *Waitrose Stores UK.*

Whisky Galore Pure Malt Aged 10 Years (60) n16 **t**16 **f**13 **b**15. Featureless. One to forget ... had there been anything to remember in the first place. **40%.** *Whisky Galore Ltd.*

Wm Morrison Islay Pure Malt Aged 10 Years (86) n21 delicate, moderately peated, seashores and that kind of stuff; **t**22 sweet with some pleasant vanilla notes to tone down the smoke, good malt firmness towards the middle; **f**21 quite light and clean then caramel toffee; **b**22 a very delicate and well-structured Islay for reflective moments. Doesn't paint the peat with a tar brush.

Wm Morrison Pure Malt Aged 8 Years ("A selection of Speyside malts") **(85) n**23 classically crisp and sharp malty notes; **t**22 a bristling array of malt and soft vanilla, absolutely deliciously tastebuds-tingling until...; **f**19 Aaaaarrrggghhhh!!!!! Bloody caramel spoils the party yet again; **b**21 this is really lovely young Speyside malt of the most mouthwatering variety. And then the caramel spreads toffee everywhere. Please stop spoiling otherwise really good whisky!!!!! **40%.** *UK.*

MYSTERY MALTS

"As We Get It" Aged 8 Years (78) n*18* t*20* f*21* b*19*. Lovely, intense malt on a dais of rich oil, but the slightly overpowering oak influence on this bottling suggests we have something a lot older then "8". **59.4%.** *J.G Thomson (bottling no. L2018BB).*

Anchor Bay (74) n*17* t*20* f*18* b*19*. Sweet overall, with a furry, bitter finish. **40%.** *Lombard.*

Blackadder Raw Cask Blairfindy (see Glenfarclas)

Pebble Beach (Speyside Distillation Area) **(79)** n*18* t*21* f*20* b*20*. Fresh, clean malt but toffee-caramel dominates. **40%.** *Lombard.*

Golden Harvest (75) n*19* t*20* f*18* b*18*. Another Lombard brand that looks promising but appears to be done to death by caramel. **40%.** *Lombard.*

Driftwood Highland Distillation Area (70) n*18* t*19* f b*17*. Flat; sinks without trace. **40%.** *Lombard.*

Tidal Ebb Islay Distillation Area (83) n*21* t*22* f*20* b*20*. Some lovely peaty tones softened by light muscovado sugar. **40%.** *Lombard.*

Smoking Ember (81) n*22* t*20* f*20* b*19*. The nose is glorious, fresh, straight from the malt kiln. But the full follow-through fails to materialise. **40%.** *Lombard.*

Spey Vintage 15 Years Old Highland Malt dist 86 **(74)** n*17* t*19* f*19* b*19*. A malt that improves with familiarity and one for those with a fruity disposition. **40%.** *Alec Harvey Private Reserve. 18,645 bottles.*

Gordon & MacPhail Christmas Malt 10 Years Old bott 02 **(85)** n*20* firm, crisp malt; t*22* big and mouthwatering malt, grassy and firm; f*21* big malt finale with some really classy oaky notes; b*22* quality malt, worth drinking more than once a year. **40%.**

Old St Andrews 5 Years Old Malt (in miniature bottle encased in plastic barrel) **(83)** n*19* t*22* f*21* b*21*. A refreshing, mouthwatering dignified young dram of good stock. **40%.** *Rarely, in 30 years of opening whisky bottles, have I made such an ass of myself as with this one. The malt inside came as a welcome relief after the ordeal. If, like me, you spend an hour wondering how to get into the thing, here's a tip: the barrel holder is detachable. I will say no more.*

Old St Andrews 15 Years Old Malt (in miniature bottle encased in plastic barrel) **(81)** n*20* t*22* f*19* b*20*. Malty and chewy with lots of vanilla and toffee. **40%.** *For barrel opening instructions, see above.*

Inverarity 10 Years Old (see Aultmore)

Inverarity Ancestral 14 Years Old (see Balmenach)

Are you member of a Whisky Club? Contact Jim Murray at
www.whiskybible.com and let him add you to the international listing.

Scottish Grain

It's a bit weird, really. Many whisky lovers stay clear of blended Scotch, preferring instead single malts. The reason, I am often told, is that the grain included in a blend makes it rough and ready. Yet I wish I had a ten pound note for each time I have been told in the last year how much someone enjoys a single grain.

The ones that the connoisseurs die for are the older versions, special independent bottlings displaying great age. Yet only a few months back I was asked if I could include a young grain at a tasting to show what melt-in-the-mouth merchants these whiskies can be.

I wasn't given enough time to get the sample in, but I will show grains at tastings any day. Because, like single malts, grain distilleries produce whisky bearing their own style and signature. And, also, some display characteristics and a richness that can surprise and delight.

Most of the grains available in (usually specialist) whisky outlets are pretty elderly. Most are made from corn. Wheat was not introduced until later when prices dropped. And that helps give them either a Canadian or, depending on the freshness of the cask, an unmistakable bourbony style. So overtly Kentuckian can they be, I once playfully introduced an old single grain Scotch whisky into a bourbon tasting I was conducting and nobody spotted that it was the cuckoo in the nest ... until I revealed all at the end of the evening.

Light whiskies, including some Speysiders, tend to adopt this north American stance when the spirit has absorbed so much oak that the balance has been tipped. Grain whiskey is made from corn, particularly, to have that Canadian feel because the mouthfeel is so similar, too.

Younger grains may give a hint of oncoming bourbon-ness. But, rather, they tend to celebrate a softness in taste. Where many malts have a tendency to pulverise the taste-buds and announce their intent and character at the top of their voice, younger grains are content to stroke and whisper.

Scotch whisky companies have so far had a relaxed attitude to marketing their grains. William Grant has made some inroads with Black Barrel, though with nothing like the enthusiasm they unleash upon us their blends and malts. And Diageo are apparently content to see their Cameron Brig sell no further than its traditional hunting grounds, just north of Edinburgh, where the locals tend to prefer single grain to any other whisky. Hats off to Kyndal, though, for actually bringing out an impressive vintage version of their Invergordon.

The news for grain lovers has not been good this year with the closure of Dumbarton. I hope Allied, as a mark of respect for the doomed distillery, each year launch a special vintage of this crisp grain. Being a distillery that distilled from both wheat and corn, it would make a fascinating addition for whisky lovers to be able to try and spot the difference in style from the same age.

The tastings notes here for grains – both single and vatted – cover only a couple of pages. With Compass Box at the vanguard of launching the first vatted grain – their 2003 bottling being easily their best yet – expect this section to increase in size in forthcoming editions.

True, a whisky mass-produced by an enormous column still that would not be lost somewhere in a chemical plant, is not something the romantics like to dwell on. Especially when it is made not from golden, malted barley but from unmalted wheat or corn. Both are known to produce less flavour than barley.

But at last the message kicking in is that the reaction of this relatively lightweight spirit – and please, don't for one moment regard it as neutral, for it most certainly is not that – to oak can throw up some fascinating and often delicious possibilities.

Blenders have known that for a long time. The word is at last filtering through to more enlightened whisky connoisseurs the world over, some alerted or even seduced by the brilliance of the Cooley pure grain in Ireland.

Interest is growing. And people are willing to admit that they can enjoy an ancient Cambus or Caledonian. Even if it does go against the grain...

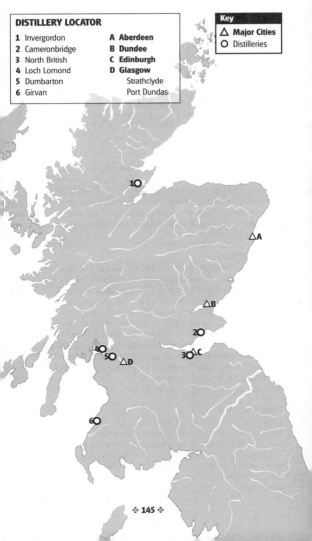

DISTILLERY LOCATOR

1 Invergordon
2 Cameronbridge
3 North British
4 Loch Lomond
5 Dumbarton
6 Girvan

A Aberdeen
B Dundee
C Edinburgh
D Glasgow
    Strathclyde
    Port Dundas

Key
△ Major Cities
○ Distilleries

Single Grain Scotch

CALEDONIAN

Cadenhead's Caledonian Aged 31 Years dist Jan 63, bott Feb 94 **(88) n**22 extremely firm grain, rigid in character; **t**23 hints of sweet bourbon but really hard corn that thumps against the teeth. **f**21 dry, soft oak with echoing corn; **b**22 the last hurrah of a grain that obviously put a metal backbone into many a blend. **48.7%**

CAMBUS

Cadenhead's Cambus Aged 31 Years dist 63, bott 94 **(87) n**21 sweet, simple, bourbony; **t**23 rich, chewy, distinct corn and oily; **f**21 remains oily and full, some lovely lingering toasty oak; **b**22 an impressive grain that has taken the years in its stride and remained upbeat and full of character. **53.2%**

CAMERONBRIDGE

Cameron Brig db **(79) n**19 **t**21 **f**19 **b**20. Toffee on the light, sweet finish. **40%**

Peerless Cameronbridge 1978 cask 003, dist Aug 78, **(84) n**20 **t**23 **f**21 **b**20. Fat chewy and very Canadian in style. Excellent. **59.9%**. *Duncan Taylor & Co. Ltd.*

DUMBARTON

Cadenhead's Dumbarton Aged 32 Years dist Feb 62, bott Feb 94 **(85) n**21 genuinely soft and floral; **t**22 much more brittle here with teasing spices and lording corn; **f**21 dry toast and bitter marmalade; **b**21 amazingly firm grain with a lovely fruity edge. **49.9%**

GIRVAN

Black Barrel db **(82) n**20 **t**20 **f**22 **b**20. Dangerously drinkable, moreish grain boasting a soft, Canadian-style oakiness. Light, spicy fizz on the long finish. **40%**

Girvan 1964 db casks filled 30/4/64, bott 10/10/01 **(88) n**22 beautiful, rich corn notes: sweet, deep, yet clean and crystal clear despite age; **t**23 sweet, oily, bourbony, sensual. Brilliant mouthfeel; **f**21 lots of liquorice, oak and subtle vanilla; **b**22 a luscious, classical well-aged grain straight from the top drawer. **48%**. *1,200 bottles.*

INVERGORDON

Invergordon Single Grain db **(84) n**20 **t**21 **f**22 **b**21. High-quality, sweet, velvety grain: a fine representative of medium-aged stock from this distillery. **40%**

Invergordon Highland Grain The Stillman's Dram Distilled 1973 db **(88) n**21 sweet, soft and lush, heaps of toffee: really attractive; **t**23 firmer and fabulously spicy. Beautiful depth with storming oak richness; **f**22 chewy toffee, enormously rich; **b**22 brilliant grain whisky that puts many malts to shame.

Cadenhead's Invergordon Aged 13 Years **(79) n**20 **t**19 **f**20 **b**20. Very oily and soft, the subtle sweetness disguising the strength. **67.8%**

Peerless Invergordon 1965 cask 15539, dist Dec 65 36-y-o **(89) n**21 sweet corn and rich, telling oak; **t**23 sumptuous natural caramel combined with chewy corn: the sweetness is in perfect rhythm with the oak; **f**23 long, sweet and more of the same; **b**22 top of the range Canadian – for a Scotch! **51.8%**. *Duncan Taylor & Co.*

NORTH BRITISH

Adelphi North British 12 Years Old cask 41147, dist 90, bott 02 **(85) n**21 firm grain, soft oak; **t**22 amazingly sweet and rum-like; **f**21 the soft oak returns with some stunning oils; **b**21 a whisky for rum devotees. **67.5%**

Adelphi North British 13 Years Old cask 52640, dist 90 **(87) n**21 soft, Canadian-style corn and oak: enticing; **t**21 delicious fat toffee with growing oak offering soft spice. Some fruit hangs around, too; **f**23 long, chewy with a hint of cocoa and increasing sweetness: stunning; **b**22 exemplary. **63.5%**

Scott's Selection North British 1974 bott 99 **(85) n**21 rich vanilla – not unlike a medium matured bourbon – deliciously sweet with the extra complexity of polished wooden floors and acacia honey; **t**22 dissolves in the mouth. It is vanilla and other delicate oaks all the way. Sweet, silky mouthfeel with the corn prominent, not unlike a superior Gibson's Canadian. Superb; **f**21 medium length and remains stubbornly sweet despite the oak trying to gather a hint of bitterness. Excepionally rich mouthfeel continues to the very last; **b**21 complexity may not be the name of the game here, but this aged grain shows what great spirit plus very good oak can produce over a quarter of a century. A minor classic. **53.1%.** *Robert Scott & Co.*

NORTH OF SCOTLAND

Scott's Selection North of Scotland 1963 bott 97 **(92) n**23 high-quality old bourbon: intense vanillas and natural caramels combine for a beautifully sweet, richly toffeed aroma. Fabulously well integrated spices and fruit add perfect complexity: damsons and dates about; **t**24 sweet and incredibly intense. Surprising viscosity for a grain that coats the mouth with pure demerara. The corn flits around in tandem with the cream-toffee oak: sensational and near flawless; **f**22 amazingly long, elements of dried vanilla and crushed pepper but it's all softly, softly and sexy; **b**23 if anyone thinks that grain whisky is inferior to malt, then grab hold of this. An appreciation and understanding of bourbon whisky would be advantageous but not essential. Much more of an ultra-fine bourbon than Scotch, but still one of the finest grains you'll ever find. Glorious. **46.8%.** *Robert Scott & Co.*

Vatted Grain

Compass Box Hedonism (first bottling, large illustration, described as "Scotch Grain") **(86) n**21 clean, waxy, cream toffee, quite dusty, showing some age; **t**22 soft, silky grain then a quick surge of oak; **f**22 amazingly soft, sweet and lethargic. The oak returns apologetically; **b**21 its strength is its coyness. Canadian style.

Compass Box Hedonism Vatted Grain (second bottling, small central illustration, described as "Vatted Grain") **(87) n**21 crisp grain, a more clipped, fruity, mildly spiced chap; **t**22 much more forthcoming and intense grain carried along with more than a hint of upfront, oaky bourbon; **f**22 long, slightly oily with a build-up of sweet banana and vanilla. Dries beautifully; **b**22 really mouthfilling and intense. Canadian style. **43%. nc ncf.**

Compass Box Hedonism Vatted Grain (third bottling, same label as second bottling, but laser jet bottling code number L3 136) **(89) n**22 light cereals, perfectly placed between sweet and dry: clean, almost ethereal with just a hint of surprising bourbon-style oak for ballast; **t**22 enormously delicate with a soft, starchy beginning building up to something oilier and sweeter. Some serious lip-smacking spices evolve; **f**22 long, spicy and drying. There is much interplay between vanilla-oak and the grain; **b**23 this is the other side of the same Hedonism coin: really classy, but in this case light and spicy rather than the overtly sweeter, oilier, more velvety texture of the previous bottling. This one, though, wins hands down for eye-closing, contemplative complexity. **40%**

Scottish Blends

If it is time for re-evaluating any one whisky type then surely it has to be Blended Scotch. For it really is quite extraordinary how people the world over, with refined palates and a good knowledge of single malts, are so willing to dismiss blends without a thought.

Perhaps it is a form of malt snobbery: if you don't drink malts, then you are not a serious Scotch whisky connoisseur ... or so some people think. Perhaps it is the fact that something like 95 out of every 100 bottles of Scotch consumed is a blend that has brought about this rather too common cold-shouldering. Well, not in my books. In fact, perhaps the opposite is true. Until you get to grips with blends you may well be entitled to regard yourself knowledgeable in single malts, but not in Scotch as a whole. Blends should be the best that Scotland can offer, because with a blend you have the ability to create any degree of complexity. And surely balance and complexity are the cornerstones of any great whisky, irrespective of type.

Of course there are some pretty awful blends created simply as a commodity with little thought going into their structure – just young whiskies, sometimes consisting of stock that is of dubious quality and then coloured up to give some impression of age. Yes, you are more likely to find that among blends than malts and for this reason the poorest blends can be pretty nasty. And, yes, they contain grain. Too often, though, grain is regarded as a kind of whisky leper – not to be touched under any circumstances. Some writers dismiss grain as "neutral" and "cheap", thus putting into the minds of the uninitiated the perception of inferiority.

But there really is nothing inferior about blends. In fact, whilst writing this book, I have to say that my heart missed more than one beat usually when I received a sample of a blend I had never found before. Why? Well, with single malts each distillery produces a style that can be found within known parameters. With a blend, anything is possible. There are many dozens of styles of malts to choose from and they will react slightly differently with certain grains.

For that reason, perhaps, I have marked blends a little more strictly and tighter than I have single malts. Because blends, by definition, should offer more.

And they do not have to be of any great age to achieve greatness. Look at the brilliance of the likes of Royal Silk, Black Bottle, Bailie Nicol Jarvie, Teachers, Grants and others. Also, look at the diversity of style from crisp and light to peat dominant. Then you get others where age has also played an astonishing role, not least a 50-years-old, such as Royal Salute.

Just like malts, blends change in character from time to time as the availability of certain malts and grains dry up. The most unforgivable reason is because the marketing guys reckon it needs a bit of extra colour and precious high notes are lost to caramel or sherry. Subtlety and character are the keys for any great blend without fail. Usually they are found in abundance in Johnnie Walker Black Label. But for this edition of the *Whisky Bible* my last two samples displayed an unusual dullness. It is a whisky I have worshipped for a quarter of a century and I am certain it is simply a blip. An irritating one, and an aspect of whisky tasting that keeps you on your toes. Get tasting and let me know what you think.

The most exciting blends show bite, character and attitude. Silk and charm are to be appreciated. But after a long, hard day is there anything better than a blend that is young and confident enough to nip and nibble at your throat on its way down and then throw up an array of flavours and shapes to get your taste-buds round?

With Blended Scotch the range and possibilities are limitless. All it takes is for the drinker not just to use his or her nose and taste-buds. But also an open mind.

Scotland Blends

100 Pipers (67) n17 **t**17 **f**16 **b**17. 100 Pipers: zero harmony. Young, less than pleasant grain. Was called 100 Pipers, then re-named Black Watch – now appears to be 100 Pipers again, though there is still a Black Watch. They keep changing the name but the same bloody awful whisky keeps appearing. **40%.** *Chivas.*

Acing Superior (76) n18 **t**22 **f**18 **b**18. A really enjoyable and impressive 5-y-o-style blend with decent malt and sparkling grain, but let down for the purists by the colouring. **40%**

Ailsa Craig (77) n18 **t**22 **f**19 **b**18. The strangely anarchic, smoky yet mildly off-key nose for a blend is compensated by an extraordinary and quite delicious mouth arrival that heads in two distinctly different directions. The grain is hard and unyielding while the malt is oily and aided by sharp and intense barley and no little smoke. Hardly a blend: more of a delicious-tasting accident. Weird and, in part, wonderful. **40%.** *A Dewar Rattray.*

The Andrew Usher Memorial Blend (92) n23 beautifully firm grain which seems attached to succulent fruit. The malts are busy and spicy: a real blender's blend; **t**24 explosive, mouth-enveloping stuff. The malts go hand-in-hand with the grain to create complex patterns all around the palate while the fruit ensures softness reigns; **f**22 much lighter with toffee-vanilla gentleness against the foraging spice; **b**23 one for the Andrew Usher hall of fame. The old man would have been proud of a blend that has it all. **49%.** *Kyndal.*

The Antiquary 12 Years Old (84) n20 **t**22 **f**20 **b**22. There is some deliciously outstanding interplay between the fussy grain and the very rich malt. But the higher notes, especially on the nose, are clobbered by toffee: it's just too delicate a blend to take it. **40%.** *J & W Hardie.*

The Antiquary 21 Years Old (88) n21 spicy with full malt and toffee to the fore; **t**24 massive spice then thinning grain before a mega tsunami of honeyed malt crashes over the tastebuds: astonishing and very beautiful; **f**21 soft, very old grains and peaty spices pick at the vanilla; **b**22 this is a stylish blend that suggests that there is a lot of whisky much older than 21 in it. The mouth arrival borders on perfection.

Asda Finest Scotch (81) n21 **t**21 **f**19 **b**20. A surprisingly complex, mouthwatering and well-balanced dram plucked off the supermarket shelf. The busy nose offers all you could ask of a young blend. *Asda UK.*

Asyla (see Compass Box)

Auld Lang Syne (81) n19 **t**21 **f**20 **b**21. A pretty good, clean blend that can barely be found these days. Easily spotted, though: thanks to a tone deaf packager in the Far East, the carton plays "Home, Home on the Range" when you open it rather than Burns' classic. **40%.** *Langs.*

Avonside (74) n17 **t**20 **f**19 **b**18. Pleasant, but a little flat. **40%.** *Gordon & MacPhail.*

Avonside 8-years-old (81) n18 **t**21 **f**22 **b**20. Beautifully honeyed: much more evidence of oak and age than on standard 8-y-o version. **57%.** *Gordon & MacPhail.*

The Bailie Nicol Jarvie (B.N.J) Over 6 Years Old. (93) n22 as fruity and mouthwatering as a riesling, but infinitely better. Green, grassy and youthful with almost perfect grain balance; **t**24 tarty and biting, the nose translates to palate with mouthwatering Speyside malt in harmony with exquisite flinty grain. It rarely gets better than this; **f**23 more grain here as the malt slowly wanders off and late oak adds to length with a brush of cocoa; **b**24 Poetry in solution: a must-have blend for every cabinet. **40%.** *Nicol Anderson & Co. (Glenmorangie plc).*

Ballantine's Finest (83) n19 **t**20 **f**21 **b**23. A soft, deceptively complex light blend that grows in stature and charm as it develops on the palate. Superb grain charisma: great blending, lads! **40%.** *Allied.*

Ballantine's Gold Seal 12 Years Old **(88)** n23 gently smoked with the most distant hints of very clean sherry: just beautiful; t21 the fruit ensures a rather too gentle entry onto the tastebuds, but excellent grain does some catching up to land a vanilla punch. The malt is lazy and relaxed; f22 some cocoa and rousing complex malty-oaky-smoky tones ensure a bitter-sweet ending; b22 very complex and alluring. **40%**. *Allied*.

Ballantine's Royal Blue 12 Years Old **(90)** n23 fabulous chalky-oak and big malt presence; t22 mouthwatering, fat, some dazzling citrus notes and then cocoa/coffee towards the spiced, complex middle; f22 sweetens with both malt and soft brown sugar The texture remains lush without ever being oily; b23 this blend has improved beyond recognition since I last tasted it: my hats off to the blender. This is for the Japanese market and, had I tasted this blind, I would have marked it down as a Japanese blend of the top order ... which is some compliment. **43%**. *Allied*.

Ballantine's 17 Years Old **(96)** n24 a floral lavender-mint combination balance with aplomb with the most intrinsic peat and grain: beguiling and wonderfully sexy; t25 this is it: balance, charm, guile, charisma ... the entire works in one voluptuous mouthful. First a sweet sheen coats the mouth then some grassy notes get you salivating before soft smoke provides the weight. Enormous with wave upon wave of intense barley sugar and peat but never heavy enough to snap a twig. This is masterful blending; f23 some oaks finally settle like sediment. Raisins and walnut complete the rich picture and spices add that extra dimension ... as if it was needed; b24 it's amazing that out of one lab comes two blends that give masterclass performances: Ballantine's 17 and Teachers. Both are outwardly weighty but reveal so much more that is gentle and complex. The point about this whisky is that you feel you never quite get to the bottom layer: labyrinthine liquid genius. **43%**. *Allied*.

Ballantine's 21 Years Old **(81)** n19 t20 f22 b20. A less than impressive sherry butt has made its way into this vatting and taken the edge off things slightly. The early finish remains impressive for its complexity with fabulously delicate peat weaving rich patterns, but the finale underlines the poor sherry. For the next edition expect this to be back in the high 80s/low 90s. **43%**. *Allied*.

Ballantine's 30 Years Old **(91)** n23 the nose is massaged by a creamy, ripe fruity, grapey and softly malt gem. Not a single sign of grain, except perhaps that cream; t23 this is too much ... now the tastebuds get the same treatment. The silky softness almost defies description; f22 mildly bitter as some grain bites, but the malt now compensates: high alcohol Horlicks; b23 I suppose the nature of the beast dictates that the style of a 30-y-o blend will move around a little: this really is very different..and superb! **43%**. *Allied*.

Ballantine's Limited **(89)** n22 excellent clarity of fruit and barley; t24 early grain and then a slow, complex delivery of malt surrounded by soft grape and the lightest coating of muscovado sugar; f21 dryer with some bitter-almond and cocoa on the oak; b22 a quality newcomer that is beautifully textured and quite fabulously constructed. **43%**. *Allied*.

Ballantine's Master's **(84)** n21 t22 f20 b21. Excellent use of lively grain and chewy malt to counter something that towards the end especially is a little too soft and gentle. **40%**. *Allied*.

Bell's Exra Special **(78)** n20 t20 f18 b20. The Bell's with no age statement. Decent arrival on palate with good biting grain to end what appears some decent Speyside maltiness through the middle. **40%**. *SA*.

Bell's Extra Special 8 Years Old **(84)** n21 t22 f21 b20. A really sound and complex whisky with good weight and no shortage of style. Lovely spice on the finish. **40%**

Bell's 12 Years Old **(90)** n22 new leather and a hint of honey; t23 both grains and malts arrive in just about equal measures for very busy, complex start.

Silky mouthfeel and some wonderful gently smoked spices; **f**22 long and clean with vanilla dominating; **b**23 absolutely quality blending, and pretty remarkable considering the mass scale on which it is achieved. No one style dominates, though it would be fair to say this is on the light side of medium in weight. **40%**

Bell's Islander (82) **n**21 **t**21 **f**20 **b**20. A blend that has been discontinued a little while, though in 2003 I have spotted it in bars as far apart as Copenhagen and Oxfordshire. These later bottlings were softer than the first run with the added Talisker not showing to great effect. Chewy, but a little toffeed. **40%**

Ben Aigen (68) **n**17 **t**18 **f**16 **b**17. Sweet caramel; bland and dusty. **40%**. *Gordon & MacPhail.*

Ben Alder (85) **n**20 yielding and sweet; **t**23 an absolute avalanche of complex fruit and barley flavours, stretched out by silky grain; **f**21 sweet and rich with much toffee and spice; **b**21 a delicious dram, especially with the massive mouth arrival. But not quite what it was at the moment. **40%**. *Gordon & MacPhail.*

Beneagles (67) **n**17 **t**18 **f**16 **b**16. Flat and lifeless. 40%

Big Ben Special Reserve (80) **n**19 **t**22 **f**19 **b**20. Solid young blend with that rush of grassy-Speysidey malt that hits the palate full on that I find irresistible. **40%**. *Angus Dundee.*

Big "T" (91) **n**22 toasty and spicy, lively grain on a very clean malt bed: excellent; **t**23 stupendous balance to the opening with both malt and grain making a bee-line for the tastebuds, complex and confrontational, with big spice kick; **f**22 the grains move in with the vanilla but there is an exceptional sweet malt theme that stays to the end; **b**24 this is my kind of whisky: busy, characterful, complex and charismatic. Available mainly in the Far East, but should be on the home and international stage. **40%**. *Tomatin Distillery Co.*

Black & White (79) **n**18 **t**20 **f**21 **b**20. Fruity but just a tad musty with all the complexity on the finish. Much richer and less grain-dominated than a few years back. **40%**. *Diageo.*

Black Bottle (95) **n**23 sizzling, jabbing grain versus heavyweight young peated malts: some match; **t**24 the outcome on the palate is explosive: rampaging peaty malts put firmly in their place by crisp grain with a unique mouthfeel style, different even to Isle of Skye; **f**25 softer, spent, sweet malts allow the more bitter cocoa-crusted grains to make a stand; **b**23 a blend that has to be tasted to be believed: it is young yet enormous, raw yet sophisticated, wild, brazen and beautiful. Here's a tip for best drinking results: take big mouthful, then open and close mouth rapidly in exaggerated chewing action. The flavours that hit you will have you searching for a chair. And another glass ... **40%**

Black Bottle 10 Years Old (89) **n**22 so age-weightedly peaty it could be almost a single malt: the grains make little discernible impact; **t**23 soft, deft malt and firmer grain. The peat arrives after a short interval; **f**22 more vanilla and other oaky tones; **b**22 a stupendous malt of weight and poise, but possessing little of the all-round steaming, rampaging sexuality of the younger version. **40%**

Black Cock (78) **n**19 **t**20 **f**19 **b**20. Overtly grainy but a surprisingly malty mouthwatering quality makes for a half-decent blend. **40%**

Blackpool (73) **n**18 **t**19 **f**18 **b**18. Grain and sweet toffee. Easy going but never hits the bright lights. **40%**. *Invergordon.*

Black Prince (68) **n**16 **t**19 **f**17 **b**16. One rich flourish apart, way off target. **40%**. *Burn Stewart.*

Black Prince 12 Years Old (80) **n**19 **t**22 **f**19 **b**20. Soft and silky, there is good fruit and crisp grain. A spicy but toffeed finish. **43%** *Burn Stewart. A discontinued blend now: a collector's item if you see it.*

Black Top Finest De Luxe (77) **n**19 **t**21 **f**18 **b**19. Silky, sweet and rich, but a touch too much caramel dulls the complexity. **40%**. *Aberfoyle & Knight. South America.*

Black Watch (for tasting notes see 100 Pipers)

Blue Eagle (80) n18 t22 f20 b20. A big, booming arrival on the palate with fresh, intense malt that glistens and sparkles. *Edrington Group. Thailand.*

Bruce and Company Scotch Whisky (79) n19 t21 f20 b19. The minimalist label – "Scotch Whisky" in black on white – somehow perfectly summarises a minimalist dram. This, for all intents and purposes, is young grain whisky with a dash of malt – and I do mean a dash. And topped up with some colouring. Yet, it's sweet, has a rich mouthfeel, there are no off-notes and perfectly enjoyable – providing you are not on the hunt for complexity. **40%.** *Exclusive to Tesco UK.*

Buchanan's De-Luxe Aged 12 Years (85) n20 some deft smoke tries to trouble the rich fruits; t23 stunningly soft texture, enormously fruity with some firm grain through the middle and then spice. Great chewing whisky; f21 the spices continue and put life into the vanilla. Slightly bitter fade; b21 a lush blend with big presence. But I have met its alter ego, the odd bottling spoiled slightly by bad sherry influence. On its day, though, a very decent dram. **40%**

Buchanan's Special Reserve (93) n22 clean grape and quite floral; t24 sumptuous, ultra-lush mouth arrival with silky grain carrying with it clean sherry and sweet malt; f23 now the complexity really begins with some smoky spices digging into the fruit and oak; b24 one of those rare whiskies that makes you groan with satisfaction as it hits your tastebuds: certainly one of the most silky around offering nothing other than sheer, supremely engineered class. **40%**

Budgen's Finely Blended Scotch (75) n18 t20 f18 b19. A high-caramel but otherwise clean blend with a very enjoyable grain bite. **40%.** *Budgens Stores UK.*

Burn McKenzie (72) n18 t19 f18 b17. Some pretty firm grain is dealt with with caramel. Coking whisky, I believe, is the term. And rightfully unashamed of it. **40%.** *Burn Stewart.*

Campbeltown Loch (71) n18 t19 f17 b17. More simplistic than of old. **40%.** *Springbank.*

Campbeltown Loch 25 Years Old (85) n21 a massive injection of oak, almost too intense, but barley and fruit balances; t22 quite massive, initially dry, oak which sweetens and develops into a honeyed barley beaut; f21 the sweet barley sheen remains with vanillas softening things further; b21 a supreme game of brinkmanship with the oak is won – just. *Springbank.*

Catto's Deluxe 12 Years Old (87) n22 deftly done: fragile, honeyed malty notes with the promise of something Speysidey and mouthwatering; t23 no disappointment: fresh malts bombard the tastebuds, then a gradual release of mouth-coating richer, oilier notes; f21 sweet with coconut milk and firmer grains; b21 a bolder and richer blend than the subtle version of a few years back. The stamp of class, though, is undeniable. **40%.** *Inver House.*

Catto's Rare Old Scottish Highland (89) n22 fresh, sensual. The grains are brilliantly chosen to allow full malt impact; t22 adorable formation of sweet Speysidey malts just melt in with the lush grain; f23 long and spicy and a touch of chalky oak adds to the balance; b22 silky and rich, this is delicious everyday fare of considerable charm. A truly classic, crisp young malt that is way above its station. For confirmation, smell the honey on the empty glass. **43%.** *Inver House.*

Chivas Brothers 1801 (92) n23 punchy oloroso: perhaps it is brittle from Glen Grant malt imitating Irish pot still, but this is so very much like a Jameson whiskey sherry cask; t24 sweet, hard and brittle again. No-one will persuade me there aren't tons of sherried Glen Grant in this. Some salt seems to bolster the flavour explosion further; f22 softer now as clean grain strikes but the spiced sherry is in close attendance; b23 the kind of dram you just can't say no to. Quality. **50%.** *This, tragically, has now been lost to us and has evolved into Chivas "Revolve".*

Chivas Brothers Oldest and Finest (94) n24 beguiling stuff of most untypical Chivas style: smoke and peat blending in with the fruit, nutmeg and allspice. The sherry influence is sublime; t24 just flows on from where the nose left off. The sherry is clean and weighty and beautiful spices arrive to flit around the palate. The malt is big with a degree of smoke and the grains do what grains should do best: polish the malts and marry the styles. Absolutely breathtaking; f22 long with smoke and a sound structure. The spices continue to sparkle and the fruit also gathers intensity; b24 it breaks my heart to announce that the blend has been discontinued, though a search through specialist outlets should reveal the odd bottle or two lurking about. Make no mistake: this is testimony to the art of brilliant, sympathetic and intuitive blending. What we have here is a masterpiece. **43%**

Chivas Regal 12 Years Old (76) n18 t22 f17 b19. The nose and finish are their usual drab selves, though this time there is a beautiful, if brief, Speyside sparkle to the early mouth arrival. The highest mark I have given this blend for some time ... which isn't saying much. **40%**

Chivas Regal 18 Years Old (82) n19 t23 f19 b21. You get the feeling that there is a great blend trying to escape the smothering clutches of some so-so grain. The early Speyside malt mouthfeel is a delight. **40%**

Chivas Revolve (81) n20 t21 f20 b20. A sherried dram that lacks complexity and direction. Not to be mentioned in the same breath as "1801", the blend it replaced. **40%**

Clan Campbell (88) n21 an old-fashioned style: slightly raw big grain kick and bite with young Speysiders who also have a punch-up; t23 the grains are side-tracked as the Speysiders go nuts: really, grassy and mouthwatering; f22 long and malty; b22 a blend that has changed dramatically, yet has somehow kept its family values. Much more bite than of old, yet the complexity and freshness on the palate has gone through the roof, while retaining its old-fashioned feel. A little stunner. **40%**

Clan Campbell Legendary Aged 18 Years (89) n22 accomplished oloroso notes are thinned by attractive grain-led vanilla: stylish stuff; t23 superb: a real outbreak of all things complex with soft grain at the centre but fruit heading from one malt to another and a very subtle smokiness from elsewhere; f22 more simple but the gentle vanilla and distant echo of spice is a tease; b22 greatly improved on recent years and now a dram of unquestionable distinction. **40%**

Clan MacGregor (88) n22 superb grains allow the lemon-fruity malt to ping around: clean, crisp and refreshing; t22 as mouthwatering as the nose suggests with first clean grain then a succession of fruity and increasingly sweet malty notes. Such a brilliant mouthful; f22 medium length with clever use of vanilla alongside very yielding grain; b22 a young blend that seems to have improved beyond recognition in recent years: maltier and perhaps a little older. A great everyday whisky of distinction. *Wm Grant's US.*

Clan MacGregor 12 Years Old (84) n21 t20 f22 b21. The suspicion is that the grains are a lot older than 12: there is a lot of bourbon-oaky character on the nose and on the mouth arrival. Great finish, but lacking the all-round fresh-faced charisma of the young MacGregor. *Wm Grant's US.*

Clan Roy (74) n18 t20 f18 b18. A clean, toffeed, blandish blend saved by a touch of spice towards the middle. **40%.** *Morrison Bowmore.*

The Claymore (76) n17 t20 f19 b20. A much more tastebud-friendly blend than the old cut-and-thrust number of yore. Still can't say the nose does much for me but the developing fruitiness on the middle and finish is silky and complex. **40%.** *Kyndal.*

Cluny (85) n20 soft grain weathers the biting malt; t21 mouth-filling and big with the grain again doing its best to lighten the load. Soft vanilla arrives early; f22 very long with more malt, even a hint of something vaguely smoky and spicy, then toffee; **b**22 I do adore this kind of blend: slightly rough-edged, and every time you take a mouthful something slightly different happens. If I were to find fault, a touch too much caramel is evident at the very death. **40%.** *Kyndal.*

Compass Box Asyla (first bottling – large picture 43% abv) **(89)** **n**22 clean and simplistic, luxuriating in the effortless interlocking of soft malt and even softer grain; **t**23 suddenly comes alive on the palate with a fabulously textured malt thrust countered by silky grains. Seriously teasing; **f**22 delicate and so beautifully spiced, with a balancing dryness; **b**22 a really excellent first issue from whisky purist John Glaser that offers nothing but quality. **ncf.**

Compass Box Asyla (second bottling (2003) – small picture, fluted bottle **40%** abv) **(93)** **n**23 charming complexity from the off with subtlety the key. The barley is rich, the grain is yielding, the result is spellbinding; **t**23 simply to die for with layers of sparkling malt, toasted and honeyed but never overly sweet. The spice teases but no more; **f**23 only now do the grains lock on. Even so, the malt runs its course and spice, if anything, intensifies; **b**24 so sexy, you could almost make love to it. Unquestionably one of the best light blends on the market. **nc ncf.**

Co-operative Group (CWS) Scotch Whisky **(79)** n19 t21 f20 b19. Young, mouth-filling, clean and quite juicy. Thoroughly decent. **40%.** *Co-op UK.*

Co-operative Group (CWS) Premium Scotch Whisky Five Years Old **(73)** n17 t21 f17 b18. Complex middle, but let down by poor cask selection. **40%.** *Co-op UK.*

Covent Garden 10 Years Old **(88)** **n**22 the style is classical and one of crystal clarity; **t**23 the marriage between those crisp, clean Speyside malts and refreshing grain is one of harmony and bliss: seems younger than its 10 years thanks to minimal oak interference; **f**21 which arrives towards the finish and dumbs down the rampaging complexity; **b**22 what an outstanding blend this is: pity – though no surprise – that the Cadenhead's shop in Covent Garden that sells it runs out so quickly. **40%** *Cadenhead's.UK.*

Crawford's 3 Star **(78)** n19 t20 f19 b20. A slightly more fragile thing than it once was with the grain a little firmer and the complexity levels upped. Very attractive. **40%.** *Kyndal.*

Crown Whisky Co. Very Rare Highland Special Reserve **(74)** n18 t19 f18 b19. A competent grainy blend with a hint of oak. **40%.** *Denmark only.*

Cutty Sark **(88)** n23 light and floral with firm grain accentuating the malt; t22 big grain surge then a slow build-up of Speyside maltiness. Grassy and sharp throughout with a lovely Tamdhu-esque oiliness; f21 lots of vanilla and a thread of cocoa on the finale; b22 always been light, but virtually all peatiness has vanished of late. Even so, a real cracker of crispy grain. **40%**

Cutty Sark Aged 12 Years **(82)** n18 t22 f21 b21. A blemish on the nose, but an otherwise lovely, fresh blend showing more sherry than of old and excellent spices throughout. **40%**

Cutty Sark Aged 18 Years **(93)** n24 outstanding clean sherry influence, softly smoked and good oak, almost bourbony, input. Beautiful; t23 big, spicy and immensely chewy; f22 lots of cream toffee, and a hint of tiring oak, but the grain is really high quality and delicious; b24 absolutely stunning. The clever use of the grain is simply breathtaking. **43%**

Cutty Sark Aged 25 Years **(90)** n23 massive acacia honey and vanilla sing sweetly; t23 as intense as an old pot-still demerara with absolutely stunning mouthfeel and fruity richness; f22 long, with gathering spices and a hint of smoke. The grains are minute but exemplary and chocolate-coated; b22 heavy and honeyed, chewy and charming, the oak has a fraction too big a say but still quite delicious! **45.7%**

Cutty Sark Discovery (see Cutty Sark Aged 18 Years)
Cutty Sark Emerald (see Cutty Sark Aged 12 Years)

Dewar's White Label (83) n21 t22 f19 b21. A decent, punchy, mildly biting blend where the grains are proud to show themselves and the malt makes enjoyable, soothing and sweetening noises. The toffee dims the sparkle somewhat, though. **40%**. *Curiously, White Label is now the possessor of a pale yellow one …*

Dewar's Ancestor Aged 12 Years (89) n22 clean, gently spiced but richly sherried nose; t23 curvaceous fruit blends superbly with crisp grains and teasing malt; f22 really gentle finish with vanilla, sherry and cold, milky coffee. The spices just take a ramble round the gob; b22 fabulous use of sherry cask as it is clean enough to allow an unusual degree of complexity. The unusual strength probably compensates for evaporation during the painfully slow pouring process … **43.5%**

Dewar's Special Reserve Aged 12 Years (91) n23 exceptionally well designed with the heavier smoke and fruit notes adding only a background noise to the slightly more three-dimensional grain and soft honey-malt; t23 big and mouthwatering with spices developing fast. Beautiful integration of the harder grains and a developing oakiness; f21 way too much toffee undoes some of the intricate complexity. The spices carry on unabated, though; b24 an unashamedly old-fashioned type of blended Scotch and closest to the traditional Dewar's style of pre-Second World War days. A seriously delicious transportation back in time to the days when blends were cherished. **43%**

Dew of Ben Nevis (76) n18 t19 f20 b19. Heavy duty stuff with a sweet finish. **40%**. *Ben Nevis Distillery.*

Dew of Ben Nevis Hector's Nectar (see Hector's Nectar)

Dew of Ben Nevis Millennium Blend (86) n20 weighty malt; t22 has that "married" feel, where the malts have combined to make a busy, impossible-to-describe whole; f22 back to the grains again: quite bitty and complex; b22 chunky and complex. **40%**. *Ben Nevis Distillery.*

Dew of Ben Nevis Special Reserve (81) n19 t20 f22 b20. Very firm malt, sweet, full-bodied and punchy grain – even a hint of honey on the spicy finale. **40%**. *Ben Nevis Distillery.*

Dew of Ben Nevis Aged 12 Years (79) n20 t20 f19 b20. Pretty straight down-the-line fare with some chunky malt but a flat finish. **40%**. *Ben Nevis Distillery.*

Dew of Ben Nevis Aged 21 Years (90) n23 citrus 'n' salt; t23 fabulous complexity with illuminating malt showing sweetness to a salty depth and toasty oak; f21 thins out towards vanilla and milky coffee, but with a little orange to lighten the load; b23 a really lovely aged blend where the complexity is mind-blowing. Go get…!! **43%**. *Ben Nevis Distillery.*

Dimple 12 Years Old (83) n21 t20 f21 b21. A puff of smoke adds a touch of clout to an otherwise light yet gently spiced and deliciously grained blend. **43%**

Dimple 15 Years Old (72) n19 t18 f18 b17. Oh, dear: a real disappointment. Just never takes off or goes anywhere. **40%**

Diners Deluxe Old Scotch 12 Years Old (85) n21 beautiful spices, intense, weighty malt, and firm grain; t22 very big, oily and chewy malt arrival that offers immediate sweetness; f21 an intriguing mixture of lingering smoke and cocoa-grain; b21 genuinely classy stuff with attitude. **43%**. *Douglas Denham for Diners Club.*

Diners Supreme Old Scotch 21 Years Old (82) n20 t21 f21 b20. A massive blend with no little bourbony-oaky style. **43%**. *Douglas Denham for Diners Club.*

The Dowans Hotel (88) n21 soft, mildly smoked; t22 more grain bite on the palate than the nose suggests; f23 weighty and majestic: really quite sweet before some clever oak rolls in against the silky grain and bubbling peat; b22 a seriously decent house blend of a style heavier than you might expect in a

Speyside hotel. Worth a detour to find it if in that part of the world. **40%**. *Inverarity Vaults for The Dowan's Hotel, Aberlour.*

Duggans (76) n17 t20 f19 b20. A young, high-grained blend which enjoys a short malty, spicy blast early on before settling for grainier, safer ground. **40%**. *Morrison Bowmore.*

The Dundee (77) n18 t22 f19 b18. Lots of upfront, grunting grain but the usual Angus Dundee superb mouth arrival. Caramel tucks away the finish, save for some lovely spice. **40%**. *Angus Dundee.*

Dunfife (75) n18 t20 f19 b18. Refreshing and chewy. **40%**. *William Maxwell.*

Dunhill Old Master (87) n20 rather caramelised, but some toasty maltiness thrives amid the well-balanced grains; t22 rich, sweet, heather-honey malt then a middle like cream toffee candy; f23 becomes even more interesting as the oak appears and spice, too: chewy and complex; b22 sadly a discontinued blend available now only in more refined outlets in the USA and Japan until stocks run dry. Something wonderfully like "Quality Street" chocolates about this one: will be sadly missed when exhausted. **43%**

Dunhill Gentleman's Speyside Blend (89) n22 excellently weighty, clean sherry; t23 subtle honey amid the fruit. The grains are North Britishy-crisp and barley mouthwatering; f21 vanilla and grape; b23 I used to prefer Old Master, but as time has progressed I have come to appreciate Gentleman's for its deft charm. Perhaps it is because I am getting older and becoming a gentleman ... Sadly lost to us: available in tiny amounts only in Japan and USA. Someone should revive a wee classic like this. **43%**

EH10 (86) n22 almost too clean to be true: the grassiest of Speyside malt input plus bracing grain. One of the most subtle noses around; t23 as mouthwatering as the nose suggests; you can chew the fresh melting, malt while the grain offers something stiffer; f20 evidence of a little oaky age, but perhaps a little too light; b21 From the same charm school as Bailie Nicol Jarvie, but lacks finish. Otherwise delicious. **40%**. *Sainsbury UK (from Glenmorangie plc).*

The Famous Grouse (83) n21 t23 f19 b20. Remains sexy, elegant and refined with a stunning opening on the palate. But I can't help feeling that caramel has recently replaced some of the crisper notes, especially on the finish. **40%**

The Famous Grouse Cask Strength (87) n22 amazingly big, fresh clean sherry for a light blend: the grains cut into the fruit with precision and no little grace; t22 seriously fruity at first then a wave of malt and toffee. The grain re-forms towards the middle; f21 quite soft with lots of toffee and vanilla; b22 a chewy, stylish dram that absorbs the strength easily. Again the toffee is a bit on the heavy side but the overall grain-malt balance is deft and delicious. **59.4%**

The Famous Grouse Gold Reserve Aged 12 Years (85) n19 honeycomb and oak make a sensuous pairing, but dulled by caramel; t23 just sensational. Honey and spice drip off the roof of the mouth. Some soft peat digs in with the oak; f21 lashing of vanilla and liquorice but again caramel dulls the picture; b22 a much more honeyed, richer and improved dram than of old. But the caramel could be cut considerably. **43%**

The Famous Grouse Islay Cask Finish (88) n21 beautifully weighted with kippery tones amid nipping grains; t22 a real chewy mouthful: sweet with lots of obvious malt; f23 more grain presence with vanilla drying out the sweeter barley. Remains smoky and very long; b22 if ever you wondered what a peaty Grouse would be like, here you go. What makes it work is the alluring softness of the smoke. Genuinely graceful for all its weight. **40%**

The Famous Grouse Port Wood Finish (75) n20 t20 f17 b18. A surprising hint of smoke, but otherwise fruity and flat. **40%**

Findlater's Finest (69) n17 t18 f17 b17. A furry, sticky palate; mildly rubbery. **40%**. *Kyndal.*

Findlater's Deluxe 15 Years Old (81) n*21* t*20* f*20* b*20*. The fruity nose is followed by a chunky arrival on the palate where the malt is thick and chewy. Some coffee on the finale. Takes time to acclimatise to this style of blend, but worth every second. **40%**. *Kydal.*

Findlater's Deluxe 18 Years Old (91) n*22* a hint of dry Lübeck chocolate marzipan; t*23* decent soft malt sprinkled with light muscovado sugar; f*22* back to bitter almonds and bourbon amid the lush grain; b*24* the cleanest, lightest yet most comfortably weighted of the Findlater clan by some margin; supremely balanced with a lush texture and lilting complexity. Some serious blending went into this one. **40%**. *Kyndal.*

Findlater's Deluxe 21 Years Old (89) n*22* subtle sherry, clean with simmering spice just below the surface; t*23* lazy and demure for a blend of such age: the malt does possess a certain countering brittleness to the softer grain; f*21* vanilla and a hint of sultana and toffee fudge; b*23* a pretty dreamy, end-of-day blend when you want your tastebuds featherdusted before retiring. **40%**. *Kyndal.*

Fortnum & Mason Choice Old 5 Year Old (83) n*20* t*21* f*22* b*20*. Good, solid grain helps propel a decent percentage of malt to rich, gently spicy deeds. An impressive 5-y-o by any standards. **40%**. *UK.*

Fraser McDonald's (74) n*16* t*20* f*19* b*19*. Attractive moments of lucid complexity between the big rubbery nose and the astonishingly sweet finale. Big stuff. Devotees of High Commissioner will know the style. **40%**. *A Bulloch.*

Frasers Supreme (77) n*19* t*19* f*20* b*19*. A dash of smoke helps add weight. **40%**. *Gordon and MacPhail.*

Gibson Glengarry (68) n*16* t*18* f*17* b*17*. Tough going. **40%**

Glen Alba (75) n*18* t*19* f*19* b*19*. Some young, sharp Speysidey notes, but pretty raw in places with the balance just failing to make the most of the mouthwatering properties. Even so, extra points for being such a clean dram. **40%**. *Brand Development Ltd.*

Glen Calder (71) n*18* t*19* f*17* b*17*. Sweet; middle of the road. **40%**. *Gordon & MacPhail.*

Glen Catrine De Luxe (77) n*17* t*22* f*19* b*19*. A dusty nose, but recovers for a rich, softly honeyed middle before caramel intervenes on the finish. **40%**. *Glen Catrine.*

Glen Crinan (72) n*17* t*19* f*18* b*18*. Oily and full in places. **40%**. *Edrington Group France.*

Glen Crinan 12 Years Old (75) n*17* t*20* f*19* b*19*. Maybe I'm being fanciful, but I'm sure I'm detecting Glenturret's hand in there somewhere. A little soapy at first, honey and spice later. **40%**. *Edrington..*

Glen Clova (70) n*18* t*18* f*17* b*17*. Grain and caramel all the way. I'm sure there must be some malt in there somewhere, but the grain is clean and decent quality, at least. *Ewen & Co for Oddbins UK.*

Glendarroch Finest 15 Years Old (91) n*21* very firm grain surrounded on all sides by peaty ancient malt and bourbony oak; t*24* impressive mouthfeel and early spice arrival, then a glorious expansion of quite stunning malt of a richness that needs tasting for comprehension. You can lose yourself in this one for some time; f*23* the grains bite back and are quite welcome to rescue you from a malty trance: you will appreciate it more if you wallow in the bourbony afterglow; b*23* this is exceptionally high-quality blending and a marriage of malts and grains that were meant for each other. **43%**. *William Gillies & Co.*

Glen Dowan (80) n*19* t*21* f*21* b*19*. Flinty and firm grain with excellent malt development. **40%**. *J& G Grant.*

Glen Dowan 21 Years Old (89) n*21* fresh, coastal and lively; t*22* a real live wire around the palate with big malt presence; f*23* lovely spices and exceptional oak control: truly brilliant; b*23* big, bold and a little salty. Delicious, especially the finale. Out of this world bitter-sweet balance. **43%**. *J&G Grant Taiwan/Jap/Asia.*

Glengarry (see Gibson Glengarry)

Glen Grigg **(71)** n16 t19 f18 b18. Young, heavy; subtlety at a premium. **40%.** Spar UK.

Glen Heather **(90)** n22 hard, unyielding and grain-heavy it may be but the ginger nut bite is engaging. Enticing, confident stuff with the faintest touch of peat; t23 fresh, young and mouthfilling. The grains remain brittle and reflect perfectly the Speysidey malts which ensure maximum salivation. Some really excellent spice. Exceptionally clean and crisply defined; f22 pretty long with a slight sweetening and softening towards the finale. Some late evidence of age; b23 a quite lovely and lively blend from the old school. Clean and distinctive with a marauding spiciness, this is a blend that takes me back 25 years in style. The colour suggests caramel should be lurking somewhere and it does show very briefly and causing virtually no damage at the death. But as a whole this is a throwback, a minor classic blend worthy of discovery. **40%** SH Jones at their shops in Banbury and elsewhere in the heart of England.

Glen Niven **(79)** n20 t19 f20 b20. Way above average supermarket stuff: the nose shows superb grain qualities while the decent malt reveals itself in the finish. Overall, silky and complex. Rip out the OTT caramel and you would have a quality blend here. Douglas MacNiven (Asda) UK.

Glen Osprey **(71)** n17 t18 f18 b18. A pageant of young grain that is generally pleasant enough, especially towards the finish. Beware, though. Another I tasted earlier in the year was off-key and seriously awful. **40%.** Duncan MacBeth & Co.

Glen Rosa **(83)** n20 t22 f21 b20. Bit of a surprise package: purists will take a look at the colour and think "caramel". However, it never seriously materialises as a brilliant firm grain stars, bringing the best out of some clean, mouthwatering malt, Arran doubtless included. Seriously tasty, cracking old-fashioned stuff. **40%.** Isle of Arran.

Glen Rossie **(80)** n20 t20 f20 b20. Grain-rich, sweet and soft. Limited variation, maximum simple charm. **40%.** Morrison Bowmore.

Glen Shira **(79)** n20 t21 f19 b19. A young blend that shows delicious citrus-fruit qualities. **40%.** Burn Stewart.

Glenshire **(69)** n17 t18 f17 b17. Clean, young and caramelised. **40%.** William Maxwell.

Glen Urquhart **(82)** n20 t21 f20 b21. Gentle and mouthwatering with a touch of spice. **40%.** Gordon & MacPhail.

Glinne Parras **(85)** n23 malt-rich and complex with evidence of some age and firm grain; t23 wonderful oily-coated malt coats the mouth allowing rich cream toffee fudge to stick alongside something very obscurely smoked. The grains tingle pleasantly; f19 flattens alarmingly and finds itself quickly spent; b20 brilliant nose and mouth-start: the real enjoyment is all upfront. The finish could do with some attention. Eaux de Vie.

Glob Kitty **(77)** n17 t20 f19 b21. Clean, firm-grained, light and biting. Good standard whisky. **40%.** Lehar Aus.

Golden Blend **(88)** n21 a teasing aroma, one minute heavy the next of a fleeting grainy lightness: intriguing and attractive; t22 honeyed and complex, major chewy sweet malt against melting grain; f22 enters overdrive here, as the softness of the grain is stupendous. The malt has every chance to form a complex liaison with the gentle oak; b23 a sound, sophisticated blend of excellent weight and evenness. At no time either bitter or sweet. **40%.** Kyndal.

Gordon Graham's Black Bottle (see Black Bottle)

The Gordon Highlanders **(85)** n21 honey and ginger; t22 pulses of grain rip through a sturdy malt wall; f21 more honeycomb and fleeting spice; b21 a seemingly light whisky but with a weighty middle of some aplomb. The arrival on the palate is almst brain-exploding: in many ways one of the most complex drams on the market. But I suspect a big caramel presence prevents this from being a genuine classic. Glorious, creamy, sweet and lip-smacking stuff. **40%**. *Wm Grant*.

The Grand Bark **(84)** **n**22 **t**22 **f**20 **b**20. The nose and malty-spicy arrival on the palate are to die for. *Symposium International*.

The Grand Bark 21 Year Old **(74)** **n**18 **t**20 **f**18 **b**18. The malt and grain just don't get on. **40%**. *Symposium International*.

Grand MacNish **(89)** **n**22 young, feral and lively. Wild grain but shackled well by some raw malt which combines lavender and gorse for a wonderfully floral blend; **t**23 I adore the way the grain and malt spark off each other. This is classic stuff; **f**22 a rare display of Speyside grassiness late on in a blend: remains sweet and clean save for some late toffee; **b**22 for those who prefer their whisky with character, eccentricity and attitude rather than water. **40%**. *MacDuff International*.

Grand MacNish 12 Years Old **(81)** **n**20 **t**21 **f**20 **b**20. Just about the softest grains you could ever wish for but the malts, though full and chewy, are just a little unbalanced. **40%**. *MacDuff International*.

Grand Old Parr Aged 12 Years **(80)** **n**21 **t**20 **f**19 **b**20. Uncompromising and rather unsophisticated, it lays the big flavours on with a trowel. Great fun, though. **43%**

Grant's (see William Grant)

Green Plaid **(87)** **n**22 buttered kippers and a sprinkling of sugar; **t**22 sweet, chewy, smoky malt is caressed by clean, yielding grain; **f**22 very long and sweet with minimum oak but surprising malt; **b**21 a touch of kindergarten smokiness does wonders for what appears to be a young dram. Really lovely stuff. And very old-fashioned. **40%**. *Inver House*.

Green Plaid 12 Years Old **(85)** **n**22 peated but deftly so, with really impressive grain softness; **t**21 early vanilla and toffee with a malty thrust towards the end; **f**21 medium length with the smoke re-forming; **b**21 a very subtle, almost whispering whisky. **40%**. *Inver House*.

Haig Gold Label **(77)** **n**19 **t**20 **f**19 **b**19. Easy going, clean but toffee rich. **40%**

Hamashkeh **(79)** **n**21 **t**21 **f**18 **b**19. A good old-fashioned blend with a delightful grain bite. Love it, but could do with dropping the caramel slightly for a crisper flavour. The only blended Scotch kosher whisky on the market. **40%**. *The Hamashkeh Co. (VDB Spirits Ltd). Specially prepared whisky, ensuring that the entire system is sherry-free, with barrels and even the bungs being thoroughly cleaned for use.*

Hankey Bannister **(80)** **n**20 **t**21 **f**20 **b**19. A mouthwateringly fresh yet toffeed young blend offering subtle spices. **40%**. *Inver House*.

Hankey Bannister 12 Year Old **(77)** **n**19 **t**21 **f**19 **b**18. Clean, sweet and syrupy. **40%**. *Inver House*.

Hankey Bannister 21 Year Old **(85)** **n**21 subtly spiced with some graceful malt; **t**22 busy, sweet and quite lush with good grain bite and clarity; **f**21 very soft oak, remains sweet, and a touch of spice; **b**21 a very easy-going dram with surprising excellent oaky control. **43%**. *Inver House*.

Harrods Finest Blended Aged 5 Years **(83)** **n**21 **t**21 **f**21 **b**20. Gives an impression of something older and wiser than five years in this one. Silky and old-fashioned in style, the grains have the leading edge and jag around the palate impressively. Too much toffee for this age, though: cut the caramel and you'd have something better still. Love it. **40%**

Hector's Nectar **(84)** **n**19 **t**22 **f**22 **b**21. A giant of a blend that takes no prisoners: young and pretty generous with the malt thrust, leaving complex grains for the biting finish. A good, rich, sweet session dram to be chewed and then the empty glass thrown in the fire!. **40%**. *Ben Nevis Distillers*.

Hedges & Butler Royal **(75)** **n**18 **t**20 **f**18 **b**19. Mouthwatering and crisp. **40%**. *Ian Macleod*.

Hedges & Butler Royal 5 Years Old (80) n17 t21 f21 b21. Try to ignore the pure caramel nose and finish: smoky, rich and beautifully weighted. **40%.** *Ian Macleod.*

Hedges & Butler Royal 15 Years Old (87) n21 heavy and fruity with real grainy bite; t22 no less weight: again the grain bites deep but there is a lot of viscous fruit to soften the impact; f22 long and chewy, delicious bitter-sweet finish; b22 bit of a throwback: not an uncommon style of blend before the Second World War. **43%**

Hedges & Butler 21 Years Old (91) n24 gently smoked and generously honeyed, this is an essay in subtlety and complexity; t23 mouth-filling, rich and lush, the grains then begin biting and nipping; f22 shows some silky ageing, offering a hint of top-order bourbon with lots of butter-toffee but also some caramel; b22 As a taster, just about impossible to spit out! Absolutely classic stuff. You cannot ask for more from an aged blend. Except the strength to be at 46% and to be non-filtered or coloured. **40%.** *Ian MacLeod.*

High Commissioner (74) n17 t21 f18 b18. A ubiquitous blend of spectacularly variable quality. This latest sample is mid-range with the usual rubbery nose, but the sweetness of the grain is a joy. Big stuff. **40%.** *A Bulloch.*

Highland Black Aged 8 Years (76) n20 t19 f18 b19. Cut the OTT caramel and you'd have a really decent blend. **40%.** *Alistair Graham Ltd (Aldi Stores).*

Highland Choice (74) n17 t19 f20 b18. Soft, silky grain, sweet and attractive. **40%.** *Alistair Graham Ltd (Aldi Stores).*

Highland Cross (89) n21 a very comfortable grain firmness; t22 mouthwatering malts arrive early and make a soft landing for the gathering grain; f22 there is a rich Speyside thread amid the oily grain; b24 This is a wonderful blend: deceptively complex and always refreshing. Love it! **40%.** *Edrington Group.*

Highland Earl (82) n20 t21 f21 b20. Rock-hard grain softened by caramel; the malt is pure Speyside. A little gem. **40%.** *Alistair Graham Ltd (Aldi Stores).*

Highland Queen (82) n20 t22 f20 b20. A clean, grassy, Speyside-led young blend, the crispness clipped by caramel. **43%.** *MacDonald & Muir.*

Highland Rose (83) n20 t22 f21 b20. Firm, high-quality blend with superb grains. Nothing withered about this one. I adore this style of whisky for everyday dramming. **40%**

Highland Stag (74) n17 t19 f20 b18. Grainy, biting, raw... but fun. **40%.** *R.N MacDonald. US.*

House of Campbell Finest (73) n18 t18 f19 b18. Very grainy and hard. **40%.** *Campbell Distillers.*

House of Peers (88) n21 a soft wave of peat is the perfect go-between as grain and malt collide; t21 the marriage between delicious, biting grain and sweet malt is harmonious; f23 really goes into overdrive as that gentle smoke returns. Additional tingling grain helps make this a long, classical finish; b23 delicate smoke gives this attractive dram something extra to chew on. A really excellent example of how to make an outwardly light blend go a long way. **43%.** *Douglas Laing.*

Ian MacLeod's Isle of Skye (see Isle of Skye)

Immortal Memory (69) n17 t18 f17 b17. Easily forgotten. **40%.** *Gordon & MacPhail.*

Imperial Classic 12 Years Old (83) n20 t22 f21 b20. A two-toned dram that is hard as nails on one hand and yielding and succulent on another. Tasty stuff on both levels. **40%.** *Allied.*

The Inverarity (83) n19 t22 f20 b22. A beautifully rich blend which would be an absolute stunner if it dropped some caramel. **40%.** *Inverarity Vaults Ltd.*

Islay Hallmark (79) n21 t20 f18 b20. Not as complex as the days when it was Islay Legend, the finish in particular being rather dull, this blend still boasts a lovely nose and mouth entry. **40%.** *Morrison Bowmore.*

Islay Mist Aged 8 Years (85) n19 not entirely in harmony but for all the peat the grain does show well; t22 sweet, rich malt with plenty of peat on show;

f22 chewy and fat; **b**22 excellent weight and freshness. Despite the youth, there is big character. **40%.** *MacDuff International.*

Islay Mist Premium Aged 17 Years (93) n23 one gets the feeling something very much older is lurking around: the gingery oakiness is big but kept in shape by the vastness of the peat. This is a balls-gripping blend you don't mess about with; **t**23 arms-behind-the-head, lean-back-and-close-the-eyes stuff. Meticulous citrus notes are bang in tune with the depth of rich, iodine-y peat. The grain is in evidence just lightening the load and offering vanilla oak; **f**23 the beautiful, lush, mildly oily texture continues. More citrus, especially lime, to combat the peat; **b**24 this is great, brave blending. I have compared it to one or two older samples of 17-y-o Islay Mist and this wins by several lengths. Brilliant. **43%**

Islay Mist Deluxe (82) n19 **t**22 **f**21 **b**20. For a blend, the grain is barely in evidence – texture apart – massacred under the weight of the fresh, young-ish peaty malt. Sweet, mildly citrussy chewy and lush. Great fun. **40%.** *MacDuff International.*

Isle of Skye 8 Years Old (93) n22 layers of peat dovetail with barley and solid grain while a wisp of honey sweetens things; **t**23 stunning. Magnificent fresh, oily peat pings round the palate, but leaves a smoky, toasty, oaky trail with a hint of marmalade fruitiness; **f**24 ridiculously long, remaining sweet and viscous with no shortage of oak and malt to bring the curtain down – eventually; **b**24 A textbook blend and an absolute must for any Islay-philes out there – in fact, a must for everybody! Your tastebuds are beaten up and caressed simultaneously. One of the most enormous yet brilliantly balanced whiskies in the world. **40%.** *Ian Macleod & Co.*

Isle of Skye 12 Years Old (91) n23 buttered kippers, big malt presence – even a hint of bourbon; **t**22 firm grain holds together the deft peat and intense vanilla; **f**23 one of the great blend finishes: smoky but allowing both oak and grain to shine for a sweetening finale; **b**23 This is a simmering blend of the very highest order: there is so much more beyond the peat. A real classic. **40%.** *Ian Macleod & Co.*

The Jacobite (76) n19 **t**20 **f**19 **b**18. A young, clean, no-nonsense, enjoyable blend with a big grain presence that puts the "bite" in Jacobite. **40%.** *Malt House Vintners.*

Jas Gordon Choice Highland Blend (77) n19 **t**20 **f**19 **b**19. Beautiful grains from an eight-year-old. **40%.** *Gordon & MacPhail.*

J&B Jet (88) n21 good, firm grain with a light Speyside shadow; **t**23 sublime mouth arrival with mouthwatering Speyside-esque malt leaping around the palate with enormous freshness, youth and energy; **f**21 mildly disappointing as some vague toffee notes dull the complexity, though gentle grainy-spice brightens the finale; **b**23 very much in the traditional J&B mould with some live-wire malt and grain keeping the tastebuds on their toes. **50%**

J&B Rare (90) n21 firm grain with a gentle Speyside edge; **t**22 mouthwatering and brittle, light yet stupendously rich as the malts fan out in all directions – other than a peaty one; **f**24 this is getting serious: the vanilla is spot on while shards of sharp malt and flinty grain rattle around the tastebuds; **b**23 for a while directly after the merger/takeover this blend went flat on us and I thought one of the great blends had been lost for good. Good news, folks, it's back! That wonderfully crisp Speyside freshness has been re-established and the blend is just like the old days. This is precious stuff: a bit of whisky heritage. Don't lose it again!!! **43%**

John Barr (75) n18 **t**20 **f**18 **b**19. A solid and honest blend with plenty of enjoyable fizz around the palate. 40%. *Kyndal.*

Johnnie Walker Black Label Aged 12 Years (89) n23 quite a thick malt presence but lighter grains and fruit, including grape, apple and tangerine lighten the load; **t**23 mouthfilling and chewy, deftly peated and boasting more lush grain; **f**21 more than normal fruit around, a bit on the sherry-ish side; **b**22 a beautifully weighted whisky but, even though scoring highly, nowhere near its best from this bottling. Normally there would be more smoke and complexity on the finish. This one has a heavier oily presence and a tad too much fruit. That said, this is still wonderful whisky: even off-form it still knocks most blends into a cocked hat. **43%**

Johnnie Walker Blue Label **(87)** n*23* the covert peat is so deep it is almost drilled into the soft oak and fruit to form the stiffest of backbones to an otherwise sultry dram; t*23* great complexity from the off with the grains hardly shy, offering a firm counter to the heathery malt; f*19* terribly disappointing as it flattens out towards toffee treacle leaving only some spice to provide entertainment; b*22* great nose and early dexterity but it is normally a lot better than this. **43%**

Johnnie Walker Gold Label **(90)** n*23* strands of honey hold together some clean, firm grain and Speysidey grassiness and the most distant toll of peat: meticulous and refined; t*23* spicy and sweet malt arrival on the palate with some much harder grains following up close behind; f*21* relatively thin and bitter with the grains dominating to an unfair degree, though some peat smoke rumbles on to ensure weight and balance; b*23* I have tasted any number of these since the very first bottling, and this is the first time it has out-scored Black Label – not least because it is so crisp, clean and beautifully defined. Also just slightly more peaty than most expressions which has guaranteed a superb balance. A blend-connoisseur's blend. **40%**

Johnnie Walker Premier **(89)** n*22* leathery and waxy with distant hints of honey and peat; t*23* big age on the malt, chewy nutty-toffee and quiet spices; f*22* more peppery now with excellent oak amid the grain with toffee returning with some sweet coffee; b*22* a luxurious blend with firm grain and big weight. A dram to take your time over. **43%**

Johnnie Walker Swing **(79)** n*19* t*22* f*18* b*20*. Grainy, biting and explosive, this blend sets itself apart from the other JW brands but is ultimately too well toffeed for its own good. **43%**

Johnnie Walker Red Label **(78)** n*19* t*22* f*18* b*19*. The salivating freshness on the palate is undermined by the heavy toffee which flattens what looked like developing into a slightly peaty finale. **40%**

John Player Special **(89)** n*23* plenty of grassy fresh malt softens the grain. Genuinely wonderful and unfettered; t*22* beautiful thirst-quenching fresh malt is lightened by good quality, clean grain; f*22* clean, long, very soft vanilla but impressive malt; b*22* Why can't more young blends be like this? Refreshing and mouthwatering, it positively basks in its youth. Of its type, utterly superb. **40%**. *Douglas Laing.*

John Player Special 12 Years Old **(81)** n*20* t*21* f*20* b*20*. Solid and quite weighty, there are some teasing spices to go with the chewy malt. **43%**. *Douglas Laing.*

John Player Special 15 Years Old **(88)** n*22* some serious age: big oak offers a bourbon style but doesn't interfere with the big apparent malt; t*22* sweet, malt start then a burst of bourbony, oaky notes; f*21* lots of vanilla and some signs of firm grain; b*23* the age states 15 years: one gets the feeling something a little more grey-bearded than that is in there ... this is a busy and complex blend. **43%**. *Douglas Laing*

Kenmore Special Reserve **(84)** n*19* t*21* f*22* b*22*. Beautifully easy going and soft. Some classic bite in there and no little complexity. A superb daily dram. **40%**. *Marks & Spencer UK.*

Kenmore Gold Special Reserve Deluxe Aged 10 Years **(79)** n*18* t*21* f*20* b*20*. Rich, well malted with a little spice and grain-cocoa on the finish. Done down by too much caramel, though. **40%**. *Marks & Spencer UK.*

King of Scots **(84)** n*20* t*21* f*21* b*22*. This is pretty raw whisky in places but what makes it a top-notch youngster is the superb balance. The grains dominate, but the malts really do make their weighty mark. Some good oiliness acts as a rich and tasty buffer. Great fun. **43%.** *Douglas Laing.*

King of Scots 12 Years Old (80) n19 **t**22 **f**19 **b**20. Some lovely oak involvement as well as rich malt and spice. But some toffee in there flattens the party somewhat. **43%.** *Douglas Laing.*

King of Scots 17 Years Old (87) n21 kumquats and a touch of honey; **t**23 early spices rendezvous with very firm grain: a serious mouthful; **f**21 slackens slightly in intensity but compensates in complexity. The oak is a little bitter but rich malt and vanilla compensate; **b**22 a beautifully aged blend. **43%.** *Douglas Laing.*

King of Scots 25 Years Old (90) n22 bourbon territory – age has given the nose a rare sheen: fruity and malty, too; **t**23 really excellent use of oak: acts as a counter to the sweet, silky grain enveloping the grapey malt; **f**23 long and richly textured with some bitter oaky tones but again the grain is absolutely outstanding; **b**22 supremely structured whisky with a most judicious and enterprising use of grain. The malts are clean and mouthwatering. A stunner. **40%.** *Douglas Laing.*

King Robert II (71) n17 **t**20 **f**17 **b**17. An otherwise honest, decent and mouthwatering blend spoiled somewhat by caramel. **40%.** *Ian MacLeod and Co.*

King's Pride (85) n20 slightly on the flat side; **t**23 fabulously complex mouth arrival, both malts and grains romping around the mouth with free expression. The grain is biting and fresh, the malt a grassy, mouthwatering mass with delicate, lightly smoked spices; **f**20 more slightly smoked malt, but gives ground a little to caramel; **b**22 take away some of the toffee effect and you have a really chewy, old-fashioned complex blend. **43%.** *Morrison Bowmore.*

Kuchh Nai (81) n19 **t**22 **f**20 **b**20. Big, bold, spicy and immensely enjoyable. **40%.** *Kuchh Nai Marketing.*

Lancelot 12 Years Old (79) n18 **t**22 **f**20 **b**19. Powerful bitter oranges on the spiced finale. **40%.** *Edrington Korea.*

Lancelot 17 Years Old (74) n17 **t**20 **f**18 **b**19. Soft and honeyed. **40%.** *Edrington Korea.*

Langs Supreme Aged 5 Years (89) n23 diced apples and sultanas, some uglifruit in there, too. Hint of something spicy and the grain is soft and crisp in equal proportion. Supreme, indeed; **t**23 soft, yielding and mouthwatering young malts are reined in by hardening grains: a bloodless coup; **f**21 some spice and vanilla but a tad too much caramel; **b**22 this is perhaps an object lesson in how to balance malts and grains. Hopefully the new owners, Ian Macleod's, will cut the caramel and raise my markings even higher next year. **40%.** *Lang Bros.*

Langs Select Aged 12 Years (77) n21 **t**21 **f**17 **b**18. Frumpy and, for all the building spice, ultimately a little passionless. **40%.** *Lang Bros.*

Lauder's (72) n18 **t**19 **f**17 **b**18. Standard, caramel-rich fare. Delicious if short-lived mouth arrival, though. **40%.** *Macduff International.*

Lauder's 12 Year Old (85) n21 massively fruity: bananas and custard meet custard cream biscuits; **t**21 sweet with velvety grain. The malt offers weight and sparkle; **f**22 delicate vanilla and quite complex malts; **b**21 a really beautifully constructed blend offering finesse. **40%.** *MacDuff International.*

Lauder's 15 Year Old (86) n21 silky sherry influence; **t**23 really superb fruit-malt combo: about as rich-textured and velvety as you could wish for; **f**21 quite long and sweet with a delightful busy grain buzz; **b**21 oddly enough it needs the grain to inject complexity into a blend that is otherwise seamless. **43%.** *MacDuff International.*

Little Frog (84) n21 **t**22 **f**20 **b**21. A big, succulent Speysidey number with considerable charm. France only. **43%.** *William Maxwell for Société Dugas France.*

The Loch Fyne (85) n21 a silky aroma with some luxuriant grain and a hint of age; **t**22 again the grain shows first but then malt slowly flickers into life and with it some spice and butterscotch; **f**21 vanilla and a slight bitter-marmalade finale; **b**21 any peat about is now covertly operating within the spice. A good session dram, a little lighter than it once was. **40%.** *Loch Fyne Whiskies Inveraray UK.*

Loch Lomond Single Blend **(85) n**21 smoky, sweet but firm; **t**22 big, oily, chewy. The grains just dissolve while the malt offers rigid resistance; **f**21 long, slightly rubbery as is the distillery trait but some vanilla to compensate; **b**21 a real heavyweight with a massive punch. A blend of malts and rains from the Loch Lomond distillery, including some crisp peaty stuff. Not exactly an exhibition of finesse, but real fun all the way. **40%**

Loch Ranza (two words, old all blue label) **(83) n**19 **t**22 **f**21 **b**21. A good, solid chewy blend of some panache. But a tad more bitter and toffeed than the present new bottling. **40%.** *Isle of Arran Distillers. Can still be commonly found in miniature form.*

Lochranza (all one word, cream and blue label) **(85) n**20 fresh grains, as one would desire for a blend, mingling with ease with a crisp maltiness; **t**22 lovely, firm mouthfeel, a hint of bitter orange then a wave of malt and caramel; **f**22 soft spices form a guard of honour around the outgoing sweet malt. The grain digs back in, but is softened by toffee-caramel; **b**21 for all its apparent lightness, a sturdy, classy blend fudged only by fudge, so to speak. **40%.** *Isle of Arran.*

Logan **(83) n**22 **t**22 **f**20 **b**19. Great nose and mouth arrival but vanishes towards the end, though it is not without a certain complexity. It seems like it's the end of Logan's run. It's been discontinued, I understand. Worth adding to a collection, though. **40%**

Long John **(72) n**17 **t**20 **b**17 **f**18. Grainy, fruity, lush but throat-gripping. **40%.** *Allied.*

McAndrews **(68) n**16 **t**18 **f**17 **b**17. A ubiquitous blend found in Britain's smaller off-licences and free houses. The caramel gives a nose not unlike a traditional Scottish west coast rum; on the palate young grains punch through the toffee-liquorice wall to offer something to bite on. **40%.** *Malt House Vintners.*

MacArthurs **(80) n**19 **t**22 **f**19 **b**20. Young, but a lot of quality malt is involved with very sympathetic grain. Silky. **40%.** *Inver House.*

McGibbons **(79) n**19 **t**19 **f**21 **b**20. A pretty fat yet medium weighted blend that gathers momentum as the complexity builds. Good spicy finale. **43%.** *McGibbons.*

Mackinlay's (see Original Mackinlay)

MacLeod's Isle Of Skye (See Isle of Skye)

Mac Na Mara **(88) n**21 salt and soft fruits; **t**22 a jazzed-up combination of brittle malts, firm grain and flavour-enlivening salt, all on a slightly oily bed; **f**22 remains malty and complex; **b**23 a very impressive blend which I adore for its mildly rugged, macho character and superb complexity. **40%.** *Praban na Linne.*

Majestic Wine Fine Oak Cask Matured Scotch **(78) n**20 **t**20 **f**19 **b**19. Youthful, biting grain forms the backbone and much of the meat of this pretty tasty and easily drinkable dram. **40%.** *Majestic Wine UK.*

Major Parka **(76) n**16 **t**20 **f**21 **b**19. Poor nose, but refreshing grain on the palate. A light but solid and enjoyable blend. **40%.** *Lehar Austria.*

Marshal **(72) n**17 **t**19 **f**18 **b**18. Very decently spiced. The nose has enough caramel to be a rum. **40%.** *Wm Maxwell Ltd.*

Martins VVO **(76) n**19 **t**20 **f**18 **b**19. Pleasant, sweet, non-committal. **40%.** *MacDonald & Muir.*

Martins 20 Years Old **(84) n**19 **t**23 **f**21 **b**21. The rich, malty, deeply satisfying, complex middle just fails to deliver on the finish. Stained slightly by a minor sherry off-note. *MacDonald & Muir.*

Martins 30 Years Old **(87) n**22 clean, ripe sherry, grains very soft, mildly spiced; **t**22 silky, melt-in-the-mouth grain gives way to some sherry and sweet ginger; **f**22 soft vanilla and spices; **b**21 it's unlikely many drams are quite as laid-back as this. What it misses in complexity (where the 20-y-o wins hands down) it makes up for in succulent, sherried sloth. *MacDonald & Muir.*

Matisse Aged 12 Years **(84) n**21 **t**23 **f**19 **b**21. Big and voluptuous, but dies on the finish. **40%**

Matisse Aged 21 Years **(63) n**14 **t**17 **f**16 **b**16. Poor sherry influence. **40%**

Matisse Royal **(81) n**21 **t**20 **f**20 **b**20. Agreeable. Makes the most of some big grain. **40%**

Mitchell's 12 Years Old **(91) n**22 pounding sea-spray of Springbank offset by hard grain: clean yet brilliantly complex; **t**22 vigorous malt and quite stunning bitter-sweet banter; **f**23 too long to be true. Some oak drifts in but can't dislodge the salty grain. Something heavy (smoke or coffee?) at the very finish; **b**24 almost too complex and beautiful to be true. Magnificent. Should increase the strength. **43%**. *Springbank.*

Monster's Choice **(69) n**18 **t**19 **f**16 **b**16. Lots of liquorice and grain. **40%**. *Gordon & MacPhail.*

Muirheads **(83) n**19 **t**22 **f**21 **b**21 A beautifully compartmentalised dram that integrates superbly, if that makes sense. In other words, the nose is crisp grain but the flavours display big Speyside malt – mouthwatering and lush. With the aid of a fatty mouthfeel, the two meet on the finish: quality blending. Old fashioned and delicious. **40%**. *MacDonald & Muir.*

Northern Scot **(76) n**18 **t**20 **f**20 **b**18. Another young grainfest from Bruce and Co., and once more very serviceable, clean, devoid of any great complexity and enjoyable for its level – and greatly improved on how it was a few years back. Marred only by too much caramel: treat as a near-grain whisky and enjoy. **40%**. *Bruce and Co. for Tesco UK.*

Old Glen **(81) n**20 **t**21 **f**20 **b**20. The grain stars despite the 60% malt content. *V&S Sweden.*

Old Mull **(83) n**22 **t**21 **f**20 **b**20. The nose offers fight and bite, but the body is lush and yielding. A real contradictory dram. **40%**. *Kyndal.*

Old Orkney "OO" 8 Years Old **(79) n**19 **t**21 **f**19 **b**20. A great improvemnet on the old "OO", with intense, delicious malt bouncing off the grain. Too much caramel, though. **40%**. *Gordon & MacPhail.*

Old Parr Superior **(87) n**23 this is great stuff: the sherry influence is clean and acts as little more than a foil for the crisp malt and light citrus; **t**22 surprisingly bitter mouth arrival but some bright malts lighten the load and sweeten things up; **f**20 quite dusty and dry with some late sherry re-surfacing with gentle grain having the very final word; **b**22 lighter than of old, but the clarity of taste is to be celebrated. **43%**

Old St Andrews 5 Years Old **(77) n**19 **t**21 **f**19 **b**18. Very soft, sweet, safe and friendly. Good middle with expansive texture. Caramel bowed. **40%**

Old St Andrews 8 Years Old **(69) n**16 **t**19 **f**17 **b**17. A flat, lifeless blend being phased out of existence. **40%**

Old St Andrews 12 Years Old **(88) n**21 fresh for age, clean, big malt and fine, clipped grain, distant hint of smoke; **t**23 outstanding Speyside-style clarity of malt, rich but never too sweet; **f**22 tapering finale with excellent vanilla; **b**22 an impressive newcomer for 2003. Loads of malt character thanks, ironically, to some excellent grain selection. Superb. **40%**. *Old St Andrews Japan.*

Old St Andrews Clubhouse **(90) n**22 clean as a whistle: both malts and grains are young but proudly so. A Speyside influence comes through loud and clear: mouthwatering; **t**23 the early arrival is identical to the nose: clear as the morning dew on the first green and no less grassy; **f**22 long with some grain gaining hold but bringing with it some soft vanillas; **b**23 a fair way to start any day. How I love young blends: fresh and lacking any sort of pretensions. It has quality enough. **40%**

Old St Andrews Golf Ball Miniatures (see Old St Andrews Clubhouse)

Old Smuggler (83) n19 t23 f20 b21. Transparently clear malt bounces off the grain like pebbles off a rock. Really flinty, crisp and deliciously fresh before some toffee arrives. **40%.** *Allied.*

The Original Mackinlay (74) n18 t20 f18 b18. This was my everyday whisky 20-odd years ago: today it is a much beefier version with, dare I say it, Fettercairn on the nose and follow-through. Tasty and weighty, but not quite the hard-grained dram I once cherished. Perhaps it should now be called The Not Quite Original Mackinlay. **40%.** *Kyndal.*

The Original Mackinlay 12 Years Old (80) n19 t21 f20 b20. Quite hefty with a spicy buzz and lingering complexity. **40%.** *Kyndal.*

Parkers (76) n17 t22 f19 b18. Flat, save for a busy early mouth rush of very decent complexity. **40%.** *Angus Dundee Ltd.*

Parkers 12 Years Old (81) n18 t19 f24 b20. Don't expect a mass market sop. Real bite to this, and for what it lacks in grace it makes up for with a finish of pure roast Brazilian coffee. Some real demerara rum style in there. **40%.** *Angus Dundee.*

Passport (80) n21 t22 f18 b19. Grainy and sharp malt at the start, but flattened by a toffee-caramel effect. Nothing like as grassy, sharp and intricate as it once was. **40%.** *Chivas.*

Peaty Craig (See Isle of Skye 8-y-o.) *From Tanner's, Shrewsbury, UK.*

Pinwinnie Royale (83) n19 t23 f20 b21. An absolutely classic, fresh young blend with crisp, rock-hard grain forming the frame on which the clean, mouthwatering malt hangs. Then a slow gathering of complex spices for good measure. Only a tad of caramel on the finish can be detected that lessens the all-round complexity and charm. **40%.** *Inver House.*

Pinwinnie Royale 12 Years Old (85) n20 more apparent malt than its younger version with a touch of smoke thrown in to soften the grain. Some zingy citrus notes grab the attention; t22 beautiful marriage between firm grain and rich malt; f21 deliciously spiced; b22 finely-textured and attractive throughout. **40%.** *Inver House.*

Politician Finest (89) n21 pretty sharp grains softened by first-class crisp malt: light and flighty; t22 really excellent used on clean young malt – probably the most of it Speyside - to refresh the tastebuds and make for a lip-smacking middle; f23 excellent complexity here as the malt and grain battle it out. It's, literally, clean fun all the way; b23 this is a terrific young blend. With its obvious reference to my favourite film of all time, Whisky Galore, it needed to be good – even go down well, if you pardon the pun – and hasn't disappointed in the slightest way. Stand up that blender and take a bow! **40%.** *Whisky Galore.*

Prince Albert De-Luxe Reserve (75) n20 t19 f18 b18. Simple, sweet and silky. **40%.** *Red Lion Blending.*

Prince Charlie Special Reserve (71) n17 t18 f19 b17. Not exactly my darling: young, sweet and shapeless, except at the end where the grains make a go of it. *Somerfield Stores UK.*

Prince Charlie Special Reserve 8 Years Old (78) n18 t19 f21 b20. Takes a bit of getting used to, and investigating, thanks to the caramel. But underneath lies an enjoyable degree of complexity, especially at the chewy sweet-liquorice finish. Good grain-malt management. **40%.** *Somerfield Stores UK.*

The Queen's Seal (73) n18 t19 f18 b18. Mildly dusty but decent Speyside input. **40%.** *Wm Maxwell Ltd.*

Real Mackenzie (80) n17 t21 f20 b22. Gets off to a flyer on the palate with fabulous grain helping the young malts to go for it. Never the gentlest of drams; great to see it maintaining its raucous spirit. **40%.** *Kyndal.*

Red Seal 12 Years Old (82) n21 t21 f19 b21. A mouthwatering blend that starts with a lovely grain kick. Overall balance is charming, but toffee numbs it down towards the finish. Still, a pretty good pub blend. **40%.** *Charles Wells UK.*

Robbie Dhu 12 Years Old **(83)** n*21* t*21* f*20* b*21*. Maintains its hallmark fruitiness but the usual soft peat is much reduced and silkiness has replaced complexity. This brand some years ago replaced the old Grant's 12-y-o. **40%**. *Wm Grant's.*

Robert Burns **(78)** n*19* t*20* f*19* b*20*. If Burns were alive today perhaps his tasting notes might be something like this. Ode to a blend: Och, wee shimmering noblest blen', tha most braken heart ye men', and this'n sets oot with grain so soft, til malt an' spice are heild aloft. **40%**. *Isle of Arran for the Robert Burns World Federation.*

Robertson's of Pitlochry Rare Old Blended **(82)** n*19* t*21* f*21* b*21*. Handsome grain bite with a late malty flourish. Classic light blend available only from Pitlochry's landmark whisky shop. **40%**

Rob Roy **(88)** n*21* lots of malt activity but the grain is firm and biting; t*23* the tastebuds are given a good going over with a really delightful array of malty tones ranging from fresh and grassy to subtly peated; f*22* tends towards dry with vanilla, cocoa, some rising peat and toffee; b*22* a profound whisky with big malt character and impressive complexity. A real no-nonsense, blend-drinker's dram. **40%**. *Morrison Bowmore.*

The Royal and Ancient **(84)** n*19* t*23* f*21* b*21*. Sort the OTT caramel on the nose and you will have back one very good blend indeed. **40%**. *Cockburn & Campbell.*

The Royal & Ancient 28 Years malt content 50% **(95)** n*24* enormously rich, floral, softly peated with stunning oak: a few molecules from perfection; t*24* big malt arrival that just swamps the mouth with the enormity of its richness. Intense bitter-sweet barley along with something smoky, but honeyed enough to keep fabulous harmony; f*23* signs of tiring oak, but forgivable. The malt is toasty, roasty, lightly peated and chewy. The grains, firm yet light, begin to glow as all else fades; b*24* an incredible blend. The mouthfeel is spot on: the whole is a sheer masterpiece! **40%**. *Cockburn & Campbell.*

Royal Castle **(51)** n*15* t*14* f*10* b*12*. Mustiness and caramel: genuinely unappealing. **40%**. *Arcus Norway.*

Royal Household **(88)** n*22* a natural harmony between crisp grain and crisper malt, wonderfully refreshing and refined; t*23* the translation onto the palate is spot on with a Speyside-style maltiness clipping alongside the rock-hard grain and a swirl of peat just about noticeable in the far distance; f*21* taken down a peg by the late caramel; b*22* this is a wonderfully sophisticated blend, far too delicate and high class to be able to support something as trade door as caramel. **43%**. *Diageo.*

Royal Salute 21 Years Old **(93)** n*23* slightly smokier than of old which means there is even more depth, which hardly seems possible: just so silky and sensuous; t*24* your tastebuds are caressed by grains that give themselves entirely to your desires, the malts provide the background music while vanilla-rich oak expresses maturity; f*22* some gentle peats arrive towards the death as the malt takes a firmer grip; b*24* just one of those whiskies you don't spit out – even when it is the 1,499th I have done for this book. Old blends are what Chivas do better than any other company and this comprehensively underlines why. **40%**. *Chivas.*

Royal Salute 50 Years Old distilled before 1953 **(95)** n*24* extremely fine strands of bourbon with suet pudding and diced apples making way for more intense raisins as the whisky warms and oxidizes; just a shaving of something peaty plus some earthy farmyardy-zooey aromas. But its all rather fantastic and supremely balanced; t*24* surprising peppery attack from the off with some very early smoke. But it's the mouthfeel that shines – no, glows! – enveloping and swamping every crevice with spiced fruit displaying exemplary composure. This is rich yet has enough bite and thrust to show shape and character. Astonishing for its age. Where the hell is the oak? Where are the cracks? Nature defying stuff;

f22 only short to medium length but sweet and genuinely barley rich with perhaps a hint of silky grain. Crisp and almost too clean to be true; **b**25 a decade ago I tasted the Royal Salute 40 Years Old. It was probably the finest blend I had ever tasted. Now they have the 50-year-old. And it has ripped up and laughed at every rule in the book: finish apart, it has just got better and better. The most extraordinary thing here is the oak involvement. At 50 years you should be picking it out of your teeth. Not here. Instead, after its appearance on the wonderful nose, it all but vanished. Instead we are left to deal with an essay in balance. This is going for £6,000 a bottle. In reality a blended whisky showing this degree of balance and elan is truly priceless. **40%** *Seagram. 255 bottles*

Royal Silk Reserve (**93**) **n**22 classically light yet richly bodied under the clear, crisp ethereal grains. The freshly-cut-grass maltiness balances perfectly; **t**24 crystal clear grains dovetail with intense, mouthwatering and refreshingly sweet malt to create a perfect pitch while the middle is heavier and livelier than you might expect with the very faintest echo of peat; **f**24 delicate oils and wonderful grainy-vanilla ensures improbable length for something so light. Beautiful spices and traces of cocoa offer the last hurrah. Sheer bliss; **b**23 I named this the best newcomer of 2001 and it has just got better and better. A session blend for any time of the day, this just proves that you don't need piles of peat to create a blend of genuine stature. Possibly the best light blend on the market in 2003. A must-have. **40%**. *International Whisky Company.*

Safeway Finest (**80**) **n**20 **t**21 **f**19 **b**20 A clean, light grainy blend. Seriously impressive for a supermarket own label and delicate despite a gentle and cleverly balancing peat input. **40%**. *UK.*

Safeway Special Reserve Double Matured Aged 5 Years (**73**) **n**18 **t**19 **f**18 **b**18. Fruity, not unlike a Manor House cake. **40%**. *UK.*

Sainsbury's Scotch Whisky (**72**) **n**18 **t**19 **f**17 **b**18. A thick, heavy, bludgeoning blend. Sublety not quite the key here. **40%**. *UK.*

Sainsbury's Finest Old Matured Aged 12 Years (**84**) **n**20 **t**22 **f**21 **b**21. Great stuff: once past the caramel the honey blossoms in all directions. A hint of smoke does no harm, either. No shame in having this around the house. **40%**. *Sainsbury UK.*

Savoy Blended Scotch (**75**) **n**18 **t**20 **f**18 **b**19. A pleasant young malt lift in the early middle palate. **40%**. *Savoy Hotel UK.*

Scotch Brothers (**70**) **n**17 **t**19 **f**17 **b**17. Grainy, hard, biting and young. **40%**. *Russia.*

Scotch Blue 17 Years Old (**78**) **n**21 **t**20 **f**18 **b**19. Salty and biting complexity makes for impressive blend, but a little too sappy and caramelised. **40%**. *Korea.*

Scotch Blue Aged 21 Years (**80**) **n**21 **t**20 **f**19 **b**20. A pleasingly spiced, rich blend with agreeable chewability. **40%**. *Korea.*

Scots Club (**72**) **n**17 **t**19 **f**18 **b**18. Young, pleasant, basic fare. **40%**. *Kyndal.*

Scots Grey De Luxe (**83**) **n**19 **t**22 **f**21 **b**21 The toffeed nose is less than promising but the quality of their grain is outstanding with very impressive malt infusion. Chewy and desirable, despite the so-so aroma. **40%**

Scottish Collie (**72**) **n**18 **t**18 **f**19 **f**17 **b**18. Starts promisingly but splutters at the finish. **40%**. *Quality Spirits Int.*

Scottish Collie Aged 12 Years (**84**) **n**22 **t**22 **f**19 **b**21 A well-constructed blend with fine character development let down by a slightly bitter finale. **43%**. *Quality Spirits Int.*

Scottish Glory (**82**) **n**19 **t**21 **f**20 **b**22. A very good standard blend with excellent grain bite but then a clean malty follow-through with some soft spices. **40%**. *Brands Development.*

Scottish Leader 12 Year Old (**77**) **n**19 **t**22 **f**18 **b**18. Fruity nose and lovely, complex mouth arrival but falters latterly. **40%**. *Burn Stewart.*

Scottish Leader 15 Year Old **(87)** n*22* fabulous, supreme mixture of deep fruity tones, soft oak, rich barley and a wisp of smoke; t*22* brilliant texture: sweet with malt and plummy fruit and natural oak-caramel; f*21* long, oily, chewy with lots of vanilla; b*22* this is big stuff, sweet and yet gentle with it. **40%.** *Burn Stewart.*

Scottish Leader 22 Years Old **(86)** n*23* mesmeric sherry influence: exceptional stuff; t*22* rich grapey-sherry influence, big malt but very sweet; f*21* fails to develop complexity save for a chocolate finale; b*20* this is a lovely dram, but would be better if it wasn't quite so sweet. Much of its complexity is hidden. **40%.** *Burn Stewart.*

Scottish Leader Aged Over 25 Years **(91)** n*24* charismatic peat offers the most sublime aroma you could imagine for a blend of this age. No off-notes whatsoever: what little grain can be detected stands firm and clean; t*22* chewy, massively intense malt framed by succulent grain; f*23* the peat returns, dovetailing with vanilla and lingering sweet barley; b*22* a changed character from a few years back: heavier and fuller yet refusing to let age dim its innumerable qualities. A real belter of a blend. **40%.** *Burn Stewart.*

Scottish Leader Blue Seal **(82)** n*21* t*22* f*19* b*20*. Impressive grain bite on the nose softened by rich malt. A fine dram by any standards. **40%.** *Burn Stewart.*

Scottish Leader Platinum **(73)** n*19* t*19* f*18* b*17*. Rather bland. **40%.** *Burn Stewart.*

Scottish Leader Supreme **(72)** n*17* t*20* f*18* b*17*. A variable dram these days: not a patch on when it had a sublime soft peating lurking about. That said, chewy, oily and pleasant with exceptional grain use. **40%.** *Burn Stewart.*

Shieldaig The Classic Uisge Beatha **(66)** n*15* t*19* f*16* b*16*. Thin and grainy. **40%.** *William Maxwell and Son (Ian Macleod).*

Shieldaig Collection Finest Old Uisge Beatha (see Shieldaig The Classic). *William Maxwell and Son France.*

Something Special **(84)** n*19* t*23* f*21* b*21*. An ordinary nose for Something Special but there is big, chewy compensation on the palate with what appears to be a solid phalanx of malt reinforcing the charming grains. A bit too toffeed on the finish, though. **40%.** *Chivas.*

Spar Finest **(80)** t*20* t*21* f*19* b*20*. A standard blend, but of a superbly-balanced style I adore. The exquisite clean grains show nip and attitude – as they should – but there is sufficient malt for depth. Love to see the toffee effect go, though, and have it raw and refreshing. **40%.** *UK.*

The Spey Cast 12 Years Old **(81)** n*18* t*22* f*21* b*20*. Lovely, complex, fruity dram. **40%.** *Gordon & MacPhail.*

Spey Royal **(76)** n*18* t*20* f*19* b*19*. Quite a young blend with a big toffee effect but not without a delicious and lush early malt-grain explosion. **40%.** *Diageo Thailand.*

Standard Selection Aged 5 Years **(92)** n*22* the rock-hard grain deflects the delicate smoke: uncompromising and enticing; t*23* fabulous collection of fruity tones, balanced by an ever-increasing peat presence, brilliantly subtle with honey-barley; f*23* the oak seems more than five years and softens the smoke; b*24* a brilliant blend that appears a lot older than its five years: a stupendously stylish interpretation of peat with sweet barley. **40%.** *V&S Stockholm.*

Stewart's Cream of the Barley **(71)** n*16* t*19* f*18* b*18*. Bubble-gum nose but a softer more malt-friendly and even complex mouth arrival than of old. **40%.** *Allied.*

Stewart's Finest **(75)** n*17* t*20* f*19* b*19*. The nose is raw, the body sweet, curvaceous, toffeed and chewy. Annoyingly and dangerously drinkable. **40%.** *Kyndal.*

Swords (74) n18 t18 f20 b18. Big grain character with some cocoa and complexity on the oak-sculpted finish. Sturdy and unpretentious. **40%.** *Morrison Bowmore.*

The Talisman (87) n21 biting grain, but enticing and malt-encrusted, young and really attractive; t22 first-class mouth arrival with some Speyside-intense malt showing early before the grains regain a foothold; f21 lovely vanilla, the toffee is creamy and malt-rich; b23 a lively blend from the same stable as The Antiquary but shows much greater verve, vitality and fun. **40%**

Teacher's Highland Cream (95) n23 hard, brittle nose where both the grains and malts are sparking off each other. A distant, kippery peatiness drifts around in the background: not a blend you muck about with; t24 one of the best mouth arrivals of any whisky in the world. It has that magical, mercurial quality of combining lush malt with crisp grain and perhaps ever crisper malt carrying soft peat: a Russian doll of a delivery; f23 long vanilla tinged with smoke, a touch of toffee and the most gentle spices. Malt bobs around until the very end, sometimes lifting the heavier veil to display a grassy, mouthwatering alter ego; b25 if I had a pound for every time I've heard this whisky rubbished I could build a distillery. Frankly, Teacher's is one of the most consistent whiskies in the world and one of unyielding quality. Its greatest asset is its quiet assertiveness, its full body and yet an ability to reveal a feminine side. This is a whisky of spellbinding complexity and of a style that is an umbilical chord to our blending forefathers. One of my desert island whiskies. **40/43%.** *Allied.*

Te Bheag (84) n19 t22 f21 b22. Well balanced with good spice bite. **40%.** *Praban na Linne.*

Te Bheag's Connoisser's Blend (pronounced Chay Vegg) **(90)** n22 coastal and salty with some ascending soft peat; t23 superbly textured with a rich digestive-biscuit, slightly salty maltiness digging in. The grains offer a distant murmur; f22 soft peats nudge at the vanilla; b23 not quite as hardy on the tastebuds or peaty as previous bottlings, this still remains a quite stupendous and satisfying dram. **40%. ncf.** *Praban na Linne.*

Tesco Special Reserve (72) n18 t20 f17 b17. Quite weighty, but much of that towards the end is the way over the top caramel. Good early body feel and complexity, though. **40%.** *Tesco UK.*

Ubique (82) n20 t22 f21 b19. Fresh, mouthwatering with lots of Speyside character. A classy job. **40%**

Upper Ten (68) n17 t18 f17 b16. Makes a point of peat on the label, but fails to deliver balance. **40%.** *Arcus Norway.*

VAT 69 (86) n20 a noseful of young, nippy grain balanced with grassy malt and a hint of toffee; t22 brilliant arrival of complex and superbly balanced young grains and malts; f21 pretty long, with the oak and grain having the lion's share of the character; b23 exemplary young blend: fresh, clean and mouthwatering. This, to me, offers the kind of balance and style that encapsulates a light blend. No problems with water and even ice on the hottest days. **43%.** *Wm Sanderson/Diageo.*

Waitrose Scotch Whisky (80) n19 t20 f21 b20. Clean, firm-grained and stylish. Excellent bite. **40%**

Walker and Scott Finest (82) n20 t21 f20 b21. Rock-hard and brittle grain gives a clean shape for the malts to develop around. High grain content, but a Speysidey grassiness is quite delicious as is the mildly citrussy nose; marks docked only for late toffee. Impressive and old-fashioned. **40%.** *Sam Smith's UK.*

The Watsonian Club Whisky (77) n19 t20 f19 b19. A soft, sweet, clean blend with a dry finish. **40%**

White Horse (92) n23 beautifully smoky: big weight with the grains shrinking by comparison; t24 magnificently rounded at first then wave upon wave of varying characteristics ranging from clean, fresh malt to heavier, smoky notes with even room for a little vanilla and sultana; f22 long, vanilla-rich with some light peat still drifting around; b23 this is one of the greatest young blends on the market: only the oiliness presented by, probably, Caol Ila, takes it out of a mark in the mid-90s. When Lagavulin was used there was a cleaner, crisper feel. But I am nit-picking: it is not entirely unknown for me to have a less than harmonious reltionship with some of the world's bigger distillers. But if I were Holmes, I would doff my deerstalker to this masterpiece of a blend, as it is one even he would fail to fathom and one that proves that greatness is not achieved by the age of the whisky but the understanding and feel for how the elements combine and interact. Proof, were it needed, that even among the big boys there are still quality blenders around who know how to make a pulse race. **43%**. *Diageo*.

Whyte & Mackay (80) n20 t19 f21 b20. Not a nose or body for the faint-hearted: big and blustery. A surprisingly tamed Fettercairn seems to be at the core, surrounded by dates and walnuts in a rich fruitcake frame with no shortage of lightly molassed sugar. Very distinctive and bold. **40%**

Whyte & MacKay 12 Years Old (84) n21 t21 f20 b22. Beautifully wallowing grain offers little shelter to some rollicking malty notes: curiously light yet weighty – totally intriguing. **40%**. *Kyndal*.

Whyte & Mackay 15 Years Old (89) n22 moist dates and walnut cake:yummy; t23 more fruitcake and some honey and mango; f22 the grains dig in and team up with some rubbery malt for a dryish finish; b22 a once-great blend that, sadly, is no longer mixed. Can still be found at some specialist outlets around the globe. A sad loss: a really great blend. **43%**. *Kyndal*.

Whyte & Mackay 15 Years Old Select Reserve (86) n21 wonderfully subtle fruit, dates and soft peat; t23 beautifully textured malt with soft grain on a hard grain field: genuine complexity here; f21 plenty of vanilla brushed with toffee; b21 a really neat blend with slightly more toffee effect than the old version. **40%**

Whyte & MacKay 18 Years Old (89) n22 dried dates moistened by sultanas: the malt hangs firm; t23 voluptuous and silky, sweet grain and malt marriage made in heaven; f22 simplifies and reverts back to the dates again; b22 a stylish, tamed brute of a blend. A whisky as expansive as its creator. But a whole lot sexier. **40%**. *Kyndal*.

Whyte & Mackay 21 Years Old (85) n20 slightly nibbled at by some vaguely off-sherry notes but this is compensated for by an exhilarating display of low-flying citrus notes; t22 the mouth luxuriates with that silky, "married" feeling you get with W&M blends; f21 nutty, points docked for the return of that mild flaw again, but it's nothing too serious; b22 this blend is so well married it wears slippers and smokes a pipe. **43%**. *Kyndal*.

Whyte & MacKay 30 Years Old (93) n24 flawless fruit, amazingly intense clean malt and the softest of vanilla-laden grain, all entwined with a waft of light smoke; t22 a very fresh sherry feel dominates at first, then behind that arrives a procession of muted malty notes; f23 so soft and gentle you could wash a baby in it. Probably the result of W&M's marrying process, the subtlety is quite astonishing. Some treacle toffee on the very finish is still outflanked by some gathering spice; b24 there is no evidence of a tired cask here at all: the tastebuds are entirely engulfed by something enormous and deeply satisfying. **40%**. *Kyndal*.

Whyte & Mackay High Strength (87) n18 rubbery, the weak link; t22 beautifully sweet with lashings of lightly molassed sugar forming the bridge between the soft grain and harder, more rigid malts; f24 long and caressing, massively intense with hints of liquorice and malt concentrate. One of the best finishes of any blend on the market: positively sensual; b23 only the poor nose prevents this from being one of the greatest blends of them all. It has enormous character and confidence and flavours attack the tastebuds from all angles. Damn it: forget the nose, just go for it and enjoy something a little special. **52.5%**. *Kyndal*.

William Grant's 100 US Proof Superior Strength **(91)** n*23* sublime chocolate lime nose, decent oak; t*23* big mouth arrival, lush and fruity with the excellent extra grain bite you might expect at this strength; f*22* back to chocolate again with a soft fruit fade; b*23* a fruitier drop now than it was in previous years but no less supremely constructed. **50%** *(100 US proof)*.

William Grant's Ale Cask Reserve **(88)** n*20* old, peculiar aroma of spilt beer: pretty malty to say the least; t*23* enormous complexity with myriad malt notes varying from sweet and chewy to bitter and biting; f*22* quite long with some toffee and hops(??) Yes, I really think so; b*23* a real fun blend that is just jam-packed with jagged malty notes. The hops were around more on earlier bottlings, but watch out for them. Nothing pint-sized about this: this is a big blend and very true in flavour/shape to the original. **40%**

William Grant's 15 Year Old **(70)** n*17* t*20* f*16* b*17*. Crushed mercilessly by caramel. No pulse whatsoever. **40%**

William Grant's Classic Reserve 18 Years Old **(93)** n*24* salty, aroma of crashing waves on a beach, seaweed, yet no more than a hint of peat. Grains are crisp and biting but the malt blunts them: sensational; t*23* big fruit kick-off followed by wave upon wave of breaking malt. The grain bites now and again. The complexity, especially with the arrival of the peat, is nothing short of mind-boggling; f*23* long, fruity and still softly peated. The grains offer gentle oak and a drifting sweetness; b*23* few whiskies maintain such high levels of complexity from nose to finish. A true classic. **40%**

William Grant's 21 Year Old **(96)** n*24* the sea crashing into the most glorious sherry butts imaginable. Salt and fruit in abundance, smoke is there too but shy, the malt and grains are almost in a passionate embrace and the sweet saltiness is almost erotic; t*25* telling fresh oloroso makes a great backdrop for the astounding passion play to unfold on the tastebuds. Mouthfeel and weight: perfect, complexity: perfect, sherry input: perfect, malt presence: perfect, grain input: perfect; f*23* more oak makes itself known, to a slightly bitter degree. Despite that, the fruit remains juicy and the malt chewy; b*24* whisky is all about balance and complexity. In my lifetime I have encountered probably a handful that come close to this. This, quite simply, is a blend of a quality rarely achieved. **40%**

William Grant's 25 Years Old **(90)** n*23* extremely clean and telling oloroso: butts of the highest standard, but they reduce the complexity somewhat; t*24* the fruit is ripe and grain offers lush softness for the malts to thrive. The complexity is massive and the tongue is working overtime against the roof of the mouth to get to grips with the gentle enormity of the blend; f*21* spicy and oak-dried; b*22* another peach of a blend. There is no other family of blends that comes close to touching the all-round brilliance of Grant's (the boring 15-y-o apart!). **40%**

William Grant's Family Reserve **(94)** n*25* this, to me, is the perfect nose to any blend: harmonious and faultless. There is absolutely everything here in just-so proportions: a bit of snap and bite from the grain, teasing sweet malts, the faintest hint of peat for medium weight, strands of oak for dryness, fruit for lustre. Even Ardbeg doesn't pluck my strings like this glass of genius can; t*23* exceptionally firm grain helps balance the rich, multi-layered malty tones. The sub-plot of burnt raisins and peek-a-boo peat adds further to the intrigue and complexity (if it doesn't bubble and nip around the mouth you have a rare sub-standard bottling); f*22* a hint of caramel can be detected amid returning grains and soft cocoa tones: just so clean and complex; b*24* there are those puzzled by my obvious love affair with blended whisky – both Scotch and Japanese – at a time when malts are all the rage. But take a glass of this and carefully nurture and savour it for the best part of half an hour and you may begin to see why I believe this to be the finest art form of whisky. For my money, this brand – brilliantly kept in tip-top shape by probably the world's most naturally gifted blender – is the closest thing to the blends of old and, considering it is pretty ubiquitous, it defies the odds for quality. It is a dram with which you can start the day and end it: one to keep you going at low points in between, or to celebrate the victories. It is the daily dram that has everything. **40%**

William Grant's Sherry Cask Reserve (84) n23 t20 f21 b20. The nose is one almost of juicy blackcurrants tinged with malt and oak. Outstanding. The follow-up, though clean and almost velvety, doesn't quite hit those same heights. **40%**

William Lawson's Finest (83) n19 t21 f21 b22. Not only has the label become more colourful, but so, too, has the whisky. However that has not interfered with the joyous old-fashioned grainy bite. A complex and busy blend from the old charm school. **40%**

William Lawson's Scottish Gold Aged 12 Years (88) n22 soft yet weighty with dulcet citrus, fruity notes; t23 crisp grains interlink superbly with very clean grape and some sweet malt; f22 a smattering of cocoa aids the spices towards a drying finish after the sweetish build-up; b21 don't get me wrong here: this is very, very good whisky. But once it was great. Something, I suspect some very good quality sherry butts, has intervened and what it gives with one hand it takes with the other ... in this case, complexity. For years Lawson's 12 was the best example of the combined wizardry of clean grain, unpeated barley and good bourbon cask that you could find anywhere in the world: a last-request dram before the firing squad. Today it is still excellent, but just another sherried blend. What's that saying about if it's not being broke...? **40%**

William Lawson's Founder's Reserve Aged 18 Years (95) n24 a sublime marriage of fresh marmalade and something delicately smoked. The grain is firm and offers a crystal clarity. The whole thing is stunning; t24 yes, it's a Lawson's and there really is something peaty on this – I am stunned. Again, just like the nose there is an almost erotic unravelling of the layers: first fruity notes, then vanilla-coffee grain then this final unbuttoning to reveal naked peat caressed by honey-toasted malt; f23 long vanilla notes with soft, smoky spice: the finish is short-ish ... probably all the excitement; b24 sensual and seductive, this quite extraordinary dram was just what I needed after the relative disappointment of Lawson's 12. The best branded whisky I have tasted for the first time while writing this book. – and this is dram number 1,604. This whisky is a real turn-on. I could be enticed to see the etching on the back of the bottle any time... **43%**

William Peel Founder's Premium Aged 7 Years (77) n18 t20 f20 b19. A decent, solid blend. **40%**. *France.*

Windsor Premier Aged 12 Years (90) n23 absolutely first-class for the age: a celebration of balance and charm with just enough fruit to soften the grain and marauding malt; t23 fresh, sweet, immensely barley-rich with engaging oak and a chocolatey-smoky-honeyed depth, excellent grain coating; f21 heaps of vanilla, dries attractively; b23 one hell of a blend. Outwardly simple, but enormous complexity lurks everywhere. Brilliant. **40%**

Windsor Prestige Aged 17 Years (87) n22 honeycomb and soft grain; t23 enormously malt-rich but thins rapidly as some grains tuck in; f20 remains a bit thin as the vanilla arrives. Some late fruit arrives; b22 at the strength this is bottled, it's like having a Jaguar and putting a Mini engine in it. I have also tasted one of these that was not up to scratch, especially on the nose. But I'm sure that was a freak. **40%**

Wm Morrison Finest Scotch (68) n17 t18 f16 b17. Way too overstacked with caramel. Supermarket fodder. *UK.*

Irish Whiskey

Is it just irony? One of those strange twists of fate? But a few years back the name Jameson was hardly synonymous with the new wave of appreciation sweeping over Irish whiskey.

People had at last discovered the brutal glory of Pot Still. They were wallowing in the outrageous magnificence and cunning of Bushmill's triple-wood 16 years old. They were taking Ireland's very own favourite, Power's, to their hearts. They were marvelling at Cooley's peated malts. They were being soothed by the velvet embrace of Blackbush. And, dare I say, trying to get to grips with the complexity of a Knappogue – not to be confused with the honeyed Gold and that essay in sherry, the 1780 – was for the true Irish whiskey lover not very high on the list of names to be encountered and conquered.

But the tasting carried out for this book succeeded only in confirming something that a few dozen glasses of assorted Irish over the last year had suggested to me. And that was while some trusty brands were going backwards, that plodding old workhorse Jameson had turned into a thoroughbred. And what was more it had moved up on the blind side of the others and was leading by a nose ...

It was only a decade ago that I regarded the standard Jameson a bit of a sham Irish. It was characterless quaffing fuel, with every last trace of Irishness wrung out of it. Today, among Irish blends, it stands almost aloof. It has not only embraced Irishness but now it radiates it. The Pot Still level has risen dramatically, the casks have been clean and uncluttered and the result is the most lucid and erudite of all Ireland's ambassadors. And that is saying something ...

Which means that other stalwarts are letting the side down. Well it is extraordinary that, while marked highly, neither Green Spot nor Redbreast have hit my awards list. Every year for the last ten they would have done, but the samples tasted here were just a little flatter than before, a trait I had first noticed late in 2002. And as for Power's ... something is not right there at all, at all. And I have pretty strong suspicions regarding the culprit. Watch future editions closely to see if they return to their traditional status.

Another Jameson also caught the eye in 2003, the newly launched 18

years old. The first batch was a classic; the second, irritatingly and confusingly, paled by comparison. Shortly before this book was completed, a third batch was made, much of it heading to the USA and that was back to being a little beaut and here's hoping it stays that way.

Cooley have been relatively quiet, though their pure grain, Greenore, has just got better and better. Along with a grain made in Spain this has to be just about Europe's finest. And they have pulled off a minor coup by now supplying the Irish whiskey to the famous Buena Vista in San Francisco for their famed Irish coffee.

But this year, as far as mass market Irish is concerned, it's time to tip your cap to Jameson. It just goes to show what positives can come from a less than flattering review in a whiskey book ...

Irish Whiskey Terms

For those of you new to Irish whiskey, or confused by the terms used, here's a simple guide to understanding the variations in Irish whiskey.

Pure Pot Still: The indigenous whiskey of Ireland. Pure Pot Still is a term used for over 130 years for a whiskey made in copper pots from a mixture of malted and unmalted barley. Once this way of making whiskey was known also to the Lowlands of Scotland, where it has long died out, and was used by distillers as a way of avoiding paying tax on malt. The flavour is entirely different from a whiskey made exclusively from malted barley, which has an all-round softer flavour and texture. Once, it was made all over Ireland, the big Dublin distilleries particularly proud exponents of the artform. But after the withering of the industry and a century of continuous closures, Pure Pot Still today is made at one last outpost: the Midleton distillery near Cork. Cooley confusingly call some of their single malt Pure Pot Still. Technically, because of the fact it is made in a copper pot, it is. But in the spirit and tradition of Irish whiskey it most certainly is not.

Single Malt: Just like Scotland, Ireland makes malt whiskey using double and triple distillation. Cooley use two stills, Bushmills and Midleton, make triple-distilled malt, though the latter has never been bottled as a single malt whiskey and instead is used in blends.

Single Grain: Amazingly no single grain whiskey was bottled in Ireland until I designed the three Clontarf whiskies and persuaded the brand owners, very much against their wishes, to include a single grain Irish. It has taken Ireland by storm. Because the Cooley grain used is as yielding yet flavoursome as any around, Cooley have a hot back, though, and their own Greenore now outpoints it.

Blended: Theoretically this could have a much wider range of styles than even Scotland. Some of Cooley's whiskey found its way into one or two Irish Distillers brands after the latter bought stocks during the aborted take-over. But these days Cooley blend from Cooley whiskies and Irish Distillers use only their own. So there is no Pure Pot Still from Midleton, mixed with peated malt from Cooley, with two types of grain to counter the flavour meltdown. Even so, blends produced from Midleton can be among the most complex on earth, especially as they have been experimenting in including whiskeys matured in virgin oak casks. But the likes of Jameson Gold or Jameson 18 are far removed from the Cooley blends, consisting of malt and grain made at the same plant and which can be variations on a theme, some much more tuneful than others. But Cooley cannot be criticised for this practice. Not only do they offer some impressive blends, but they are doing no different from Irish Distillers, who boast the extraordinary Black Bush – made up simply from a single grain from Midleton and a single malt from Bushmills. And, it has to be said, that no harm is being done, either, by Irish Distillers having their hands on the best sherry butts I have seen sourced from Jerez in the last ten years by the Scotch, Japanese and Irish whisky industries combined.

Pure Pot Still
JAMESON

John Jameson Academy bottled by M D Daly & Sons, Academy Street, Cork. **(92) n**23 shining, shimmering pot still, clean, intense and gently honeyed with some peppered celery, too; **t**23 massive barley then a surge of rock-hard pot still, crisp yet silky with generous malt fusing with oak. Mouthwatering and chewy, this is perfectly weighted for a Jameson of this era; **f**22 medium to long with lingering flinty barley merging with late grapey fruitiness, finishing with a sprinkling of demerara; **b**24 living history – a bottled time machine. Jameson pot still at its very finest preserved with stunning freshness from its heyday. A once-in-a-lifetime treat. This single bottle produced from the old, now lost, Jameson distillery in Dublin dates probably from the early 1950s. It is found only at the Lidsay House Restaurant in London's Soho. No strength stated.

MIDLETON (old distillery)

Midleton 25-y-o Pot Still db **(92) n**24 astonishing aroma: fabulously fruity and fresh despite its great age. Even so, there is a wonderful oaky-vanilla depth that not only displays age but actually highlights the richness of the unmalted barley. A lovely toffee sweetness hangs over the proceedings and an unmistakable hint of bourbon-character has begun to win through, softened by a Canadian-style vanilla lightness – yet always unmistakably and uniquely Irish! Excellent complexity throughout; **t**24 a tantalising, lively palate-buster from the off with an oily sweetness immediately clinging to the roof of the mouth. An astonishing and most delicate spiciness balances superbly against the stark crispness of the mouth-watering, rye-ish unmalted barley; **f**21 only medium length but with a big, dark chocolate depth, a rich echo of the aged oak; **b**23 a really enormous whiskey that is in the truest classic Irish style. The un-malted barley really does make the tastebuds hum and the oak has added fabulous depth. Interesting when tasted against an American rye – the closeness of the character is there to be experienced, but also the differences. A subtle mature whiskey of unquestionable quality. Superb. **43%**

Midleton 30-y-o Pot Still db **(85) n**19 heavier, more deeply brooding with some honey and oily, crushed pine nuts. A molassed sugar sweetness is also evident. An oaky, substantial, well-balanced aroma, but with great age in evidence; **t**22 immediately mouth-watering, grassy and spicy. Beautifully sweet and malty but it's the almost bitter un-malted grain which gains the upper hand and is soothed by the deep and fabulously balanced oak; **f**22 clean and slightly oily with a build-up of vanilla and malt, very crisp and firm, almost hard; **b**22 a typically brittle, crunchy Irish pot still where the un-malted grains have a telling say. The oak has travelled as far as it can without having an adverse effect. A chewy whiskey which revels in its bitter-sweet balance. An impressively tasty and fascinating insight into yesteryear. **45%**

MIDLETON (new distillery)

Green Spot **(92) t**23 mouthwatering and fresh on one level, honey and menthol on another; **t**23 crisp, mouthwatering with a fabulous honey burst, alarmingly sensuous; **f**23 faint coffee intertwines with the pot still. The thumbprint thread of honey remains; **b**23 has remained in this honey state for a few years now, once previously a bit sharper. Soft yet complex throughout. Unquestionably one of the world's greatest branded whiskies. **40%**. *Irish Distillers for Mitchell & Son, Dublin.*

Jameson 15 Years Old **(89) n**24 the raisiny, deftly honeyed brittle pot still eventually dominates the spice. Brooding stuff and very old fashioned; **t**23 Jameson Gold-like shafts of honey pierce the oaky, barley rich intensity. Outstanding bittersweet shape, but just tending towards the sweeter side of things; **f**20 docked marks for the surprising brevity of the finale, though some cocoa makes a guest appearance; **b**22 finish apart, this is sensational stuff of a style universally unique to Ireland, the Midleton Distillery in particular. **40%**. *Irish Distillers. A limited edition to mark the year 2000.*

Redbreast 12 Years Old (90) n23 an unhurried display of ripe fruits which, together with the sharpness of the pot still, reminds me of a firm, pure rye, only this is a tad spicier; **t**23 more lazy spice, though not before the shock waves of complex, mouthwatering barley notes on a field of clean sherry; **f**22 lingering fruity toffee-sherry; **b**22 remains an all-Ireland great institution and one of the few pure pot-still whiskeys still around. Amazing to think this was a dead duck until my book Jim Murray's Irish Whiskey Almanac was released in 1994 when the brand was due to be withdrawn. The only change in the whiskey over those near 10 years is that the sherry today is a fraction lighter, the heavy effect once being similar to that found in the equally glorious Jameson 1780. Not to be confused with the rare blend Redbreast Blend (see Irish Blends) **40%**. *Irish Distillers.*

OLD COMBER

Old Comber 30 Years Old Pure Pot Still (88) n23 glorious and quite unique combination of pure pot still and honey. Sweet with traces of malt with the bourbony wood doing slightly less damage than one might imagine. The resiny threat of oak circles like a vulture, however; **t**24 begins with a soft, breezy maltiness which is attractive for its gentle character, but this is abruptly cut short by a surge of oak; **f**20 woody-mentholy traits as the oak takes grip. Dries as some sap appears. The sap still battles gamely to the end; **b**21 a classic example of a whiskey spending a few summers too many in wood: increasing age doesn't equal excellence. That said, always very drinkable and early on positively sparkles with a stunning mouthfeel. Out of respect for the old I have made the markings for taste cover the first seven or eight seconds ... **40%**

TULLAMORE

Cadenhead's Tullamore 38 Years Old dist 52, bott 91 **(63) n**16 **t**16 **f**15 **b**16. A collector's whiskey that, if unwisely opened, reveals an essay in oak.

Cadenhead's Tullamore 41 Years Old dist 49, bott 91 **(89) n**22 sap burns off quickly to reveal something extraordinary. Pot still remains intact and proud, bolstered by coffee and molassed sugar. Fresh hay and sturdy but perfectly weighted oak ensure balance and a feeling of great age; **t**22 the pot still, aided by juicy-fresh barley rigidity, shows first and does so strongly. Lashings of oily honey, coated with oak, add a cinnamon-like spice and some cocoa; **f**22 long and very clean. The unmalted barley retains its shape and a honeycomb bitter-sweetness also shines through; **b**23 one of those rare whiskies which has incorporated excess oak and converted it into something quite stupendous. A great testament to the Tullamore distillery, and one I opened a bottle of at a tasting in Germany not so long ago. Outstandingly beautiful. **65.4%. nc ncf sc.**

Cadenhead's Tullamore 42 Years Old dist 48, bott 91 **(72) n**18 **t**19 **f**17 **b**18. Drinkable despite big oak dominance, but on its last legs. **65.3%. nc ncf sc.**

Knappogue Castle 1951 bott 87 **(93) n**23 a heady mix of over-ripe – almost black – banana and big oak. A blend of molasses and demerara sugar mixed with honey, ripe greengages and pepper ... almost rum-like; **t**24 big and booming. Rich start, attractively oily and mouthwatering. The unmalted barley and even oats show well while the middle provides plenty of estery Jamaican pot-still rum; **f**22 long, hard and brittle – as to be expected from an Irish of this genre. Bourbon-style vanilla with chewy liquorice. An estery, vaguely honeyed finale; **b**24 highly individualistic. Another year in cask might have tipped this over the edge. We are talking brinkmanship here with a truly awesome display of flavour profile here ranging from traditional Irish pot to bourbon via Jamaican pot-still rum. A whiskey of mind-boggling duplicity, tricking the tastebuds into one sensation and then meandering off on a different tangent altogether. About as complex and beguiling as a straight Irish whiskey ever gets. **40%**. *Great Spirits*.

Single Malt
COOLEY

Connemara db **(82)** n*22* t*21* f*19* b*20*. Delicate, almost apologetic peat; quite flinty and hard on the nose; sweet, gristy malt with the peat at first coming out to play and making a feeble, begrudging appearance. Not the same old smoky Connemara we have come to know and love. **40%**

Connemara Cask Strength db **(88)** n*22* buttered kippers, oily, gentle smoke; t*23* sweet and sweetens further as the peat makes a dignified entrance with lovely chewy malt: exceptionally creamy and lush; f*21* a threat of spice never quite materialises, but the vanilla is clean and dry; b*22* not one of those big, blistering Connemaras where you could stand a spoon in the peat reek, but rather a more subtle and sophisticated Irish requiring time to explore. **58.5%**

Locke's Malt 8 Years Old db **(76)** n*20* t*20* f*18* b*18*. Not unpeated Cooley at its best by any means: other expressions of this brand have been far nearer the mark. Pleasant citrus on the nose and chewy malt on the mouth arrival, but rather wan after that. **40%**

The Tyrconnell db **(89)** n*22* oranges and cedar, clean malt and courteous oak; t*23* blemish free, so clean and mouthwatering but with a hint of something almost salty; f*21* pretty long with the malt continuing to buzz around the palate. The vanilla also begins to show well; b*23* this is easily the best Tyrconnell yet. Enormous thought and work has gone into the cask selection. **40%**

The Tyrconnell (Limited Edition) (84) n*19* t*21* f*22* b*22*. Lots of lovely citrus on nose and palate, but goes curiously flat at point of entry. Even so, lots of charm and sophistication, especially on the finish, even when all cylinders aren't used. **40%**. *Cooley. 5000 bottles. Confusingly, the label says "Single Malt" and "Pure Pot Still". This is a single malt.*

Avoca (76) n*19* t*20* f*18* b*19*. Chewy and sweet at first but turns bitter as the grain and oak bite. **40%**. *Cooley for Aldi.*

Cadenhead's Cooley 10 Years Old dist 92, bott 03/03 **(84)** n*21* t*22* f*20* b*21*. Cooley in its malty splendour with some delicate peat hanging around. Just a bit raw around the edges, though. **59.8%**

Clontarf Single Malt (85) n*20* citrus and coal smoke; t*22* clean, busy, toasted if slightly toffeed malt: elegant and lip-smacking; f*21* fades for a while but returns with vanilla and spices; b*22* a malt I created as a consultant blender in the late 90s which is of a similar style to the blueprint I drew up. Very drinkable indeed ... but I would say that. **40%**

James MacArthur 1992 Peated Irish Single Malt (85) n*21* Irish Arbroath smokies, sweet at first then something oilier and oakier coming through; t*22* full texture holding together soft molassed sugar, hints of liquorice and full-bodied peat; f*21* long with the smoke drifting happily until some drier oaky tones begin to develop into cocoa powder; b*21* surprising that at this young age a few aged cracks are noticeable amid the beauty. **61%**

Knappogue Castle 1990 (91) n*22* crisp, dry riesling, extremely winey. Even so, a fabulous development of grassy malt and an undercurrent of vanilla oakiness adds depth; t*23* light, fresh and mouthwatering followed by a malty follow-through which develops into a honeyed sweetness with a trace of vague fruitiness; f*22* dryer with vanilla depth and a hint of cocoa; b*24* for a light whiskey this shows enormous complexity and depth. Genuine balance from nose to finish; refreshing and dangerously more-ish. Entirely from bourbon cask and personally selected and vatted by a certain Jim Murray. **40%. nc.** *Great Spirits.*

Knappogue Castle 1991 (90) n22 delicate, teasing maltiness with soft suffusion of oak and sharper, almost youthful malt notes: grassy, crisp and clean with a hint of butterscotch; **t**23 an immediate malt clarity waters the mouth while a subtle pepperiness tingles the tastebuds. Although the body is light, a fresh malt intensity now fills the mouth. Excellent bitter-sweet balance with some delayed oak arriving offers extra dryness; **f**22 medium length but long for an 8-y-o. The oak hangs on to offer cocoa-chocolatey bitterness that wonderfully counterbalances the flitting honeyed sweetness; **b**23 offers rare complexity for such a youthful malt especially in the subtle battles that rage on the palate between sweet and dry, malt and oak and so on. The spiciness is a great foil for the malt. Each cask picked and vatted by the author. **40%. nc.** *Great Spirits.*

Knappogue Castle 1992 (94) n23 heavy oil and rich with a hint of spice, enormously intense with a vague stratum of honey. Big and well structured, strengthened by the massive depth of malt; **t**23 big oily arrival on the palate ensures a biscuity maltiness and a slightly molassed sweetness clings to the roof of the mouth. Lush, chewy and deep with a subtle bitter-sweet balance. Delicate peppers make for a teasing but controlled middle; **f**24 the lingering spice tends to play peek-a-boo with the oily, almost unbelievably intense maltiness. At the death dries fabulously to show surprising age; **b**24 a different Knappogue altogether from the delicate, ultra-refined type. This expression positively revels in its handsome ruggedness and muscular body: a surprisingly bruising yet complex malt that always remains balanced and fresh – the alter-ego of the '90 and '91 vintages. I mean, as the guy who put this whiskey together, what do you expect? But it's not bad if I say so myself and was voted the USA's No. 1 Spirit. Virtually all vanished, but worth getting a bottle if you can find it (I don't receive a penny – I was paid as a consultant!). **40%. nc.** *Great Spirits.*

Knappogue Castle 1993 (see under Bushmills)

Limerick Cooley Aged 9 Years cask 10839, dist 91, bott 00 **(83) n**19 **t**22 **f**20 **b**22. Typical Cooley: heaps of delightfully intense malt with a slight bitterness as the oak progresses. **67.3%.** *Adelphi under their green, Irish flag of Limerick Distillery.*

Sainsbury's Irish Single Malt (87) n22 clean, slightly citrussy; **t**22 beautifully fresh and crisp with a wonderful spreading of an almost gristy maltiness; **f**21 vanilla, oak and a little prickle; **b**22 refreshingly crisp and clean. A thoroughly good malt. **40%.** *UK.*

Scotch Malt Whiskey Society Irish Malt Cask 117.1 Aged 12 Years (Cooley unpeated – unstated) dist Nov 89, bott Jun 02 **(83) n**18 **t**22 **f**22 **b**21. Typically early Cooley make: off-key aroma but a veritable malt bomb to follow. **49.5%**

Scotch Malt Whiskey Society Irish Malt Cask Aged 13 Years (Cooley unpeated – unstated) 117.2 **(85) n**19 mildly dusty, biting nose, but powerful malt to compensate; **t**23 that malt arrives with a vengeance on the palate then mildly austere and mean the barley feel intensifies to the exclusion of all else; **f**22 barley sugar and soft vanilla; **b**21 a closed kind of Cooley that almost implodes into its barley-rich core. **48.3%. nc ncf sc.**

Scotch Malt Whiskey Society Irish Malt 118.1 Aged 9 Years (Cooley peated – unstated) dist Aug 92, bott Jun 02 **(91) n**23 oily kippers, salt and vanilla; **t**24 sweet, clean peat which fades to reveal an orangey-malty middle of some magnitude; **f**22 perhaps over-sweet barley amid lingering smoke; **b**22 a minor classic here, certainly one of the best Cooley malts in bottled form. This is beautifully made whiskey by any standards. **58.2%**

Scotch Malt Whiskey Society Irish Malt 118.2 Aged 10 Years (Cooley peated – unstated) **(91) n**21 pretty low, oily phenols intermix with some vanilla notes to present something strangely and attractively earthy and floral; **t**24 sweet and silky with nip and bite, the smoke forms a friendly, protective carpet for interplay to develop; **f**23 the peat is now pretty confident and thick, the initial sweetness is fading and some oak plays gently with the phenols; **b**23 exceptionally attractive, well-made malt with a stunning peat personality. **56.6%. nc ncf sc.**

Shanagarry (76) n19 **t**20 **f**18 **b**19. Pleasant, but lacks depth. **40%.** *For Intermarche France. Note: Label says "Pure Pot Still". But it is single malt.*

Slieve na Gcloc (84) n21 **t**20 **f**22 **b**21. No, I wasn't drunk when I typed the name. And I was sober enough to detect a slight feinty note that reappears towards the death. Until then, curiously thin. A pleasant cocoa and peat malt, but one not quite gelling as it perhaps might. **40%.** *For Oddbins.*

Waitrose Irish Single Malt (83) n20 **t**22 **f**20 **b**21. Pulsating sweet malt: clean as an Irish whistle and beautifully mouthwatering. Really impressive. With the slightly flat finale I suspect it has caramel: without it, it would be better still. **40%.** *UK.*

OLD BUSHMILLS

Bushmills 10 Years Old (82) n22 **t**21 **f**19 **b**20. A beefed-up, sherried number compared to a few years back; attractive but in need of finding some complexity from somewhere. **40%.** *Irish Distillers*

Bushmills 12 Years Old Distillery Reserve (84) n20 **t**22 **f**21 **b**21. Quality malt that boasts a complex middle. A decent dram for quiet reflection. **40%**

Bushmills 16 Years Old Triple Wood (93) n23 a basket of ripe fruit, with apples, pomegranates and grapes to the fore. Just so delicate! **t**24 seismic waves of spicy fruit, juicy and salivating in effect; **f**22 vanilla and a sprinkling of cocoa represents the moderate oak presence; **b**24 this has become the leader of the Bushmills tribe. Few whiskies can maintain this degree of sophistication. Love it! **40%**

Bushmills 21 Year Old (74) n19 **t**19 **f**18 **b**18. Full-flavoured yet strangely off-key: never quite gels. **40%**

The Old Bushmills Distillery Single Cask Rum Barrel 1988 db cask no. 14355 **(88) n**21 a sharp, punchy addition to the soft malt, but impossible to pinpoint exactly what. Lively nose prickle with some Demerara-style weight; **t**22 spicy and hawkish from the start while a bitter-chocolate shadow forms early on; **f**23 quietens and sweetens slightly, the malt has a very sweet edge and a distant touch of liquorice adds an oaky feel; **b**22 I do a lot of work with rum, but it is quite impossible to distinguish just what sort of spirit had been in the cask before the whiskey. At a guess – though mainly from the nose I'd say Demerara. A real mouthful, with only an extra sweet dimension revealing a rummy connection. Quite lovely, though. **53.8%** *for La Maison Du Whisky. Fr.*

The Old Bushmills Distillery Single Cask Distiller's Reserve Bourbon Barrel 1990 db cask no. 4650 **(91) n**20 quite harsh oak at first but settles as the malt slips into gear; hints of marshmallows; **t**24 profound citrus character with melting barley, a sensational marriage all the more harmonious for some striking spice; **f**23 medium length but a continuation of the fruity, mouthwatering mêlée of before. Soft vanillas see this classic Irish out; **b**24 don't be put off by the non-committal nose: the arrival on the palate is a thing of beauty and legend. A Bushmills you will never forget. **54.4%** *for La Maison Du Whisky. Fr.*

Knappogue Castle 1990 (see Cooley)
Knappogue Castle 1991 (see Cooley)
Knappogue Castle 1992 (see Cooley)
Knappogue Castle 1993 (91) n22 an uplifting, lively nose, lightly malty and grassy and exceptionally clean; **b**22 intense malt vies for supremacy with a surge of controlled spice. The dominant cloves are well contained and are met with mouthwatering sweetness that is rather brittle yet fresh – like warm toffee-apple; **f**23 soft spice suffuses with natural cream-toffee sweetness, gentle with a tantalising hint of cocoa and toast. Lush, oily and exceptionally long on the finish;

b24 this is a malt of exceptional character and charisma. It is almost squeaky clean but proudly contains enormous depth and intensity. The chocolate finish is an absolute delight. Quite different and darker than any previous Knappogue but not dwarfed in stature to any of the previous three vintages. Created by yours truly. **40%. nc.** *Great Spirits.*

Single Grain
COOLEY

Clontarf (black label) **(86) n**21 hard and crisp and enticing; **t**22 rigid grain again, this time softened by gentle oak and toffee; **f**21 lazy spices tack onto the oak. The toffee dies more quickly than expected; **b**22 when I created this whiskey some years back as a consultant I was putting on to the market the first-known pure Irish grain whiskey ... against the wishes of the Clontarf Company. But it has been an enormous success, not least because of Cooley's consistently high quality of grain. This is a bit more caramel-rich than in my day, but still a very, very drinkable drop. **40%.** *Clontarf Irish Whiskey Co.*

Greenore 8 Years Old db **(89) n**23 soft, sweet corn, delicious hints of bourbon; **t**22 rich, soft oils, melt-in-the-mouth grain and just a hint of barley for good measure; **f**22 crisps up as the oak returns; **b**22 just a lovely grain whiskey from one of the world's finest grain distilleries. **40%.**

Blended

Ballygeary (80) n20 **t**21 **f**20 **b**19. Fresh and mouthwatering with an impressive malty thrust. Decent oak, too. **40%.** *Cooley for Malt House Vintners.*

Black Bush (see Bushmills Black Bush)

Brennan's (86) n21 malty and pleasantly sweet and fruity despite some oakiness adding weight; **t**22 big, lush malt kick softened and thinned by grain while oak adds some excellent spice; **f**21 pretty long, oaky yet never loses balance; **b**22 a very well put together blend with impressive malt magnitude. **40%.** *Cooley for Shaw Ross USA.*

Buena Vista old stock (74) n17 **t**20 **f**18 **b**19. Muscovado sugar and soft vanilla. **40%.** *Irish Distillers, San Francisco, USA only.*

Buena Vista new stock (74) n17 **t**19 **f**19 **b**19. A softer, lusher dram than the original bottling with bigger toffee input. Qualitywise, on a par. **40%.** *Cooley, San Francisco, USA only.*

Bushmills Black Bush (91) n24 amazingly spicy – a bit like the old 1608! – with clean but lively sherry and freshish malt. This is one crackerjack nose; **t**23 stunning: the sweetness is exemplary as it sits snugly between the enormity of the fruit and the clarity of the malt. Somewhere in there is a raisiny sheen; **f**21 dropped points for a toffee-caramel finale, which undermines some of the complexity. Even so, the sherry remains lip-smacking and the spices behave themselves; **b**23 the quality of the sherry used boggles the mind. Remains a true classic. My word, though, what I would do to see a 46% non-coloured, non-chill filtered version. **40%.** *Irish Distillers.*

Bushmills Original (79) n19 **t**20 **f**19 **b**21. A light blend that has improved dramatically in recent years. The aroma is of Fox's Biscuits Party Rings, as is the finish topped with some toffee and chocolate. **40%.** *Irish Distillers.*

Bushmills 1608 (88) n22 massive surge of fruit and malt all intermingling with light spices with hardly any grain evidence; **t**23 pure silk: the sherry holds the foreground allowing spices to build up from the rear; **f**21 at last a little grain appears, accentuating the sherry; **b**21 a beautiful Irish that on the evidence of this bottling has turned away from big and spicy to a more velvety sherry number. *Irish Distillers.* **40%**

Cassidy's (77) n19 **t**20 **f**19 **b**19. Uncomplicated and refreshing. **40%.** *Cooley for Marks & Spencer UK.*

Castelgy (81) n20 t20 f20 **b**21. Strange name, familiar blend style from Cooley. This one does have a little extra fruit from somewhere on the nose and excellent young malt grip on the finish. **40%.** *Cooley for Lidl.*

Clancey's (82) n20 t21 f21 **b**20. A curiously sweet and nutty affair, not unlike Nutella. Fabulous grain use. **40%.** *Cooley for Wm Morrison UK.*

Clontarf Reserve (gold label) **(83)** n20 t22 f20 **b**21. Big, complex chewy blend with some detailed and delicious grain and vanilla involvement. A whiskey I created some years back, but I don't quite remember the toffee influence being quite this telling on the finish. Very sound whiskey, still, though. **40%.** *Clontarf Irish Whiskey Company.*

Coleraine (74) n18 t21 f18 **b**17. Another improved offering than compared to recent years: less firebrand and more sweet and sultry. Still lacks any real complexity although the mouth arrival is much, much more fulfilling than it once was. **40%.** *Irish Distillers.*

Crested Ten (see Jameson Crested Ten)

Dunphys (68) n16 t18 f17 **b**17. Hard-as-nails blend: rigid grain allows little other development. At least what appears a little pot still does give an Irish feel to it. **40%.** *Irish Distillers IR.*

Delaney's (71) n18 t19 f16 **b**18. Half decent, but lacking finish or depth. **40%.** *From Cooley for Co-operative Group.*

Finnegan (75) n19 t19 f18 **b**19. A simple blend with good malt showing. **40%**

Golden Irish (93) n24 firm yet deeply complex with fabulous malt/grain texture. Text-book stuff; **t**22 voluptuous, silky, ultra malty and fresh; **f**23 long, with gathering grains and sublime vanilla; **b**24 a stunning, brilliantly balanced blend that groans with mouthwatering complexity. **40%.** *Cooley Distillers for Dunne's Stores IR.*

Jameson (95) n23 crisp pot still bounces off some firm and clean grain. Fresh sherry offers a softer dimension; **t**24 melt-in-the-mouth sherry is the prelude to brilliant pot-still sharpness. A real mouthful that you can suck and chew at the same time with some real bite in there; **f**24 vanilla, fruit and some prickly spice; **b**24 from a pretty boring bit-of-a- nothing whiskey to a sheer classic in the space of a decade: not bad going. The inclusion of extra pot still is one thing; getting the balance as fine as this is something else. Truly magnificent: this is the current Irish masterpiece. As classically Irish as someone called Seamus O'Crimmins. **40%.** *Irish Distillers.*

Jameson 12 Years Old (89) n22 first sturdy sherry and crisp grain then a clean but understated pot-still clarity; **t**23 fresh, first-fill sherry offers a velvety contrast to the prickly barley and oak combination: sensuously bitter-sweet; **f**21 very light with the sherry now carried on the back of the grain; **b**23 a clean, flighty blend with superb use of spices. The sherry and pot still both appear light in character and the balance is charming. **40%**

Jameson 15 (see under Pot Still section)

Jameson 18 Years Old first batch JJ18-1 db **(92)** n23 vigorous and vivid pot still with no little shortage of honey, lovely oak only softens rather than adds weight; **t**24 this is Irish blended to its complex best: chewey, corny oils counter the sparkling unmalted barley which is firm and crisp; gentle hints of very fine bourbon; **f**22 soft cocoa tones work well with the persistent oil but the pot still continues to guarantee high notes to the very last. Wonderful spices flourish throughout; **b**23 this is using pot still with enormous imagination and sympathy. A really top range Irish tht celebrates its roots and reminiscent of the first-ever bottlings of Jameson Gold. **40%** *Irish Distillers*

Jameson 18 Years Old second batch JJ18-2 db **(76)** n19 t20 f18 **b**19. Some barley and honey does poke out through the cream toffee, but it's all relatively blandish by standards set by the first stupendous bottling. **40%** *Irish Distillers*

Jameson 18 Years Old third batch JJ18-3 db **(89) n**21 soft honey permeates some light sherry tones and more rigid pot still, some hints of bourbon; **t**23 mouthwatering start and then a lift off of big spice. The pot still is pounding and relentless, the grain firm and the malt sweet. Excellent complexity; **f**22 the honey returns while the pot still begins to tighten and harden. A grapey sub-plot attempts to soften the punches but with only limited success; **b**23 this is big Irish with attitude. Much closer to the first bottling, it cuts down on the honey slightly and offers a more bourbony character. That said, the pot still guarantees this as uniquely Irish. The spices amaze. Beautiful stuff. **40%** *Bottled at 75cl especially for launch into American market but will be available at 70cl elsewhere.*

Jameson 1780 Matured 12 Years (94) n23 lush and confident, spicy and warming: there is a prevailing oloroso undercurrent head on against some sharp pot still; **t**24 a whiskey that fills the mouth with thick, bitter-sweet sherry, then the unmistakable delights of old pot still coupled with a short but effective fly-past of spice. The pot still dominates – towards the middle after the early sherry lead; **f**23 pretty long with neither pot still nor sherry showing any signs of wanting to leave; **b**24 this blend has now been discontinued and if you should see one hanging around an old off licence grab it with both hands. The 12-y-o that has taken its place appears to be using as much sherry, but it appears to be a lighter style, as is the pot still. The 1780 was the last commercial link with the old Irish whiskies I fell in love with in the early 70s. A colossus of an Irish, of a sherry type now entirely lost which couldn't come from any other country in the world. **40%.** *Irish Distillers.*

Jameson Crested Ten (88) n23 the enormity of the pot still is awesome: lovely sherry-ginger balance; **t**23 amazingly clean sherry then traces of malt and vanilla; **f**19 too much toffee but some decent spice helps compensate; **b**23 a beautifully balanced whiskey let down only by the weak finish. **40%.** *Irish Distillers.*

Jameson Distillery Reserve (available at Jameson, Dublin) **(74) n**20 **t**20 **f**17 **b**17. Starts well but becomes flatter than the Irish Midlands. Nothing like as good as previous bottlings I have tasted. Just a one-off, I am sure. **40%.** *Irish Distillers Dublin.*

Jameson Distillery Reserve (available at Midleton – see Midleton Distillery Reserve)

Jameson Gold (94) n24 layered elements of soft honey and subtle, mildly bourbony oak criss-crossing the crisp pot still; **t**24 honey and barley all the way, wonderfully rich and silky, cocoa shows early too with a fruit chocolate character; **f**22 some age apparent towards the bitter-sweet finale, as is butterscotch; **b**24 if you don't enjoy this, then you just don't get what Irish whiskey is all about. Vattings vary from bottling to bottling, but this is quite representative and falls comfortably within its colourful spectrum. **40%.** *Irish Distillers.*

Hewitts (87) n22 big, intense, heavy malt-rich with some clean fruity-grapey notes in the background. Dark cherries and chocolate complete the mix; **t**22 intriguingly fresh, packed with even more grapey fruitiness. The malt clings to the mouth in tandem with crisp grain, though the body is curiously oily and full; **f**20 custard creams and dry, thinner grain with just a late hint of malt; **b**23 a lovely blend that somehow manages to be light, medium and heavy at various stages. **40%** *Irish Distillers. The only blend from Midleton using exclusively malt and grain and no pot still (mixture of malted and unmalted barley).*

Inishowen (73) n18 **t**20 **f**17 **b**18. Someone's stolen the peat and replaced it with cream toffee. **40%.** *Cooley.*

Kilbeggan (76) n19 **t**20 **f**18 **b**19. Fruity in part but the bite is sharp and attractively relentless. **40%.** *Cooley.*

Locke's (73) n18 **t**20 **f**17 **b**18. Big malt through the middle, but it all just fizzles out. **40%.** *Cooley.*

Midleton Distillery Reserve (85) n22 punchy barley; t22 rich, intense barley with some mouthwatering fruit and spices; f20 vanilla-toffee; b21 a whiskey which, for all its muscovado sweetness offers some memorable barley moments. **40%.** *Irish Distillers Midleton Distillery only. Was once bottled as Jameson Distillery Reserve exclusive to Midleton. Changes character slightly with each new vatting. This one is some departure.*

Midleton Very Rare 1984 (70) n19 t18 f17 b16. Disappointing with little backbone or balance. **40%.** *Irish Distillers.*

Midleton Very Rare 1985 (77) n20 t20 f18 b19. Medium-bodied and oily, this is a big improvement on the initial vintage. **40%.** *Irish Distillers.*

Midleton Very Rare 1986 (79) n21 t20 f18 b20. A very malty Midleton richer in character than previous vintages. **40%.** *Irish Distillers.*

Midleton Very Rare 1987 (77) n20 t19 f19 b19. Quite oaky at first until a late surge of excellent pot still. **40%.** *Irish Distillers.*

Midleton Very Rare 1988 (86) n23 integrated rock-hard pot still and softer vanilla. Touches of honey and mint add to the complex equation; t21 the first MVR to offer immediate Irishness; busy and attractively muddled; f21 a late chalky dryness counters a building malty sweetness; b21 a landmark MVR as it is the first vintage to celebrate the Irish pot-still style. **40%**

Midleton Very Rare 1989 (87) n22 citrussy and spicy, the malt is hard-chiselled into the overall chararacter: some formidable pot still, too; t22 very vivid pot still which follows the firm grain; f22 the hard, brittle unmalted barley makes itself heard: you could break your teeth on it; b21 a real mouthful but has lost balance to achieve the effect. **40%.** *Irish Distillers.*

Midleton Very Rare 1990 (93) n23 carrying on from where the '89 left off. The pot still doesn't drill itself so far into your sinuses, perhaps: more of a firm massage; t23 solid pot still again. There is a pattern now: pot still first, sweeter, maltier notes second, pleasant grains third and somewhere, imperceptibly, warming spices fill in the gaps; f24 long and Redbreast-like in character. Spices seep from the bourbon casks; b23 astounding whiskey: one of the vintages every true Irish whiskey lover should hunt for. **40%.** *Irish Distillers.*

Midleton Very Rare 1991 (76) n19 t20 f19 b18. After the Lord Mayor's Show, relatively dull and uninspiring. **40%.** *Irish Distillers.*

Midleton Very Rare 1992 (84) n20 t20 f23 b21. Superb finish with outstanding use of feisty grain. **40%.** *Irish Distillers.*

Midleton Very Rare 1993 (88) n21 pot still with sub plots of honey and pepper; t22 the pot still makes use of the dry hardness of the grain; f23 beautiful elevation of the pot still towards something more complex and sharp balancing superbly with malt and bourbony-oak texture; b22 big, brash and beautiful – the perfect way to celebrate the 10th-ever bottling of MVR. **40%.** *Irish Distillers.*

Midleton Very Rare 1994 (87) n22 pot-still characteristics not unlike the '93 but with extra honey and ginger; t22 the honeyed theme continues with malt arriving in a lush sweetness; f21 oily and a spurt of sharper, harder pot still; b22 another different style of MVR, one of amazing lushness. **40%.** *Irish Distillers.*

Midleton Very Rare 1995 (90) n23 big pot still with fleeting honey; t24 enormous! Bitter, sweet and tart all together for a chewable battle of apple and barley. Brilliant; b21 some caramel calms proceedings, but Java coffee goes a little way to restoring complexity; b22 they don't come much bigger than this. Prepare a knife and fork to battle through this one. Fabulous. **40%.** *Irish Distillers.*

Midleton Very Rare 1996 (82) n21 t22 f19 b20. The grains lead a soft course, hardened by subtle pot still. Just missing a beat on the finish, though. **40%**

Midleton Very Rare 1997 (83) n22 t21 f19 b21. The piercing pot still fruitiness of the nose is met by a countering grain of rare softness on the palate. Just dies on the finish when you want it to make a little speech. Very drinkable. **40%.** *Irish Distillers.*

Midleton Very Rare 1999 (89) n*21* malt and toffee: as sleepy as a night-time drink; **t***23* stupendous grain, soft enough to absorb some pounding malt; **f***22* spices arrive as the blend hardens and some pot still finally battles its way through the swampy grain; **b***23* one of the maltiest Midletons of all time: a superb blend. **40%.** *Irish Distillers.*

Midleton Very Rare 2000 (85) n*22* citrus and new-mown straw; **t***21* so soft it barely troubles the tastebuds. Some harder unmalted barley makes itself heard; **f***21* toffee and bitter cocoa, but still very soft mouthfeel; **b***21* an extraordinary departure even by Midleton's eclectic standards. The pot still is like a distant church spire in an hypnotic Fen landscape. **40%.** *Irish Distillers.*

Midleton Very Rare 2001 (79) n*21* **t***20* **f***18* **b***20.* Extremely light but the finish is slightly on the bitter side. **40%.** *Irish Distillers.*

Midleton Very Rare 2002 (79) n*20* **t***22* **f***18* **b***19* The nose is rather subdued and the finish is likewise toffee-quiet and shy. There are some fabulous middle moments, some of flashing genius, when the pot still and grain combine for a spicy kick, but the finish really is lacklustre and disappointing. **40%.** *Irish Distillers*

Millar's Special Reserve (87) n*21* attractive grains lighten and interact with the clean malt: we have complexity here; **t***22* big malt arrival then a wonderful development of spice tinged with muscovado sugar; **f***22* vanilla and even more malt with the grains pulsing in the background; **b***22* this is a complex dram from Cooley that needs time to understand it. Delicious, so it is. **40%.** *Cooley.*

O'Brien's (77) n*18* **t***20* **f***19* **b***20.* Big grain shape with softening grains. **40%.** *Somerfield UK.*

O'Hara (80) n*20* **t***21* **f***19* **b***20.* A genuinely fine blend from Cooley. **40%.** *For Millar's.*

Old Dublin (73) n*17* **t***20* **f***17* **b***19.* A clean blend that rarely troubles the inner tastebuds. Sweet with no pretensions of grandeur whatsoever. **40%.** *Irish Distillers.*

Old Kilkenny (86) n*21* really biting pot still and grain ... on an own-label blend?! **t***22* mouthwatering rich pot still and then diffusing grain; **f***21* not even the toffee from the caramel can ruin the richness of the grain; **b***22* a real shock to the system. Traditional pot still character in an own-label product, and real quality stuff to boot. However, gather up as many of the labels as you can that tell you it's triple distilled. Cooley are likely to take over the blend from Irish Distillers later in 2003 so the biting barley character will be lost for a softer malt-based blend. In this form a collectable one for Irish whiskey lovers worldwide. **40%.** *Asda UK.*

Old Midleton Distillery Blended Whiskey 1967 35 Years Old (92) n*24* a really cut-glass clean, pot still character and, although sharp, soft marmalady grain lightens the experience: some honey wanders from the emptied glass; **t***23* rock-hard barley chips at the tastebuds, wonderfully fruity and mouthwatering. The grain offers something much sweeter and softer: two separate tales being told simultaneously; **f***22* mainly clean grain with soft vanilla drifting in. The barley does offer some late sharpness and some late bitter almond reminds you of the enormity of the age; **b***23* this is a real one-off bottling of a quite unique Irish whiskey (actually coming from the old Midleton distillery, surely that should be "whisky"?). Apparently this one cask was filled in 1967 from a mixture of Midleton pure pot still and Midleton grain. After all this time, no-one knows why. But it was rescued by enthusiasts David Radcliffe and Sukhinder Singh and bottled for their respective businesses. I'm delighted to report (unlike Sukhinder's soon-to-become legendary Dunglass) that this is a little stunner. **41.1%** www.potstill.com and www.thewhiskeyexchange.com

Paddy (68) n*16* **t***19* **f***16* **b***17.* Good old Paddy: I knew it wouldn't let me down. While other lesser Irish whiskies have improved, Paddy has steadfastly refused to budge: dusty, cloyingly sweet and shapeless. Like an ugly duckling, I'm almost becoming fond of it. Hang on a minute, I'll have another taste: no, actually

I'm not. About as unclassicallly Irish as someone called Pedro Manchovitz. **40%.** *Irish Distillers.*

Powers (87) n22 rugged pot still, but not quite as butch as it once was; **t**24 brilliant mouth arrival, one of the best in all Ireland: the pot still shrieks and attacks every available tastebud. Too short-lived, though; **f**20 the ending, once the final traces of pot have vanished, is long and dull, save for some lovely spice. Sweet beyond recognition with toffee and ... toffee; **b**21 is it coincidence that as Jameson has become more pot-still accentuated, Power's – once the very last bastion of grizzled pot-still blend – has become cissified? If they cut the colouring many of the problems will disappear, I feel. But at the moment it is a pale – or should I say dark? – shadow of its once magnificent self. **40%.** *Irish Distillers.*

Powers 12 Years Old (77) n21 **t**20 **f**18 **b**18. Disappointing: surely should be seeing more out of this baby? **40%.** *Irish Distillers.*

Redbreast Blend (88) n23 some genuinely telling pot-still hardness sparks like a flint off the no less unyielding grain. Just love this; **t**23 very sweet and soft, the grain carrying a massive amount of vanilla. Barley offers some riches, as does spice; **f**20 a climbdown from the confrontational beginnings, but pretty delicious all the same; **b**22 really impressed with this one-off bottling for Dillons the Irish wine merchants. Must try and get another bottle before they all vanish. **40%.** *Irish Distillers for Dillone IR (not to be confused with Redbreast 12-y-o Pure Pot Still).*

Safeway Irish Whiskey (86) n21 stupendous, top-quality grain rarely seen in supermarket own-label brands marrying comfortably with some sharp, fresh malt; **t**22 the oiliest Irish I have come across for a while: any silkier and this will have been distilled in Macclesfield! But the freshness of the malt is superb and telling; **f**22 stunning vanilla delivery and soft malt; **b**21 a brilliant own-label brand but ... arrrrgggghhhh!!! This is where I get militant: please don't confuse the words pot still on an Irish whiskey label with traditional Irish Pot Still of malted and unmalted barley. This is a superb blend of grain and single malt. **40%.** *Cooley for Safeway UK.*

Tesco Special Reserve Irish Whiskey (87) n21 belligerent malt, young but well directed, spices the more docile grain; **t**23 the malts are stupendously juicy and have no problems punching their way entirely through the rich, clean grain; **f**21 really it's the grains that have the day here, but such is their superb quality, no problem; **b**22 delicious! Underlines the fact that Cooley produces one of the world's best grain whiskies and a very sharp, decent malt. **40%.** *Cooley for Tesco UK.*

Tullamore Dew (75) n18 **t**20 **f**18 **b**19. Less than inspiring, maybe. But it has picked up on the pot still in recent years. Less throat-ripping, more balance. There is hope yet. **40%.** *Irish Distillers for Campbell and Cochrane.*

Tullamore Dew 12 Years Old (81) n21 **t**21 **f**20 **b**19. Enjoyable citrussy, pot-still tones criss-cross from the nose to the toffeed, Canadian finale. **40%.** *Irish Distillers for Campbell & Cochrane.*

Tullamore Dew Heritage (79) n20 **t**22 **f**19 **b**18. Fat and lush, the mouthwatering action is upfront on the tastebuds before the long toffeed, mildly spiced finale. **40%.** *Irish Distillers for Campbell & Cochrane.*

Waitrose Irish Whiskey (77) n20 **t**19 **f**20 **b**18. Very sweet but the grain is stupendous. **40%.** *UK.*

Wm Morrison (see Clancey's)

American Whiskey

Bourbon has long ruled the roost in America. It has had an almost clear run since Prohibition encumbered upon Americans a lighter palate and rye began to fall from grace in favour of its cornier cousin. But now rye is making a comeback, with interest growing internationally for this most full-flavoured of spirits. At least one distillery is looking at increasing the number of mashes they produce each year, and with good reason. It is beginning to slowly creep into new markets the world over, often stunning whiskey lovers who discover it for the first time. Already Sazerac Rye is being regarded by some converts as the Holy Grail of rye. It's a hard one to argue against.

Rye, though, is not alone in adding diversity to the American whisky scene. The last decade has seen the birth of four malt distilleries – three making from barley, the other from rye. Only one has yet to bottle, the Triple Eight Distillery in Nantucket, Massachusetts, whose single malts are currently maturing away in former Jim Beam barrels. The oldest has now reached three years of age and plans are already afoot to begin filling into sherry butts.

It is not the first time malt has been made on the East Coast. Until the 1970s it was distilled and bottled in Maryland. This, though, will be America's first island whiskey and the historic initial bottling of "Notch" should be sometime in 2005. By American single malt standards, it will be an old man by the time it sees the inside of a bottling hall.

Because, some 3,000 miles away in California, St. Georges have again bottled at 3-years-old, their second batch being a great improvement on the over-fruity first offering. And further north up the coast at Portland, Oregon, Clear Creek have just launched their latest batch of Macarthy's – another 3-year-old – a delicately peated number that this time sets new standards among the world's smaller distilleries.

It is even on a par with the very best of the extraordinary malted rye brilliance of Old Potrero. The Anchor Distillery in San Francisco has continued to bring out "essays" of the mouthwatering, above-weight punching giant that has set American whiskey distilling alight in recent years and, like Macarthy's, has earned a place among the world's elite whiskies.

So small-batch American single malt is in good shape at the moment. Which it has to be to catch the attention of drinkers in a country that has so many first-class ryes and bourbons to choose from. I have long held the belief that America today makes the best quality whisky in the world and the exercise of tasting most of what is on offer has confirmed that.

Whisky would not be whiskey and I wouldn't be me if I didn't find an exception to that rule. And that comes in the form of what was one of the great blended whiskeys in the world: Seagram 7 Crown. For years I have championed its cause and if you ever spot me at Chicago Airport or somewhere else in the United States reading or writing in a bar you are likely to find a glass of the stuff by my side. Usually it ranks in the low to mid-90s in my rating system. Not this time: it didn't even hit the 90 mark. Usually a bold, rye-fest of a beast, the sample I received was still deliciously drinkable. But it had lost that cutting edge, it shone where once it sparkled. I detected a slight rye reduction, but enough to change its shape. Some institutions are above tampering with. Seagram 7 Crown is one.

CALIFORNIA
○ Anchor (San Francisco)

MO: Missouri	**TN:** Tennessee
IN: Indiana	**PA:** Pennsylvania
KY: Kentucky	**VA:** Virginia

Key
△ **Major Cities**
○ Distilleries

DISTILLERY LOCATOR

1 Weston
2 Seagram
3 Michter's
4 Virginia Gentleman
5 Wild Turkey
  Four Roses
6 Clermont
  Boston

7 Makers Mark
8 George Dickel
9 Jack Daniel
A Nashville
B Louisville
  Early Times
  Bernheim
  Stitzel Weller

C Frankfort
  Ancient Age
  Labrot & Graham
D Bardstown
  Heaven Hill
  Willett
  Barton

American Single Malt
ANCHOR DISTILLERY (see Rye)

CLEAR CREEK DISTILLERY

McCarthy's Oregon Single Malt Aged 3 Years db **(94)** n24 just a hint of fusel oil, but – hey – who cares? The nose is astounding, incredibly delicate peat combined with an almost industrial oiliness, similar to that my old dad brought home with him each night from the machine shop. Distillers just can't buy an aroma like this; t23 this is too good to be true: the malt and peat melt into the mouth with startling complexity and the sweetness is beautifully disguised behind soft oak; f23 very long, soft oils drifting around the palate with peat which fluctuates between big and deft; b24 this is a dram I could drink any day ... and would if I had the supplies. And, although I may be stoned to death for saying so, the closest whisk(e)y I have come across to how Ardbeg was 20 years ago – but it's a fact. Not as good, admittedly, but some of the similarities are spine-tingling. This is landmark American whiskey and one of extraordinary quality.

ST GEORGE DISTILLERY

St George Single Malt Aged 3 Years db **(75)** n17 t19 f20 b19. Without doubt the fruitiest whisk(e)y I have tasted in nearly 30 years of sampling the stuff. The nose in particular is some kind of raspberry or similar fruit, more eau de vie than whiskey. That said, this is beautifully distilled and clean with a wonderful bite near the finish: it is just that the malt has been lost along the way. **43%**

St George Single Malt Aged 3 Years Lot 2 db **(82)** n19 t21 f21 b21. Much better. The fruit still clings to the nose, but this time malt rings loud and clear round the tastebuds and there is superb interaction with the oak. Once more, supremely made and, once that fruit is lost, we will have an absolutely top-rank malt on our hands. **43%**

Bourbon

Bourbon confuses people. Often they don't even realise it is a whiskey, a situation not helped by leading British pub chains, such as Wetherspoon, whose bar menus list "whiskey" and "bourbon" in separate sections. And if I see the liqueur Southern Comfort listed as a bourbon one more time I may not be responsible for my actions.

Bourbon is a whiskey. It is made from grain and matured in oak, so really it can't be much else. To be legally called bourbon it must have been made with a minimum of 51% corn and matured in virgin oak casks for a minimum of two years. Oh, and no colouring can be added other than that which comes naturally from the barrel.

Where it does differ, from, say Scotch, is that the straight whiskey from the distillery may be called by something other than that distillery name. Indeed, the distillery may change its name which has happened to two this year already and two others in the last three or four. So, to make things easy and reference as quick as possible, I shall list the distilleries first and then their products in alphabetical order.

BARTON

Located close to downtown Bardstown, Barton specialises in young, inexpensive bourbons for the US market. At their best Barton whiskeys possess a unique bite and crispness that helps create impressive complexity ... and the firm rye character does little harm, either. With the loss of the Heaven Hill distillery and closure of other plants since World War II, Barton is now the last distilling outpost in a town once famed for bourbon production and now the home of the industry's museum.

BUFFALO TRACE

For too long the venerable whiskeys of the Ancient Age distillery were known only by Kentuckians and bourbon connoisseurs across the United States. Owners

Sazerac, though, have slowly given the ruggedly handsome old place at Leestown, on the outskirts of Frankfort, a really big spruce up. No more so than with the name itself, which was changed from Ancient Age to Buffalo Trace to attract a younger, more international market. For those not in the know, a Buffalo Trace is a track made by herds of buffalo; and this distillery sits by the banks of the Kentucky River, where buffalo made their regular crossing. To add a little confusion, Japanese distillers Takara Shuru own the Blantons brand, perhaps the most internationally recognised of all the distillery's top-of-the-range products. Buffalo Trace is now finding more and more markets globally and it is no surprise to us who have long admired the distillery's make that it is receiving a warm welcome wherever it goes. Irritatingly, years of slight underproduction means that growth of all Buffalo Trace whiskies will, at least for a little while, be at walking pace rather than a stampede.

BROWN-FORMAN

Until April 2002, the Brown-Forman distillery in Shively, Louisville, was better known as Early Times. Perhaps having that distinctly non-21st century feel to it, like Ancient Age, it was a name that had to go. Mind you, it has taken Brown-Forman 62 years to put their name on the place, having bought it in 1940 when it was known as the Old Kentucky Distillery ... even though it had been standing only five years. Three major brands are distilled here: Old Forester, Early Times and Woodford Reserve. Early Times was the odd one out for being distilled with a higher corn and lower rye content; Woodford Reserve was the odd one out for having its barrels matured at Labrot & Graham; and Early Times was the odd one out for having some of its make being matured in second-hand barrels to make American whisk(e)y as opposed to Bourbon.

FOUR ROSES

For years the beautiful Four Roses distillery in Lawrenceburg was protected under the mighty umbrella of Seagram. Today it is owned by Japanese distillers Kirin, who perhaps have a greater desire for the lightest of all Kentucky's bourbons to hit a wider audience. For a while, Four Roses as a bourbon vanished off the US radar altogether, but now is back. Unlike most of the other distilleries, Four Roses does not own an enormous number of brands, concentrating on those that carry its distinctive name. However there is a move towards the single barrel market that should be watched carefully – and explored whenever possible.

HEAVEN HILL

If you buy a bourbon anywhere in the world that is mildly quirky in appearance or name, or that is own-label, the probabilities are that the whiskey contained therein originates from Heaven Hill. Exactly where it will have been distilled is another matter. In 1996 the original, stupendous Heaven Hill distillery was consumed by fire and for a while the stills at Early Times were rented to work on a beer made from the original Heaven Hill recipe. Now their whisky is made at the state-of-the-art Bernheim distillery in Louisville, a good distance away in style and miles to the original Heaven Hill distillery in Bardstown. On top of that, the company had to buy in surplus bourbon stocks from elsewhere to replace some of the 90,000 barrels destroyed in the inferno. The possibility of the old distillery being rebuilt is still a twinkling in the eyes of some. And not without good reason. From seven years onwards HH is bourbon you overlook at your peril, but when reaching 12 years the original Bardstown Heaven Hill bourbon ranks among the world's greatest whiskies.

JIM BEAM

Two distilleries serve Jim Beam. The last time I really had a good look – a few years back I admit – the lesser known (in fact virtually unknown) distillery at Boston Clermont was making the most characterful bourbon. Amongst bourbons freely available around the world these days, Jim Beam Black, a rich and chewy individual ranks among the best ... and usually costing little more than the standard and much more famous White Label version despite having a few extra years in the wood. Even standard Jim Beam is showing a touch more attitude these days. But pride of place, for me, in the entire Jim Beam portfolio is the astonishing Jim Beam Rye. Its distinctive mustard-yellow label is enough to get connoisseurs salivating at 50 yards and any liquor store outside the United States having it on their shelves makes them a very serious and knowledgeable whisky outlet indeed.

LABROT & GRAHAM

A picture postcard distillery that has recently been rescued from little more than a pile of rubble to be far the most attractive distillery on the American continent. It is remarkable not least for triple distilling its bourbon using old-fashioned pot stills, not unlike those once found four miles along Glenns Creek at the now dead Old Crow distillery. Distilling was re-introduced at Labrot & Graham as recently as 1996 and now its make is in a bottle for the first time. I never quite believed the predictions that it would be a perfect fit for the Woodford Reserve that was launched from the richest barrels of Old Forester they could find, despite originally sharing the same generously ryed mashbill. Instead we have the Woodford Reserve Four Grain which is, as John Cleese might say, something completely different. And no less delicious. There had been talk about re-naming the distillery Woodford Reserve, but so far wiser counsel has prevailed.

MAKER'S MARK

A small and attractive distillery located in stunning country at Loretto, making it Kentucky's southern-most distillery. Also probably the most stable and consistent of all bourbons quite capable at times of being nothing short of sublime. From using a wheat rather than rye recipe, the small copper stills make a full bodied bourbon that matures majestically and, to date, I cannot remember being let down by a bottle yet. Seemingly being the inventors of plastic-wax seals – red for the standard brand, gold and black for older, smaller batch versions – this style of closure has been much imitated in recent years and has a lot to answer for. For a time it was one of the unlikely stars of the Australian soap *Neighbours*: a bottle of Maker's Mark would be seen most days behind the left shoulder of pub landlord Lou Carpenter. Despite its neck level failing to plunge in about three years, one day it suddenly vanished. Obviously a member of the cast had discovered its myriad charms. Despite its weighty body, Maker's Mark is a classic anytime anywhere bourbon. Even in Australia.

WILD TURKEY

For me, a world heritage whisky, if there is such a thing. Both for its whiskey and for the distillery which is perched precariously it seems on a cliff with a sheer drop of 259 feet into the Kentucky River. The whiskey is no less dramatic, especially when it has passed eight years of age. Like Buffalo Trace it ranks in my top three of world distilleries for the extraordinary magnitude of its bourbon. For some time my preferred Wild Turkey was the Rare Breed which simply rejoiced in its honeyed richness and complexity, even though batches could vary from time to time. Today the distillery has a new Champion, the Wild Turkey Russell Reserve, a 10 Year Old named after distillery manager Jimmy Russell (a true master distiller if ever there was one), who will soon be retiring after more than 40 years at the plant. Jimmy prefers to see his whiskeys bottled at 101 proof (50.5% abv) and this is no exception. At younger years Wild Turkey can be ordinary and even the 8-year-old these days is outshone by similar whiskeys its age from around Kentucky. But it is part of the right of passage for every whisky connoisseur to get to grips with Wild Turkey in its most exulted state.

Bourbon

1492 Bourbon (see Heaven Hill 80 Proof)

American Star (86) n21 enormous small-grain character; **t**22 big and roasty yet with plenty of sweet corn to balance out, lovely rye follow-through; **f**21 some hints of cocoa amid the vanilla and fruity grains; **b**22 a seriously good rye-recipe bourbon with enormous full-bodied and fruity character. Sweet and lingering. **40% (80 proof).** *Bernkasteler Germany.*

Ancient Age (75) n18 **t**19 **f**19 **b**19. Light, pleasant but half cooked. **40% (80 proof).**

Ancient Ancient Age 10 Star (89) n22 lavender and soft rye amid the rich corn; **t**23 complex small grain, centring around the rye, but also slightly nutty with some raisiny fruits; **f**22 oak comes steaming in to gently dry the broadening corn. Spices begin to bite; **b**22 what we have here is a bourbon that knows how to offer complexity: a thinking man's bourbon. Much better than it once was. **45% (90 proof).**

Ancient Ancient Age 10 Years Old (94) n23 superb oak richness with the corn floating around and the rye biting and nipping; **t**24 Kentucky heaven: this is bourbon as it should be. The small grains just play around offering a fruitiness of under-ripened greengages and the sweet nuttiness of sunflower seeds, bristling with complexity; **f**23 remains long and playful: the rye is a fraction bitter and cocoa adds to the dryness, but the corn offers all the sweetness required; **b**24 this is my everyday drinking whiskey when back home in Kentucky. A tiny fraction heavier now than previously, I actually prefer it when they choose barrels from the bottom of the warehouse to make the complexity even more nerve-tingling. Then, usually, it scores around 95. But you really can't complain about this: find me a Scotch of the same price or age to match its complexity and I'll show you a British whisky magazine publisher not in it just for the money. **43% (86 proof).**

Anderson Club (see Heaven Hill Aged 6 Years 90 Proof)

Aristocrat (see Heaven Hill 80 Proof)

Baker's Aged 7 Years batch B-85-001 **(88) n**22 excellent rye bite to the very firm and sweet nose. Fabulously fruity: mature plums and slightly over-ripe banana star; **t**23 again the rye kicks off early and allows a slightly bitter and prickly, softly spiced middle to ensure this is a characterful, multi-layered bourbon that follows a deliciously unique agenda; **f**21 massively complex follow-through, with quite enormous and beautiful cocoa notes; **b**22 a chocoholic's bourbon if ever there was one. Changed shape slightly in the last few years with a bigger rye firmness. Tasty, armchair stuff. **53.5% (107 proof).** *Jim Beam.*

Baker's Aged 7 Years batch B-90-001 **(85) n**21 soft, corn dominant, vanilla-rich with sexy rye sub-plot; **t**22 clean corn with a chewy toffee-apple middle; **f**21 extremely soft and undemanding despite some late small grain; **b**21 not quite in the same league as the bigger batch 85, but pretty timeless, enjoyable stuff. **53.5% (107 proof).** *Jim Beam.*

Barclay's Bourbon (79) n20 **t**21 **f**18 **b**20. Economical in development, there is still enough rye and nutty oiliness to keep the tastebuds amused. Little sparkle on the finish. **40% (80 proof)**

Basil Hayden's (77) n21 **t**19 **f**18 **b**19. Some attractive rye riches, but overall disappointingly thin and lacking in depth. **40% (80 proof).** *Jim Beam.*

Benchmark (see McAfee's Benchmark)

Blanton's (89) n20 relatively raw, grainy, hot and unwieldy for a Blanton; **t**23 goes into honeyed overdrive with a superb rye-based back-up; **f**23 bitter, slightly fruity rye and some major oak incursions, but still the honey continues; **b**23 forget the nose: once on the palate you are entering honeyed bliss. **42.5% (93 proof).** *Buffalo Trace.*

Blanton's Gold Edition barrel no. 226 w/house H Rick 32 dumped 12 March 02 **(93) n**23 stunning rye and small grains hammering into the oak; **t**24 beautiful, silky arrival of honeyed oak and lush, busy grains; **f**22 more vanilla, chills out ... or would do if a massive spice surge didn't want to have the last word; **b**24 brilliant complexity: top-order bourbon. Grab any bottle you spot. **51.5% (103 proof).** *Buffalo Trace.*

Blanton's Barrel no. 239 w/house H Rick 49 dumped 21 Oct 02 **(91) n**23 bourbon concentrate, and absolutely stunning, complex bourbon at that, with big age and heavy, sweet oak; **t**23 dry, mouth-puckering oak sweetens as the juicy corn arrives. A beautiful shimmer of honey, but kept in check by peppery spice; **f**22 sweet corn forms a juicy interlude before the softer, saner vanillas return; **b**23 massive whiskey, and not because of the natural strength. Age and nature have had a big input here. The results are enormous and breathtakingly enjoyable. **67.7% (135.2 proof).** *Buffalo Trace.*

Blanton's Single Barrel barrel no. 520 w/house H Rick 55 dumped 23 Aug 01 **(89) n**22 superb oak of quite perfect weight; **t**23 big and oily mouthfeel, a toffeed middle that you can chew indefinitely; **f**22 soft vanilla and a touch of marmalade and spice; **b**22 simply a quality bourbon. **46.5%.** *Buffalo Trace.*

Blanton's Special Reserve barrel no. 180 w/house H Rick 10 dumped 6 Aug 02 **(79) n**20 **t**21 **f**19 **b**19. Pleasant, but surprisingly flat for Blanton's. **40% (80 proof).** *Buffalo Trace.*

Blue Grass State (77) n19 **t**19 **f**20 **b**19. Clean, good toast and vanilla. **40% (80 proof).** *Somerfield UK.*

Bowman's Bourbon (81) n20 **t**20 **f**21 **b**20. A very decent, well-balanced, softly spiced and rich young-to-medium-age bourbon originating from Heaven Hill. A fine everyday shot. **40% (80 proof).** *A Smith Bowman.*

Booker's 7 Yrs 3 Months batch C92-I-15 **(92) n**24 a stunningly integrated aroma: fresh rye and almost green corn in perfect harmony with dry toasty oak and sweet chestnuts; **t**23 corn and sweetened cocoa in equal measures, slightly lush but the rye pops up to make a very complex middle; **f**22 remains sweet but with fade-out of the constituent flavours as graceful as the setting sun; **b**24 of the batches I have come across over the years, the finest yet, not just because of the extra sweetness, but the complexity required to keep that sweetness at bay. Brilliant. **63.25% (126.5 proof).**

Booker's 7 Years 4 Months batch no. C90-D-11 **(88) n**22 burnt raisins and heavy sweet corn; **t**23 incredibly sweet: the sweet corn is thick enough to stand a spoon in, velvety and chewy; **f**21 decent liquorice as the oak kicks in; **b**22 clever Booker Beam: he's picked a different style, but kept the quality bang on course. This really is a treat for corn whiskey lovers! **63.25% (126.5 poof).** *Jim Beam.*

Booker's 8 Years 8 Months batch no. C87-D-21 **(86) n**22 light and quite malty, almost dank hessian amid some growing rye; **t**23 corn much more prominent, then a hugely satisfying surge of honey and spice: delicious; **f**20 slightly flat compared to the excellent build-up. Some decent rye lingers, though; **b**21 a rich bourbon that varies in style from batch to batch. This one has a better than average middle with no shortage of rye, but is let down in the final stages. **62.45% (124.9 proof).** *Jim Beam.*

Bourbon Falls (see Heaven Hill 86 Proof)

Bourbon Royal (see Heaven Hill 80 Proof)

Buffalo Trace (94) n23 sharp rye screams above the complex corn, citrus and oak: seriously absorbing; **t**24 stupendous, softly oiled mouthfeel with the corn absorbing some prickly rye and spice; **f**23 sweet, remains oily with some cream toffee. The small grains re-emerge for a last battle with the corn; **b**24 I simply adore this whiskey: the weight is just about perfect as is the corn-oak, bitter-sweet harmony. The small grains add great colour and complexity. A whiskey gem of the world. **45%. (90 proof).** *Buffalo Trace.*

Bulleit Bourbon Frontier Whiskey (88) n22 light and teasing: mallows roasting on an open fire plus pine nuts and vanilla. Honest, folks; **t**22 the faintest dry oak start vanishes within seconds for a rich follow-through of sweet chestnut, a busy complexity of malted barley and rye and then spice; **f**22 mildly oily, softly honeycombed and chocolatey for a chewy, bitter-sweet finale. Like all that's gone before, exceptionally well balanced and satisfying; **b**22 absolutely excellent from first to last, an essay in balance and control: I doubt if any frontier whiskey of Boone's day was half as good as this. **45% (90 proof)**

Cabin Hill (see Heaven Hill 80 Proof)

Champion (see Heaven Hill 80 Proof)

Chapin & Gore (see Heaven Hill 80 Proof)

Chapin & Gore 86 Proof (see Heaven Hill 86 Proof)

Chesapeake (see Heaven Hill 80 Proof)

Chillie Gone Crazy (see Heaven Hill 80 Proof)

Classic Cask Bourbon Aged 17 Years Distilled 1983 batch GL-106 bott 00 **(87) n**21 an oily, roasty aroma, full of mocha, a sliver of liquorice and some excellent small grains with the rye having greater say than the delicate malt. Superb grip on the nose; **t**21 a classic explosion of sweet, oily liquorice and simmering spice. The middle becomes a simple mixture of toffee and dried dates; **f**23 medium length vanilla with a hint of hickory, honey and nuts on the finale; **b**22 a beautiful bourbon that shows no sign of fade whatsoever. Simplistic towards the middle and finish but the journey there is sensational. **45.4% (90.8 proof).** *The Classic Cask Co. Bardstown. 600 bottles.*

Classic Cask Bourbon Aged 17 Years Distilled 1985 batch GL-108 bott 02 **(86) n**20 for the big colour and age, this is light and minty with extra emphasis on the corn; **t**22 beautifully delicate with a fine sharp rye kick against the much sweeter corn and oak; **f**22 soft, gracious exit, the vanilla taking the lead with liquorice following tamely behind. Some lovely late roast notes and a little sap emphasise the age; **b**22 talk about gentle giants – really charming bourbon that looks like it wishes to bludgeon you, but instead sings lullabies. **45.4% (90.8 proof).** *The Classic Cask Co. Bardstown. 600 bottles.*

Colonel Lee (69) n17 **t**17 **f**18 **b**17. Grim stuff. **40%.** *Barton.*

Colonel's Pride (see Heaven Hill 80 Proof)

Daniel Stewart Aged 8 Years (88) n22 rich, leathery and pipe-tobacco-sweet but underneath a second stratum of young grain: unusual; **t**22 brilliantly spiced yet sweet corn forms an oily-textured middle; **f**22 lots of blistering small grain and spice; **b**22 a very sweet yet complex bourbon of light-to-medium weight. **45% (90 proof).** *Heaven Hill.*

Daniel Stewart Aged 12 Years (95) n24 floral, honey and outstanding clean oak and corn: a classy act; **t**24 heather, honey, hints of citrus and then some serious oak, but always sweetened by the rich corn. The rye offers a spicy and even more complex background; **f**23 such a delicate fade: the sweetness falls over aeons, the oak gathering density at the same rate. But the rye continues its merry tune; **b**24 it is pretty obvious that the original old Heaven Hill peaks at 12: it always has in the time I have known it. Awesome, spellbinding bottlings like this place it amongst the world's elite. **53.5% (107 proof).** *Heaven Hill.*

Dierberg's (see Heaven Hill 80 Proof)

Distiller's Pride (see Heaven Hill 80 Proof)

Don & Ben's (see Evan Williams Aged 7 Years 86 Proof)

Dowling Deluxe Aged 8 Years 100 Proof (84) n21 **t**22 **f**20 **b**21. Simplistically sweet and oaky. **50% (100 proof).** *Heaven Hill.*

Eagle Rare Single Barrel Bourbon 10 Years Old (89) n23 big: touches of honey add to the peek-a-boo rye and distant demerara; **t**23 initial sweet arrival of rye, then chewy oak and corn, followed by peppery, toffee attack; **f**21 very long, remaining on the vanilla-caramel theme; **b**22 a delight. *Buffalo Trace.*

Eagle Rare 10 Years Old (78) n21 **t**20 **f**18 **b**19. Lush, big and chewy toffee but very limited complexity. Decent whiskey, but I never seem to get on with this one as I do with other Buffalo Trace bourbons, either for one reason or another. Strange. **50.5% (101 proof).** *Buffalo Trace.*

Eagle Rare 17 Years Old (94) n24 fabulous combination of roasted almonds and pecan pie, all topped with brown sugar, stewed apples and the faintest dash of honeycomb. Brilliant – almost a template for how aged bourbon should be; **t**23 lighter, cleaner initial mouthfeel than would be expected and the cranking up of rich, leathery, liquoricy, slightly phenolic oak notes takes a little time; **f**23 plateaus out with lots of demerara sweetness, a drying vanilla and toffee. Spices begin to rise towards the finale like a phoenix from the ashes: big but manageable; **b**24 the nose is wondrous, the taste is lighter, but only marginally less awesome, though the spice on the finish is a masterstroke. Such a consistent, reliable whiskey over the years. One of the all-time great bourbons. **45% (90 proof).** *Buffalo Trace.*

Early Times (brown label) (80) n19 t21 f20 b20. A very light but well-made bourbon. Clean, with hints of cinnamon and citrus. Quite refreshing. **40%. (80 proof).**

Early Times (yellow label) (83) n20 t21 f21 b21. A heavier, more vanilla-rich bourbon that offers a consistent, delicate, sweet theme throughout with butterscotch on the finish. **40% (80 proof).**

Echo Spring (see Heaven Hill 80 Proof)

Elijah Craig 12 Years Old (96) n24 gentle lavender and violets merge into a rye-oak soup. As heavy as it seems, it just floats around the glass, and as dry as the oak appears, the inherent mildly honeyed sweetness offers the perfect riposte: fabulous; **t**24 now the honey is so much more apparent, but some rye-weathered spice keeps it under control; **f**23 long, spiced cream toffee, but doesn't even begin to soften or undermine the enormous depth to this whiskey; **b**25 this whiskey is all about contrast and balance, power and subtlety. It is a world masterpiece, the kind of whiskey that makes you glad to be alive. My heartfelt praise and thanks to the boys at HH for keeping this one of the world's most consistently astounding treats. **47% (94 proof).** *Heaven Hill.*

Elijah Craig 18 Years Old Single Barrel barrel no. 821 barrelled on 22 Oct 82 **(81)** n19 t22 f19 b21. Surprisingly low key with little on the nose but picking up for a burnt honey finish, though the finish is a bit on the tired side. **45% (90 proof).** *Heaven Hill.*

Elijah Craig 18 Years Old Single Barrel barrel no. 495 barrelled on 18 Nov 82 **(88)** n22 vanilla and milky coffee. The rye shows well; **t**22 beautiful sweet corn in tandem with some big oak notes; **f**22 small grains to the rescue as the oak fails to gain control. Really delicious, complex stuff; **b**22 breaks all the rules: how can a bourbon survive this number of Kentucky summers and come out sweet as a nut? **45% (90 proof).** *Heaven Hill.*

Elmer T Lee Single Barrel (88) n22 distinct citrus and light corn-rich notes; **t**23 sweet corn again with hints of banana and rye; **f**21 a very settled, toffeed finale with a hint of spicy rebellion; **b**22 a more delicate and less rye-infested bottling than some. Really delicious. **45% (90 proof).** *Buffalo Trace.*

Evan Williams (see Heaven Hill 80 Proof)
Evan Williams 100 Proof (see Heaven Hill 100 Proof)
Evan Williams Aged 7 Years (83) n22 t21 f20 b20. Sweet, corn-rich with caramel on the middle and a dry, oaky finish. **43%.** *Heaven Hill.*

Evan Williams 15 Years (90) n23 heavy duty age, but enough sweetness to absorb the oaky impact; **t**22 too thick to drink through a straw, again the oak dominance thwarted by amazingly active corn. The spices buzz blissfully; **f**22 liquorice and demerara sugar head-to-head; **b**23 there is no way that a bourbon carrying this amount of oak should be enjoyable. But it is much more than that: a grizzly arm-wrestle in which you come out a smiling victor. Macho stuff ... and magnificent. **50.5% (101 proof).** *Heaven Hill.*

Evan Williams 23 Years Old (86) n*21* the oak is creaking a bit with a hint of sap on the aroma, but a thread of sweetness keeps it together; t*22* massive mouth arrival with enough small grain to offer complexity enough to drive off the oak, even time for some orangey notes to arrive; f*21* soft vanilla and a build-up of sweetish corn; b*22* hats off to this bourbon. It defies nature by surviving this amount of time in the barrel: the original richness of the spirit must have played a significant start. This is some beast and, by the second glassful, a bit of a beauty, too. **53.5% (107 proof)**. *Heaven Hill.*

Evan Williams 1783 (see Heaven Hill 10 Years 86 Proof)

Evan Williams Old (see Heaven Hill 100 Proof)

Evan Williams Vintage 1989 Single Barrel (87) n*22* heavy-ish oak thinned by soft lime: a gentle giant; t*22* enormous corn dominance and then a chewy layer of toffee; f*21* incredibly soft with the small grains rising without anger; b*22* for all the early puff, one of the more gentle single-barrel expressions from Kentucky. **43.3% (86.6% proof)**. *Heaven Hill.*

Evan Williams Vintage 1990 Single Barrel (91) n*23* a stunning herbal start blossoms into a ginger-honey sweetness. The small grains are lively, with the malt and rye becoming a fruity and citrussy one; t*23* a fresh and clean start allows the corn to develop beautifully before the rye takes hold. Brilliant bittersweet balance and complexity that dances around the palate; f*22* medium length only, but the quality is outstanding with a new layer of fresh rye on soft corn bringing the curtain down; b*23* a bourbon that celebrates the part rye and malt notes can play against the more neutral background of corn. At times, almost too complex to be true. **43.3% (86.6 proof)**. *Heaven Hill.*

Evan Williams Vintage 1993 Single Barrel (89) n*22* busy citrus battling with fresh and fruity rye; t*22* delicate small grains dominate at first, then a wave of oak followed by sweet corn; f*22* pretty long and quite dry with some chalky oak enlivened by returning rye and liquorice; b*23* a steady, sexy, delicate bourbon that is a lot more complex than it initially seems. **43.3% (86.6%).**

Ezra Brooks (79) n*19* t*20* f*20* b*20*. A light-to-medium weight bourbon with a standard nose but offering good sweet liquorice on the rich finish. **45%**

Fighting Cock Aged 6 Years (84) n*22* t*22* f*20* b*20*. Brilliant nose of old, waxy wooden floors and a really battling palate arrival of almost fruity corn. Quite hot. **51.5% (103 proof)**. *Heaven Hill.*

Four Roses (84) n*22* t*21* f*20* b*21*. A sweet and charming bourbon that is light and sophisticated but always pulls up short of being a world beater. Now that the distillery is on its own I expect this perennial under-achiever to go through the roof quality-wise. The stocks are there, as the single-barrel expressions illustrate, and as I have seen over the years when inspecting the warehouses. Keep your eyes peeled and tastebuds at the ready. Four Roses is likely to become a thorn in their competitors' sides. **40% (80 proof)**

Four Roses Single Barrel barrel 2-13-926, bott 22 Oct 99 **(89)** n*23* small grains to the fore with a lovely malt-rye interplay – certainly more rye apparent on this batch than normal, fittingly delicate and floral; t*22* denser on the palate, surprisingly heavy. It all hangs on the rye base, but fans out with roasty, burnt raisins, a hint of coffee and burnt fudge. Unbelievably chewy; f*22* more of the same, though the fade-out is slow, roasty and tantalising; b*22* the best bottled sample from this distillery I'd tasted at the time. **43% (86 proof)**

Four Roses Single Barrel barrel 2-1093E, bott 7 Dec 00 **(90)** n*23* just so delicate with the rye making a proud stand against equally crisp corn. Hedgerow flowers with a touch of honey; t*22* initially much sweeter than the nose suggests, hints of molasses sugar doubling with the rich corn; f*22* lovely arrival of oak doesn't quite bother the general sweetness; b*23* pips the previous bottling thanks to stupendous rye involvement. A benchmark whiskey for the distillery. **43% (86 proof)**

Four Roses Single Barrel Reserve (80) n22 t21 f18 b19. Starts promisingly and the rye gives good weight but fades alarmingly. This is now a discontinued line but the odd bottle can still be seen in specialist outlets the world over. **43% (86 proof)**

Gentleman Earl (see Heaven Hill 80 Proof)

George T Stagg (97) n25 I cannot really find a fault here: the oak is big enough to add a herbal almost medicinal quality, which on its own could be a downer were it not for the extraordinary, just about perfect, counter provided by sharp, juicy rye fruitiness and sweetening corn. Stick your nose in this – but only after you have warmed it to body temperature and you have about 15–20 minutes to spare. Really, tasting notes are pointless in some ways: look for it and you will find it there. This in some way redefines complexity; t24 the enormity of the age and strength at first wrinkles and shrivels the palate, but when your eyes have stopped watering and you can focus, you will see you're in Eden. The splendour of the rye leads the way, with a soft oily body forming from which much more succulent corn springs. The oak is a vaguely bitter pulse somewhere in the background. In the midst of this a buttery, small-grain anthem is played over and over again; f23 much quieter by comparison but the fruits remain and now a natural, caramelised corn sweetens the building, coffeed oak; b25 I have tried this with water at varying strengths, but to get the best out of this bourbon you must be brave. Take at full strength, but only in very small amounts. Such is the enormity of this whiskey it will soon spread around the palate offering its full service. Along with a certain Ardbeg, this George T Stagg is without any shadow of a doubt one of the two best whiskies it has ever been my luck and privilege to taste in nearly 30 years. **72.3% (144.6 proof).** *Buffalo Trace.*

Gold Label (see Heaven Hill 80 Proof)

Hancock's Reserve Single Barrel (83) n21 t21 f20 b21. A tad butyric but still employs enough sweet liquorice charm to make for a very decent whiskey. **44.45% (88.9 proof).**

Heaven Hill 80 Proof (75) n18 t20 f18 b19. Green, young and lively; no shortage of flavour for all its tender years. **40% (80 proof).** *Comes with gold, blue, green and white labels.*

Heaven Hill 86 Proof (83) n20 t22 f20 b21. Probably the maltiest bourbon I have tasted in 29 years of savouring the stuff: barley springs out at you from all directions. Fresh, juicy and mouthwatering: delicious and a real surprise package. **43% (86 proof)**

Heaven Hill 100 Proof (78) n19 t20 f19 b20. There is lots of rye and toffee here. **50% (100 proof)**

Heaven Hill Aged 6 Years 80 Proof (88) n22 green corn but lively rye; t22 lots of fresh rye and massive spice sparkle; f22 hints of sweet liquorice as the oak says, "hello"; the corn remains youthful and a fun antidote to the oak; b22 this is wonderful, sophisticated whiskey: the jump from five to six years is a chasm. **40% (80 proof)**

Heaven Hill Aged 6 Years 90 Proof (88) n22 pine alongside the fresh rye; t23 brilliant rye and barley complexity swamped by a wave of sweet corn: unbelievably tasty; f21 soft oak with hints of liquorice and demerara sugar; b22 weighty bourbon with excellent small-grain complexity. **45% (90 proof)**

Heaven Hill Aged 6 Years 100 Proof (85) n20 flattish, toffeed; t22 big oak kick takes the breath away; f22 some spice and shy rye, flattens slightly as the toffee returns; b21 tasty, but a bit of a lazy one, this. Natural, caramel-dependent and short of oomph. **45% (90 proof)**

Heaven Hill Aged 10 Years 86 Proof (86) n21 attractive weight with hickory and liquorice combining; the vanilla is sweet, the grains subdued except for some dogged rye; t21 spicy, chewy kick off with a firm rye development;

softly oiled and slowly gathers sweetness; **f**22 quite long and the building grain offers great complexity and balance; **b**22 takes a little time to get going but a sophisticated number in some ways showing greater age than expected with the whole being better than the parts. **43% (86 proof)**

Heaven Hill Ultra Deluxe (see Heaven Hill 80 Proof)

Heaven Hill Ultra Deluxe 5 Years (76) **n**20 **t**19 **f**18 **b**19. In a bit of a toffeed trough here, halfway between the juicy, lively 4-y-o and the more, small-grain pounding, oak-heavy 6-y-o. **40% (80 proof).**

Heaven Hill Ultra DeLuxe 6 Years (see Heaven Hill Aged 6 Years 90 Proof)

Henry McKenna (see Heaven Hill Aged 6 Years 80 Proof)

Henry McKenna Single Barrel Aged 10 Years Bottled in Bond barrel no. 208 barrelled on 1 May 92 **(91)** **n**23 no prisoners here at all: minty toothpaste after a marmalade breakfast then black coffee with muscovado sugar and spice ... phew! **t**23 chewy with enormous oak presence from the first moment. The spice is magnificent; **f**22 back to Jamaican Blue Mountain coffee, reasonably heavy roast with a fluttering of cocoa and more brown sugar; **b**23 knife and fork bourbon with stupendous character and presence. A sublime selection. For grown-ups only. **50% (100 proof).**

Jacob's Well batch B-0230-JW459 **(84)** **n**22 **t**20 **f**21 **b**21. Still seen around from time to time (though pretty rarely), this small-batch bourbon concentrates on a lavender delicacy and subtle sweetness. **42% (84 proof).** *Jim Beam.*

Jefferson's Reserve 15 Year Old batch no. 2 **(94)** **n**24 this is to die for: gently oiled, which means the rye and corn stick to the nose, the sweetness and sharp fruit in equal measure; **t**24 brilliant corn/rye entry on the palate then a shimmering honey. Great age, but always elegant and refined while the complexity dazzles; **f**22 very soft landing with vanilla and rye to the fore. The complexity remains superb; **b**24 a great whiskey: simple as that. **45.1% (90.2 proof).**

Jim Beam (85) **n**21 charmingly floral with a soft rye undercurrent; **t**21 sweet corn arrival then soft oaky-vanilla notes; **f**22 hints of soft liquorice and then much drier mouthwatering vaguely malty tones; **b**21 this whiskey has improved enormously in recent years. Still light and easy going, there appears to be an element of extra age, weight and complexity. **40% (80 proof)**

Jim Beam Black (90) **n**23 big and bruising, there is weighty oil and liquorice; **t**23 beautifully sweet, manuka honey and then liquorice, candy and rich rye; **f**22 soft vanilla and liquorice; **b**22 I just so love this bourbon. The closest in style to a Jack Daniel's because of a mildly lumbering gait. Any time, any day whiskey of the very top order. **43% (86 proof)**

Jim Porter (see Heaven Hill 80 Proof)

John Hamilton (see Heaven Hill 80 Proof)

J T S Brown (see Heaven Hill 80 Proof)

J T S Brown 86 Proof (see Heaven Hill 86 Proof)

J T S Brown 100 Proof (see Heaven Hill 100 Proof)

J T S Brown 6 Years 80 Proof (see Heaven Hill Aged 6 Years 80 Proof)

J T S Brown 6 Years 100 Proof (see Heaven Hill Aged 6 Years 100 Proof)

J T S Brown 8 Years (see Old Heaven Hill Very Rare Aged 8 Years 86 Proof)

J T S Brown 10 Years (see Heaven Hill 10 Years 86 Proof)

J W Dant (see Heaven Hill 80 Proof)

J W Dant (see Heaven Hill 100 Proof)

J W Kent (see Heaven Hill 80 Proof)

Kentucky Beau (see Heaven Hill 80 Proof)

Kentucky Crown Aged 8 Years (88) **n**22 pipe-tobacco-sweet, sensual; **t**22 there is a layer of oily, sweet corn before spices arrive; **f**22 sweet vanilla and corn; **b**22 a charmingly sweet yet spicy bourbon. **45% (90 proof).** *Germany.*

Kentucky Crown Very Rare Aged 16 Years (87) n22 distinct kumquat and over-ripe pears, really excellent oak; **t**23 sweet, oily corn followed by liquorice and citrus: big, threatening yet mouthwatering; **f**20 levels out with a tad too much natural caramel; **b**22 a mildly abrupt toffeed end just when it was getting good. **53.5% (107 proof).** *Germany.*

Kentucky deLuxe (see Heaven Hill 80 Proof)

Kentucky deLuxe 86 Proof (see Heaven Hill 86 Proof)

Kentucky Gentleman (89) n23 improbable small-grains complexity for a whiskey so young; **t**23 lots of rye charging around the palate and malt adds something sweet and weighty. The corn imposes itself gently; **f**21 quietens and becomes a little bitter; **b**22 this was always a little belter for its age, but this is the best I have tasted yet. The small-grain quality is unimpeachable. Delicious. **40% (80 proof).** *Barton.*

Kentucky Gold (see Heaven Hill 80 Proof)

Kentucky Spirit Single Barrel barrel 10 warehouse A, rick 51, bott 9 May 02 **(89) n**23 very dry despite the subtle oranges and burnt honey; **t**23 explodes on entry: punchy, rye-based spices and then big toffee-liquorice, genuinely spectacular early middle; **f**21 very dry, the oak offering toasty vanilla; **b**22 this is big bourbon but the complexity is lost towards the finish as the oak kicks in. **50.5% (101 proof).**

Kentucky Tavern (86) n22 some age and weight amid the rye-led small grains; **t**22 mouthwatering, fresh and very busy; **f**21 a touch of liquorice; **b**21 typical fare from Barton distillery: for Scotch drinkers, their whiskey is the equivalent of young Speyside malt, refreshing and mouthwatering. This is no exception. **40% (80 proof).** *Barton.*

Kentucky Supreme (see Old Heaven Hill Very Rare Aged 8 Years 80 Proof)

Kentucky Vintage batch 02-38, dist 22 Feb 94, bott 9 Mar 02 **(83) n**21 **t**22 **f**20 **b**20. Pretty hefty in places, sweet with some citrus fruit. **45% (90 proof)**

Knob Creek Aged 9 Years (90) n24 marmalade on slightly burnt toast, beautiful, sweet fruit, mainly pears, and then a dash of soft rye and an edge of saltiness, some honey as a side-dish; **t**22 softly spiced, oaky, busy start; then a powerful delivery of natural toffee. A playfully biting, tastebud-nipping character tries to add momentum; **f**22 chocolate toffee balances out the vanilla and ensures a dry, slightly oily and long finish; **b**22 the best aroma from the JBB Small Batch selection; softer on the tastebuds than previous bottlings, but still a power player. **50% (100 proof).** *Jim Beam.*

Lone Oak Aged 12 Long Years (89) n23 really sexy oak involvement with the small grains making some noise and good, controlled age; **t**24 astonishingly silky mouth arrival with some very oily and sweet corn being countered superbly by bitter oak. Honeydew melon and muscovado sugar offer the counterbalance while the small grains go wild; **f**20 heaps of toffee, then a quick fade; **b**22 the short, simple finish is a bit of a surprise package in one of the silkiest bourbons on the market shelf. **50.5% (101 proof).**

McAfee's Benchmark (79) n20 **t**21 **f**19 **b**19. Light, young and corn-rich. **40% (80 proof).** *Buffalo Trace.*

McAfee's Benchmark 8 Years Old (83) n21 **t**21 **f**20 **b**21. Fruity, mouthwatering and refreshing. **40% (80 proof).** *Buffalo Trace.*

McScrooge's (see Heaven Hill 80 Proof)

Maker's Mark (Red Wax Seal) (black on buff label) **(89) n**23 wispy aroma with delightful strands of exotic fruit and honey. The old fruitcake is still there, but these days the complexity and balance are nothing short of stunning. Beguiling oak adds to the overall feeling of class; **t**23 lush, pleasingly deep and quite malty. A firm nuttiness adds extra oily, chewability to the toffee and liquorice; **f**21 perhaps drier than of old with signs of a little extra age. Caramel toffee continues its interplay with the oak to guarantee a bitter-sweet edge; **b**22 an old faithful of a bourbon. Never lets you down and being from the wheaty school always shows good oak balance. **45% (90 proof).**

Maker's Mark (Black Wax Seal) (gold on black label) **(93)** n23 thick, charred notes, deep, mildly waxy, hints of cordite; t24 oily and immediately mouthfilling with a quite stupendous soft honey, grainy sweetness that balances almost to perfection with the toasty, liquorice-caramel, burnt sugar deeper tones. A pepperiness is on a wavelength almost too subtle to be heard. This is cerebral drinking; f22 much less taxing on the tastebuds with a more toffeed departure. Vanilla and other well-ordered oaky tones are also present and correct; b24 simply outstanding bourbon with the most clever weight ratio. A whiskey that demands solitude and the ability to listen. The story it tells is worth hearing again and again. **47.5% (95 proof).**

Mark Twain (see Heaven Hill 80 Proof)

Mark Twain Aged 12 Years 100 Proof **(88)** n22 the obvious oak remains light and corny; t22 hard rye and fruity, the sweetness is well camouflaged; f22 slightly burnt toast, very roasty; b22 a well-disciplined bourbon that looks at one point as though the oak has taken too firm a grip but the complexity never ends. **50% (100 proof).** *Heaven Hill.*

Martin Mills (see Heaven Hill 80 Proof)

Mattingly & Moore (see Heaven Hill 80 Proof)

May's (see Heaven Hill 80 Proof)

Mellow Bourbon (see Heaven Hill 80 Proof)

Military Special (see Heaven Hill 80 Proof)

Mound City (see Heaven Hill 80 Proof)

Noah's Mill batch 02-71, dist 2 Jul 87, bott 1 Nov 02 **(91)** n23 stunning small grain, the rye in particular starring; t23 excellent transfer from nose to palate with busy grains pounding the tastebuds; f21 takes a breather as some corn and oak give a softer landing; b24 this is one of Kentucky's most complex whiskies by far. Small grains, big heart. **57.15% (114.3 proof)**

No Face (see Heaven Hill 80 Proof)

No Face 86 Proof (see Heaven Hill 86 Proof)

Old 1889 (see Heaven Hill 80 Proof)

Old 1889 Aged 10 Years 86 Proof **(85)** n22 mango has somehow slipped into the equation here: one of the fruitiest Heaven Hill numbers I've ever known; t20 really light with the corn glowing on the palate; f22 the small grains offer a nutty dimension to the gentle corn; b21 really quite different HH from what I usually see. This is much more light and delicate with less of the usual richness those old big copper stills guaranteed. A real one-off. **43% (86 proof).** *Heaven Hill.*

Old Charter 8 Years Old **(77)** n19 t19 f20 b19. A simple, sweet, toffeed bourbon with limited complexity. On this evidence, not quite what it once was. **40% (80 proof).**

Old Charter 10 Years Old **(82)** n21 t21 f20 b20. Sweet corn but fails to develop on the rich start. **43% (86 proof).**

Old Charter 12 Years Old **(87)** n22 some dazzling oak but always enough room for the small grains to flourish; t23 small-grain arrival on palate; genuinely complex with a spicy kick all the way; f20 surprising amount of natural toffee flattens it a little; b22 until that toffee arrives this is a deliciously complex dram. Well worth an investigation. **45% (90 proof).**

Old Charter Proprietor Reserve 13 Years Old **(89)** n23 kumquats and lemon peel, marmalade on light toast; t22 fruity from the word go then a wave of corn and very soft rye; f21 gentle vanillas; b23 what an enormously delicate bourbon for such great age. Graceful and charming. **45% (90 proof).**

Old Fitzgerald **(79)** n18 t20 f21 b20. One of the sweetest bourbons around: the nose does it no favours but a chewy toffee fightback. **43% (86 proof).**

Old Fitzgerald Very Special 12 Years Old (80) n18 t23 f20 b19. Warming spice paves the way for a crashing wave of corn and oak. But that excellent middle apart, something is curiously lacking. **45% (90 proof).**

Old Fitzgerald's 1849 8 Years (90) n21 ethereal corn and wheat; t23 lush and sweet arrival with a mixture of sugar and honey on the corn: the wheat fizzes around the roof of the mouth; f23 remains sweet with a late citrus surge and then drier vanilla tones; b23 light yet big. The sweetness is enormous but avoids going OTT thanks to excellent oak balance. A delight and the best of the Old Fitz range by a country mile. **45% (90 proof).**

Old Forester (89) n22 an explosion of small grains pepper the nose, hints of marmalade; t23 chunky and deep with liquorice-toffee but it's the softly spiced apple and pear juiciness that wins the day; f22 the liqorice factor increases as oak makes a stand; b22 if anyone asks me to show them a classic rye-rich bourbon where the small grains really count, as often as not I'll show them this. **43% (86 proof).** *Brown-Forman.*

Old Forester Birthday Bourbon Vintage 1989 (94) n22 big fruit only partially masked by telling oak; t24 superb: absolutely perfect weight on the palate with soft oil, but a cauldron of frothing small grains. The rye input is extraordinary but completely under control. Toffee apple provides the extra sweet juiciness but balances things perfectly; f24 one of the longest controlled finishes not just in bourbon but any whiskey. Those small grains just simmer away, nibbling playfully at the tastebuds, the sweetness level varying with the depth of the oak. Pulsating and rhythmic, it just seems to go on forever; b24 a bourbon for toffs and swells. Sheer class, offering complexity on a silver platter: a bourbon connoisseur's bourbon if ever there was one. Unquestionably one of the bourbons of the decade. **47.5% (95 proof).** *Brown-Forman.*

Old Forester Birthday Bourbon Vintage 1990 (90) n23 apples and cinnamon, over-ripe figs, a fraction smoky and rye-rich; t23 delicate vanilla arrives early, then a wave of rye and yet more powering oak. Pretty dry; f22 sweetens with corn, then the dry oak returns; b22 seriously delicate and sophisticated bourbon. **44.5% (89 proof).** *Brown-Forman.*

Old Forester Birthday Bourbon Vintage 1990 95 Proof (91) n22 compressed, heavyweight oak and rye; t23 chewy and molassed, the small grains punch delicious holes through the spicy morass; f23 long, lingering, spiced at first, then trailing off towards a dry, burnt toast, cold black coffee finale; b23 not for the squeamish: there is enormous complexity, but laid on with a trowel. **47.5% (95 proof).** *Brown-Forman.*

Old Forester 100 Proof (89) n23 beautifully weighted clementine, hickory and coffee: a real nose full; t22 cream toffee sweetens out with fat corn and a sprinkling of molassed sugar. The rye thuds in alongside some glittering spice; f22 the spice just continues its tingling journey around the palate, soft toffee and vanilla offering a softer finish than predicted; b22 as ever, very high quality bourbon from one of Kentucky's most consistent distilleries. **50% (100 proof).** *Brown-Forman.*

Old Heaven Hill (see Heaven Hill 80 Proof)

Old Heaven Hill 100 Proof (see Heaven Hill 100 Proof)

Old Heaven Hill Very Rare Aged 8 Years 80 Proof (82) n20 t21 f21 b20. Unusually citrussy for this distillery: lemon and lime knitting with green corn. Amazingly youthful for its age. **40% (80 proof)**

Old Heaven Hill Very Rare Aged 8 Years 86 Proof (86) n22 lording oak offers honey to the corn; t22 two-tiered: very light corn battles the more compelex small grain and growing oak; f21 more small grains and soft vanilla; b21 intriguing bourbon with greater maturity than the 80 proof version: delightful in its own right, but just on the edge of something significant, you feel. **43% (86 proof)**

Old Heaven Hill Very Rare Aged 10 Years 80 Proof (84) n21 t21 f21 b21. Very soft, sweet corn-laden and even. **40% (80 proof)**

Old Heaven Hill Very Rare Aged 10 Years 86 Proof (see Heaven Hill 10 Years 86 Proof)

Old Heaven Hill Very Rare Aged 10 Years 100 Proof (93) n23 heavier and rich, fruitcake style. Really beautiful and subtle but telling rye involvement; t24 weighty and just so spectacularly rich. Really is prize-winning heavy British fruitcake with raisins and cherries to chew on before a lovely walnut oiliness arrives, followed by corn concentrate; f23 the lull after the storm, but the birds sing sweetly because the rye re-appears for a gentle but wonderfully complex finale; b23 this is astonishing bourbon, the type that makes you glad to be in the know. Brilliant. **50% (100 proof)**

Old Heaven Hill Aged 15 Years 100 Proof (86) n21 thinnish for its age; t22 biting grain with a surge of sweet corn; f22 remains sweet with the oak keeping its distance until very late on; b21 for all the whiskey's colour, this doesn't have much of a 15-years-old's normal belligerent attitude. This is sweet and flighty and a little oily, too. Most un-Heaven Hill. **50% (80 proof)**

Old Kentucky Amber Aged 10 Years (87) n22 soft, sweet toffee apple; t21 very gentle arrival with some nipping grain and sweet corn, but some toffeed oak dominates; f22 there is a clever build-up in complexity with the small grains beginning to really delight; b22 a chilled-out, relaxed bourbon at first finally gets the rye to talk. **45% (90 proof).** Germany.

Old Kentucky No. 88 Brand Aged 13 Years (92) n22 excellent rye nip and oak weight, great balance; t24 mouthwatering, fresh and fruity despite the great age: the corn is sharp but a malty character fights through. The complexity is awesome; f23 slightly smoky in style with vanilla and figs; b23 stunning whiskey of classic proportions: hard to find, but grab a bottle if you can. **47% (94 proof).** Germany.

Old Rip Van Winkle 10 Years Old 90 Proof (88) n23 chocolate marzipan and corn; t22 sweet, slightly oily and demerara sugar; f21 spicy vanilla; b22 really well balanced and weighty whiskey. **45% (90 proof)**

Old Rip Van Winkle 10 Years Old 90.4 Proof (85) n21 vanilla; t22 spicy, chewy rye; f21 spice and vanilla plus some sweet corn; b21 light-bodied but packing a spicy punch. **45.2% (90.4 proof)**

Old Rip Van Winkle 10 Years Old 107 Proof (86) n21 biting rye; t22 more rye from the off, but quite hot; decent corn oil sweetens things; f21 vanilla and cocoa; b22 a hotter than average bottling and it has nothing to do with the alcohol! **53.5% (1-7 proof)**

Old Rip Van Winkle 12 Years Old (89) n21 light and fruity, figs and distant liquorice; t23 juicy, a hint of malt at first, grass and grapes and then harder rye and soft corn: deliciously complex; f22 liquorice and some gritty rye; b23 wonderful balance and drive to this bourbon: for something so outwardly light, the flavours just keep on coming. **45.2% (90.4 proof).**

Old Rip Van Winkle 15 Years Old (88) n22 attractive banana-sandwich aroma, topped by some unusual smokiness; t21 fragile, uncluttered, corny; f22 the small grains begin to bite and show great complexity; b23 one of those bourbons where the sum is better than the parts. Really superb balancing act and holds back the years supremely. **45% (90 proof).**

Old Rip Van Winkle 15 Years Old (93) n24 intense honey-nut and corn, like breakfast cereal in which you could happily bury your nose; t23 biting corn forms the bitter-sweet, slightly oily background with some oak arriving early, but adds only depth and something else to chew on; f23 enormously complex: again the corn leads the way but the honey returns with some cocoa and a bit of mouth prickle keeps the tastebuds occupied further; b23 this is a cracker. It always was. It was once a wheated bourbon, and still could be because rye doesn't make any kind of telling contribution here. A classic for sure. **53.5% (107 proof).**

Old Weller 7 Years Old (86) n22 kumquats, tangerines and crushed walnuts: could be Santa's stocking! t22 syrupy liquorice-toffee sweetness then drier oak; f21 lazy spices mingle with toffee; b21 a heavyweight wheated bourbon that's a bit lethargic but thoroughly entertaining. **53.5% (107 proof).** *See also Weller and WL Weller for other members of the same "family".*

Original Barrel Bourbon Aged 12 Years (see Daniel Stewart Aged 12 Years)

Pappy Van Winkle 20 Years Old (78) n21 t20 f18 b19. Nothing like as bone-crushingly dry as some previous bottlings, but this still has way too much oak for me. There are some honeycomb moments on the nose and early arrival, but after that the balance is lost. **45.2% (90.4 proof).**

Pennypacker (87) n22 rye-rich small grains bury themselves deeply into the fruit and oak; t22 a firm, brittle mouthfeel, again with the rye showing brightly; f21 lots of honeyed vanilla and hazelnuts amid the vanilla; b22 the PR blurb from the importers that came with this bottle said the whiskey is three years old. It's a lot older than that, I can assure you. Seriously well made bourbon with big small-grain presence and decent age. **40% (80 proof).** *Borco Hamburg.*

Pure Kentucky XO batch 02-19, dist 14 Nov 89, bott 8 Feb 02 **(88)** n22 seriously impressive small-grain complexity, pretty light and enlightening despite age; t23 masses of honey, hickory and demerara sugar, the balance coming from drier oak; f21 plateaus out; b22 really firm, confident, well-aged whiskey. **53.5% (107 proof)**

Rebecca (see Heaven Hill 10 Years 86 Proof)

Rebel Yell (86) n22 strawberries and corn, beautifully fruity and rich; t21 still fruity, more strawberry – plus melon this time – then a slow assimilation of oak and some oily corn; f21 an oaky layer dries the palate; b22 my word: this brand has moved on some. The fiery, spicy peppery attack has vanished entirely and the citrus notes have been replaced by softer strawberries, but stays true to its fruity style. Lovely wheated stuff. **40% (80 proof)**

Rock Hill Farms (89) n21 thin, but honeyed; t22 slightly hot at first with developing sweet corn; f24 slowly awakens and the small grains go wild: the rye kicks in to give a hard fruit edge, a hint of malt but the sweet corn and oak combining is superb; b22 rock by name, rock by nature: a very hard whiskey which rewards patient study handsomely. **50% (100 proof).** *Buffalo Trace.*

Rowan's Creek batch 02-72, dist 26 Feb 85, bott 5 Nov 02 **(78)** n21 t20 f18 b19. Loads of honey and liquorice, but way too heavily oaked. **50% (100 proof)**

Safeway Bourbon (77) n18 t19 f20 b20. Exceptionally light and lemon-zesty. As refreshing a bourbon as you are likely to find in the UK. **40% (80 proof).** *UK.*

Sam Clay (see Heaven Hill Aged 6 Years 80 Proof)

Sam Clay 8 Years (see Old Heaven Hill Very Rare Aged 8 Years 80 Proof)

Sam Sykes (see Heaven Hill 80 Proof)

Samuels 1844 (see Heaven Hill Aged 6 Years 101 Proof)

Seven Hills (see Evan Williams Aged 7 Years 86 Proof)

Smokey Jim (85) n21 excellent small-grain complexity; t22 rich, full arrival on the palate; brilliant mouthfeel; f21 back to a dark, juicy, fruity rye character towards the end; b21 genuinely complex and satisfying everyday bourbon. Excellent. **40% (80 proof)**

Ten High (70) n17 t18 f17 b18. Light, clean and untaxing. Good for mixing. **40% (80 proof).** *Barton.*

Tesco Old Kentucky (78) n19 t20 f19 b20. Young, sweet, very clean with a hint of hickory. **40% (80 proof)**

Tom Moore (83) n21 t20 f22 b20. The rye on the nose pops up at regular intervals on the palate, but overall this is a really deft, undemanding whiskey yet offering above-average complexity. **40% (80 proof).** *Barton.*

Tom Sims (see Heaven Hill Aged 6 Years 80 Proof)

T W Samuels (see Heaven Hill 80 Proof)

T W Samuels (see Heaven Hill 86 Proof)

T W Samuels 100 Proof (see Heaven Hill 100 Proof)

T W Samuels 6 Years 90 Proof (see Heaven Hill Aged 6 Years 90 Proof)

Red Eye Aged 6 Years (86) n*21* spot-on rye involvement: very complex; **t***22* honeyed and chewy; **f***21* lovely vanilla climb-down, with the grains having as big a say as the oak; **b***22* a bourbon of attractive complexity and weight. **45% (90 proof).** *Bardstown.*

Van Winkle Special Reserve (82) n*19* **t***22* **f***20* **b***21.* Subdued nose, then a sweet, almost molassed explosion before a quick fade. Good early oak, though. **45.2% (90.4 proof)**

Very Old Barton Aged 6 Years (88) n*22* green and lively with the rye really getting in amongst the powering corn. Green tea is also about; **t***22* brittle small grains melt into the sweetening corn: a touch oily; **f***22* remains sweet despite the onset of some drying oak; **b***22* it's a bit like sweetened green tea in alcohol with a strong rye kick-back. Unique as a style amongst bourbons and wholly enjoyable. **40% (80 proof).** *Barton.*

Vintage Bourbon 1976 bott 7 Mar 01 **(94) n***23* light muscovado sugar sprinkled over rye and even a touch of malt, the oak very relaxed; **t***24* stunning mouthfeel, gently oiled with a slow arrival of sweet corn and then a fruitier rye: again the oak is delicate and sympathetic; **f***23* gentle spices and a build-up of honey; **b***24* this barrel must have sat on the bottom level of a warehouse somewhere for it to be this unscathed and beautifully rounded after a quarter of a century of Kentucky sunshine. A freaky and fantastic bourbon you must find at all costs. **43% (86 proof).**

Vintage Bourbon 1980 bott 26 Oct, 00 **(90) n***22* surprisingly green corn and greener rye: enormous fresh grain despite weighty oak; **t***22* wonderul medium-sweet mouthfilling corn, a hint of tangerine and apple; **f***23* now it gets heavy with big rye kicking in with the liquorice oak; **b***23* outstanding whiskey offering different levels of complexity and enjoyment. A little classic. **43% (86 proof).**

Vintage Bourbon 1983 bott 10 Nov 00 **(87) n***22* mint, mango and liquorice; **t***22* enormous rye depth and bite; **f***21* softer vanilla; **b***22* very good weight and balance to a quite complex if a little oaky bourbon. **43% (86 proof).**

Virgin Bourbon Aged 7 Years 101 Proof (88) n*22* very gentle oak with distant and intriguing hints of rice paper and pine; **t***23* vaguely honeyed with lots of liquorice-toffee; **f***21* dries with rye-tingling spices; **b***22* seriously complex, big and lip-smacking. We are talking serious bourbon, here. **50.5% (101 proof).** *Heaven Hill.*

Virgin Bourbon Aged 15 Years 101 Proof (89) n*23* chunky oak, liquorice and a touch of lemon; **t***22* dry, crushing oak with just enough corn and demerara sweetness to keep on course; **b***22* small grains take control while the oak lifts slightly to leave a soft vanilla; **b***22* a drier version than some 15-y-o but substantial and stupendous all the same. **50.5% (101 proof).** *Heaven Hill.*

Walker & Scott Bourbon (84) n*23* **t***20* **f***20* **b***21.* A delightful pub bourbon of good age and impressive complexity. The nose in particular is an orgy of superb small grain. **40%.** *Samuel Smith UK.*

Weller Centennial 10 Years Old (85) n*23* soft fruit, citrus and freshly shelled peas: a delight; **t***21* very dry start with a soft oak kick and spices: very warming; **f***20* enormous natural toffee sweetens it at the finish; **b***21* as gentle as a cruise on the old Kentucky river. **50% (100 proof).**

Weller 12 Years Old (90) n*23* oak is the star here, and at several levels, offering heavier liquorice notes and soft vanilla. Mint and apple also get in on the act; **t***23* sublime corn attack but the oak gives it a bitter edge: this is enormously intense stuff; **f***21* back to that toffee again: sweet and creamy and seeing off the oak; **b***23* immensely deep and satisfying with a magnificent chewability. **45% (90 proof).**

Westridge (see Heaven Hill 80 Proof)

Wild Turkey (80) n20 t19 f21 b20. An improvement in recent years: the orangey nose is striking and impressive while the palate is thin. The finish toffees up for a rich finale. **40% (80 proof)**

Wild Turkey Aged 8 Years (86) n21 spicy orange with salt; t22 corn dominant but lovely coffee; f21 dry vanilla and other oaky notes, the spice returns; b22 not quite such a pressure cooker bourbon as a decade ago, subtlety replacing flavour power. **50.5% (101 proof).**

Wild Turkey Russell's Reserve Aged 10 Years (96) n23 stunning rye-citrus combo pans out to reveal a mint and oak-encrusted, leathery corn sweetness; t24 seriously mega for its age, not so much in the firm cocoa-oak but the utter enormity of the small-grain depth. Once more all paths lead to clean and chewy corn; f24 gentle, minty spices cool the mouth; b25 this is dream-time whiskey, entirely befitting the name of my close friend and mentor Jimmy Russell. This is a controlled explosion of complexity, the constant light sweetness overseeing those darker, brooding passages. Only Yoichi in Japan offers a stated 10-y-o whisky which can stand shoulder to shoulder with this, though not always. Entirely flawless whiskey. **50.5% (101 proof).**

Wild Turkey Aged 12 Years (90) n22 peaches and cream, topped with demerara sugar, beautiful nutty fruitcake; t22 pretty sweet on the uptake with that sugary quality bursting forward, and estery like an old Jamaican rum; f23 liquorice and corn interweave beautifully; b23 this is great whiskey, perhaps not the most complex from this stable but the effect is uplifting. **50.5% (101 proof).**

Wild Turkey Rare Breed batch W-T-02-91 **(94)** n24 gorgeous honey threading its way through diced dates, old leather and rye with a teasing sprinkling of spice: magnificent; t24 massively intense launch, waxy honeycomb with fabulously controlled demerara sweetness and an edge of rye; f22 long, lightly liquoriced toffee with the honey hanging on, as does the rye and a soft build-up of cocoa; t24 a big bourbon with the proportions being generous and almost perfectly proportioned. The classiest of class acts. **55% (110 proof).**

Wild Turkey Rare Breed batch W-T-01-99 **(89)** n23 toffee and nuts with big corn thrust; t22 sweet, soft, with building rye and spice; f22 spicy with liquorice and hints of honey; b22 compared to previous Rare Breeds this is relatively sweet and simple. Still beautiful, though. **54.2% (108.4 proof).**

W L Weller Special Reserve 7 Years Old (84) n21 t22 f20 b21 A bigger whiskey than of old with lots of orangey tones on the nose and a lush, sweet and peppery body. **45% (90 proof).** *For other members of the Weller "family" see also Old Weller and Weller.*

Woodford Reserve Distiller's Select (88) n22 some striking levels of light and heavy oak glued together by firm corn; the rye offers the excitement; t22 some sweetened coffee notes hit the tastebuds running; heavy muscovado sugar takes on the rye; f22 vanilla heavy at first then a hint of liquorice candy; b22 great balance: a whiskey with pretensions of being light but seems to fail at every turn. Busy, chewy and rye-enhanced. **45.2% (90.4 proof).** *Brown-Forman.*

Woodford Reserve Four Grain (90) n20 highly unusual with a different nose to any other bourbon I know: very light liquorice, kind of Old Forester but without the intensity, and extraordinary floral tones; t24 big and rambling with a quite massive flavour explosion. The small grains are working overtime to provide a deep spicy-fruit texture to the oak. The liquorice comes through, but so does the rye by the spadeful and much softer oilier corn notes. Sensational; f23 calms down, though it takes its time: very rarely have I experienced the small grains in a bourbon working with such complexity: the oak barely gets a look in; b23 what a supreme bourbon. The nose is a bit confusing, but once it hits the tastebuds it has one thing on its mind: to blow you away. I shall ensure a bottle of this is always somewhere near my desk in future. **47.2% (94.4 proof).** *Brown-Forman.*

Woodford Reserve Personal Selection (83) n21 t21 f20 b21. Heaps of toffee character, which tends by definition to make for a soft ride but at the expense of the complexity which is a byword of Woodford Reserve. Delightful in its own right with lovely rye-spice sub-plot, but the brilliance of Four Grain and Distillers' Select tends to spoil you a little. **45.2% (90.4 proof).** *Brown-Forman.*

Wm Morrison Old Kentucky Special No. 1 Brand (76) n18 t20 f19 b19. A very decent cooking bourbon with some weight, spice and natural toffee. A genuine chewing bourbon. **40% (80 proof).** *Wm Morrison UK. Ignore the back label nattering on about three years and blended and all that rubbish. This is a straight bourbon.*

Yellow Rose of Texas (see Heaven Hill 80 Proof)

Yellow Rose of Texas 8 Years (see Old Heaven Hill Very Rare Aged 8 Years 86 proof)

Tennessee Whiskey
GEORGE DICKEL

George Dickel Aged 10 Years Distilled in or Before 1986 (71) n17 t19 f17 b18. The only Dickel I have seen being sold either on a shelf or bar in the last 12 months. And my least favourite. Weirdly musty and out of alignment. Dickel is usually a lot, lot better than this load of tat. **43% (86 proof).**

JACK DANIEL

Gentleman Jack Rare Tennessee Whiskey (79) n19 t21 f20 b19. One of America's cleanest whiskeys, sweet and improbably light. An affront to hardened Jack drinkers, a blessing for those with a sweet tooth. **40% (80 proof).** *Brown-Forman.*

Jack Daniel's (Green Label) (84) n20 t21 f22 b21. A light but lively little gem of a whiskey. Starts as a shrinking violet, finishes as a roaring lion with nimble spices ripping into the developing liquorice. A superb session whiskey. **40% (80 proof).** *Brown-Forman.*

Jack Daniel's Old No. 7 Brand (Black Label) (87) n21 thick, oily, smoky, dense, corn syrupy ... it's Jack Daniel; t23 sweet, fat, chewy, various types of burnt notes: tofffee, toast etc. etc; f21 quite a sweet, fat and toffeed finale; b22 a quite unique whiskey at which many American whiskey connoisseurs turn up their noses. I always think it's worth the occasional visit; you can't beat roughing it a little. **43% (86 proof).** *Brown-Forman.*

Jack Daniel's Single Barrel (88) n22 more fruit on this than most Jacks, still plenty of liquorice and burnt toast; t22 spicy and immediately warming: some real kick to this with the blows softened by the sweetness of the corn and the surrounding thick oils; f22 very consistent with the sweetness fading, despite some rye input, then oak starting to make a stand; b22 a characterful, rich whiskey, with plenty of corn sweetness and some excellent spice. **40% (80 proof).** *Brown-Forman.*

VIRGINIA BOURBON

Virginia Gentleman 80 (cream, sepia and red label) **(84)** n20 t22 f21 b21. A very light bourbon with a distinctive, easy-going sweet corn effect then spicy, mildly bitter oak and cocoa. **40% (80 proof).** *A Smith Bowman.*

Virginia Gentleman 90 (coloured label) **(89)** n21 the leathery oak has much more to say than the corn, but it's all done in whispers; t23 charming entry onto the palate with, first, chewy oak then more teasing rye and a dash of honey here and there; f22 the small grains really come out to play, accompanied by spices, superb mouthfeel with excellent drying towards the very end; b23 you know, forget about this being the only Virginia whiskey. Romance apart, this is one hell of a whiskey where complexity is the foundation stone. Marvellous stuff. **45% (90 proof).** *A Smith Bowman.*

Corn Whiskey

Dixie Dew Kentucky Straight Corn Whiskey (89) n22 some very decent oak and vanilla to add to the dryish corn, complex by corn whiskey standards; **t**22 wonderfully balanced, starting dry and oaky then the corn building up with the sweetness; **f**22 long with even a dash of spice – much improved than in recent years; **b**23 brilliant whiskey that should have a far wider market. **50% (100 proof).** Heaven Hill.

J W Corn 100 Straight Corn Whiskey (87) n21 oily and rich with some much drier oak present; **t**22 thumping early oak offsets the sweet corn which fails to quite take off; **f**22 really spicy and big; **b**22 this has the biggest oak character on the market at the moment, which means a drier style and no shortage of spice. **50% (100 proof).** Heaven Hill.

Mellow Corn (85) n21 slight cooking oil aroma, but the oak adds a delicate spice; **t**22 full-bodied and textured, the oils helping the corn to stick to the roof of the mouth while a softly spiced sweetness develops; **f**21 sweet and chewy like a Barbadian rum; **b**21 I first drank this brand back in 1974 and I can safely say that I've never encountered it, or any other whisk(e)y, with an oilier texture: if you don't like the whiskey, you could always fry your eggs in it. Seriously delicious, though! **50%** Medley Company. (Heaven Hill).

Rye; Single Malt Rye
ANCHOR DISTILLERY

Old Potrero Single Malt Whiskey Aged One Year Essay 6-RW-ARM-3-A "a distilled spirit produced from rye malt mash aged ... in new uncharred oak barrels". In barrel 18 Apr 96, bott 8 Jan 98 **(86) n**18 a hint of feinty oil can be detected over the sharp rye but the worst of this burns off as it warms in the glass to reveal stupendous honey; **t**23 enormous presence, oily as one would expect, but the build-up over ever-sweetening fruit is astonishing; **f**23 the oils have burnt off early and now we are left with soft vanilla and a rye residue: it is sublime, even for something so young; **b**22 here we have a collector's item: a slightly flawed Old Potrero – a bit like finding an English stamp with the queen's head missing. These were early days in the company's distilling life and the middle cut is a little too wide affecting the nose ... but hey: they wanted to create a rye people would recognise 200 years ago, and this would be exactly it! But the other side of the same coin is that those oils give fabulous extra richness to the body. Still a beaut! **62.3% (124.6 proof).** 814 bottles.

Old Potrero Single Malt Whiskey Aged One Year Essay 7-RW-ARM-5 "a distilled spirit produced from rye malt mash... aged... in new uncharred oak barrels". In barrel 3 June 97, bott 25 May 99 **(88) n**20 oily, wide middle cut allows the rye a full, bitter-sweet run and lovely trademark honey bloom follows the rye wherever it goes; **t**23 very soft arrival on the palate, despite the strength, with gentle honey dovetailing with the much sharper, fruitier rye. The oil on the palate is a masterstroke as it clings to the roof of the mouth and won't let go; **f**22 amazing degree of vanilla for a year-old barrel but it's there with hints of orange; **b**23 this is just such expressive whiskey: I adore the extra oil and richness it brings. Something different but certainly not diffident. **61.75% (123.3 proof).** 2,175 Bottles.

Old Potrero Single Malt Whiskey Aged Two Years Essay 7-RW-ARM-6 "a distilled spirit produced from rye malt mash ... aged ... in new and used uncharred oak barrels". In barrel 31 Dec 97, bott 14 Jul 00 **(92) n**22 the extra year has introduced spice and a little dryness, bitter orange and biting rye; **t**24 sensational mouth arrival: the rye simply explodes on impact scattering rock-hard fruity debris around the palate. The honey takes time to arrive, but does so on the back of some mouthwatering grainy notes – extraordinary; **f**23 long and lusty with the rye still holding court. Citrus notes rise and fall, the rye fades and re-emerges, the brilliance is a constant; **b**23 in July 1900 this was the best two-year-old bottled whiskey the world had ever seen. **62.1% (124.2 proof).** 3,448 bottles.

Old Potrero Single Malt Whiskey Aged Two Years Essay 8-RW-ARM-7A/8A "a distilled spirit produced from rye malt mash ... aged ... in new and used uncharred oak barrels". In barrel 9 Dec 98, bott 20 Apr 01 **(85) n**21 spiced-up citrus, very firm grain with some sweetening toffee; **t**22 the toffee remains a constant but the rye pricks enough with its accompanying oil to give plenty to chew on; **f**21 constant: more of before, but with less rye bite and settling for a more bitter edge; **b**21 the complexity levels are down on this one thanks mainly to the rich vein of toffee than runs naggingly through the whiskey. **62.2% (124.4 proof).**

Old Potrero Single Malt Straight Rye Whiskey Aged Three Years Essay 5-RW-ARM-2-A (93) n24 textbook stuff: liquorice-embossed rye, hard as nails, but caresses the senses. You beauty! **t**24 big, uncompromising, bold and fruity. Just so sweet with hints of honey and demerara, but the firmness of the rye is the spine to it all and cocoa provides a perfect counterweight; **f**22 slightly toffeed with rich oaky-vanilla but all the time the rye peppers the tastebuds; **b**23 this is what makes rye whiskey, for me, the most enjoyable style in the world. Brazen and bedazzling. **62.6% (125.2 proof).** 1,880 bottles.

Old Potrero Single Malt Straight Rye Whiskey Aged Three Years Essay 8-RW-ARM-8-A (94) in barrel date 9 Dec 98, bott 19 Apr 02 **n**23 much drier and subtle. The rye is relatively closed, but open enough to get you salivating; **t**25 nothing closed about the rye now as it erupts from the first mouthful. Brilliant fruit (wild cherries)-honey balance, as good as any rye currently on the market. Faultless and fabulous, the candy sweetness is kept in check by the impervious rye. One of the greatest whiskey-tasting experiences money can buy; **f**23 much softer and well behaved now, going back to the comparative serenity of the nose. A hint of toffee-vanilla towards the finish; **b**23 when you open a bottle of this, you go for the long haul: this is no splash of water or coke job, and forget the ice. This, for its age and style, is the most unique whiskey in the world: expect to be thrown a few times before you learn to ride it. A very dear friend and colleague of mine is quoted as saying that the Old Potrero ryes are "the most noteworthy development in American whiskey in living memory." I kind of know what he means but cannot begin to agree. I was playing and coaching soccer in Maryland when they were still making rye there and I remember the deep sadness I felt when I was notified of the closure of the last distillery in the state where it more or less all began. And the shock and dismay at the news that Old Crow, Old Taylor and Old Grand-dad distilleries were all being closed to devastate bourbon-making in the Frankfort area. And never will I forget the tears I shed as Heaven Hill burned and the joy as I watched, stone by stone, Labrot & Graham rise from a pile of charming rubble (and the play area for my son and me) into Kentucky's one and only pot-still distillery. Rather, back in 1998 I wrote of Old Potrero in my book *Classic Bourbon Tennessee and Rye*, "This is the most exciting taste in world whiskey at the moment. The youngest classic of them all." Five years on every word still rings true.

Rye; Straight Rye

Classic Cask Straight Rye Aged 15 Years Distilled 1984 batch RW 101, bott 99 **(88) n**23: a voluptuous overture of spring flowers and under-ripe fruit. Quite brittle and clean with a surprising malt undertone; **t**23 the hardness of the rye arrives early and spreads sensuously around the mouth, painting an oily, spicy glow: mouthwatering and dangerously moreish; **f**21 somewhat tired with the oak suppressing the sweeter rye notes; **b**21 shows excellent balance early on but diminishes in style and complexity as the oak gathers and the age shows. Very enjoyable, nonetheless. **45% (90 proof).** *Classic Cask Co. Bardstown.*

Classic Cask Straight Rye Aged 15 Years Distilled 1986 batch RW 103, bott 01 **(75)** n20 t20 f17 b18. Pleasant and soft, but disappointingly missing the usual complexity and intensity one expects from a rye. **45% (90 proof)**. *Classic Cask Co. Bardstown.*

Jim Beam Rye (93) n24 lemon zest, mint and lavender: a stunning bag of tricks; t24 early rye broadside followed by some tender fruit and oak. This battle between rock-hard rigidity and gentle fruit is astonishing; f22 long and flinty with cocoa rounding things off; b23 almost certainly the most entertaining and consistent whiskey in the entire Jim Beam armoury. A classic without doubt.

Old Rip Van Winkle 12 Years Old Time Rye (90) n23 two-toned rye, both chunky and light and flitting: seriously attractive; t23 big crunchy, brittle rye kick from the very first moment, really beautifully fruity; f22 remains bitter and crisp at first but then softens as natural oaky-caramels appear; b22 a profound, fruity, refreshing and old-fashioned rye that's hard to find. **45% (90 proof)**. *Mac Y Denmark.*

Old Rip Van Winkle 13 Years Old Family Reserve Rye (91) n23 big and belligerent, the rye forms a fruity, rock-hard crust; t24 vroom ... !! Off she goes on a massive ryefest. Brilliant bitter-sweet grain stomps with hob-nailed boots around the palate, both fresh yet well aged. Everything is a contradiction – so complex; f21 quietens down alarmingly as the caramel kicks in which sweetens it a little while some bitter coffee/rye notes still chatter in the background; b23 an alarmingly complex whiskey that seems to make the rules up as it goes along. Anarchic and adorable. **47.8% (95.6 proof).**

Old Rip Van Winkle 15 Years Old (1985) Family Reserve Rye (91) n22 minty, firm oak but the rye does show good, fruity shape; t23 brilliant rye ruggedness, really hard at first but showing a feminine, fruity side: an intriguing mixture of molasses and demerara sugar sees off the oak; f23 that sweetness lasts the course, allowing the rye open season on the tastebuds; b23 a supremely improbable rye that has managed to retain a zesty freshness over 15 summers. Brilliant. **50% (100 proof).**

Old Rip Van Winkle 15 Years Old (79) n22 t20 f18 b19. Spicy rye, but the oak cuts deep on the nose while to taste mildly sappy but some rye does leak out of the oakiness. This is for the guy who buttonholed me at a tasting I gave in Zurich in 2002 and wanted to know about a Van Winkle 15-y-o rye he had recently tasted in a bar over 100 proof which had been there for some time and he felt was out of condition. Dug this out of my library: this bottling dates to around 1994/95. Seems to fit the bill: amazed it is still around. **53.5% (107 proof).**

Pikesville Supreme Straight Rye (87) n23 a curious and delicious mixture of traditional British scrumpy cider and new car interior: this is traditional straight rye at its freshest and fruitiest; t21 much lighter arrival than the nose suggests, even a hint of corn in there. The fruit slowly starts to return, but only after a sprinkling of brown sugar then a thumping measure of rye; f21 that usual Heaven Hill rye bitterness on the ending plus some caramel-vanilla to sweeten things a little; b22 not quite as in your face with the rye as was once the case. **40% (80 proof)**. *Heaven Hill.*

Rittenhouse Straight Rye (85) n21 the rye is barely awake but offers soft fruit amid the toffee-vanilla; t21 clean and sweet, the rye takes a little time to make its mark but eventually does so to add warming spices: all very subdued, though; f21 bitter-sweet with accent on the bitter, pretty oily; b22 this, the only rye in America I'm aware of spelt "Whisky" rather than "whiskey", has always been the least rye-pronounced. But this bottling makes a virtue of it. **40% (80 proof)**. *Heaven Hill.*

Rittenhouse Straight Rye 100 Proof Bottled in Bond (86) n21 the extra alcohol still does little to rouse the rye from its slumbers; t22 much earlier rye thrust, subsides as the body sweetens, then reappears; f21 more oily and clingy to the palate with a late, slightly burned toasty finale; **b**22 a weighty guy. **50% (100 proof).** *Heaven Hill.*

Sazerac Rye 18 Years Old (96) n25 traditonal straight rye doesn't come more complex, confident or clean than this: there is a hard grainy edge, but it is softened by over-ripe juicy cherry and blackberries. Subtle and sophisticated; **t**24 the brittle quality of the rye shows to full effect here, but there is a softness – a tad oily – which also beguiles. Fruity and improbably flavoursome: close your eyes and wallow; **f**23 takes a little rest as the toffee makes a mark, but such is the intensity of the rye and oak that waves of spices and fruit continue to break against the tastebuds; **b**24 I remember being given my first sample of this: it was in the lab at Buffalo Trace before it went into bottle and a legendary brand was born. I was standing at the time ... I had to sit down. I wondered what it would be like to sample away from the romance of the beautiful distillery where the casks were laying ... well, now you know. I was presented with the first-ever bottle of Sazerac Rye as a token of thanks for my help in identifying its qualities and (some hope) weaknesses. I trust the person who stole it out of my bag while I was giving a tasting in New York appreciated it as much as I. If he/she still has it, I would be grateful if it is returned, care of my publishers, no questions asked. And one final thing: my late father was born in 1916. This is the 1,916th whiskey I have tasted for this book. Need I say more? **45% (90 proof).**

Wild Turkey Kentucky Straight Rye (88) n21 very gentle rye on a decent oak base; **t**23 the extra strength helps propel the lush rye forward, but it remains sweet and refrains from nipping and biting ... at first; **f**22 nips and bites and becomes more bitter; **b**22 an improved rye with much better integrated rye fruitiness than of old. **50.5% (101 proof).**

Kentucky Whiskey

Early Times Kentucky Whiskey (71) n17 **t**18 **f**18 **b**.18 Lightweight and thin, the corn tends to go it alone with a touch of toffee to prop it up. **40% (80 proof).** *Brown-Forman.*

American Whiskey Blend

Seagram's 7 Crown (89) n23 rich with heavy vanilla and rye; **t**22 complex grain and oak battle: the softness of the neutral grain acts as the perfect foil for the crisper rye; **f**22 silky, sweet, soft corn and vanilla; **b**22 this is beautiful whiskey, but on this evidence not a patch on the rye-infested giant it has been for the last couple of decades. The rye level seems to have been reduced and I trust that this is just a rogue batch. Still a little mouthwatering stunner for sure, but it was much better the way it was: semi-wild and flavour-explosive. Like that it was an American institution – something too rare and precious to be tampered with ... **40% (80 proof).**

Japanese Whisky

Sadly, if you want to discover Japanese whisky you must still go to Japan. Of the 115 Japanese whiskies I have tasted for this book, only a handful are available in markets outside the nation in which they were distilled or blended. This is very frustrating when you see that many of the distilleries are nowhere near on full production and some are either silent or closed.

Part of the problem has been the Japanese custom of refusing to trade with their rivals. Therefore a Japanese whisky, if not made completely from home-distilled spirit, will instead contain a percentage of Scotch rather than whisky from fellow Japanese distillers.

This, ultimately, is doing the industry no favours at all. The practice is partly down to the traditional work ethics of company loyalty and an inherent, and these days false, belief that Scotch whisky is automatically better than Japanese. Back in the late 1990s I planted the first seeds in trying to get rival distillers to discuss with each other the possibility of exchanging whiskies to ensure that their distilleries worked more economically.

In the meantime word is getting round that Japanese whisky is worth finding. Indeed, there is so much interest in these little-known brands (outside Japan that is) that last year I even gave an all Japanese whisky tasting in Holland.

Two leading lights are getting whisky drinkers switched on to just what oriental delights we are missing: the malts of Yoichi and Hakushu. Both make whiskies that rank unquestionably among the very finest in the world, though Yoichi – the brilliance of which I'm proud to have first brought to the world's attention in 1997 – these days has to be a little more careful with their use of sherry. Less than a handful of Scotch distilleries, though, can match their and Hakushu's supremely complex makes.

As if stirred by the recent success and fame of Yoichi, other distillers in Japan have begun looking at bringing out single cask bottlings and I hope to have reviews of a number of them for the 2005 edition. However, they can be hard to find for the whisky drinker – even in Japan. Some sell out almost as soon as they are released.

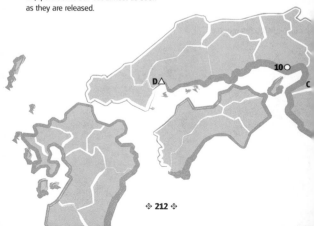

But, perhaps above all, it has been a breath of fresh air to see the Scotch Malt Whisky Society also recognise the beauty of Japanese malt. Some of their bottlings of Hakushu, Yoichi and Yamazaki have already hit legendary status, coming as a bit of a shock to quite a number of Scotch whisky connoisseurs.

The next, more tricky bit, is to find a way of getting a wider range of blends on to the world's markets. Although both Tsuru and Super Nikka are regular relaxing drinks for me, there is a wonderful delicacy to Suntory's blends that remain fresh and irresistible.

What I would like over the next few years is the ability to discuss their merits (or otherwise) with whisky lovers around the world, rather than simply explain to them what they are missing.

Key	
△	**Major Cities**
○	Distilleries

DISTILLERY LOCATOR

1	Hokkaido	8	Gotemba
2	Yoichi	9	Mars Shinshu
3	Sendai	10	Yamazaki
4	Shirakawa	**A**	**Sapporo**
5	Karuizawa	**B**	**Tokyo**
6	Hanyu	**C**	**Osaka**
7	Hakushu	**D**	**Hiroshima**

Single Malts
CHICHIBU

Golden Horse Chichibu db **(80) n**19 t21 f20 b20. Light, toasty and delicate yet the oak is prominent throughout. Good balancing sweet malt, though. **43%**. *Toa.*

Golden Horse Chichibu 10 Years Old Single Malt db **(82) n**19 t22 f21 b20. Developing citrus notes lighten the weight as the oak and sweet malt go head to head. **43%**. *Toa.*

Golden Horse Chichibu 12 Years Old Single Malt db **(85) n**20 tangerine peel and rice paper, a hint of bourbon, perhaps? t22 juicy, fruity, mouthwatering then spicy. A real working-over for the palate with the faintest hint of something bourbony about to happen; f21 some excellently well behaved oak shepherding the malt; b22 a malt that proudly boasts its own style. One of those whiskies that grows on you each time you taste it. **50%**. *Toa.*

Chichibu 14 Years Old Single Malt db **(89) n**20 tangerine peel and rice: two years older than the 12-y-o, that hint of bourbon has now become a statement; t23 brilliantly eclectic arrival on the palate with no organisation at all to the flurry of malt and bourbony oak and tangerine-fruity spices that are whizzing around; f23 pretty long with firm vanilla and a distinctive oiliness. Something approaching a whiff of smoke adds some extra ballast to the oak; b23 we are talking mega, in-your-face taste explosions here. A malt with a bourbony attitude that is unquestionably superb. **57%**. *Toa.*

FUJI GOTEMBA, 1973. Kirin Distillers.

Fuji Gotemba 20th Anniversary Pure Malt db **(84) n**21 t20 f22 b21. The nose is a lovely mixture of fruit and mixed oak; the body has a delightful sheen and more fruit with the malt. Handsome stuff. **40%**. *Kirin.*

HAKUSHU, 1973. Suntory.

Hakushu 1982 db **(86) n**23 dense but very clean oloroso with a touch of medium-roast Santos coffee tossed in for extra depth. Plenty of cereal amid soft oak and smoke; t22 silky arrival and immediately juicy and then a spicy spread across the palate forming into distinct, burnt raisin; f20 quick and closed with some coffee notes returning as the oak dries; b21 starts outstandingly but finishes too quickly to be a Japanese great. **61%**

Hakushu 1984 db **(95) n**22 delicate banana and malt with a gentle fly-past of peat. The oak is unbowed but sympathetic; t25 staggeringly beautiful: wave upon wave of astonishing complexity crashes against the tastebuds. The malt is intense but there is plenty of room for oak in varying guises to arrive, make eloquent speeches and retire. The intensity of spice is spot on – perfect; f24 long, more spice and greater malt intensity as the oak fades. Only the softest hints of smoke; mouthwatering to the last as mild coffee appears; b24 a masterpiece malt of quite sublime complexity and balance. The sort of experience that gives a meaning to life, the universe and everything ... **61%**

Hakushu 1988 db **(92) n**21 overtly peaty and dense, pleasant but lacking usual Hakushu complexity; t24 mouthwatering start with massively lively malt and fresh peating hanging on to its coat-tails. Some amazing heather–honey moments that have no right to be there; the peat intensifies then lightens; f23 lots of rich peat and then intense vanilla; crisp and abrupt at the finale with late bitter chocolate; b24 like all great whiskies this is one that gangs up on you in a way you are not expecting: the limited complexity on the nose is more than compensated for elsewhere. Superb. If this were an Islay malt the world would be drooling over it. **61%**

Suntory Pure Malt Hakushu Aged 10 Years db **(89) n**23 exemplary grassiness, fresh malt: mouthwatering and refreshes the senses; t24 spot-on, top-of-the-range malt. The freshness and integrity of the barley is beyond belief:

thirst-quenching whisky of the highest order; f20 becomes rather toffeed and less well defined. A subtle display of spice compensates; b22 beautifully crafted whisky that's fresh and rewarding. **40%**. *The name Hakushu appears in small writing on the front label.*

Suntory Pure Malt Hakushu Aged 12 Years bott 2002 db **(95) n23** fresh clean malt with the vaguest hint of peat imaginable, but such is the clarity of the nose it can be spotted; t24 just wonderful crispness to the mouthwatering barley, gristy and fresh with a building of stupendous peaty spices; f24 beautifully refined with some oak just offering extra chewability; b24 this is one of the best distillery-bottled whiskies since the turn of the new millennium. Simply magnificent. **43%**

Suntory Pure Malt Aged 12 Years (no bottling date) db **(84) n20 t23 f20 b21.** Deliciously malty with no little fruit, but the finish is disappointingly flat save for some welcome spices. **43%**

Suntory Pure Malt Hakushu 15 Years Old Cask Strength db **(92) n21** curiously muted: one assumes it is a fruit-oak influence that is keeping the higher barley notes at bay; t24 gets back into the old Hakushu groove with a truly stunning display of mouthwatering malt in all its regalia: honeycomb too. Somehow manages to be big and chewy and light and flighty all at the same time; f23 good length, toasted honey, marmalade and spices; b24 if only the nose had been right, this would have been one of the truly great whiskies. The enormity on the palate is something you are unlikely to forget for a long time while the balance between barley, honey and oak is extraordinary. **56%**

Suntory Pure Malt Hakushu Aged 20 Years db **(94) n23** fresh, mildly grapey fruit combined with subtle waves of peat; t24 the peat is now less subtle: wave upon wave of it bringing with it flotsam of drifting oak and then a very sharp malt tang; f23 long, sweet spice but the oak forms a chunky alliance with the firm peat. The bitter-sweet compexity almost defies belief; b24 a hard-to-find malt, but find it you must. Yet another huge nail in the coffin of those who purport Japanese whisky to be automatically inferior to Scotch. **56%**

Scotch Malt Whisky Society Cask 120.1 Aged 21 Years **(93) n23** fruit and nuts sprinkled with fresh malt, very muesli in style, fresh oak, clean yet astonishingly complex; t23 voluptuous mouthfeel, the barley is intense and so mouthwatering. Some lovely nip and bite adds extra complexity; f22 slightly shot but clean and enormously malty; b25 a malt of genuine class and integrity. The entire balance of the whisky is flawless. **60%**

Scotch Malt Whisky Society Cask 120.2 Aged 14 Years **(92) n23** no more than a dusting of peat over soft cocoa, sensuous and teasing, like fingers running down your spine, barely touching the skin; t23 a firm, biting malt again uncloaks its peat slowly and with more than a degree of eroticism; f22 a slight bourbony-oaky sweetness intervenes on the keyhole peat show; b24 do you drink this whisky or make love to it? I'm not altogether sure. One of the few whiskies I recommend with water ... in the form of a cold shower! **62%. nc ncf sc.**

KARUIZAWA, 1955. Mercian.

Karuizawa Pure Malt 12 Years **(862) n19** slightly iffy: borderline between good and so-so sherry; t21 firm, crisp malt and sweet vanilla; f24 orange marzipan topped by black chocolate; b22 the finish is absolutely astonishing, one of the best in the business. **40%**

Karuizawa Pure Malt 15 Years **(76) n17 t21 f20 b18.** Some vague sulphur notes on the sherry do no favours for what appears to be an otherwise top-quality malt. (Earlier bottlings have been around the 87–88 mark, with the fruit, though clean, not being quite in balance but made up for by an astonishing silkiness with roast chestnut puree and malt). **40%**

Karuizawa Pure Malt Aged 17 Years **(90)** n*20* bourbony, big oak and pounding fruit; t*24* enormous stuff: the link between malt and fruit is almost without definition; f*23* amazingly long and silky. Natural vanilla melts in with the almost concentrated malt; b*23* brilliant whisky beautifully made and majestically matured. Neither sweetness nor dryness dominates, always the mark of a quality dram. **40%**

KOMAGATAKE

Komagatake 10 Years Old Single Malt db **(78)** n*19* t*20* f*19* b*20*. A very simple, malty whisky that's chewy and clean with a slight hint of toffee. **40%**. *Mars.*

SENDAI, 1969. Nikka.

Sendai 12 Years Old (code 06C40C) db **(83)** n*17* t*22* f*23* b*21*. To put it politely, the nose is pretty ordinary; but what goes on afterwards is relative bliss with a wonderful, oily, fruity resonance. For those thinking in Scotch terms, this is very Speysidey with the malt intense and chewy. **45%**. *Nikka.*

Sendai 12 Years Old (code 08J48B) **(86)** n*19* very crisp, clean but slightly closed; t*23* an eruption of magnificent cut-grass-fresh malts with some spicy citrus back-up; f*22* lots of vanilla and other soft oaky tanginess; b*22* good, solid whisky which, though decent and enjoyable as a single malt, offers the blender much more excitement. **45%**. *Nikka.*

SHIRAKAWA

Shirakawa 32 Years Old Single Malt **(94)** n*23* ripe mango meets a riper, rye-encrusted bourbon. We are talking a major aroma here; t*24* the most intense malt you'll ever find explodes and drools all over your tastebuds. To make the flavour bigger still, the oak adds a punchy bourbon quality. Beautiful oils coat the roof of the mouth to amplify the performance; f*23* long, sweet and malty. Some fruitiness does arrive but it is the oak-malt combination that just knocks you out; b*24* just how big can an unpeated malt whisky get? The kind of malt that leaves you in awe, even when you thought you had seen and tasted them all. **55%**. *Takara.*

YAMAZAKI, 1923. Suntory.

Yamazaki 1979 db **(86)** n*22* sweet local oak, mildly bourbony but curiously vegetative besides. A soft sprig of mint freshens it further; t*21* resounding oak from the start, some bite and then a wave of ultra-sweet malt; f*22* surprisingly soft with rich vanilla and further, confident and continuous waves of malt and natural caramel tones. The oak has calmed superbly; b*21* many signs of tiredness, but sheer charm and richness of character wins through. **56%**

Yamazaki 1991 db **(88)** n*21* bourbony and light with a substratum of soft malt; t*23* astonishing unfurling of mouthwatering malt tones that spreads over the mouth revealing a subtle hint of smoke and beautifully graceful oak; f*22* long, lashings of cocoa powder and again soft barley hand-in-hand with gentle oak; b*22* closed when cold, improves dramatically when warmed on the hand. But the mouth arrival really does deserve a medal. **61%**

Yamazaki 1993 db **(87)** n*23* smoky and clean; gristy and Port Ellen-ish with a bit of extra exotic oak; t*23* sweet, spicy, vaguely Islay-ish start with the peats developing but not at the expense of dense malt. The oak is refined and there is something unusually coastal for a non-Scottish peated malt; f*20* rather hard, closed and brittle. Metallic malt scrapes against rock-like peat; b*21* a real surprise package. At times quite Islay-ish in style – Port Ellen in particular – but the finish is more realistic. A really delicious experience nonetheless.

Suntory Pure Malt Yamazaki 10 Years Old db **(79)** n*20* t*21* f*19* b*19*. Almost unnatural fruitiness, as though wild fruit yeast spores have been at work. Malty and sweet, nonetheless. **40%**

Suntory Pure Malt Yamazaki 12 Years Old db **(86) n**21 butterscotch and jam tarts, a slight chalky oakiness; **t**22 mouthwatering malt, fresh and then slow, gathering vanilla; **f**22 long and remaining intensely malty and clean; **b**21 an enormous leap in quality from the 10-y-o. On the market you might also find darker versions of Yamazaki 12, usually slightly older bottlings containing a peaty substratum and fruit and toffee replacing the intense, lighter malt. Over the last 10 years or so my average score for these has been: (86) n20 t23 f21 b22 ... so little difference in quality, just style. **43%**

Suntory Pure Malt Yamazaki 18 Years Old db **(86) n**22 a bourbony fanfare suggests great age, pipe smoke and creaking leather. Sweet with a beeswaxy texture. Some spice suggests the faintest of peat. Hangs together imperiously; **t**22 a slightly battered array of oaky notes limps alongside the strained malt. A charming sweetness overcomes the excesses of the big age; **f**21 superficial smoky malt notes adhere to an embracing waxiness. Quite estery and almost like pot-still rum in style; **b**21 not a dram I was once over-keen on, it has, in recent bottlings, shown much more guile and complexity. **43%**

Suntory Pure Malt Yamazaki 25 Years Old db **(91) n**23 quite intoxicating marriage between grapey fruitiness and rich oak: supremely spiced and balanced with a wave of pure bourbon following through; **t**23 big, big oloroso character then an entrancing molassed, burnt raisin, malty richness; **f**22 subtle spices, poppy seed with some late bitter oak; **b**23 being matured in Japan, the 25 years doesn't have quite the same value as Scotland. So perhaps in some ways this can lay claim to be one of the most enormously aged, oak-laden whiskies that has somehow kept its grace and star quality. **43%**

Suntory Pure Malt Yamazaki Cask Strength db **(88) n**22 very light, flimsy weight but the malty grassiness impresses; **t**23 absolutely pure Yamazaki in concentrate: refreshing malt that sweetens and fattens; **f**21 a light, toffeed finale without the complexity of either the nose or early palate; **b**22 a malt of indisputably high quality. **56%**

Scotch Malt Whisky Society Cask 119.1 Aged 22 Years **(81) n**20 **t**22 **f**20 **b**19. Enormous amounts of natural toffee from the bourbony oak. Missing some complexity but the overall experience is pretty rewarding. **51%. nc ncf sc.**

Scotch Malt Whisky Society Cask 119.4 Aged 10 Years **(92) n**22 young, thumping peat, very clean and curiously non-coastal in style; **t**24 a peat explosion of almost unbelievable intensity. Nothing quite like this the world over (now) as the intense barley sweetness is both gristy and mashy; **f**24 a long, long, long finale as it takes a while for all that peat to disperse. It does so with both elegance and eloquence with the melt-in-the-mouth malt simply knocking you out; **b**22 not many marks for balance here, as it's pretty one-sided. But anyone missing out on this experience will kick themselves. Perhaps it should be re-named Banzai! **58%**

YOICHI, 1934. Nikka.

Hokkaido 12 Years Old db **(87) n**23 a mixed bag of citrus and oak, really very beautifully balanced; **t**22 very firm malt and crisp-textured, even the fruit is hard; **f**21 very light with crisp barley and drying vanilla; **b**21 full-flavoured malt with absolutely zero yield. Just ricochets around the palate. **43%.** *Nikka.*

Nikka Single Cask Malt Whisky 10 Years Old dist 14/12/88, bott 14/12/98 db **(93) n**23 big oak influence: bourbony in character with ripe plums, too. One assumes local oak has been used; **t**24 seriously big bourbon character: massively sweet, rich deep barley and the lightest rumble of peat; **f**22 gentle, oily with some molassed sugar on the rolling smoke; **b**24 this is a seriously big whisky for the serious whisky drinker. Amazingly high-quality malt where the wood plays the dominant role but leaves space enough for malt development. **62.2%.** *Nikka. From the Yoichi distillery.*

Nikka Single Cask Malt Whisky 10 Years Old dist 21/1/89, bott 3/12/99 db **(86) n**22 telling fruit is fresh yet confident enough to form an alliance with the oak: pretty heady; **t**21 dry and spicy start with first malt then fruit making an impact, lots of bite and bristle; **f**21 remains dry and biting and a small burst of smoke makes a late entrance, becoming a little silkier towards the end; **b**22 a Japanese malt with attitude. **59.5%. Nikka. From the Yoichi distillery.**

Yoichi 10 Years Old (code 02C42 new "Yoichi" distillery label) db **(86) n**18 Oh, no! Only once before in 15 years have I ever nosed a Yoichi with an off-note, and for this book I find a second! A minor blemish, but sulphured sherry butt has intervened, but such is the character of the malt the damage has been limited; **t**23 silky, ultra-intense, almost concentrated malt actually outguns the rich fruit; **f**23 very long with some beautiful vanilla harmonising with the malt. There is wave upon wave of complexity offering, finally, a buttery finale; **b**22 for a malt scarred by a poor cask, this has recovered brilliantly. The complexity levels think about heading through the roof. **45%. Nikka.**

Yoichi 10 Years Old (code 14B22 new "Yoichi" distillery label) db **(88) n**18 fruity but sulphur blemish then fine malt notes maintain the shape; **t**23 very hard, biting malt: firm in style, almost like a blended whisky, but some fruit softens the impact; **f**23 a build-up of gentle, peaty spices all the more remarkable for there having been little sign of smoke on the nose or early palate; **b**24 typical Yoichi. Even when it shows a flaw it recovers to an unbelievable degree: like a champion ice skater who falls at the first leap and then dances on as if nothing happened. Keeps you guessing to the very last about what is to happen next. Fabulous verve and complexity. **45%. Nikka.**

Yoichi 10 Years Old (code 12I32 old Hokkaido "Yoichi" distillery label) db **(91) n**22 the peat brushes the nose like a feather over skin: just so delicate; **t**23 immediate flinty malt, amazingly hard and tooth-cracking then softened slowly by a salty, peaty edge; **f**23 peaty, delicate and now as soft, thanks to vanilla, as it was previously uncompromisingly hard. Some toffee and coffee aid the finale; **b**23 yet another teasing, unpredictable dram from Yoichi. **43%. Nikka.**

Yoichi 10 Years Old (code 14H62A old Hokkaido "Yoichi" distillery label) db **(91) n**23 big malt but it is the delicate quality of the peat that is most remarkable. Oak is present, but this is almost too clean to be true; **t**23 sweet and soft, then that Yoichi trademark gradual build-up of peat; **f**22 hard and brittle despite the softness of the peat, long and chewy with a hint of liquorice and honey; **b**23 the crispness and bite of this whisky makes it almost blend-like in style – which goes to underline the complexity. **43%. Nikka.**

Yoichi 10 Years Old (code 14H62B old Hokkaido "Yoichi" distillery label) db **(89) n**23 fruity, oranges, a sprinkling of peat and fresh malt; **t**21 enormously malty with the peat arriving late; **f**22 soft vanilla and more grapey fruit then the peats come into their own; **b**23 soft and delicate with beautifully chewy peat throughout. **43%. Nikka.**

Yoichi 10 Years Old (code 24G48C old Hokkaido "Yoichi" distillery label) db **(93) n**23 for an aroma carrying smoke this is almost austere: but this is an illusion. Some crisp malty, softly peated notes give it a delicate depth and massive sophistication; **t**23 enormous malt, absolutely brimming with lusty barley. Refreshing and mouthwatering, yet all the time that soft peat is present; **f**24 a quite brilliant marriage between rich barley and soft oak. No more than the slightest hint of very distant smoke; **b**23 a Yoichi in its "Old Speyside" phase, with just a waft of peat-reek to add some ballast to the enormous, clean malt. The fade is nothing short of fabulous. A Japanese version of Ardmore: whisky for grown-ups. **43%. Nikka.**

Yoichi 10 Years Old (code 24H18C old Hokkaido "Yoichi" distillery label) db **(89) n**20 firm, very lightly peated malt with softening vanilla, fruity; **t**23 honeyed and much sweeter than the nose suggests, mouthfilling and oily; **f**23 gentle

‍‍‍
~ Yoichi ~

peppers mix with the barley but the sweetness pervades on the very long, mildly peated finish; **b**23 another bottle of understated genius. **43%. Nikka.**

Yoichi 12 Years Old (code 06C14 new Yoichi label with distillery drawing) db **(91) n**21 spicy fresh oloroso; **t**24 big, clean sultana-fruit with a gathering intensity of ripe dates and sweet, gently smoked malt; **f**22 dies slightly, but the dates remain, as does the smoke. The oak kicks in with a late bitter finale; **b**24 absolutely magnificent malt with a no-holds-barred intensity of fruit and malt. **45%. Nikka.**

Yoichi 12 Years Old (code 16J32 new Yoichi label with distillery drawing) db **(87) n**20 clean fruit and soft oak; **t**22 massive malt and toffee, almost like a night drink; **f**23 major complexity kicks in with some incredibly juicy fruity notes marrying into a ripping malt theme; **b**22 a pretty light Yoichi almost devoid of peat. After getting over a toffee-led lull the malt comes to life with impressive results. **45%. Yoichi.**

Yoichi 12 Years Old (code 20F18D old cream label) **(86) n**23 a two-tiered nose, both yielding and biting. There seems to be something of a cut-grass maltiness that is nipping away, while a softer, loftier fruit note soothes; **t**22 big, big malt arrival then a firm oak; **f**21 a fraction soapy but malt sweetens; **b**20 after the great nose, this one fails to really get cracking in Yoichi's usually sophisticated way. **43%. Nikka.**

Yoichi 15 Years Old (code 10J44 old green back label) db **(94) n**23 roast chestnuts plus salty, soft peat and dried dates: awesome complexity; **t**24 the dates have moistened, the peat positively glows, having been seasoned with salt, the fruitiness is full but in perfect proportion; **f**23 for the enormity of the nose and mouth arrival, the soft peated spices offer a charming sophistication to the intense barley. The fruit remains yielding and the oak no less soft and accommodating; **b**24 the kind of whisky that propels a distillery into super league status. A classic. **45%. Nikka.**

Yoichi 15 Years Old (code 06C10 new buff-coloured back label) db **(90) n**22 nutty, intense clean malt with just a light dusting of peat. The fruits are light and plummy; **t**22 very clean malt, almost gristy in its delicate nature. The peat no more than tickles the tastebuds. A weak grapejuice sweetness offers further complexity; **f**23 amazingly delicate, a beautiful combination of barley and vanilla. The peat remains playful and wonderfully balanced; **b**23 this is a succulent malt of enormous complexity. Typical Yoichi. **45%. Nikka.**

Yoichi 20 Years Old db **(95) n**23 magnificently intense oloroso (a tiny fleck of sulphur burns off in about 10 minutes when warmed), the background malt oak-laden; **t**23 again it's oloroso that leads the way, apparently too intensely at first but quickly settling to allow some stupendous spices to unravel and create balance. Fabulous bitter-sweet harmony; **f**25 Okay, guys, help me out here. Spot the fault. I can't. The fruit is now spotlessly clean and displaying a grapey complexity, the spices are warming but not entirely engulfing, the oak is firm and adds no more than a hint of dryness and at last the malt comes into full play to offer both mouthwatering barley and something slightly smoky. If you can pick a defect, let me know; **b**24 I don't know how much they charge for this stuff but either alone or with mates get some for one hell of an experience. What makes it all the more remarkable is that there is a slight sulphury note on the nose: once you taste the stuff that becomes of little consequence. **52%. Nikka.**

Scotch Malt Whisky Society Cask 116.1 Aged 16 Years (94) n24 a style of Yoichi I know so well and so adore: half bourbon-oaky character, half proud malt. The intensity and complexity is nothing short of brilliant; **t**23 a perfect match to the nose: sweet bourbony tones, then oak-extracted toffee intensified by stunning malt; **f**23 long, rich, chewy, mildly spiced and clean as a whistle; **b**24 brilliantly made malt in total harmony with its oaky confines. If this were Scotch, it would be about 30-y-o in style; if it were bourbon, it would be from Frankfort. Need I say more? **56.6%. nc ncf sc.**

Scotch Malt Whisky Society Cask 116.2 **(91)** n*22* big and bourbony, sweet malt and oak infusing to form a marmalade fruitiness; t*23* some age on this, with again some major bourbon-style sweetness lifting from the vanillins. The malt follows later, clean, intense and chewy; f*23* and so it goes on: more of the same, wave upon wave as if in a loop; b*23* totally top rate. This is where single malt meets bourbon in style. The battle is long and bloody and only one winner emerges: the person lucky enough to be drinking it.

Scotch Malt Whisky Society Cask 116.3 Aged 11 Years **(84)** n*22* t*21* f*20* b*21*. Chewy, bourbon-caramel character with decent spice on the finish. Perhaps lacks the usual Yoichi complexity, though. **60.6%. nc ncf sc.**

Scotch Malt Whisky Society Cask 116.4 Aged 13 Years **(88)** n*23* east meets west: ol' West Virginia, that is. Massive bourbony kick before the amazingly complex and light malty notes filter through. Intriguingly delicious; t*22* some citrus tones fleetingly come to life before rich oak and richer malt take command; f*21* bitter-sweet and drying before a mildly molassed sugary oakiness wins through; b*22* a pretty challenging whisky to Scotch malt lovers, as the style is very Japanese. It allows a bourbony-oaky incursion so far before setting down its limits. Will that incursion have gone too far for some purists, I wonder? **64.9%. nc ncf sc.**

Unspecified Malts

Nikka Whisky From the Barrel **(89)** n*20* carries some weight; good age and subtle malty sugars; t*23* exemplary mouthfeel: delightful oils and nipping spices but the malt remains clean and very sweet; f*22* some dryer oakiness but the malt keeps its balancing sweetness; b*24* a whisky that requires a bit of time and concentration to get the best out of. You will discover something big and exceptionally well balanced. **51.4%.** *Nikka.*

Vatted Malts

All Malt **(86)** n*22* delicate yet intensely malty: a bit like it says on the bottle, in fact! Those who drink Scotch will recognise the style as Speyside in its grassy, mouthwatering tones and as clean and clear on the nose as a crystal spring. When warmed, some smoke appears (aromatically, I mean!); t*21* fresh and then sharply intense, with a fleeting hardness more associated with unmalted barley. Brilliantly mouthwatering and chewy with a slow unravelling of distant peatiness; f*21* late arrival of drier vanilla, oaky tones and Java coffee: long and delicious; b*22* the best example by a mile of an almost unique style of vatted whisky: both malt and "grain" are distilled from entirely malted barley, identical to Kasauli malt whisky in India. Stupendous grace and balance. **40%.** *Nikka.*

Malt Club **(77)** n*18* t*20* f*18* b*21*. Young in character with attractive vitality from the moment it crunches the tastebuds. Really lovely balance throughout. **40%.** *Nikka.*

Mars Maltage Pure Malt 8 Years Old **(84)** n*20* t*21* f*21* b*22*. A very level, intense, clean malt with no peaks or troughs, just a steady variance in the degree of sweetness and oak input. Impossible not to have a second glass of. **43%.** *Mars.*

Pure Malt Black batch 02C58A **(95)** n*24* an exquisitely crafted nose: studied peat in luxuriant yet deft proportions nestling amid some honeyed malt and oak. The balance between sweet and dry is faultless. There is neither a single off-note nor a ripple of disharmony. The kind of nose you can sink your head into and simply disappear; t*23* for all the evident peat, this is medium-weighted, the subtlety encased in a gentle cloak of oil; f*23* long, silky, fabulously weighted peat running a sweet course through some surging malt and liquorice tones with a bit of salt in there for zip; b*25* well, if anyone can show me a better-balanced whisky than this you know where to get hold of me. You open a bottle of this at your peril: best to do so in the company of friends. Either way, it will be empty before the night is over. **43%**. *Nikka*.

Pure Malt Red batch 02C30B **(86) n**21 firm vanilla gives an oaky lead to this one; **t**21 light and malty with the vanilla again coming up fast: light-bodied otherwise with a dash of honey; **f**22 bang on course in character with the oak sticking gently to its task while the malt weaves tasty patterns on the tastebuds; **b**22 a light malt that appears heavier than it actually is with an almost imperceptible oiliness. **43%**. Nikka.

Pure Malt White batch 02C30C **(92) n**23 massive, Islay-style peat with a fresh sea kick thanks to brine amid the barley; **t**24 again, the peat-reek hangs firmly on the tastebuds from the word go, the sweetness of the barley tempered by some drying oaky notes suggesting reasonable age. Lots of subtle oils bind the complexity; **f**22 liquorice and salt combine to create a powerful malty-oak combo. An oily, kippery smokiness continues to the very end; **b**23 a big peaty number displaying the most subtle of hands. **43%**. Nikka.

Pure Malt White batch 06J26 **(91) n**22 soft peat interrupted by gentle oak; **t**23 biting, nippy malt offering a degree of orangey-citrus fruit amid the building smoke; **f**22 sweet vanilla and light smoke that dries towards a salty, tangy, liquorice finish; **b**24 a sweet malt, but one with such deft use of peat and oak that one never really notices. Real class. **43%**. Nikka.

Southern Alps Pure Malt (93) n24 bananas and freshly peeled lemon skin: one of the world's most refreshing and exhilarating whisky noses; **t**2t crisp youngish malts, as one might suspect from the nose, mouthwatering and as a clean as an Alpine stream; **f**22 some vanilla development and a late slightly creamy flourish but finished with a substantial and startling malty rally boasting a very discreet sweetness; **b**24 this is a bottle I have only to look at to start salivating. Sadly, though, I drink sparingly from it as it is a hard whisky to find, even in Japan. Fresh, clean and totally stunning, the term "pure malt" could not be more apposite. Fabulous whisky: a very personal favourite. **40%**. *Suntory*.

Super Nikka Vatted Pure Malt (76) n20 **t**19 **f**19 **b**18. Decent and chewy but something doesn't quite click with this one. **55.5%**. Nikka.

Taketsuru Pure Malt 12 Years Old (80) n19 **t**22 **f**19 **b**20. For its age, heavier than a sumo wrestler. But perhaps a little more agile over the tastebuds. Lovely silkiness impresses, but lots of toffee. **40%**. Nikka.

Taketsuru Pure Malt 17 Years Old (89) n21 firm oak, but compromises sufficiently to allow several layers of malt to battle through with a touch of peat-coffee; **t**22 massive: a toasted, honeyed front gives way to really intense and complex malt notes; **f**23 superb. Some late marmalade arrives from somewhere: the toast is slightly burnt but the waves of malty complexity are endless; **b**23 not a whisky for the squeamish. This is big stuff – about as big as it gets without peat or rye. No bar shelf or whisky club should be without one. **43%**. Nikka.

Taketsuru Pure Malt 21 Years Old (88) n22 middle-aged bourbon with a heavy, vaguely honeyed malt presence; **t**21 the oak remains quite fresh and chewy. Again, the malt is massive; **f**22 sweet, oily and more honey arrives; **b**23 a much more civilised and gracious offering than the 17-y-o: there is certainly nothing linear about the character development from Taketsuru 12 to 21 inclusive. Serious whisky for the serious whisky drinker. **43%**. Nikka.

Zen (84) n19 **t**22 **f**22 **b**21. A sweet, gristy malt that is light and clean. **40%**. *Suntory*.

Blends

Ajiwai Kakubin (see Kakubin Ajiwai)

Amber (75) n18 **t**20 **f**18 **b**19. Similar in style to "Old" but with more toffee caramel. A silky experience. **40%**. *Mars*.

Black Nikka (72) n17 **t**20 **f**17 **b**18. Big grain presence and decent middle; carries a caramel tang. **37%.** *Nikka.*

Black Nikka Special (70) n16 **t**20 **f**17 **b**17. Simliar to ordinary Black Nikka, except weighed down by extra caramel **42%.** *Nikka.*

Black Nikka Aged 8 Years (82) n20 **t**21 **f**21 **b**20. Beautifully bourbony, especially on the nose. Lush, silky and great fun. Love it! **40%.** *Nikka.*

The Blend of Nikka (90) n21 a dry, oaky buzz infiltrates some firm grain and sweeter malt; **t**23 brilliant! Absolutely outstanding explosion of clean grassy malts thudding into the tastebuds with confidence and precision: mouthwatering and breath-catching; **f**22 delightful grain bite to follow the malt; **b**24 an adorable blend that makes you sit up and take notice of every enormous mouthful. Classy, complex, charismatic and brilliantly balanced. **45%.** *Nikka.*

Boston Club (Brown Label) **(73) n**17 **t**20 **f**18 **b**18. "More Boston Strangler than Boston Club", I wrote somewhere on tasting this some years back. Certainly they have sorted out the dreadful finish on the old bottling, and this is pleasant enough, but devoid of any challenge thanks possibly to caramel although the spice does. **40%.** *Kirin.*

Boston Club (70) n16 **t**19 **f**18 **b**17. Less opaque than the Brown Label, lighter in body with a fraction less toffee-caramel **37%.** *Kirin.*

Crescent (82) n19 **t**22 **f**20 **b**21. Fresh, grassy, lightweight malt dominates. A spot of the old caramel toffee, perhaps? Without it, this would be a stunner. **43%.** *Kirin.*

Diamond Whisky (73) n17 **t**20 **f**18 **b**18. Another blend where complexity takes second place to caramel though it does have some sweet, attractive moments. **43%.** *Nikka.*

Emblem (76) n18 **t**20 **f**18 **b**20. Richly textured bend with a deliciously clean and salivating malt character. **40%.** *Kirin.*

Evermore (90) n22 big age, salt and outstanding malt riches to counter the oak; **t**23 more massive oak wrapped in a bourbony sweetness with glorious malts and a salty, spicy tang; **f**22 long, sweet malt and crisp grains: plenty to chew on and savour; **b**23 top-grade, well-aged blended whisky with fabulous depth and complexity that never loses its sweet edge despite the oak. 40%. *Kirin.*

Gold & Gold (83) n21 **t**22 **f**20 **b**20. Some lovely, crisp malty moments set against firm grain and softened by honey. Something to get your teeth into, but perhaps a touch too much toffee. **43%.** *Nikka.*

Golden Horse Bosyuu (80) n20 **t**21 **f**19 **b**20. Soft grain melts beautifully in the mouth. **40%.** Toa.

Golden Horse Busyuu Deluxe (93) n22 some decent signs of age with some classy oak alongside smoke: sexy stuff; **t**24 enormous flavour profile simply because it is so fresh: massive malt presence, some of it peaty, bananas and under-ripe grapes; **f**23 clean malt and some sharpish grain with a touch of bite, continuing to tantalise the tastebuds for a long time; **b**24 whoever blended this has a genuine feel for whisky: a classic in its own right and one of astonishing complexity and textbook balance. **43%.** *Toa. To celebrate the year 2000.*

Golden Horse Grand (78) n19 **t**21 **f**19 **b**19. Decent malt, sweet and a little chalky. **39%.** *Toa.*

Golden Horse Musashi (86) n20 the soft, dry oak counters the rich malts pleasantly; **t**22 big mouth arrival, again with the malt prominent: fresh and mouthwatering; **f**22 grains arrive to add a luxuriant dash; **b**22 really attractive, sweetish blend balanced with aplomb. **43%.** *Toa.*

Hibiki (82) n20 **t**19 **f**23 **b**20. The grains here are fresh, forceful and merciless, the malts bouncing off them meekly. Lovely cocoa finale. A blend that brings a tear to the eye. Hard stuff – perfect after a hard day! Love it! **43%.** *Suntory.*

Hibiki 17 Years Old (74) n17 **t**20 **f**19 **b**18. Hmmm, an odd cask or two got into this one I think. The fruity effect has gone OTT and we have quite a syrupy sweetness which doesn't quite fit with sharp finish. Not the usual house style at all. I suspect the next bottling will be a lot better. **43%.** *Suntory.*

Hibiki 21 Years Old (93) n*24* fruitier notes of cherry and sherry with a triumphal triumvirate of intense malt, the subtlest of peat smoke and leathery oak combining for maximum, stupendous complexity, also a dash of kumquats; t*22* fat and oily, like the nose hinting slightly at bourbon but the grains thin the middle out sufficiently to let the malt, mildly peaty and otherwise, through; f*23* long and intense with more lightly orchestrated smoke and lashings of late, grapey fruit and a build-up of, first, sweet malts, then a drier, spicier oak; b*24* when people refer to Yoichi as the exception that proves the rule about Japanese whisky, I tend to point them in the direction of this. If I close my eyes and taste this, cherry blossom really does form in my mind's eye. Yet this is a classic whisky in any language or any culture. **43%.** *Suntory.*

Hibiki 30 Years Old (87) n*21* curious mix of peat and bourbon; t*22* sweet, fat oak: bourbon all the way; f*22* the glorious rich-textured sweetness continues forever; b*22* Kentuckians would really go for this one: the smoke might confuse them a little, though. Pretty unique the world over. **43%.** *Suntory.*

Hi Nikka Whisky (68) n*16* t*18* f*17* b*17.* Very light but lots of caramel character. A good mixer. **39%.** *Nikka.*

Imperial (81) n*20* t*22* f*19* b*20.* Flinty, hard grain softened by malt and vanilla but toffee dulled. **43%.** *Suntory.*

Kakubin (80) n*19* t*21* f*20* b*20.* A beautifully constructed, fresh, bright and mouthwatering blend. Refreshing and so dangerously moreish! **40%.** *Suntory.*

Kakubin Ajiwai (82) n*20* t*21* f*20* b*21.* Usual Kakubin hard grain and mouthwatering malt, with this time a hint of warming stem ginger. **40%.** *Suntory.*

Kakubin New (90) n*21* gritty grain with very hard malt to accompany it; t*24* stunning mouth arrival with heaps of mouthwatering young malt and then soft grain and oil. Brilliant stuff; f*21* some beautiful cocoa notes round off the blend perfectly; b*24* seriously divine blending: a refreshing dram of the top order. **40%.** *Suntory.*

Kingsland (81) n*21* t*22* f*17* b*21.* An ultra-lively and mouthwatering blend with a short, dry finish. Overall, quite impressive, refreshing and moreish. *Nikka.*

Master's Blend Aged 10 Years (87) n*21* integrated fruit and flinty malt; t*23* mouthwatering and massively fruity, very sweet, light muscovado sugar and malt; f*22* trails off towards vanilla; b*21* chewy, big and satisfying. **40%.** *Mercian/Karuizawa.*

New Kakubin Suntory (see Kakubin New)

New Shirokaku (74) n*18* t*19* f*19* b*18.* Grain-heavy, hard and toffeed. **40%.** *Suntory.*

The Nikka Whisky Aged 34 Years blended and bottled in 99 **(93)** n*23* bourbony and rich: over-ripe cherries and wet tobacco with chunks of moist Melton Mowbray fruitcake. The oak, for all its weight, remains charming; t*23* big and fruity and then a surge of oak, perhaps mildly over-aged, but still intact and firm, excellent waxy sweetness through the middle; f*24* wonderfully spicy and mouth-filling. Excellent oily texture guarantees a good malt presence as the oak dries and takes final control; b*23* a Japanese whisky of antiquity that has not only survived many passing years, but has actually achieved something of stature and sophistication. Over time I have come to appreciate this whisky immensely. It is among the world's greatest blends, no question. **43%.** *Nikka.*

Oak Master (78) n*19* t*20* f*19* b*20.* Foraging malts on the nose and palate counter a big grain surge. Decent, silky whisky, though a little on the bitter side. **37%.** *Mercian.*

Ocean Luckey (70) n*17* t*18* f*17* b*18.* Grainy, chalky and pretty weightless. **37%.** *Mercian.*

Ocean Whisky Special Old (83) **n**20 **t**21 **f**21 **b**21. Deliciously rich malt is absorbed effortlessly into melt-in-the-mouth grain. Good blending. **40%**

Old (77) **n**18 **t**20 **f**20 **b**19. Light, sweet, chewy. Good, clean session whisky. **43%.** Mars.

Old Halley (71) **n**18 **t**19 **f**17 **b**17. Flat, not unpleasant but toffee-reliant. **37%.** Toa.

Red (75) **n**17 **t**19 **f**20 **b**19. On the thin side: the grains are to the fore and aft but there is good late spicy bite amid the toffee. **39%.** Suntory.

Robert Brown (74) **n**19 **t**20 **f**17 **b**18. What a pity! Too much toffee has overshadowed some lovely spice. **40%.** Kirin.

Royal 12 Years Old (89) **n**22 chalky and dry, but malt and oranges add character; **t**23 fabulously complex arrival on the palate with some grainy nip countered by sparkling malt and a hint of smoke; **f**21 the grains and oak carry on as the spice builds; **b**23 a splendidly blended whisky with complexity being the main theme. Beautiful stuff. **43%.** Suntory.

Royal 15 Years Old (91) **n**23 kumquats and lime give a fruity start to an immensely malty aroma; **t**23 the grain kicks off early bringing with it some oak, then an immediate malt explosion with a spicy drop-out, lashings of clean, juicy fruit; **f**22 the grain rules OK. But the oaky vanilla is a joy; **b**23 this is outstanding blended whisky. **43%.** Suntory.

Ship Bottle (86) **n**22 young, hard grain: classic old-fashioned blend nose; **t**22 first-class grain forms a firm alliance with some crisp malt; **f**21 long, subtle grain and oak, some caramel on the slightly spicy finish; **b**21 not totally unlike how that once-classic Scotch, The Original Mackinlay, was 20 years ago. Now that is a compliment. **40%.** Mercian.

Special Reserve 10 Years Old (94) **n**23 magnificent approach of rich fruit buttressed by firm, clear grain. Some further fruity spices reveal some age is evident; **t**24 complex from the off with a tidal tsunami of malt crashing over the tastebuds. The grain holds firm and supports some budding fruit; **f**23 a touch of something peaty and pliable begins to take shape with some wonderful malty spices coating the mouth; **b**24 a beguiling whisky of near faultless complexity. Blending at its peak. **43%.** Suntory.

Special Reserve 10 Years Old Matured in Sherry Cask (86) **n**22 intricate fruits are outgunned by firm malt and firmer grain; **t**22 malty and a little spicy, the grain and fruit mingle contentedly; **f**21 soft fruit and toffee; **b**21 a subtle and subdued blend. **40%.** Suntory.

Suntory Old (89) **n**19 dusty and fruity. Attractive nip and balance; **t**24 mouthwatering from the off with a rich array of chewy, clean fresh malt: textbook standard, complete with bite; **f**23 subtle oak on the grain offers texture alongside the silky malt; **b**23 this is a blend that seems to offer both old and new whiskies something of genuine class. The nose is average, but from then on this is about as sure-footed a blending as you will find. A gem. **43%.** Suntory.

Suntory Old Mild and Smooth (84) **n**19 **t**22 **f**21 **b**22. Chirpy and lively around the palate, the grains soften the crisp malts wonderfully. **40%**

Suntory Old Rich and Mellow (89) **n**20 very lightly smoked with healthy maltiness; **t**23 complex, fat and chewy, no shortage of deep malty tones, including a touch of smoke; **f**23 sweeter malts see off the grain, excellent spices; **b**23 a pretty malt-rich blend with the grains offering a fat base. Impressive blending. **43%**

Super Nikka (93) **n**23 excellent crisp, grassy malt base bounces off firm grain. A distant hint of peat, maybe, offers a little weighty extra; **t**23 an immediate starburst of rich, mouthwatering and entirely uncompromising malt that almost over-runs the tastebuds; **f**23 soft, fabulously intrinsic peaty notes from the Yoichi School give brilliant length and depth. But the cocoa notes from the oak-wrapped grain also offer untold riches; **b**24 a very, very fine blend which makes no apology whatsoever for the peaty complexity of Yoichi malt. The grain really is melt-in-the mouth stuff. A better sample, this, for having kicked out some – though not all – of the totally unnecessary caramel of old. Now it's pretty classy stuff. However, Nikka being Nikka you might find the occasional bottling that is entirely devoid of peat, more honeyed and lighter in style (21-22-23-23 Total 89 – no less a quality turn, obviously). Either way, an absolutely brilliant day-to-day, anytime, any place dram. One of the true 24-carat, super nova commonplace blends not just in Japan, but in the world. **43%**. *Nikka*.

Torys **(77)** n*19* t*20* f*19* b*19*. Lots of toffee in the middle and at the end of this one. The grain used is top class and chewy. **37%**. *Suntory*.

Torys Whisky Square **(80)** n*19* t*20* f*21* f*20*. At first glance very similar to Torys, but very close scrutiny reveals slightly more "new loaf" nose and a better, spicier and less toffeed finale. **37%**. *Suntory*.

Tsuru **(93)** n*23* apples, cedar, crushed pine nuts, blood oranges and soft malt, all rather chalky and soft – and unusually peatless for Nikka; t*24* fantastic grain bite bringing with it a mouthwateringly clean and fresh attack of sweet and lip-smacking malt; f*22* a continuation of untaxing soft malts and gathering oak, a slight "Malteser" candy quality to it, and then some late sultana fruitiness; b*24* gentle and beautifully structured, genuinely mouthwatering, more-ish and effortlessly noble. If they had the confidence to cut the caramel, this would be even higher up the charts as one of the great blends of the world. As it is, in my house we pass the ceramic Tsuru bottle as one does the ship's decanter. And it empties very quickly. **43%. Nikka.**

The Whisky **(88)** n*22* fresh barley sugar and oaky, bourbony tones; t*22* good weight and hard barley rigidity against the softer grains; f*21* quite simplistic with soft vanilla; b*23* a really rich, confident and well-balanced dram. **43%**. *Suntory*.

White **(75)** n*20* t*19* f*18* b*18*. After a classically nippy nose, proves disappointingly bland. **40%**. *Suntory*.

White Super Clean **(86)** n*22* delicate citrus notes and under-ripe apples, while the malt is playful against the firm grain; t*22* mouthwatering "Speyside"-style malts impress enormously with their freshness, the grains adding clean support; f*21* becomes slightly buttery with some toffee fudge slowly welling towards the end; b*21* another fresh blend exuding clarity, at least until the end when it weakens a little. Even so, delightful. **37%**. *Suntory*.

Za **(79)** n*19* t*21* f*19* b*20*. Some lively boisterous grain offers a suet-pudding chewiness. A little bitter on the finish. **40%**. *Suntory*.

Canadian Whisky

Sad to say, but Canadian whisky remains a style that fails to turn on whisky connoisseurs. Only three times during the whole of the 2002/03 whisky tasting season did I manage to persuade organisers to include a Canadian. An "All-Canadian" was out of the question.

Certainly Canadian, by and large, is the least challenging of the whisky styles. Yet when it hits top form it is up there amongst the best – just look to see how many brands made the 93 mark. It just takes time and a little understanding. Classic Canadian is all about subtlety rather than charisma.

Good to see the two small independent guys, Glenora and Kittling Ridge, finding their way on to the market place and staying there. But I am fascinated to see which direction the better known brands go, especially now there has been a major change of hands with two of the better distilleries. Allied still, thankfully have the Walkerville Distillery, home to Canadian Club, while its twin sister distillery at Dumbarton in Scotland awaits the demolition man's ball and chain. And Jim Beam Brands have kept hold of Alberta Distillery. Now, though, Diageo have the old – or perhaps I should say new – Seagram's distillery at Gimley while Barton, under the guise of Schenley, have the wonderful Valleyfield distillery in Quebec.

Please check out **www.whiskybible.com** for fuller details on each distillery.

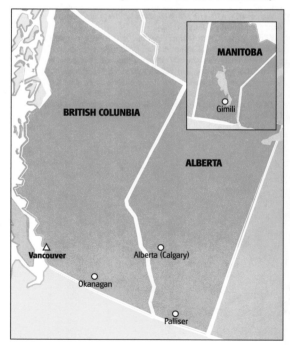

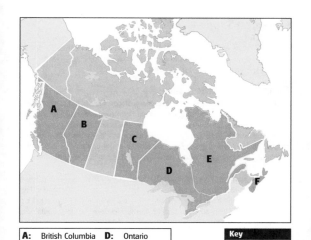

A:	British Columbia	**D:**	Ontario
B:	Alberta	**E:**	Quebec
C:	Manitoba	**F:**	Nova Scotia

Key
△ **Major Cities**
○ Distilleries

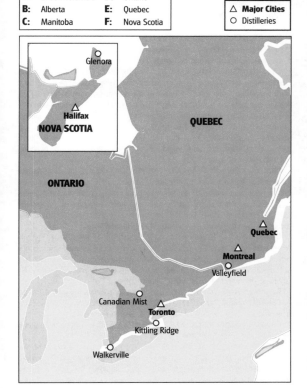

Canadian Single Malt
GLENORA

Glen Breton db **(81)** n*19* t*21* f*20* b*21*. Enormously sweet malt, in almost concentrated form with a tantalising whiff of smoke hanging around; mildly spiced and slightly oily, soapy finale. **43%**

Canadian Blended Whisky

Alberta Premium **(89)** n*23* so brittle, just one tap should crack it into a thousand pieces, yet it still offers enormous floral complexity; t*23* an indecent amount of flavours hits the tastebuds running, the grains are chewy and busy – this is hard as nails and superb! f*21* the downside as toffee takes over, sweet and soft; b*22* what I would give to see this whisky in the bottle without a drop of colouring: the complexity would blow the mind. As it is, just settle for mere brilliance. **40%**

Alberta Springs Rye Whisky 10 Years Old **(86)** n*23* signs of some crispness: beautiful fruit amid excellent oak; t*21* gentle grains melt into a toffeed softness, fruity and full-bodied; f*20* the toffee envelops the finale but some oak makes its way through; b*22* a softer, considerably less rye-rugged Canadian. Still an honour to drink Canadian rye that is just that. **40%**

Barton's Canadian 36 Months Old **(78)** n*19* t*20* f*19* b*20*. Sweet, toffeed, easy-going. **40%**. *Barton.*

Black Velvet DeLuxe **(80)** n*20* t*20* f*20* b*20*. Consistent, clean, toffeed Canadian with rich body and decent fizz on the finish. **40%**. *Schenley.*

Canadian Club Premium **(78)** n*19* t*20* f*19* b*20*. Lovely nip and pinch on the nose and some bite on the finish. Enlivening and, in parts, lush. The most visible Canadian whisky in the world, and pretty consistent, too. **40%** *Hiram Walker.*

Canadian Club Sherry Cask Aged Eight Years **(76)** n*22* t*17* f*19* b*18*. The problem with putting Canadian whisky into what here appears to be a very high-quality sherry fresh-fill cask or two is that the spirit is naturally too light to withstand the grapey onslaught. The result is less whisky and more high-proof sherry. I admire the effort; the nose is quite lovely and the late finish also has some delightful fruit-spice moments. But the middle is just too one-dimensional. I'd keep the faith, but some tinkering is needed here. If you don't like it first time round, give it a year and see what happens. **41.3%**. *Hiram Walker.*

Canadian Club Reserve 10 Years of Age **(88)** n*21* intriguing mixture of soft fruit and rich corn; t*23* delicately sweet mouth arrival, then a slightly oily development and an almost heathery, floral complexity as the oak appears; f*22* beautiful play-out: the oaky vanilla dries attractively against the sweeter corn; b*23* this is great blending: a whisky sympathetic to the idea of balance and poise. An everyday dram of distinction. **40%**. *Hiram Walker.*

Canadian Club Premium Classic Aged 12 Years **(86)** n*22* pretty chunky cream toffee; t*22* more toffee but the corn is quite voluptuous and gentle spices hover; f*21* curious bitter-sweet affair with the oak quite pronounced; b*21* a busy Canadian which fails to match the Reserve's all round-charm and guile. No shortage of character, though. **40%**. *Hiram Walker.*

Canadian Host **(74)** n*19* t*18* f*19* b*18*. Sweet, light, weirdly fruity. **40%**. *Barton.*

Canadian Mist **(74)** n*19* t*18* f*19* b*18*. One of those helium-light blends with lots of sweet fruitiness. Lots of vanilla. **40%**. *Brown-Forman.*

Canadian Supreme **(74)** n*18* t*19* f*19* b*18*. A light, banana-ry blend that is young but extremely fruity. **40%**

Corby's Canadian 36 Months Old **(85)** n*20* subtle variants of vanilla; t*21* sweetcorn to start, oils up and then fills the mouth; f*22* develops into something almost sawdusty. Impressive complexity for one so young; b*22* always attractive with fine bitter-sweet balance and I love the late spice kick-back. **40%** *Barton. Interesting label: as a keen ornithologist, I had no idea there were parrots in Canada. Must be related to the Norwegian Blue.*

Crown Royal (93) n23 seriously big rye offers a hard and fruity edge to the soft corn and oak; **t**24 rock-hard and crisp mouth arrival thanks to the early rye, softens for the corn and then the rye sends some fruity shockwaves around the palate; **f**22 bitter and booming: big controlled oak finale on gentle oil; **b**24 this has definitely changed in the last seven or eight years, as all blends must. It has a slightly larger rye dependency than of old but the mouthwatering effect is sublime. An international great. **40%**

Crown Royal Limited Edition (91) n24 floral tones to the fore as the rye shows its hand with a wonderful and perfectly matched hint of citrus, too; **t**23 hard at first, then softens as the corn gets a grip; **f**21 a touch bitter and dry at first but becomes fruity and complex as the small grain re-emerges; **b**23 delicious whisky which shows great sleight of hand in dealing with some powerful rye. Depending on the bottling, this vies alongside Crown Royal for sheer élan. **40%**

Crown Royal Special Reserve (88) n23 great subtlety: various small grains – you could swear barley was in there somewhere – gang together to offer a nose worth five minutes of anyone's time; **t**23 firm rye impact and then a rich development of sweet corn; **f**20 lots of vanilla but disappointingly flat with too much toffee at the death; **b**22 re-introduce some life back into the finale and you'd have a classic on your hands. Quite brilliant until the finish. **40%**

Forty Creek Barrel Select (new bottling) **(84) n**23 **t**19 **f**21 **b**21. Beautifully made clean whisky which appears to have a big fruit input, sherry-cask in style. The nose offers a delicious apricot jam and, though it goes a bit fat and confused on mouth entry, it re-forms to complete a fruit and nut finish unique in the whisky world. Very different and really worth finding. **40%**

Forty Creek Barrel Select (old bottling) **(79) n**20 **t**20 **f**19 **b**20. A well-made but curiously dry whisky despite some fruity edges. **40%**. *Kittling Ridge.*

Forty Creek Three Grain (84) n20 **t**20 **f**22 **b**22. Dry with a very attractive evolution of complex grain notes, coupled with decent oak. I have found the odd bottling that has been a touch feinty on the nose, but that hasn't affected its performance on the palate. **40%**. *Kittling Ridge.*

Gibson's Finest Aged 12 Years (86) n23 great aroma, brilliant balance between firm oak and even firmer corn; **t**22 lush mouthfeel, medium sweet with dry oak; **f**19 toffee kicks in and dulls things down way too much; **b**22 an otherwise great whisky spoiled by caramel. Nothing like the whisky it was. **40%**

Gibson's Finest Rare Aged 18 Years (93) n23 serious oak here, but the oily intensity of the corn balances out perfectly; **t**24 honey and corn combine wonderfully, drier oak notes act only as a counterweight; **f**23 long with less honey now, more demerara sugar brushed over the corn, with the oak continuing to offer a drier backdrop; **b**23 this is like one of those honied cereals you always have to have a second bowl of. It takes Canadian whisky into a new dimension. Truly brilliant. **40%**

Gibson's Finest Sterling Edition (88) n23 gentle, almost green corn and good oak, natural and unblemished; **t**21 oily and sweet, mildly hot then a wonderful delivery of molten corn; **f**22 a delicate, softly oaked finish with the spices reforming for a second attack; **b**22 a refreshing Canadian whisky in that I detect very little caramel interference. Great stuff! **40%**

Golden Wedding (see Schenley Golden Wedding)

Gooderham & Worts Ltd (90) n23 excellent trilogy of fresh corn, soft rye and something fruity; **t**23 a supremely weighted and deliciously sweet start bursts from the off. Not as much rye as I remember, though, as I was involved in the blending development of this brand; **f**22 lots of rich corn and deep oaky vanilla. Pure Canadian on a golden platter; **b**22 sensational Canadian, though on this bottling the rye input has been taken down a peg or two, which is a shame. Even so, a real stunner for its genre. **45%**

Hamilton (77) n*18* t*20* f*20* b*19*. Young grains are kept on the leash to offer very sweet toffee. Very well made and easy-going. **40%**

Hiram Walker Special Old Rye Whisky (86) n*22* clean corn with hints of oak and toffee; t*21* superb bitter-sweet arrival; f*22* some corn oil develops and vanilla frames the busy grain involvement; b*21* a rich, solidly constructed, sweet whisky with some excellent late grain development. Good old-fashioned Canadian. **40%**

Lot No. 40 (93) n*24* one of the most magnificent and rarest noses in the world: malted rye. Hints of spearmint chewing gum, kumquats, boiled sugar candy, all enveloped in that unique rye fruitiness; t*24* brittle and hard at first then soft rye-powered fruit arrives, slightly peppery towards the middle, heavy roast cocoa and soft rye oil; f*23* decent oak presence and some straggling fruity rye notes; b*23* this is great whisky, irrespective of whichever country it came from. As for a Canadian, this is true rye whisky, one with which I was very proud to be associated in the early blending days. Elegant stuff. **43%**

McGuinness Silk Tassel (78) n*19* t*20* f*19* b*20*. As silky as the name suggests: fruity, bitter orange and spice. **40%**

McMaster's (80) n*19* t*20* f*21* b*20*. Velvet-textured and buttered sweet corn. Dangerously easy-to-drink session whisky. **40%**. *Barton.*

Northern Light (82) n*20* t*21* f*20* b*21*. A young, natural, unpretentious Canadian grain blend with a good, clean character and first-class bite. Very attractive. **40%**. *Barton.*

Pike Creek finished in port barrels **(87)** n*21* curious amalgam of corn and fresh wine; t*23* soft, silky mouthfeel and then a whoosh of sweetness; f*21* some spices prosper as the port makes a stand, genuinely fruity at first then becoming a little more bitter as the oak arrives; b*22* much more complexity now than from the first bottlings. A Canadian of genuine style and character. **40%**. *Allied.*

Royal Reserve (85) n*21* lots of lively corn ... and even a hint of rye; t*21* clean, chewy, oily corn with decent oak presence; f*22* really takes off as almost imperceptible rye gives a subtle deeper, richer edge; b*21* a lovely Canadian which doesn't suffer from too much fruit interference and actually appears to have some discernible rye in the blend. **60%**. *Corby.*

Safeway Canadian Rye Whisky (75) n*18* t*18* f*20* b*19*. A reasonable, clean, sweet if uninspiring Canadian. **40%**. *UK.*

Seagram's 83 Canadian Whisky (68) n*18* t*17* f*16* b*17*. Caramel-dominated these days. **40%**. *The "83" refers to 1883, not a 1983 vintage, and certainly nots its rating ...*

Seagram's Five Star Rye Whisky (77) n*19* t*19* f*20* b*19*. Corn-dominated despite the name. Enjoyable tail-off. **40%**

Seagram's VO (94) n*24* the wonderfully weighted rye input offers lavender and violets, the oak input is quite beautiful: delicate and sexy; t*23* corn oil softens the arrival and then a swathe of grainy-corny notes hits you head-on; f*23* rye returns to declare open season on the tastebuds; b*24* brilliant whisky not afraid to take on its rye roots. I guess the rye is malted and comes from Lawrenceburg, Indiana: I may be wrong ... it has been a few years since I was in the old Seagram lab, while they have had to take on the losing of stocks from the old Waterloo and LaSalle distilleries. And my blender mate there has retired. But such is the richness and complexity of this blend someone is still doing a supreme job there and understands what makes rye tick. If you don't have a bottle of this, then you don't possess a true, traditional Canadian. **40%**

Schenley Golden Wedding (83) n*20* t*21* f*21* b*21*. Beautifully silky textured and rich. Great distillate used here which is both prickly and luxurious. Lovely stuff. **40%**

Schenley OFC Aged 8 Years (93) n24 brilliant nose: awesome complexity here as the grains tease around the vanilla. Perfectly weighted; **t**23 again, outstanding balance on the sweetness as you chew at the grain and lick at the thin sugary coating; **f**23 soft spices, vanilla and traces of late honey; **b**23 some re-writing of history here: the label says "Original Fine Canadian" under OFC. Actually, I'm pretty convinced it originally meant Old Fire Copper. I can think of other things OFC stand for, perhaps not suitable for this book, but I will settle instead for Outstandingly Flavoured Creation, for this remains one of Canada's top three finest traditional blends, one which comes back at you with each mouthful with greater and greater complexity. **40%**

Silk Tassel (see McGuinness Silk Tassel)

Tangle Ridge Aged 10 Years (67) n17 **t**17 **f**16 **b**17. One of the worst Canadians I have tasted in years: something sweet and unpleasant has been added. The mouthfeel and effect are dreadful, the nose isn't much better. Considering this is based on rye whisky, you could almost cry. Still see it in specialist outlets from time to time: one to avoid. **40%**

Tesco Canadian Whisky (75) n18 **t**18 **f**20 **b**19. As close as makes no difference to Safeway own label. **40%**. *UK.*

Wiser's De Luxe (86) n21 youngish: banana and soft vanilla teams with rich corn; **t**21 immediate soft spice but the corn dominates; **f**22 teasing vanilla and corn weave complex patterns; **b**22 one of the most dangerously quaffable drams you'll find in Canada. All the better for having minimal fruit interference. **40%**. *Hiram Walker.*

Wiser's De Luxe 10 Years Old (93) n23 a blueprint for Canadian noses: firm and hard-grained then, below the surface, soft, subtly sweetening vanilla. Clean and brittle; **t**23 big grain push that's hard and biting then gently yielding as the corn sweetens and fattens; **f**23 long and buttery with the cleanest, most gentle and softly sweetened corn imaginable. Hints of rye ping around the tastebuds at the death: you'll have no doubt why this is one of my regular whiskies when I'm working in Canada; **b**24 feeling this whisky come alive on the palate is like watching the dawn break: slow, sometimes imperceptible, but when it's over you feel you have experienced a timeless, simple beauty. **40%**. *Hiram Walker.*

Wiser's Special Blend (72) n18 **t**19 **f**17 **b**18. A pretty cramped blend with little expression. **40%**

European Whisky

Mainland Europe has gone whisky mad. When I looked about six years ago there was one large distillery in Segovia, Spain, a couple in the Czech Republic and little else: unless you count Turkey. But I had accidentally overlooked one or two very quiet distilleries in Germany and Austria (even their embassies did not appear to know they existed), which was very much my loss. Until recently, that is. Then I made a whirlwind tour of some of the stills operating in Germany, Austria and Switzerland – and was greatly impressed: in some cases enormously surprised with what I found.

Certainly, at the moment, Austria has Europe's leading distillers in terms of quality. To my knowledge there are three distilleries, of which I have visited two. And although Herr Haider's distillery at Roggenreith, with its extraordinary and wonderfully chunky rye, rich malt and curious hybrids of both, is by far the most impressive, the one big whisky shock I received in the last twelve months occurred at a farm distillery nearby at Kottes.

There Oswald Weidenauer makes the only whisky I have found anywhere in the world consisting purely of oats. At its best it is quite wonderful. It's different, certainly, but there is no mistaking that it is whisky. This is very refreshing, because it is only a relatively short, if spectacular, walk through vineyards to the Danube. It is not often you find whisky being produced in a wine-making region.

Another remarkable whisky I came across in the last year was Swissky. Where was it made? Hard to say, because the owner has a distillery on wheels and moves it from its base at Baar – which I visited (along with the nearby brewery that makes his mash) – all over Switzerland. I have even seen it in operation in the centre of Zurich.

The Germans are also impressing. The pick of their malts have been the ever dependable bottlings from the oldest of them all, Blaue Maus, and one from one of the newest: the charming and genteel Slyrs in the heart of Bavaria. Where Blaue Maus specialises in heavy malts, Slyrs has a tendency towards refined Speysiders. It's impressive, encouraging and very drinkable.

Further north, the Swedes are coming. A distillery north of Stockholm, at Mackmyra, has already been expanded even before their unique malts hit the market. For a short time it was the world's northern-most distillery. But one recently opened in Finland has deprived them of that honour.

Even the old Eastern Bloc countries are getting in on the act. Poland has its own whisky now: since the fall of the Berlin Wall, the number of agricultural distilleries has plummeted from around 400 to something nearer 100. Now it is possible to find Polish whisky, made from either rye or wheat, distilled at first from a single column before being transported elsewhere for rectification and maturation. It is they who claim to be the whisky makers. And even the Bulgarians have launched their own whiskies, of which so far I have managed to taste only one.

France is distilling and I am aware of at least one other country where plans are seriously afoot to make either malt or rye whisky. Whatever, it looks as though whisky lovers will soon be able to start spending fewer holidays in Scotland and head for towns and villages all over mainland Europe and Scandinavia. Because while politically and economically Europe may seem to find it hard to agree on many points, there is one that seems to be increasingly obvious among more and more nations: they tend to like making whisky.

AUSTRIA
HAIDER

J H **Feinster Roggenwhisky L21/98** (81) n18 t20 f22 b21. Very sweet with excellent oak weight and even rye distribution. Lovely spice v demerara at the finale. **41%**

J H **Feinster Roggenwhisky Fassstarke L42/97** (91) n20 sharp, hard and flinty. The grains really kick hard here; t24 brilliant weight on the mouth and then a series of slow spicy explosions, each unleashing clear, chewy rye on the palate: a pyrotechnical display of rye at near enough perfection; f24 superb chocolate adds sublime balance to the fruity rye and bitter oranges; b23 look at this from any angle and you have a minor masterpiece on your hands: quite sublime. **54%**

J H **Gersten-Malzwhisky L10/99** db (80) n19 t21 f19 b21. Slightly chalky with a tad more oak interference than it needs. That said, the malt is gristy, chewy and clean with a slight buzz of spice. Impressive. **41%**

J H **Gersten-Malzwhisky L10/99 Fassstarke** db (83) n20 t21 f21 b21. Holds together better on the nose at a fuller strength plus an extra hint of honey on the finish. More compact and not far off delicious. **54%**

J H **Gersten-Malzwhisky Karamell L66/98** db (74) n16 t19 f20 b19. An off-beam nose – well it was a very early barrel – is rescued to a degree by a sweet malt surge towards the death. **41%**

J H **Gersten-Malzwhisky Karamell L66/98 Fassstarke** db (77) n16 t21 f20 b20. Much more early intense malt offers a sugared coating at the start and a hint of liquorice on the finale. A big difference. **55%**

J H **Roggen-Malzwhisky L20/98** db (90) n22 intense, sweet rye and clean, spicy, fruit; t23 outstanding clarity of crisp, hard rye that sweetens by the second, quite plummy and juicy; f22 the bitterness returns – and then some – and dry pounding oaky tones add a late chalkiness. Hints of honey lurk in the background; b23 simply excellent and quite classic rye whisky. Congratulations to all concerned for a delicious job well done. **41%**

J H **Roggen-Malzwhisky Fassstarke L6/98** db (88) n20 surprisingly closed nose; t25 high octane, faultlessly clean rye that completely hammers the palate with a welter of fruity, cherry-laden punches. Clean, chewy and breathtaking: man, this is rye whisky!!!! f21 just like the nose, flattens alarmingly; b22 if it could be like the arrival on the palate from nose to finish, we'd have a world classic! **55%**

J H **Roggen-Malzwhisky Nougat L3/99** db (74) n17 t19 f19 b19. The rye has been flattened into submission. **41%**

J H **Gersten-Malzwhisky Nougat L3/99 Fassstarke** db (78) n17 t20 f21 b20. The rye sparkles much more here than at the lower strength, especially on the long finish. **50%**

WELDENAUER DISTILLERY

Waldviestler Hafer Whisky 1998 db (79) n20 t21 f18 b20. An oily, assertive whisky that, while sweet, shows signs of a bitterness and imbalance despite the enormous fruitiness on the nose. That said, the oats do come through loud and clear and make quite a porridge, if a slightly salted one. **42%**

Waldviestler Hafer Whisky 1999 db (89) n23 oat-crunchies breakfast cereal combined with soft honey and a sprinkling of sugar: amazingly clean yet so much going on; t21 initially hard on the palate then it softens as a grainy sweetness spreads across the roof of the mouth, excellent texture; f22 pure oats: just so pure and clean, you could almost chew it: remarkable; b23 this is unique whisky and as such deserves time in the glass to oxidise and warm. Once you become accustomed to the taste, the complexity is spellbinding. **42%**

Waldviestler Hafer Whisky 2000 db (94) n23 some delicate spices link beautifully with oak 'n' oats; t24 sumptuous, just about perfectly weighted with the most sublime oil involvement, then that unique oaty quality that is sweetish, but softly so, yet with a drying mealiness; **f24** long, really intense oat character which dries in the most delicious manner of any whisky I have ever encountered! **b23** this was the best new whisky worldwide of 2002. Totally unique in character, flawless in distillation and awesome in subtlety. **42%**

BULGARIA

12 Years Finest Bulgarian db **(81) n19 t21 f21 b20**. Some whisky! Takes no prisoners with an onslaught of what appears to be fresh European oak: more like a 35–40-year-old Scotch. Chewy, sweet with a big liquorice finish. Some decent malt does makes it through and shows at the end. Beautifully textured, clean and obviously well made. Very drinkable whisky indeed, but not for the lily-livered. **43%**

FRANCE
Single Malt
ARMORIC

Armorik db **(63) n15 t18 f14 b16**. Too feinty and what appears to be caramel dependent. Some of the fat, oiliness is pleasant for a while, but a long way to go on the learning curve here. **40%**

Blended

Whisky Breton **(80) n19 t20 f21 b20**. An altogether better effort; malty and assertively drinkable with attractive, firm, chewy grains and a late, lingering sweetness. A lively, characterful and creditable blend. **40%**

GERMANY
BLAUE MAUS

Blaue Maus Single Malt Whisky Fassstarke 2, dist 8/93, bott 9/02 db **(84) n19 t22 f21 b22**. This is more of a man than a maus: big, oily, heavy-weighted deep molassed sweetness. Lovely spices, too. Really well balanced and a better nose would catapult it into the top bracket. **40%**

Glen Mouse Pure Malt Whisky Fassstarke 2, dist 8/86, bott 1/98 db **(81) n20 t19 f21 b21**. Exceptionally clean distillate with massive oak richness. **40%**

Krottentaler Single Malt Whisky Fassstarke 1, dist 6/94, bott 7/02 db **(77) n16 t21 f21 b19**. On the feinty side but, as ever, the result is a big whisky with chewy sweet oils and intense malt. Once over the nose, it's a lovely journey. **40%**

Mouse db **(92) n22** rich, big vanilla and thick malt: a touch of distant honey to a nose more akin to bourbon than malt; **t24** sensational: the mouthfeel is near perfect with just the right amount of subtle sweetness leaking into the big oak; **f23** more bitter as the tannins mount, roast Java coffee; **b23** this is an outstanding whisky that any bourbon lover will cross a few countries for. And you will have to: this is malt kept in a small barrel at the distillery bar at Egolsheim/Neuses. You cannot get it anywhere else. Strength unknown.

Schwarzer Pirat Single Malt Whisky Fassstarke 3, dist 7/94, bott 9/02 db **(77) n17 t20 f20 b20**. Again the nose is hard going but this is compensated for by a sweet, spicy, charismatic malt on the palate. **40%**

Spinnaker Single Malt Whisky Fassstarke 3, dist 9/93, bott 9/02 db **(82) n19 t22 f21 b20**. Superbly made malt, delicate in its weight and possessing a light muscovado sugar sweetness the entire voyage. Just a little heavy on the nose to be a ship-shape great whisky, but I could drink this one any time any place. Especially Germany ... **40%**

GRUELS'

Schwabischer Whisky Single Grain db **(80) n19 t21 f19 b21**. Full credit for an excellent first attempt. The nose is good if a tad off-key and the dying embers a little bitter. But the intense oily, rich, sweet, buttery middle is a delight. Familiarity breeds anything but contempt with this characterful whisky. **43%**

SLYRS

Slyrs Bavarian Single Malt 1999 db **(84)** n20 t21 f22 b21. A very competently made malt whisky that celebrates its clean simplicity. The nose is vanilla-bound but on the palate it takes off slowly, first clearing a soft oak hurdle and then really letting the malt go into overdrive. Thoroughly enjoyable, high-quality quaffing whisky that will need to be made in greater amounts if they keep up this standard. **43%**

SONNEN SCHEIN

Sonnen Schein Single Malt Whisky 1989 bott 00 db **(69)** n17 t17 f18 b17. Very unusual stale tobacco aroma and possibly (I am guessing as a lifelong non-smoker) taste. A whisky that tastes slightly better second time round, though not by much. Room for improvement here, I think. **43%**

POLAND
LIEBONA GIORA

Dark Whisky **(77)** n19 t19 f20 b19. Lots of grain character with perhaps a tad too much toffee, but the texture is alluring and appealing and finishes well with decent oak and lustre. **40%**

SPAIN
Blended

DYC **(81)** n20 t21 f19 b21. Thin and grainy in parts but the bite is attractive and assertive while the malt comfortably holds its own. **40%**

SWITZERLAND

Swissky (label shows boxed drawing of pot still) db **(84)** n19 t22 f21 b22. Only the most distant hint of feintiness takes away from the beauty of this rich malt. The oils are sublime, as usual from this distillery, and the malt is sweet and chewy. If anything, I am marking down. **42%**

Swissky (label shows man working a pot still) db **(83)** n20 t21 f21 b21. A thinnish, clean malt at first with some decent oak depth to bolster the copper-rich finale. **42%**

Swissky '00 Selection db **(89)** n21 intense, clean malt tinged with hints of citrus and hazelnut; t23 stunning mouth arrival: the texture is near enough perfect and the development of the sweet malt is a delight; f22 soft vanilla works well with the light oil and generous malt, praline on the finale; b23 what a fabulous whisky! The texture is to die for and the malty-nutty complexity is extraordinary. Probably a nation's finest whisky yet. **42%**

TURKEY

Ankara Turk Viskisi **(80)** n20 t20 f19 b21. Soft and gentle despite the clear grain with soft delicate oak on the finish. Quite beautifully balanced: a genuinely charming whisky to be taken seriously. **43%**

World Whiskies

I have long said that whisky can be made just about anywhere in the world; that it is not writ large in stone that it is the inalienable right for just Scotland, Ireland, Kentucky and Canada to have it all to themselves. And so, it seems, it is increasingly being proved.

Perhaps only sandy deserts and fields of ironstone can prevent its make physically and Islam culturally, though even that has not been a barrier to malt whisky being distilled in both Pakistan and Turkey. While not even the world's highest mountains or jungle can prevent the spread of barley and pot.

Outside of North America and Europe, the whisky's traditional nesting sites, you can head in any direction and find it being made. South America may be well known for its rum, but in the south of Brazil, an area populated by Italian and German settlers many generations back, malt whisky is thriving. In even more lush and tropical climes it can now also be found, with Thailand leading the way. Japan has long represented Asia with distinction and whisky-making there is in such an advanced state and to such a high standard the *Whisky Bible* has given it its own section. But while neighbouring South Korea has ended its malt distilling venture, further east, and at a very unlikely altitude, Nepal has forged a small industry to team up, geographically, with fellow malt distillers India and Pakistan.

And Africa is also represented. There has long been a tradition of blending Scotch malt with South African grain. Now I am receiving reports of a South African malt distillery in operation. Check the website between now and the next 2005 edition to see if I can find samples of a straight malt – and the distillery itself.

This section is a lot shorter than I originally planned. The reason is simple: rather than use old, outdated tasting notes, my aim had been to gather fresh samples, preferably by visiting or re-visiting these far off distilleries. However, the chaos surrounding the Sars outbreak made travelling to the Far East worth postponing for a year.

However, one new whisky-making region is due immediate study: Australia. I will be travelling there to visit the distilleries for the first time while the book is being printed. For reports on what I find, click on to **www.whiskybible.com**.

From a distance of 12,000 miles, the waters around Australia's distilleries appear to be muddied. Quality appears to range from the very good to extremely poor, and during late 2003 I shall endeavour to find out why and report back. The good news is that Australian distillers are taking their craft seriously and there is a strong move for them to form their own industry body. The thinking behind this is for distillers to help pass on knowledge in order for the overall quality to improve and for Australian whisky, as a genre, to be regarded in a more wholesome light.

Certainly they would do well to make malt as well as it was made at the old Wilson Distillery in Dunedin, New Zealand. Although that distillery – once part of Seagrams – has now closed for good, with its distilling apparatus being used – I believe – to make rum in Fiji, the stocks that are being made available are underlining just what a loss to the whisky world the old Lammerlaw brand will be when the characterful contents of all the remaining barrels are finally consumed.

Which leaves Antarctica as the only continent not making whisky, though what some of those scientists get up to for months on end no one knows. Still, effluent might be a problem there, though it should make the perfect whisky with ice ...

AUSTRALIA
BAKERY HILL DISTILLERY, 1999. Operating.

This is a small distillery in North Bayswater on the outskirts of Melbourne, Victoria. The owner David Baker has been distilling since 3rd March 2001 and plans to bottle for the first time either late 2003 or some time in 2004. He is likely to be bringing out up to four styles of whisky which I have tasted – unbottled, at two years – and have given marks below. This should not be confused with the late Corio Distillery in Melbourne which went under two decades before.

The first is a Double Wood, begun in bourbon but given a fair percentage of time rounding off in French oak **(79)** n17 t20 f21 b21. The faintest feinty trace doesn't hinder a distinctly fruity nose. The malt development on the palate is quite beautiful and, despite being unpeated, a soft, distant smokiness adds excellent weight to the lilting malt-oak richness.

Even better still is a malt that has gone down the same road but spent much less time in the French oak **(85)** n19 t21 f23 b22. American oak has given the whisky great complexity on the nose; and on the palate we are talking something in the style of a Glenmorangie. The finish is pure cocoa. Startling malt-oak complexity, offering easily the most stylish Australian malt I have found.

Truly astonishing is a cask-strength version planned at 65%. This is unpeated, from bourbon barrel and breathtaking **(86)** n23 t20 f22 b21. It may be pretty youthful on arrival on the palate, but the nose is a riot of complex oaky-malty tones, very well distilled with only the odd minor blemish. The finish is as profound as the start is young, with some lively, mouthwatering malt sparkling with clarity. Again cocoa has a late say. Lovely stuff.

Doubtless, though, the collectors will be heading for the Bakery Hill Peated Malt **(81)** n21 t21 f20 b19. Lightly smoked, it is dry at first but gathers sweetness as the oils close in. Unbalanced at this age but still entertaining on the palate with plenty of character and scope.

TASMAN DISTILLERY

Great Outback Rare Old Australian Single Malt **(92)** n24 I could stick my nose in a glass of this all day. This is sensational: more a question of what we don't have here! The malt is clean, beautifully defined and dovetails with refined, orangey-citrus notes. The oak is near perfection adding only a degree of tempered weight. I don't detect peat, but there is some compensating Blue Mountain coffee; t24 just so beautifully textured with countless waves of clean, rich malt neither too sweet nor too dry. This is faultless distillate; f21 lightens considerably with the oak vanilla dominating; b23 What can you say? An Australian whisky distillery makes a malt to grace the world's stage. But you can't find it outside of Australia. This will have to be rectified. Strength not known

LARK DISTILLERY

Lark Distillery Single Malt Single Cask Bottled April 01 db **(88)** n22 apples and cinnamon: other peppery spices dig in to the oily malt; t22 massively malty, clean and fruity with a powdery oak offering further complexity; oily and fat; f22 beautifully spiced and delicate with fluttering malty tones caressing the palate; b22 this is lovely whisky, superbly made and offering both guile and charisma. Congratulations: Australia has entered the ranks of serious whisky distilling nations. **40%**

Lark Distillery Single Malt Single Cask Bottled Sep 02 db **(82)** n18 t22 f21 b21. A touch feinty but the malt is intense and recovers superbly on the palate for a genuinely delicious dram. Certainly one of the maltiest bottlings you'll find worldwide, almost Cardhu-like. **40%**

Lark Distillery Single Malt Single Cask Bottled Jan 03 db **(83)** n19 t21 f22 b21. Again big malt intensity but the body is thinner, the finish, as the malts begin to show their complexity, is brilliant. A superb dram with a slight nose blemish. **40%**

Lark Distillery Single Malt 2nd Release October 1999 **(78) n**17 **t**21 **f**20 **b**20. Mildly feinty and fruity, it does offer a mouthwatering malty theme which is realised on the palate. A dram best served if a small proportion is put into a smallish bottle and kept warm overnight. This will burn off some of the feints and you are left with a very drinkable Aussie malt. **40%**

TASMANIA DISTILLERY

Old Hobart db **(69) n**16 **t**19 **f**17 **b**17. The nose still has some way to go before it can be accepted as a mainstream malt, though there is something more than a little coastal about it this time. However, the arrival on the palate is another matter and I must say I kind of enjoyed its big, oily and increasingly sweet maltiness and crushed sunflower seed nuttiness towards the end. Green (and yellow) shoots are growing. The whisky is unquestionably getting better. **60%**

Sullivan's Cove Classic (capped with a black seal) db **(64) n**15 **t**16 **f**17 **b**16. A feinty dram, off-key and in need of a good tidy-up, though much better and cleaner than the gold seal. As this is a distillery's first attempt, I would rather encourage than fire off shells at a soft target. My advice is always to buy a bottle and see how a new distillery evolves. Again, the whisky can be improved dramatically by heating the glass in your hand to burn off the excess oils. **40%**

Sullivan's Cove Classic (capped with a gold seal) db **(58) n**12 **t**15 **f**16 **b**15. Feinty with a weird aroma of rotting vegetables on top. Some malt gurgles through, but it's not a pleasant experience. The gold cap and seal at the top was used only by the founders of the distillery and therefore represents the first-ever bottlings from Sullivan's Cove. **40%**

WHISKY TASMANIA

Based in Burnie, have yet to bottle.

BRAZIL
HEUBLEIN DISTILLERY

Durfee Hall Malt Whisky **(81) n**18 **t**22 **f**20 **b**21. Superbly made whisky; the intensity of the malt is beautifully layered without ever becoming too sweet. Very light bodied and immaculately clean. Good whisky by any standards. **43%**

UNION DISTILLERY

Barrilete **(72) n**18 **t**19 **f**18 **b**17. Nothing particularly wrong with it technically; it just lacks vitality. Thin but extremely malt intense. **39.1%**

NEW ZEALAND
WILSON DISTILLERY

Milford Aged 10 Years Limited Edition dist 91 bott Aug 02 batch no. F9/0/08 **(89) n**22 mildly minty, dry oak suppressing slightly the barley-sugar sweetness; gentle peat adds lovely depth; **t**23 rich, clean malt then that superb, trademark Wilson distillery fizz accompanying that delicate smoke; **f**21 softer oaky notes but some brittle peat offers some length to an otherwise abrupt finish; **b**23 charming yet always busy on the palate. **43%** *New Zealand Malt Whisky Co. 5573 bottles.*

Milford Aged 12 Years Limited Edition dist 90 bott Oct 02 batch no. E50/0 **(88) n**22 firm, crisp barley; the oak is dry despite a faint burbony character; a slight shake of black pepper; **t**24 beautifully mouth-watering and rich, the malt is stunningly intense and its usual ultra-clean self. A little bite and fizz towards the middle; **f**20 quite light, short and a touch thin; **b**22 the mouth arrival and barley lift-off is the stuff of New Zealand whisky legend; only the closed finish prevents this being a major classic. Excellent whisky. **43%** *New Zealand Malt Whisky Co. 2840 bottles.*

Lammerlaw Aged 12 Years Peated Malt Sherry Cask Finishing (85) **n**22 softly and delightfully peated: gentle malt and oak with a thread of honey; **t**19 abrasive and uneven at first then a surge of lightly honied malt leads to a decent oaky-malty middle; **f**23 now the peat kicks in for a sensuous finale. Sweetens brilliantly on the light but chewy finish. Great complexity; **b**21 gets over the hurdle of the rough start to finish how it began on the nose: wonderfully! **50%. nc ncf.** *From Wilson Distillery, though it says Willowbank on the label.*

Cadenhead's Lammerlaw 10 Years Old (88) n22 big, fresh malt with a drying, chalky oak influence; **t**23 mouthwatering, clean, juicy malt. A touch of salt seasons it and the complexity is further aided by warming spices and the most subtle hints of citrus; **f**21 back to that drying, chalky oak; **b**22 seriously sensuous and complex malt from a tragically lost distillery. Pure New Zealand, but Speyside in style, and puts a good number of Speysiders to shame with its balance and complexity. **48.2%**

Meenan's Lammerlaw 12 Years Old (90) n23 beautifully honeyed, with lavender and a very distant rumble of peat: the oak suggests something older; **t**23 an outstanding delivery of soft, fruity malts, a layer of sweet honey and some oak and distant smoke; **f**21 heaps of vanilla and soft spice and a gradual build-up of something peaty; **b**23 this is a genuinely complex, beautifully made malt where the oak makes a wonderful divergence. A classic from any continent. **50%.** *Available only in New Zealand.*

SOUTH AFRICA

Harrier (77) n17 **t**20 **f**21 **b**19. Perfumy and sweet; very easy to drink soft grain. **43%.** *South African/Scotch Whisky.*

Knights (77) n16 **t**21 **f**20 **b**20. Spot-on grain: a sumptuous blend with genuinely impressive and high-quality bite and balance. **43%.** *South African/ Scotch Whisky.*

Three Ships sample A, **(78) n**20 **t**21 **f**18 **b**19. Some excellent grain and complexity kicking about with subtle vanilla spices. Bit of caramel influence, too, I'm afraid. **43%.** *South African/Scotch Whisky.*

Three Ships sample B, **(87) n**21 thin, hard grain offset by softer, Islay (Bowmore-ish style) smoke. Delicate and attractive; **t**22 again it's grain first to show, then a slow evolution of malt with peat drifting in as the spices arrive; **f**22 excellent sweet-dry balance with toffee taking out the top notes; **b**22 seriously drinkable blended whisky offering excellent balance. Has improved beyond recognition in recent years: now the pride of the fleet. **43%.** *South African/ Scotch Whisky.*

Stop Press...

Late bottled and additional whiskies.

Scotch Single Malt

ARDMORE Old Master's Ardmore 1980 **(94)** n23 a supreme dovetailing of soft yet confident peats and mouthwatering, grassy malt. Clean and much younger than you might expect from the age, despite some background oak; **t24** classic Ardmore with the sweet peat with a controlled explosion on lift off but then a fabulous follow-through of crisp, brittle barley. The complexity and clarity is glorious; **f23** the most subtle oak is around but it's mainly cocoa on the finale, all slowly drying. Still the peat remains a nagging whisper and the backbone malt remain erect and sturdy and, miraculously, salivating to the very end; **b24** what can you say? Yet another example of why Ardmore is probably the world's greatest undiscovered malt. This is surely one of the most mouthwatering drams for an 18-year-old year-old-malt you'll ever find, and the luscious subtlety of the peat is more than a bonus. With such fabulous balance and complexity, if you want to discover what a subtlety in whisky is all about, have a gander at this. For this is a Masterpiece Malt. **51.4%** James MacArthur.

BEN NEVIS Ben Nevis Ten Years Old db **(88)** n21 typically weighty, nutty and oily, though there are some powering, over-ripe orange tones. Mountainous stuff; **t24** no less massive on the palate: the intensity of the malt is awesome. Much cleaner than the nose, and the degree of sweetness is surprising. Fat, chewy and entirely delicious with no shortage of fruity notes countering a vague hint of smoke; **f20** much, much harder as the sweetness dissolves. Firm vanilla and brittle malt and a faint echo of cocoa; **b23** bottled exclusively for the Japanese market, this expression shows Ben Nevis at its most colourful, characterful and complex: no shrinking violet, this. The mouth arrival is spellbinding. The definitive 10-year-old Ben Nevis for whisky clubs to chase. **43%**. bott 03 Japan only

BRUICHLADDICH Berry's Own Bruichladdich 1993 bott 03 **(89)** n22 exceptionally clean, light and young. It's almost as if you can still get the CO_2 off the washbacks; **t24** a wonderful arrival of mouthwatering barley: fresh, lively and mouth-puckeringly sharp; **f21** soft oak and slowly dawning layers of increasingly oily malt; pretty dry and spent at the death; **b22** an absolute charmer, full of fizz and vitality. The most Speysidey Islay you're ever likely to find. **57%**. Berry Bros

DAILUAINE Berry's Own Dailuaine 1975 bott 03 **(91)** n22 appears at first to have oaky bags under its eyes, but a distant echo of spiced smoke plus some intense barley offers life and intrigue enough; **t23** enlivened further by an intensely malty, chewy middle. The sweet, succulent barley is wonderfully clean and invigorating for its great age; **f23** again trails off towards oak at the finale, but the middle and finale sparkle with no little complexity. Quite estery at the death: very rum-like; **b23** a seriously impressive and enjoyable old malt that takes a little time to fathom. Really outstanding stuff and unquestionably one of the great bottled Dailuaines of our time. **46%**. Berry Bros

DUFFTOWN Berry's Own Dufftown 1979 **(78)** n21 t20 f18 b19. Promising at first, especially with the deep and rich malt intensity on mouth arrival. But there is that trademark, odd – dirty almost – kick and residue to be countered. **46%**. Berry Bros

GLENDRONACH Berry's Own Glendronach 1990 bott 03 **(81)** n18 t22 f20 b21. A very curious Glendronach, having absorbed very little colour but enough on the nose to suggest this is not from the greatest of casks. A hint of peat and some beautifully intense malt make for a magic few moments on entering the mouth, but the finish is closed and hard. **46%.** Berry Bros

GLEN GRANT Berry's Own Glen Grant 1972 bott 03 **(87)** n23 absolutely top class sherry, whistle-clean, dry, weighty yet subtle enough to allow the development of vanilla and various floral-oaky notes; t23 lush, soft arrival of sherry on the palate: a mouthwateringly juicy affair at first; followed by a wave of barley; and then firmer oak, chocolate eclairs and faint peat; f20 pretty dry, flint embedded in chalk; b21 rock hard Glen Grant with a grey beard, but the sherry really has that touch of class. **46%.** Berry Bros

Berry's Own Glen Grant 1973 bott 03 **(86)** n23 sultanas and warming spices; clean, clear and crisp; t23 brilliant delivery of intense fruit coupled with enormous spices that nip, bite and chatter around the palate. The oak takes its time before arriving, allowing the barley-sherry combo full and unrestricted reign; f19 rock-hard and almost impenetrable in the most classic of Glen Grant styles. The oak is bolder now and showing a little sap along with some very late cocoa. Still the spice persists; b21 an old malt that at first displays Glen Grant in a near classic pose, but ultimately just a fraction too sappy around the gills. **52%.** Berry Bros

GLENLIVET Berry's Own Glenlivet 1971 bott 03 **(82)** n23 t22 f18 b19. A heavyweight, yet nimble, bout between massed ranks of oak and tar-brushed sherry. Sherry, it must be said, that is dry and of the very finest order; to taste, though, an enormous spice attack, heaps of prickle and pepper and early wave of thick oak. A subtle, sweet backdrop softens the thudding blows but even traces of cocoa fail to entirely shield us from the OTT oak. Not without charm, character and quality but, alas, several summers too old. **55%.** Berry Bros

INCHGOWER Berry's Own Inchgower 1975 bott 03 **(87)** n23 weighty and very well balanced; barley sugar and the faintest hint of smoke merges effortlessly with some crushed green leaf and oaky notes; t22 a very sweet, fat chap with massive chewing power. The malt rules the roost but in the background earthier, smokier notes are lightened, highlighted even, by hints of citrus; f20 dry with subtle vanilla on one plain, deft, sweeter smoke on another; b22 an impressively balanced dram that shows really good weight. **46%.** Berry Bros

MORTLACH Berry's Own Mortlach 1989 bott 03 **(92)** n22 a hint of new make, but it has seen just enough oak to pick up balance with the intense and tart young malt. Fresh and mouth-watering: those who remember the old Glenfiddich will recognise this guy; t24 bracing and clean, there is wave upon wave of succulent malt, interspersed with vague sugar-biscuit notes. Wonderful liveliness and youth; f23 remains clean and mouth-watering to the very death, with some vanilla weight to balance the barley onslaught; b23 once I wrote an article saying how Mortlach made one of Speyside's great whiskies, based on tasting samples of the stuff since the 1970s. Recent bottlings have been disappointing to almost heartbreak proportions. This, though, is a stupendous example of first-class distillate in aspic. The cask was probably on its third lap around the warehouses, which has given the tastebuds free access to what makes this distillery tick. Light and lacking its complexity of old, this is still the best Mortlach bottled in the last five or six years. Refreshingly brilliant: the perfect pre-prandial malt. **46%.** Berry Bros

Whisky Bible Dictionary

* **Age:** The age of any bottled whisky refers to the very youngest whisky used in the vatting.
* **Ageing:** The process by which whisky gathers its individual character by maturing within the confines of an oak cask. Once the whisky has been bottled the ageing process has been ended, irrespective of the time it may spend in that bottle.
* **Alcohol by Volume:** Also known as ABV. The alcohol strength of the whisky measured as a percentage part in relation to the liquid as a whole, e.g. 40% ABV equals 40% alcohol, 60% water, congeners, etc.
* **Angel's Share:** The name given to the whisky which each year evaporates from barrels stored in warehouses. On average this works out at around 2% of the barrel's contents per annum, most of which is alcohol.
* **Backset:** Peculiar to North American whiskeys, this is the "Thin Stillage" added to both the "Mash Tub" and fermenter to an amount totalling no less than 25% of the overall mash. This is carried out to help prevent bacterial contamination.
* **Ball of Malt:** A peculiarly Irish expression for a glass of whiskey.
* **Beading:** A rough method used to tell the alcoholic strength of a whisky. When a bottle is shaken bubbles, or beads, will form. The bigger they are and longer they last, the greater the alcoholic strength of the spirit.
* **Beer:** "Wort" or "Mash" that has had yeast added which is either partly or completely fermented. Known also as "Wash".
* **Beer Still:** Mainly North American term for the first still to be used in the distillation process, whether pot or continuous.
* **Blending:** In general terms the mixing together of a straight whiskey (be it pure malt, bourbon or rye) and grain whisky. In Canada, the blending process allows for 9.09 per cent to include non-Canadian whiskies (i.e. distilled fruit juices, fortified wine or whiskies from other countries, e.g. bourbon). The result is a blended whisky.
* **Bond:** The warehouse(s) in which whisky stocks are held until excise duty is levied against them.
* **Bothie:** A small, usually one-roomed building, sometimes even a hidden underground den, in which illicit distillers in the Scottish Highlands made their whisky.
* **Bottled in Bond:** North American (nearly exclusively bourbon) whiskey which is bottled at four years old and at a minimum of 50% alcohol by volume.
* **Bourbon:** A whiskey produced anywhere in the United States made from a mash of a minimum 51% corn, distilled to a strength of no more than 80% alcohol by volume (160 proof) and entered into new charred oak barrels at a strength not exceeding 62.5% alcohol by volume.

※ **Bourbon Whiskey - A Blend:** A whiskey containing a minimum 51% straight bourbon whiskey with the remainder being made of whiskey matured in used casks or neutral spirit.

※ **Brewing:** The process of infusing cereal grains in hot water (mashing) which, with the aid of yeast (fermentation), produces alcoholic liquids (wash/beer) from the dissolved sugars present.

※ **Canadian Whisky:** A grain spirit made within the boundaries of Canada and matured for a minimum three years. Uniquely, by law, Canadian whiskey is allowed to contain non-Canadian whiskey, which could be whiskies from other countries, pure sherry, distilled fruit juices, etc. (see "Blending").

※ **Cask Strength:** A term used for whisky which has not been reduced by water to a standard strength of, say, 40% ABV before bottling. Often, however, the strength may have been reduced down fractionally to perhaps 57% ABV in order that labels do not have to be constantly changed.

※ **Charcoal Mellowing:** The process which sets Tennessee whiskey apart. The spirit runs off the stills into tanks holding around 10 feet of charcoal. Only after it has been filtered through this is it entered into barrel. Some whiskey is also filtered a second time after maturation but before bottling.

※ **Charring:** The dramatic firing of the inside of a new barrel. The contact of the naked flame on the oak opens fissures into which the spirit can run and form types of sugars which will assist the flavouring and colouring of the maturing spirit. The term sometimes applied to the process being carried out on old barrels is re-charring.

※ **Chill Filtration:** The removal by the chilling of whisky of congeners. This is a purely cosmetic precaution used to prevent hazing when the bottled whisky is stored at cold temperatures. The greater the spirit is chilled during filtration, the greater the number of congeners will be removed.

※ **Column Stills:** Also "Continuous Stills" or "Coffey Stills". These are used in the process of continuous distillation, a cheaper and faster method than batch-distillation pot stills. These stills work by the use of plates, made from either copper of stainless steel, through which an upward thrust of steam meets alcoholic liquid, thus stripping the alcohol as it passes.

※ **Congeners:** Chemical compounds found within whisky and formulated during fermentation, distillation and maturation carrying properties that have direct relevance to the taste and smell of the sprit. Some of the more delicate congeners can be lost during chill filtration.

※ **Couch:** A second tank in which barley is placed after it has been taken from the steep and dries sufficiently before being spread on the floor.

※ **Distillation:** This is the simple process of extracting alcohol from a fluid substance by the application of heat. Because alcohol vaporizes quicker than water, it can be collected during condensation.

※ **Doubler:** A pot still used for the second distillation off a beer still in order to increase alcoholic strength.

※ **Draff:** The Scottish term for spent grains after it has been exhausted of all sugar-like properties during fermentation. Used as nutritious food for livestock.

※ **Dram:** The Scottish term for a glass of whisky.

※ **Enzymes**: Carried within grain, especially after malting, acting as an organic catalyst which converts large non-fermentable molecules of starch into smaller, fermentable ones. During mashing, brewers must beware that the grain does not enter the waters at too hot a temperature as these enzymes can be destroyed or damaged.

※ **Feints:** Also known as "Tails", this is the flawed end portion of the run from the final distillation. Being unpotable, re-distillation is required.

※ **Fermenters:** These are the vessels, made from either metal or wood, used for the mash to be turned into beer. This is achieved by the addition of yeast which feeds off the soluble sugars held within the wash. Because of the energy created by the activity of the yeast, fermenters are never filled to the brim. Distilleries using all malt in their fermentation use either switchers to help keep down the foam, or use temperature control.

※ **Fillings:** Barrels containing spirit freshly run off the still and which is to be allowed to mature in whisky.

※ **Floor Maltings:** The building within a distillery in which the practice of malting is carried out by hand. Very few distilleries now continue this ancient practice.

※ **Foreshots:** The very first runnings off the still during the second distillation (see "Heads").

※ **Fusel Oil:** One of the principal and heavier congeners produced during fermentation.

※ **Gauger:** The old name given to the exciseman, whose job it was to put down illicit distillation and smuggling.

※ **Grain Whisky:** A whisky distilled by a continuous method to a high alcoholic strength from either wheat or maize and used to blend with a straight whisky.

※ **Green Malt:** Barley that has begun germination but has not yet been hot-air dried either by kiln or in a drum. This is sometimes used in the making of grain whisky.

※ **Grist:** Ground grains that will be used in mashing.

※ **Heads:** The very first runnings off the still, an undesirable distillate containing compounds even more volatile than alcohol. These are unsuitable for whisky and must be re-distilled.

※ **High Wine:** The alcoholic product from the first distillation which is ready to be pumped into a second still for re-distillation.

※ **Indian Whisky:** As the Indian government does not give a specific definition of whisky, a bottle of Indian whisky may be found to contain pure single malt, a blend of Indian malt and grain whiskies; a mixture of Indian and Scotch whiskies; a spirit distilled from molasses or a mixture of all of these.

※ **Irish Pot Still Whiskey:** A spirit produced in a copper pot and made from a mixture of malted and unmalted barley.

※ **Jigger:** A now disused name for an illicit distillery which has lived on to mean an American measure of spirit, usually one and half fluid U.S. ounces.

※ **Kieve:** The Irish term for mash tun, these days rarely heard.

※ **Leaching:** One of the most common terms applied to the filtration process carried out in Tennessee Whiskey, the others being Charcoal Mellowing, Mellowing and sometimes, though accurately, The Lincoln County Process (see "Tennessee Whiskey").

※ **Liquor:** Hot water that is specially prepared for the mashing process.

※ **Lomond Still:** A type of pot still, squat in shape, designed to produce a heavier, oilier spirit. Named after the Lomond Distillery where first used.

※ **Low Wines:** The third and final portion of the distillate from the first distillation following High Wines and the middle cut. This is relatively weak in alcohol and joins the High Wines for re-distillation.

※ **Lyne Arm:** Pertaining to pot stills, this is the pipe which slants from the head of the still to condenser or worm along which the alcoholic vapours travel.

※ **Malt:** (1) A name given to a grain – usually to barley, sometimes rye – which has undergone a process of artificial growth. This is a achieved by steeping in cold water and then allowing to germinate. The growth is arrested by rapid drying. The grain will then be rich in sugar-type chemical compounds on which yeast can feed to produce alcohol. (2) The simple name given to malt whisky; a whisky made entirely from malted barley, be it single malt or vatted malt.

※ **Maltings:** The building in which malt is made.

※ **Marrying:** A process, a lot less common than of old, when blended whisky is given time to mingle in large containers of either wood or stainless steel before being bottled.

※ **Mash:** A sweet, yellow-brown liquid containing the sugars extracted from the crushed grains that is cooled before passing into the fermenter.

※ **Mash Bill:** North American term for the percentage make up of the ingredients (corn, barley, wheat, rye, etc.) that is being used for mashing.

※ **Mashing:** The process by which the grist is added to hot water in order to dissolve the fermentable starches.

※ **Mash Tub:** The large metal vessel in which milled grains (grist) are added to hot water in order to make all grain starch soluble in preparation for fermentation.

※ **Mash Tun:** (Scottish) see "Mash Tub".

※ **Middle Cut:** The fraction of the spirit which runs from the stills through the spirit safe which is regarded as potable. Also known as the "Heart of the Run".

※ **Mouthfeel:** The term applied to the effect a whisky has on the palate. It could be smooth, fiery, soft, light, cloying, etc.

※ **Nose:** The aroma of the whisky.

※ **Noser:** One who smells whisky usually within the distillery or for the distilling company to ensure that its quality meets the required standard.

※ **Organic Whisky:** Made exclusively from brarley gown in ground free of inorganic fertilizer and treated with natural, non-chemical pesticides.

※ **Peat:** Known as turf in Ireland, or moss, this is a combustable fuel made from compressed vegetable matter, but unlike coal is soft enough to be cut from bogs and is dark brown, sometimes black in colour. Produces a very pungent smoke, known as peat-reek and it is this that is sometimes used in the malting of barley, especially on the Scottish island of Islay. Waters used in distillation that has run over peat will also pick up certain peaty character traits.

※ **Peated Malt:** Malt whisky showing strong, smoky flavour characteristics peculiar to a spirit made from barley kiln-dried with peat.

※ **Piece:** The term given in Scottish distilleries still practising floor malting to the barley that has been spread on the floor to germinate at one particular time. Therefore a floor maltings may have a number of pieces at any one time.

※ **Pot Stills:** Containers, usually made of copper, occasionally stainless steel, used for the purpose of distillation.

※ **Premalt:** Used in North America. Here malt is added to the grist before cooking in order to help agitation. The enzymes within this malt will be damaged and unusable so far as fermentation is concerned.

※ **Quaich:** An ancient two-handled Celtic drinking vessel; its use these days is synonymous with whisky.

※ **Reflux:** Alcohol-rich vapours that have already undergone the distillation process and which for reasons of control in column stills or, in pot stills, the individual shape of the lyne arm, return into the still for additional distillation, usually to produce a lighter spirit.

※ **Rummager:** Found only in coal-fired pot stills, a mechanical device consisting of arms and chains which rotate within the bottom of the still to prevent solids sticking to the surface and burning in the direct heat.

※ **Run (or Runnings):** The colourless spirit at various strength and purity which passes from the still through the spirit safe via the condensing apparatus.

※ **Rye Whiskey:** A spirit produced in the same manner as bourbon but with the mash bill containing no less than 51% rye.

※ **Saladin Box:** Found with a mechanical maltings; the trough-like container named after its French inventor in which barley germinates while being turned by mechanical rather than manual means.

※ **Scotch Whiskey:** A spirit made exclusively in Scotland either from barley, wheat, maize or a mixture of all three which has been matured for a minimum three years in oak casks.

※ **Single Barrel Whisky:** A whisky from an individual cask and which had been made at a single distillery.

※ **Single Malt Whisky:** A whisky produced exclusively from malted barley and is not blended or vatted with any other whisky.

※ **Small Grains:** The term applied to all cereal grains used in the making of Bourbon, Tennessee and Rye whiskey which are smaller than corn.

※ **Sour Mash Whiskey:** Bourbon or Tennessee whiskey which during its making met prescribed government requirements. These include the mash containing a minimum 25% backset stillage; the use of a lactic bacteria soured yeast mash and a minimum fermentation period of 72 hours. In fact, all Bourbon and Tennessee is Sour Mash, irrespective of whether the label tells you so or not (see Backset).

※ **Spent Beer:** See "Stillage".

※ **Spirit Still:** The second still (or third when triple distillation is practised) which takes the high wines from the previous still and re-distils them. It is from this final distillation that the potable spirit is entered into cask.

※ **Steep:** The tank found at a maltings in which barley is soaked – steeped – in cold water to begin the process of germination and then malting.

※ **Stillage:** Pertaining particularly to North American distillation, the residue at the bottom of a still; beer that has been stripped of alcohol and containing solids (see "Thin Stillage").

※ **Sweet Mash:** A mash where yeast only has been used in fermentation without the addition of backset.

※ **Tails:** The last runnings off a still, weak in alcohol (see "Feints").

※ **Tennessee Whiskey:** A type of whiskey made and matured to the same specifications as bourbon but with the exception of undergoing a filtering process before barrelling. This consists of the spirit passing through at least 10 feet of charcoal made from burned sugar-maple wood.

※ **Thin Stillage:** The alcohol free liquid that remains when solids have been removed from the stillage.

※ **Thumper:** A type of doubler, this contains water which vapours from the beer still passes through causing a noisy, thumping effect.

※ **Uisce Beatha:** The Gaelic name meaning "water of life" and the derivative term for whisky: "uisce" was corrupted to "uisgey" and then whisky.

※ **Vatting:** A term used for the mixing together of malt whisky from one distillery or more. Likewise with grain whisky.

※ **Vatted Malt:** A bottled whisky made entirely from malt whisky but from more than one distillery.

※ **Wash:** See "Beer".

※ **Wash Back:** Celtic term for "Fermenter". Made either from wood or stainless steel.

※ **Wash Still:** Performing the same job as the continuous beer still, this is the first pot still used in the distillation process, producing high wines to be re-distilled in the "Spirit Still".

※ **Worm:** The coiled copper tube along which alcoholic vapours travel and assist in condensation by being submerged in cold water. Most distilleries these days prefer to use condensers, also made of copper tubes, but smaller in area used through not being coiled.

※ **Wort:** The liquid high in dissolved sugars which is the product of the mash-tun; a liquid sweetened usually by malt by mashing and is cooled before entering the "Wash Back" for fermentation (see "Mash").

※ **X-Waters:** An ancient term for distilled spirits in Ireland.

※ **Yeast:** A living micro-organism of the fungus family essential for the purpose of fermentation. By feeding on sugar it produces alcohol and carbon dioxide as a by-product.

※ **Zzzzzz:** The happy and peaceful result of drinking too much whisky!

Advice on Drinking Whisky

How do you prefer it, then? Fizzed up with coke or ginger ale? In a fruit juice for healthier dramming? In freezing milk, a way someone I know eulogises over? Or do you like it hot with boiling water, lemon and sugar; or perhaps Siberian with the whisky poured over ice? Long, maybe, with loads of water reducing taste to a minimum, or with just a splash to bring out the aroma? Or could it be you are a traditionalist, that dying breed who tops it up with soda? Whichever way you prefer to drink your whisky, please don't let me stop you. However ... perhaps you may allow me to show you an alternative way.

Each and every mark given in this book is for the whisky as it comes from the bottle. It makes sense: it is the one starting point that is the same for you and me. If, for instance, I added ginger ale, it might be a different brand to the one you prefer, or in slightly different amounts. So here in the *Whisky Bible* you can gauge – thanks to the marking system – which whiskies may benefit from something (in some cases, anything) added to them. And, likewise, my marks may indicate that the whisky you have been drowning in a mixer each night in your glass is worth further investigation on its own.

Do I drink all my whisky neat? No. In Kentucky, for instance, in high summer when the humidity reduces the muscles in your legs to the consistency of a Tunnocks mallow, then you need fluids. And you will not find me averse to my whisk(e)y being long and even iced. For years I would enjoy a whisky and ginger ale with my old Uncle Dave – I would always drink my whisky straight when alone, but to keep him company, so to speak, would enjoy the odd evening of whisky and ginger with him. These are the times when you are thinking not so much about the whiskies themselves, rather their background effect: the whisky becomes elevator music for the tastebuds. However, I entirely admit that when I'm drinking whisky seriously I never add anything. Not even water and certainly not ice.

The first thing to remember about ice is that it closes down the tastebuds and the cold physically constricts the movement of the molecules within the whisky. If ever you need to know how much softer a warm fluid is simply run a tap of warm to hot water and then the cold tap. Listen to the sounds they make: the cold water makes a much harder noise on the basin.

So it is that I never need to add water my whisky ... against what just about everyone one else in the industry says. Actually, I know one blender who also prefers his whisky straight but admits he daren't go public as his stance may be seen as a little too controversial!

Instead, I find a stemmed glass, put my fingers underneath to warm the whisky. As thousands of you who have attended my tastings will testify, the effect is dramatic. A whisky that may originally taste hard and bitter when first poured will open like a flower in the warmed glass and sweeten. Its overall complexity is exposed and for a much longer time than when you add water. Granted, adding water can automatically lift the nose and release characters you had not previously spotted. But they quickly vanish and you need another splash again.

Before you know it you have a stewed whisky with little discernible flavour on the palate. It is no uncommon sight at a tasting to see people lose the whisky completely by adding too much water. Rarely can the same be said for those who drink it neat, but by warmed hand. Of course some people have a problem with the strength. But with experience you learn when the alcohol ends and the natural whisky flavours start.

For those of you who take whisky very seriously indeed I suggest you should learn to spit. I taste some 3,000 whiskies (and a few hundred rums besides) each year, many at full cask strength. If I didn't use a spittoon I would by now be dead. Using a spittoon means that you can taste more whiskies in an evening and keep your wits about you. At the whisky festivals I attend round the world I can easily spot those who are spitting. By the end of an evening they take on a new whisky and can soon pinpoint its weaknesses. Those who have been enjoying a little too much of the spirit of the event begin to enjoy any whisky proffered them, no matter how bad it is.

Please remember: as much as whisky is fun, it is best enjoyed when consumed in moderation. Spitting now and again will do you no harm at all if you are on a quest to discover more.

Glasses

In recent years various companies have come out with whisky glasses designed for maximum enjoyment. Oddly enough they tend to have either short stems or none at all, thereby completely overlooking the need to warm the whisky in the glass. I suggest that you use, if possible, a tulip- or thistle-shaped glass which allows both the aroma to be collected and held, plus a degree of oxidisation which also – in the short term – helps benefit a whisky. And it must have a long enough stem for your fingers to comfortably fit around the bowl in order to cup the glass.

Preparing your palate

Usually I drink a black coffee without sugar before tasting whisky. At home, I roast, blend and grind my own coffee – often using up to six different types of bean – to create whatever taste I feel my palate needs. The beauty of black coffee is that it has the ability to neutralise all other tastes and the bitterness means that your palate is primed to detect any sweetness lurking within a whisky. The balance and complexity of a whisky can be easily overlooked or misunderstood by residual sweetness on the palate.

A decade ago, Kyndal blender Richard Paterson suggested that I also use dark chocolate and in my lab I now keep slabs of 99% pure cocoa chocolate which I sometimes nibble at between tastings, when the whiskies are beginning to gang up on me. However, if I detect either cocoa or coffee in a whisky – neither are uncommon flavour profiles – I will go back to it again (with an untreated palate) to make sure it wasn't an echo of what I'd either drunk or tasted before. So far it hasn't been the case. For those of you who are not coffee lovers and cannot find 99% cocoa I suggest you make a cocoa drink using as high percentage of cocoa powder as you can bear. Your palate will eventually thank you for it.

Whisky and food

I have turned down several offers to make television programmes about whisky and food. The reason is simply because they, unlike barley and a pot, were not made to go together. Others will tell you otherwise, which is their right. However, the true fact for me is that I have never enjoyed a whisky when eating food at the same time. And I have been to quite a few dinners where the chef has prepared this dish to go with that whisky. I have applauded their efforts but only out of politeness: I have yet to come across one that works yet.

Eating while drinking tends to make a whisky bitter, for the reasons I touched upon above. Yes I do drink whisky with a haggis. But it burns my throat out as often as not. I have had a venison steak to go with an Islay. But the sweet sauce with the game obliterated all the complexity and even without the sauce I was pining for a big red Bordeaux or even a 10% barley wine.

Instead, I suggest you drink before you sit down at the table. My preferred choice before a meal is something that will make you salivate: in Scotland a Bailie Nicol Jarvie, a J&B perhaps, or maybe Royal Silk; amongst malts: a light, crisp but by no means effete Speysider like a young Glen Grant (oh, and how I wish they would return to us the original, no age statement Glenfiddich); or from outside that region a standard, truly classic Glenmorangie 10 or a fresh-faced Glengoyne. In Ireland I prefer, before eating, a common-or-garden yet entirely luscious Jameson or the Pot Still succulence of a Green Spot. Or if there is any around, one of my own Knappogue creations. Each and every one gets the tastebuds on full alert. In Japan Suntory tend to offer the lightest in style and before a meal they have nothing better than Southern Alps Pure Malt, though a Tsuru from Nikka can also hit the spot. America is a bit trickier because of the fuller weight of bourbon, so I tend to delve into a Jim Beam Rye before eating. Also I would go for the Ancient Age 10 Years Old, but that is much oakier now and would be an after dinner contender. And as for Canada: you are spoiled for choice.

After the meal, it's all a matter of mood. Always drink a black coffee first before tucking into your whiskies to kill off the dessert sweetness. But I always adore something heavily smoked after dinner ... and I don't mean a cigar.

Finally, a word for those determined to use whisky in their food. Here's a couple of tips. If you enjoy a good steak then marinate it for a few hours in a powerfully flavoured bourbon or Tennessee. And for dessert a Jack Daniels goes a long way when tipped into a chocolate mousse.

Food for thought ... but whisky is for drinking. Neat.

Tasting Notes

Space is provided below for you to evaluate your own dramming experiences using the rating system of the "Whisky Bible".

Whisky ABERLOUR 12 YEARS OLD SHERRY CASK MATURED (40%)
Type SCOTTISH SINGLE MALT
Nose BIZARRELY TOOTHPASTEY; WHAT IS IT ABOUT MINT AND
ABERLOUR WHISKIES?   (20)

Taste STUNNINGLY TEXTURED, RICH FRUIT, WITH SUCCULENT GRAPE
EDGING OUT THE MALT.   (22)

Finish LONG, WITH FINGERS OF OAK ON THE MALT.   (22)

Balance THIS IS A BIG, CLEAN DRAM WHERE THE MALT IS JUST
ABOUT STRONG ENOUGH TO HOLD ONTO THE SHERRY.   (21)

Total Points awarded   (85)

Whisky
Type
Nose   ( )

Taste   ( )

Finish   ( )

Balance   ( )

Total Points awarded   ( )

Whisky
Type
Nose   ( )

Taste   ( )

Finish   ( )

Balance   ( )

Total Points awarded   ( )

Whisky
Type
Nose

Taste

Finish

Balance

Total Points awarded

Whisky
Type
Nose

Taste

Finish

Balance

Total Points awarded

Whisky
Type
Nose

Taste

Finish

Balance

Total Points awarded

Whisky

Type

Nose

Taste

Finish

Balance

Total Points awarded

Whisky

Type

Nose

Taste

Finish

Balance

Total Points awarded

Whisky

Type

Nose

Taste

Finish

Balance

Total Points awarded

Other Carlton Books by Jim Murray

"The most highly respected whisky writer ever." Irish Times

Jim Murray's Complete Book of Whisky
The lavishly illustrated, definitive guide to the whiskies of the world
"Essential reading for any prospective whisky buff." *The Independent*
224pp
ISBN 185568 184 7
Price £25.00
Published by Carlton Books

Classic Blended Scotch
Fully illustrated guide to the complete range blended Scotch whisky.
"Informative and well researched." *Yorkshire Evening Press*
256pp
ISBN 1 85375 297 5
Price £12.99
Published by Prion Books, an imprint of Carlton Publishing

Classic Irish Whiskey
A beautiful volume descibing the varieties of Irish whiskey, illustrated in full colour.
"An authoritative guide to the drink." *Irish Times*
256pp
ISBN 1 85375 241 X,
Price £12.99
Published by Prion Books, an imprint of Carlton Publishing

Classic Bourbon Tennessee & Rye Whiskey
An informative and honest insight into America's fascinating and diverse whisky
production. "Provides essential information." *Maryland Beverage Journal*
272pp
ISBN 1 85375 218 5
Price £12.99
Published by Prion Books, an imprint of Carlton Publishing

whiskybible.com

Let Jim Murray keep you in touch with what's going on around the world's whiskies

www.whiskybible.com

Jim will be regularly updating the site, filing reports about distilleries in his multi-award-winning prose from Scotland to Scandinavia, from Austria to Australia. If a new whisky distillery pops up somewhere in the world be sure that Jim Murray will be paying it a visit....

Also look out for details of new whiskies to be launched in 2004 and find out how to get his exclusive review and ratings of the bottlings.

The site will include an international guide to which distilleries welcome visitors, contact numbers for whisky clubs and organisations, liquor stores offering a choice of over 250 whiskies and lots, lots more.

In fact, **www.whiskybible.com** will have all the things we wanted to put in Jim Murray's Whisky Bible but just didn't have the room.

Keep in touch with Jim Murray. The most passionate and independent voice in world whisky.

Slàinte

It seems that you can't have a Bible without a whole lot of begetting. And without all those listed below – and few others besides whose details I have mislaid amid the chaos – this Bible would never have been begot at all. Tasting over 2,000 whiskies single handedly took a lot of time: the logistics in getting them to my lab took a whole lot more. So my heartfelt appreciation goes to all those listed below in supporting me in one way or another. Special thanks are due to my good friend in Japan Takeshi Mogi for his enormous input from afar and slightly nearer home Soren Norgaard of MacY in Denmark for allowing me to use his personal bar as my second tasting lab. Finally a big thank you for my team-mates, editor Martin Corteel and art guru Darren Jordan, for their patience and enormous help in aiding me to hit very tough deadlines. Saint Darren, your reward was that taste of the sublime Royal Salute 50-year-old. Martin, yours will be in Heaven... .

Esben Andersen; Paul Aston; David Baker; David Ballheimer; Liselle Barnsley; Rachel Barrie; Jim Beveridge; Borat; Neil Boyd; Karen Brown; Andy Burns; Bill Caldwell; Tina Carey; Alex Carnie; Candy Charters; Julie Christian; Ricky Christie; Andy Crook; Rick Connolly; Paula Cormack; Andy Cornwall; Silvia Corrieri; Isabel Coughlan; James Cowan; Ronnie Cox; Fergal Crean; Andrew Currie; Bob Dalgarno; Craig Daniels; Martin Dawson; Jürgen Deibel; Gordon Doctor; Ed Dodson; Lucy Drake; Jonathan Driver; Colin Dunn; Lucy Egerton; Duncan Elphick; Richard Evans; Roy Evans; Robert Fleischmann; Angela Forsgren D'Orazio; Emma Gill; Fiona Gittus; Richard Gordon; Ed Graham; George Grant; Lynn Grant; Donald R Greeter; David Hallgarten; Archie Hamilton; Andy Hart; Donald Hart; Julian Haswell; CJ Hellie; Lincon Henderson; Irene Hemmings; Robert Hicks; Vincent Hill; Aaron Hillman; Sandy Hislop; Mark Hunt; Ford Hussain; Ily Jaffa; Richard Joynson; Naofumi Kamaguchi; Larry Kass; Daniel Kissling; Dennis Klindrup; Mana Kondo; Lex Kraaijeveld; Libby Lafferty; Fred Laing; Stuart Laing; Bill Lark; Walter Lecocq; Patricia Lee; Darren Leitch; Jim Long; Martin Long; Linda Love; Bill Lumsden; Stuart MacDuff; Sarah McGhee; Helen McGinn; Doug McIvor; Kirsty McLeod; Janice McMillan; Steven McNeil; Patrick Maguire; Norman Mathison; David Maxwell-Scott; Clare Meikle; Rick Mew; Tatsuya Minagawa; Euan Mitchell; Matthew Mitchell; Jürgen Moeller; Takeshi Mogi; Daniela Dal Molin; Les Morgan; Chris Morris; Mary Morton; Gordon Motion; Arthur Motley; Malcolm Mullin; Alison Murray; Andrew Murray; Charles Murray; James Murray; Marc Neilly; Margaret Nicol; Micke Nilsson; Sir Iain Noble; Edel Nørgaard; Johannes Nørgaard; Lis Nørgaard; Søren Nørgaard; Lucy Pritchard; Richard Paterson (also belated double thanks for his help with my book *Classic Blended Scotch* but whose name did not appear in the credits despite having originally been included by me!); Rupert Patrick; Plamen Petroff; Dave Phelan; Simon Pointon; Warren Preston; Annie Pugh; David Radcliffe; John Ramsey; Alan Reid; Geraldine Roche; Colin Ross; Duncan Ross; Jim Rutledge; Christine Sandys; Charlie Saunders; Leander Schadler; Gerd Schmerschneider; Mick Secor; Tammy Secor; Tara Serafini; Catherine Service; Euan Shand; Sukhinder Singh; Emanuel Solinsky; Sue Stamps; Tamsin Stevens; David Stewart; Kathleen Stirling; Kaj Stovring; Derek Strange; Noel Sweeney; Graham Taylor; Corinna Thompson; Stuart Thompson; Terry Threlfall; Hamish Torrie; Sarah True; Robin Tucek; Ian Urquhart; Billy Walker; Jamie Walker; Barry Walsh; Oswald Weidenauer; Jan H Westcott; Alex Williams; Arthur Winning; Lance Winter.